"Can one generation bind another, and all others, in succession forever? I think not. The creator has made the earth for the living, not the dead. . . . A generation may bind itself as long as its majority continues in life; when that has disappeared, another majority is in place, holds all the rights and powers their predecessors once held, and may change their laws and institutions to suit themselves. Nothing is unchangeable but the inherent and unalienable rights of man. . . ."

—*Jefferson to John Cartwright, June 5, 1824*

THE
ESSENTIAL

JEFFERSON

Edited, and with an Introduction by
ALBERT FRIED

COLLIER BOOKS
NEW YORK, N.Y.

A Collier Books Original

First Edition 1963

Collier Books is a division of The Crowell-Collier Publishing
Company

Contents

Part VII.   Democratic–Republican: 1794–1801

General Introduction

1

THOUGH JEFFERSON formulated his ideals in the cool, lucid, rational form common to eighteenth century intellectuals, he always sought to give them concrete form, to embody them in laws and institutions, and he succeeded to an astonishing degree. The seminal power of Jefferson's ideals lay precisely in their union with action. He served Virginia and the nation during the formative years of their development under republican rule—years when his convictions were bound to carry greatest weight. In the three decades following the Declaration of Independence (of which he was chief author) there were few important events which he failed to participate in, to influence considerably, or to dominate altogether.

Jefferson's private life was equally rich and fruitful. His versatility is famous. To all his activities—inventor, architect, musician, naturalist, planter as well as philosopher—he gave full intensity of consciousness. His travel accounts, for example, would make a fascinating book—as would his views of religion, wine, education, language and a host of other subjects. He published two books: the great *Notes on Virginia* and the still useful *Manual of Parliamentary Practice*. Despite the ocean of words which poured from him the lucidity and elegance of his style remained uniformly high. Only Lincoln, among American politicians, wrote more skillfully.

Jefferson was driven by a peculiar tension throughout his forty years in politics. He repeatedly complained of how his family, home, books and interests were being neglected because of his duty to his people and country. There is no reason to question the depth of Jefferson's feelings on the matter. But they are more ambiguous and complex than he allowed. Nothing could have *compelled* him to engage actively in politics for so long and at so great a cost had he not wanted to. He could have been a planter-philosopher like his friend John Taylor of Caroline. The fact is that long stretches of retirement bored Jefferson. For some reason, he needed to feel that his political and private lives were opposed, that one was his duty and the other his pleasure. Judging from his Faustian accomplishments in both, each must have acted as a stimulus upon the other. But we will not conjecture on the reason for this.

2

Jefferson was born on April 13, 1743, at Shadwell in the Piedmont region of Virginia. Had he not been born to wealth and prestige, it is unlikely that his immense talents could have been devoted to intellect, statesmanship and the arts. Probably he would have led a life similar to that of his father. Peter Jefferson, whose forbears came to Virginia from Wales generations before, created with his own hands the best part of the wealth inherited by his son. The elder Jefferson was unquestionably a man of parts. He became an expert surveyor, served as judge in Albemarle County and sat for several years in the House of Burgesses. He saw to it that his son Thomas received a good classical education and was encouraged to develop habits of study and reflection.

Little is known about Thomas Jefferson's mother. In his "Autobiography" he mentions her only in passing. Jane Randolph came from a better family—or one, at any rate, that had greater aristocratic pretensions—than Peter Jefferson's. (In his "Autobiography" Jefferson writes that the Randolphs "trace their pedigree far back into England and Scotland, to which let everyone ascribe the faith and merit he chooses.") When they married in 1739, Peter Jefferson was thirty-one and Jane Randolph nineteen. Neither lived to old age.

Three years after his father died, Jefferson, at sixteen, left his mother, six sisters and brother and went to William and Mary College in Williamsburg. He hoped to pursue his studies "in the Greek and Latin" and "likewise learn something of the Mathematics." Jefferson learned less from the college (an Anglican establishment presided over by clergymen and attended by young squires) than from his friendships with Dr. William Small and George Wythe.

Dr. Small, of Scotland, who taught mathematics as well as ethics, rhetoric and belles-lettres, imparted to Jefferson the exciting avant-garde thought of the Enlightenment. From Small's conversations, Jefferson later recalled, he got his "first views of the expansion of science, and of the system of things in which we are placed." Small's friend, Wythe, was a lawyer of strong republican principles who became Jefferson's legal mentor in 1762 and remained his "most affectionate friend through life." Without doubt, these two men had a seminal influence on the young Jefferson, who easily deduced republicanism from "the system of things in which we are placed." At all events, he practiced law only five years after serving his apprenticeship with Wythe. Dissatisfied, he gave up the practice in order to divide his time between public and private life—his family, his plantation and his multitude of interests.

Jefferson was twenty-nine when he married Martha Skelton, a widow five years younger than he. His marriage seems to have been happy, but it was tragically brief. His wife died after ten years, and he never remarried. Of the six children born to them, only two, Martha and Mary, survived infancy. Martha, the older daughter, lived to a ripe age and bore twelve children. Mary died at twenty-six after bearing two children. Jefferson wrote little about his family. Practically nothing is known of his wife beyond her birth, marriage and death, and the only information about his children and their lives is that which is contained in their dry correspondence with him. Only one scandal marred his personal life, and that —an alleged liaison with a friend's wife—occurred before he was married, and came to light while he was President.

3

Joining the House of Burgesses as a member from Albemarle County in 1769, Jefferson at once fell in with the group of young men who persistently challenged British authority. The time of trouble between Colonies and mother country began immediately after the conclusion of the French and Indian War in 1763. Parliament, attempting to force the Colonies to assume their share of imperial responsibilities, imposed, for the first time, a direct tax upon them. The Stamp Act of 1765 could not be enforced because it produced too much resistance, and it was withdrawn the following year. The Townshend Acts of 1767, cunningly designed to counteract the Colonies' objections to internal taxes by levying external ones, were likewise resisted by such measures as the Virginia Resolves and Association. The British yielded again, and by 1770 only the duty on tea remained. The next four years were quiet.

The crisis which began in 1774 and led to revolution and independence brought Jefferson to the foreground. That year Parliament passed a series of Coercive Acts to chastise the patriots of Massachusetts who, several months before, had stolen aboard a British vessel and thrown its consignment of tea into Boston Harbor in a protest against the Tea Act of May 1773. Besides closing the port of Boston, the Coercive Acts virtually did away with representative government in Massachusetts. Parliament also blatantly passed a Quartering Act enabling British troops to quarter in private residences anywhere in the thirteen colonies. These direct acts of coercion, which were far more serious than the previous disputes over taxation, provoked the colonies into holding a Continental Congress.

Unable to attend the First Continental Congress, Jefferson, for the edification of the Virginia delegates, wrote his *Summary View of the Rights of British America*, which asserted the equality between colonial legislature and Parliament under the strictly limited powers of the crown. In 1775 he was elected delegate to Congress and became the incipient Revolution's most eloquent spokesman. He was appointed to a Committee of Five called together in June 1776 to present Congress with the draft of a Declaration of Independence. The Committee, knowing him to be a talented writer, asked him to draw up the draft.

Though the Committee and then Congress made many changes in Jefferson's original draft, the design, the conception and the vocabulary remained his. To Jefferson, then, fell the privilege of announcing to all mankind that a new nation existed whose hopes rested on the revolutionary principles of human equality, liberty and happiness.

In the fall of 1776 Jefferson returned to Virginia where he remained for the next seven years. Before the Virginia legislature elected him governor in 1779 he spent his time helping to codify and reform the state laws—an heroic achievement in itself. It was a credo of eighteenth century rationalist faith to judge common and statutory law by the canons of scientific sociology and psychology—essentially, by the greatest happiness, or pleasure–pain, principle. In this respect, Jefferson was in the direct radical tradition of Beccaria, Helvétius, Bentham and the Utilitarians.

But custom in Virginia proved recalcitrant, and only a modest number of Jefferson's reform bills passed. The most important piece of legislation which Jefferson wrote was the Statute for Religious Freedom, which severed all relations between church and state in Virginia and reduced religious "truths" to "opinions." Its influence spread far beyond Virginia's borders. In 1787 the Federal Constitution prohibited religious tests as qualifications for public trust. In effect, Jefferson's bill became the law of the land.

As governor for two years, Jefferson endured a series of disasters culminating in a rout of the government by the forces of British General Cornwallis in the spring of 1781. Hostility and suspicion toward executive authority was so great that the governors in every state lacked power to cope with the exigencies of war. The government of Virginia simply ceased functioning during and for a time after Britain's brief occupation of the capital. Much of the obloquy for the humiliation fell on Jefferson's head. After he left office, the legislature, prodded by Patrick Henry, inquired into Jefferson's conduct. Though the inquiry exonerated him, and complimented him to boot, Jefferson was not appeased. He withdrew sulkily into the solace of his family and property.

4

Never again did Jefferson serve the state of Virginia. Though he championed the cause of state's rights, he spent the last twenty-five years of his public career with the United States government: as commissioner, then minister, to France; as Secretary of State in Washington's Cabinet; as Vice-President under John Adams; finally as President for two terms.

Coming out of a long seclusion following his wife's death, Jefferson consented to join John Adams and Benjamin Franklin in Paris as member of a commission charged to negotiate treaties of peace and commerce with European countries. Before embarking, he remained in the United States long enough to define for Congress, in his famous Ordinance of 1784, the government's liberal policy toward western territories, and, in an extraordinary special report, to lay down the conditions for establishing a uniform monetary system. The force of Jefferson's intelligence and convictions made itself felt wherever he went and in whatever he did. His work for Congress, during a stopover before going to Europe, affected the whole subsequent territorial policy of the United States and laid the groundwork for the uniform monetary system later adopted by the federal government.

In his five years in Paris (he replaced Franklin as minister in 1785) Jefferson was able to pursue his private interests— travel, love, philosophy, science (all pursued with his particular intensity)—to his heart's content at the same time as he carried on his ministerial functions. Had he not been in France, he would no doubt have played a part in drawing up the federal Constitution. In the course of an illuminating correspondence with Madison, he emphasized his support for a new Constitution giving the federal government greater power, but he disagreed with his friend over how much power the states ought to yield. Jefferson deemed it imperative that the Constitution include a bill of rights as its insuperable limit. While in Paris, Jefferson was privileged to witness the opening phase of the French Revolution, which lifted his spirits as no single event had done since America declared her independence thirteen years before. His ebullience was reflected in an important letter to Madison, written on the eve of his return, in which he upheld the revolutionary position that "the earth belongs, in usufruct, to the living; that the dead have neither power nor rights over it."

5

In the period between his appointment as Secretary of State and his election to the Presidency, Jefferson had to put his radical ideals to the test of political conflict. His great adversary during the period was, of course, Alexander Hamilton, who, as Secretary of the Treasury, was the most powerful man in Washington's administration. It is rare that two men of such extraordinary talents, differing so markedly in so many ways, and moreover so thoroughly conscious of their differences, should confront each other at the formative moment of a nation's history. Hamilton was a brilliant advocate of a strong central government secured and made durable by alliance with financial and mercantile interests. To accomplish this end, he applied all his powers of political thought and even yielded up his personal ambitions. Hamilton rarely dispersed his intellectual energies. He pursued the main chance with narrow and concentrated purpose. And he possessed a genius for administration and party leadership. Yet in the end Jefferson defeated him because Jefferson's mightiest ally was Hamilton himself.

Hamilton prevailed in the two central issues which divided them in the Cabinet—the scope of federal responsibility and America's relations with France and Britain. Washington was less disposed to accept Jefferson's objection to Hamilton's policies after the French Revolution entered its most radical phase early in 1793. To Jefferson, a kindred destiny linked republicanism in the United States with the success of the Revolution. He saw Hamilton's extreme Federalism—manifested by the assumption and funding of the debt, the creation of the Bank of the United States and the desire for an economy based on manufacturing—as simply the obverse side of Hamilton's pleading the cause of Britain at every turn. By a sort of inevitable descent, Jefferson believed, Hamiltonian policies must lead to the triumph of the "monocratic" principle and the death of republicanism. Hamilton got his way: Congress adopted his domestic program and Washington adopted his policy of unconditional neutrality toward all belligerent powers, which in reality meant partiality toward Britain (Jefferson also desired neutrality, but as a *quid pro quo* to exact concessions from Britain).

6

In the three years that Jefferson spent at Monticello following his resignation from the Cabinet, the anti-Federalist or Republican Party, under his leadership, grew into a formidable opposition.

Most Americans were yeomen farmers whose interests were not served by the Federalists. This became increasingly apparent as the decade wore on. Imposition of the excise tax on whiskey in 1791 alienated farmers who used whiskey as a means of exchange. Suppression in 1794 of the Whiskey Rebellion of western Pennsylvania intensified their rancor. Jay's Treaty, ratified in June 1795, finally convinced a majority of farmers and planters that the Federalists were willing to compromise their interests in order to appease Britain. Leadership of the Republican Party was supplied by a remarkably durable coalition of Virginia squires and shrewd New York politicians. They were dedicated to the one end of overthrowing the party of Hamilton and Hamiltonianism.

Moreover, the Federalist Party was riven and disorganized. Washington's departure and John Adams' election to the Presidency in 1796 (by a narrow margin over Jefferson, who was elected Vice-President) brought the conflicts within the party to a head. Adams felt much the same way about Hamilton as Jefferson did. Adams' political philosophy, furthermore, was implicitly opposed to Hamilton's. Though both assumed the natural depravity of men, each deduced different conclusions: Adams, that the power of government should be limited and checked; Hamilton, that it should be both concentrated and extended. Adams was in the conservative tradition of Hume, Blackstone and Burke; Hamilton was in the conservative tradition of Machiavelli and Hobbes. Despite the presence of their common enemy, Jefferson, their factions were unable to come to terms.

The crisis over relations with France sealed the fate of the Federalist Party. Republican France, still at war with Britain, reacted to Jay's Treaty by intensifying her attacks upon American vessels and, in effect, breaking off diplomatic relations with the United States early in 1797. Hoping to negotiate a treaty, Adams sent a commission to Paris. Three agents of foreign minister Talleyrand (designated X, Y and Z by the commission) offered cooperation in return for a loan and a bribe. The news of the XYZ affair shocked the American public. Preparations were soon made for war. A direct property tax was imposed to pay for it. The skeleton staff of an army was established, with the aged and ill Washington as commander in chief and Hamilton his second in command. All previous treaties with France were abrogated. The American people were closer to war than at any time since 1783.

At the height of the fever, in the summer of 1798, Congress passed the oppressive Alien and Sedition Acts, aimed at radicals and Francophiles and revolutionary emigrés. To Jefferson—the Vice-President of the country—the Alien and Sedition Acts justified extreme opposition. The Federal Government, he argued, was exercising excessive power which the states had never granted in the Constitution. For the states to resist the Alien and Sedition Acts was therefore to uphold the Constitution. Such was the burden of Jefferson's argument in the Resolutions he drew up for the Kentucky legislature in the fall of 1798. But only Virginia, of the other fifteen states, concurred. In any case, Adams relieved the crisis by appointing, over the opposition of Hamilton and of his friends in the Cabinet, a commission to negotiate with France. By thus outraging the Hamilton wing of the Federalist Party, Adams assured Republican victory in the election of 1800.

7

The Federalist Party never recovered. Jefferson and the Republicans took power at just the right moment. The country stood at the threshold of a prodigious westward expansion. In championing the West—anathema to Federalism—Jefferson was not only affirming his own deeply felt principles; he was securing the future of his party. Jefferson further consolidated his advantage when peace came temporarily to Europe in 1801. For the first time in a decade, American vessels plied the oceans freely, while farmers and planters grew abundant crops to fill their holds. The taxes and restrictions that had been imposed by the Federalists were conspicuously withdrawn by a government whose standard read liberty and rights, not authority and duties.

Jefferson believed that his election finally scotched the threat, implicit in Federalism, to undermine republican institutions. Immediately upon taking office he pardoned the victims of the Alien and Sedition Acts, and the Acts became dead letters. One of the first moves of Congress in 1802 was to repeal the Judiciary Act of the previous year which, by expanding the federal court apparatus, had enabled Adams, just before quitting office, to appoint a multitude of Federalist judges, marshals, attorneys and clerks. Congress also repealed all internal taxes, while the administration, through Secretary of the Treasury Albert Gallatin, cut back federal expenses, especially in the War and Navy departments, and reduced the national debt. To emphasize the avowedly republican style of his government, Jefferson eschewed pomp and ceremony in social and even in diplomatic intercourse. All in all, Jefferson could lay legitimate claim to having led a second revolution in America.

Jefferson ruled the federal establishment—the Supreme Court alone excepted—with unchallenged authority. Congress followed his wishes implicitly in choosing its leadership, its policies, its legislation. Although Jefferson—in his first term —contracted the domain of executive power, within that domain his power was complete. This was possible because the Federalist Party steadily ceased to be a viable opposition. In Congress, Federalists were reduced to a fraction. Nearly every state legislature, including New England's, went Republican. Jefferson's shrewd political policies contributed to the comminution of the Federalist Party. He scrupulously avoided alienating Federalists who could be won over to his party. Nor did he remove them from appointive offices unless he had good cause; on principle Jefferson abhorred spoils and respected talent whatever the policies of the officeholder.

While Jefferson's election affirmed republican ideals—in a world where those ideals were turning to ashes—it nevertheless forced him and his party to accept the responsibility of governing. Rarely do governments, when faced with hard choices, relegate power to ideology. Had international affairs remained as calm during Jefferson's second term as they had during his first, he would not have found it necessary to exceed the Federalists in the broad use and construction of federal power. The Louisiana Purchase of April 30, 1803, which nearly doubled the size of the country and promised to remove a persistent threat from the West, was an augury of the future. Jefferson in effect served notice that doctrine would be modified to suit the desired action. He was not a hypocrite—as the Federalists thought—only a pragmatist.

Jefferson stretched the limits of his pragmatism in his determination, nearly an obsession, to enforce the three Embargo Acts passed by a docile Congress between December 1807 and March 1809. He thought that an embargo against Napoleonic France and Great Britain, who had resumed war in 1803 and depredations of American shipping after 1805, would be preferable to military conflict in securing American neutrality rights. But as the violations of the embargo increased, so, too, did the degree of government coercion. Never before, in fact, had the government so directly and so drastically interfered in the lives of individuals. Nor would it again until the Civil War. The round of coercion and disobedience, each feeding on the other, finally broke when Jefferson signed the law repealing the embargo four days before leaving office.

The embargo produced many ironies. Jefferson had once opposed manufacturing. Now he saw its necessity and virtue. The North as a whole, thanks to its manufacturing and to the greater thrift of its people, adjusted more easily to the embargo than did the South. Virginia suffered most of all. Her livelihood depended on exporting tobacco—all the more because tobacco was a commodity that had been declining in value long before the embargo. (Jefferson's own estate came one step closer to bankruptcy.) The embargo, finally, encouraged massive violation of *republican* law, the people's own law. Many of Jefferson's erstwhile supporters concluded with John Randolph of Virginia, who led a dissident Republican faction, that Jefferson was basically no different than the Federalists. In little more than a year, Jefferson had dissipated most of his previous popularity. But the Federalist Party was too feeble to take adequate advantage of this.

8

Jefferson's long retirement was an epoch in itself. Thousands of letters came from his pen. Eloquent, fresh, trenchant as ever, they covered an astonishing range of subjects. Especially noteworthy was the vast and illuminating correspondence with John Adams which began in 1812 and ended only with their deaths. Throughout his retirement Jefferson remained an unyielding defender of democracy over privilege, of human rights over property rights, of science and knowledge over power bottomed on ignorance and religious superstition. He reiterated these ideals with customary *brio* in the very last letter he wrote, two weeks before his death: "All eyes are opened, or opening, to the rights of man. The general spread of the light of science has already laid open to every view the palpable truth, that the mass of mankind has not been born with saddles on their backs, nor a favored few booted and spurred, ready to ride them legitimately, by the grace of God."

Jefferson's greatest deed during his retirement was establishing the University of Virginia. He had always hoped Virginia would have a university, part of a comprehensive system of public education, which would be open to men of talent and which would spread the truths of science, republicanism and human rights. From the moment that the opportunity for such a university arose in 1814, when he was seventy-one, to its opening eleven years later, Jefferson planned and presided over it from its inception to the coping-stone of its last building. He wrote volumes of letters to generate support, he drafted legislation, secured the site, raised money (nearly $300,000), brought together an impressive faculty, planned the curricula, designed the buildings, etc. It was a prodigious achievement, worthy of its creator, and he wanted it mentioned along with the Declaration of Independence and the Statute of Virginia for Religious Freedom as the legacy to his countrymen and to all men of which he was most proud.

Jefferson stoically bore the suffering and pathos of old age. His once great estate, now bankrupt and irretrievably in debt, headed toward dissolution. His wife, five children, five sisters and only brother were dead. But his immense family of grandchildren and great-grandchildren was his consolation. Tall and straight and self-willed to the end of his life, Jefferson stood in their midst, welcoming the multitude of visitors who paid him homage, like the revered patriarch that he was. Jefferson died on the very day that John Adams died: the fiftieth anniversary of the Declaration of Independence.

9

When Jefferson wrote the Declaration of Independence "the pursuit of happiness" was the privilege of kings and nobility and the dream of philosophers. Jefferson devoted his political life to the end that happiness could be realized for the greatest number of people. He believed that the possibility of happiness inhered in the nature of things and that only falsehood, ignorance and tyranny prevented men from obtaining it. But for the institutions which batten on these evils—essentially governments and formal religions—men would act and think in accordance with the laws of nature. Jefferson set himself the task of transforming—or overthrowing—these institutions so as to enable all men, regardless of class and station, to share in the happiness which was theirs by birthright.

What Jefferson understood by natural law and natural rights had been defined by John Locke in the seventeenth century and dominated American political thought in the eighteenth. According to Locke all men are born with the power to create property by applying their labor to nature. This property is inalienable; it is theirs by the same natural right which enabled them to create it. To secure this right they establish by an original contract a government invested only with the power of trusteeship. Should the government transgress its natural limits the original contract commands its removal, by force if necessary. Jefferson's contribution to politics consisted in creatively adapting Locke's philosophy to the United States.

For Jefferson the right to pursue happiness transcended the right to property, though he hoped the two would not conflict. He believed that the uneven distribution of property must lead to political and ecclesiastical privileges and thus to the denial of happiness for the many. He opposed Hamilton and Federalism because they sought in his view to create a strong central government leagued with the large commercial and banking interests of the East. As the condition of happiness for the majority Jefferson favored the broadest and most equal distribution of property possible. His ideal was a society of independent, self-sufficient, yeoman farmers. For this reason he always championed expansion westward into the vast interior of the American continent. Jefferson distrusted all government other than the individual's government over himself. He most favored small local governments in which every inhabitant of the community could participate to fullest measure. The function of the federal government as Jefferson envisaged it was to act as the trustee for these local governments and thereby to promote the happiness of all the people of the United States. Jefferson was convinced that happiness was possible only when all the people and not the few owned the nation's property.

Jefferson lived long enough to see his party and its ideals triumph, to see the habits and thoughts and feelings of the country cast in his, not in Hamilton's mold. Americans affirmed their faith in the unlimited possibilities of common men and in the priority of human rights over property rights. Like Jefferson they exulted in their liberty, certain that "the laws of nature and of nature's God" sanctioned it to all eternity.

I should like to thank Miss Emily Bernstein for her splendid assistance throughout the preparation of the manuscript.

To Miss Edith Firoozi I am grateful beyond measure for her indispensable help in writing and organizing this book.

ALBERT FRIED
New York City
May 1962

PART I

EARLY YEARS: 1743–1774

Introduction

JEFFERSON WAS BORN IN THE WILDERNESS, like millions of Americans before and since. His father, Peter Jefferson, a man of prodigious strength and accomplishment, had wrested a huge estate from the forests of Virginia and peopled it with slaves. By the age of thirty-one, Peter had earned the right to marry Jane Randolph, who came from one of the best families in Virginia. Eight children were born to them, six daughters and two sons. Thomas, the third eldest, was the first male (his brother Randolph was twelve years younger).

Thomas Jefferson acquired his robustness and love for the outdoors from his father. From his father too, he learned to relentlessly improve his mind and character. Young Jefferson received an education in the classics and arts befitting a gentleman. When he was fourteen his father died, leaving him in charge of the entire family, "without," as he later put it, "a relation or friend qualified to advise or guide him." It was a measure of his wisdom that he decided at the age of sixteen to attend William and Mary College in Williamsburg.

During the time Jefferson attended William and Mary, the entire faculty, save one, were Anglican priests. But their influence on Jefferson must have been negligible. He read widely in the classics, in religion, in science and in moral philosophy, displaying in college the same habits of industry that he was to display throughout his long life. After two years he left college to become a lawyer.

The doors of society in Williamsburg easily opened to Jefferson. He was tall, ruddy, red-haired, quiet-spoken, an aristocrat of unusual intelligence and learning. In his early twenties he was admitted into the best circle in Williamsburg, a "partie quarree" as he called it, consisting of the amiable and cultivated governor, Francis Fauquier; the Scotsman William Small, professor of natural philosophy and mathematics at the college, from whom Jefferson acquired his "first views of the expansion of science & of the system of things in which we are placed"; and the eminent lawyer and political philosopher, George Wythe, to whom Jefferson was especially close. Jefferson much later wrote of their gatherings: "I have heard more good sense, more rational and philosophical conversation, than in all my life besides. They were truly Attic societies."

33

While the protégé and legal apprentice of George Wythe, he continued to read voraciously and deeply—and not alone in law. Volumes of notebooks attest to the wide range of subjects and books he absorbed—and to the breadth of imagination he applied to them—during this five year period of his life. Fifty years later he remembered that he had been "bold in the pursuit of knowledge, never fearing to follow truth and reason whatever results they led [to], and bearding every authority which stood in the way." Jefferson learned after he began practicing law—and practicing it successfully —that he was a better scholar, philosopher, statesman, than he was a lawyer. He found it difficult to accommodate himself to the moral ambiguities of the profession (see, for example, his letter below to Thomas Turpin) and after five years of practice he gave it up forever.

Jefferson's marriage on January 1, 1772 ended a bachelorhood long for those days—a bachelorhood in which he had roistered little, spending his time to good purpose. He chose for his wife a young, pretty and wealthy widow, Martha Wayles Skelton. Little is known of Martha Jefferson—Jefferson maintained an uncompromising reticence about his personal life—except that she was a charming hostess, entertained well, and that Jefferson was deeply attached to her. Her father's death a year after the marriage doubled Jefferson's estate, making him one of the wealthiest men in Virginia. Before Jefferson's wife died on September 6, 1782, she bore six children of whom six lived to maturity.

Jefferson's status and talents enabled him to enter politics at an early age. He served as justice of the peace and member of the county court before Albemarle County elected him to the House of Burgesses in 1769. There he was privileged to sit with an extraordinary aggregation of men—George Washington, Patrick Henry, Peyton Randolph, George Mason, Richard Henry Lee, Edmund Pendleton, among others— during the most critical years in Virginia history. Thanks to their presence, Virginia, the largest colony, more than bore her weight of leadership in the conflict with Great Britain. Jefferson himself did little that was noteworthy in his first five years in the legislature. He served on minor committees; he also drew up the pusillanimous resolution answering Governor Botetourt's speech. Not until the crisis of 1774 did Jefferson emerge as a political leader in Virginia—and in the nation.

A More Universal Acquaintance

To John Harvie, January 14, 1760

This is Jefferson's first known letter. Both John Harvie and Peter Randolph were his guardians.

Sir,—I was at Colo. Peter Randolph's about a Fortnight ago, & my Schooling falling into Discourse, he said he thought it would be to my Advantage to go to the College,[1] & was desirous I should go, as indeed I am myself for several Reasons. In the first place as long as I stay at the Mountains the loss of one fourth of my Time is inevitable, by Company's coming here & detaining me from School. And likewise my Absence will in a great measure put a Stop to so much Company, & by that Means lessen the Expences of the Estate in House-Keeping. And on the other Hand by going to the College I shall get a more universal Acquaintance, which may hereafter be serviceable to me; & I suppose I can pursue my studies in the Greek & Latin as well there as here, & likewise learn something of the Mathematics. I shall be glad of your opinion.

[1] William and Mary College in Williamsburg.

Overwhelmed with Misfortunes

To John Page, December 25, 1762

Jefferson's best friend at William and Mary, John Page, later became governor of Virginia. Rebecca Burwell (or Belinda as Jefferson often referred to her) was the sister of Lewis Burwell, Jr., Jefferson's classmate at William and Mary. She was an orphan whose uncles were well-connected in the Virginia aristocracy.

Dear Page,—This very day, to others the day of greatest mirth and jollity, sees me overwhelmed with more and greater misfortunes than have befallen a descendant of Adam for these thousand years past, I am sure; and perhaps, after excepting Job, since the creation of the world. I think his misfortunes were somewhat greater than mine; for, although we may be pretty nearly on a level in other respects, yet, I thank my God, I have the advantage of brother Job in this, that Satan has not as yet put forth his hand to load me with bodily afflictions. You must know, dear Page, that I am now in a house surrounded with enemies, who take counsel together against my soul; and when I lay me down to rest, they say among themselves, come let us destroy him. I am sure if there is such a thing as a Devil in this world, he must have been here last night, and have had some hand in contriving what happened to me. Do you think the cursed rats (at his instigation, I suppose) did not eat up my pocket-book which was in my pocket, within a foot of my head? And not contented with plenty for the present, they carried away my jemmy-worked silk garters, and half a dozen new minuets I had just got, to serve, I suppose, as provision for the winter. But of this I should not have accused the Devil (because, you know rats will be rats, and hunger, without the addition of his instigations, might have urged them to do this), if something worse, and from a different quarter, had not happened. You know it rained last night, or if you do not know it, I am sure I do. When I went to bed, I laid my watch in the usual place, and going to take her up after I arose this morning, I found her, in the same place, it's true, but *Quantum mutatus ab illo!*[1] all afloat in water, let in at a leak in the roof of the house, and as silent and still as the rats that had eaten my pocket-book. Now, you know, if chance had had anything to do in this matter, there were a thousand other spots where it might have chanced to leak as well as at this one, which was perpendicularly over my watch. But I'll tell you, it's my opinion that the Devil came and bored the hole over it on purpose. Well, as I was saying, my poor watch had lost her speech: I should not have cared much for this, but something worse attended it: the subtle particles of the water with which the case was filled, had, by their penetration so overcome the cohesion of the particles of the paper, of which my dear picture and watch-paper were composed,[2] that, in attempting to take them out to dry them, good God! *Mens horret referre!*[3] My cursed fingers gave them such a rent as I fear I never shall get over. This, cried I, was the last stroke Satan had in reserve for me: he knew I cared not for anything else he could do to me, and was determined to try this last most fatal expedient. *Multis fortunæ vulneribus percussus, huic uni me imparem sensi, et penitus succubui!*[4] . . . However, whatever misfortunes may attend the picture or lover, my hearty prayers shall be, that all the health and happiness which Heaven can send may be the portion of the original, and that so much goodness may ever meet with what may be most agreeable in this world, as I am sure it must be in the next. And now, although the picture be defaced, there is so lively an image of her imprinted in my mind, that I shall think of her too often, I fear, for my peace of mind, and too often, I am sure, to get through old Coke this winter: for God knows I have not seen him since I packed him up in my trunk in Williamsburg.

Well, Page, I do wish the Devil had old Coke, for I am sure I never was so tired of an old dull scoundrel in my life. What! are there so few inquietudes tacked to this momentary life of ours, that we must need be loading ourselves with a thousand more? Or, as brother Job says (who, by-the-bye, I think began to whine a little under his afflictions), "Are not my days few? Cease then, that I may take comfort a little

[1] "How changed from what it was!"
[2] This is a picture of Rebecca Burwell.
[3] "The mind shudders to recall it."
[4] "Pierced through by the many wounds of fate, I felt myself unequal to this one and succumbed utterly!"

before I go whence I shall not return, even to the land of darkness, and the shadow of death." But the old fellows say we must read to gain knowledge; and gain knowledge to make us happy and admired. *Mere jargon!* Is there any such thing as happiness in this world? No. And as for admiration, I am sure the man who powders most, perfumes most, embroiders most, and talks most nonsense, is most admired. Though to be candid, there are some who have too much good sense to esteem such monkey-like animals as these, in whose formation, as the saying is, the tailors and barbers go halves with God Almighty; and since these are the only persons whose esteem is worth a wish, I do not know but that, upon the whole, the advice of these old fellows may be worth following.

You cannot conceive the satisfaction it would give me to have a letter from you. Write me very circumstantially everything which happened at the wedding. Was she there? Because, if she was, I ought to have been at the Devil for not being there too. If there is any news stirring in town or country, such as deaths, courtships, or marriages, in the circle of my acquaintance, let me know it. Remember me affectionately to all the young ladies of my acquaintance, particularly the Miss Burwells, and Miss Potters, and tell them that though that heavy earthly part of me, my body, be absent, the better half of me, my soul, is ever with them, and that my best wishes shall ever attend them. Tell Miss Alice Corbin that I verily believe the rats knew I was to win a pair of garters from her, or they never would have been so cruel as to carry mine away. This very consideration makes me so sure of the bet that I shall ask everybody I see from that part of the world what pretty gentleman is making his addresses to her. I would fain ask the favor of Miss Becca Burwell to give me another watch-paper of her own cutting, which I should esteem much more, though it were a plain round one, than the nicest in the world cut by other hands: however I am afraid she would think this presumption after my suffering the other to get spoiled. If you think you can excuse me to her for this, I should be glad if you would ask her. Tell Miss Sukey Potter that I heard, just before I came out of town, that she was offended with me about something: what it is I do not know; but this I know, that I never was guilty of the least disrespect to her in my life, either in word or deed; as far from it as it has been possible for one to be: I suppose when we meet next, she will be *endeavoring* to repay an imaginary affront with a real one: but she may save herself the trouble, for nothing that she can say or do to me shall ever lessen her in my esteem, and I am determined always to look upon her as the same honest-hearted, good-humored, agreeable lady I ever did. Tell—tell—in short tell them all ten thousand things more than either you or I can now or ever shall think of as long as we live.

My mind has been so taken up with thinking of my acquaintances, that, till this moment, I almost imagined myself in Williamsburg, talking to you in our old unreserved way; and never observed, till I turned over the leaf, to what an immoderate size I had swelled my letter: however, that I may not tire your patience by further additions I will make but this one more, that I am sincerely and affectionately Dear Page your friend and servant.

Perfect Resignation

To John Page, July 15, 1763

Jefferson's love for "Belinda" was evidently not so deep as to prevent him from being philosophically detached about it. The rival to whom Jefferson refers was Jacquelin Ambler who married Rebecca in May of the following year.

Your's of May 30'th came safe to hand. The rival you mentioned I know not whether to think formidable or not as there has been so great an opening for him during my absence. I say "has been" because I expect there is one no longer since you have undertaken to act as my attorney. You advise me to "go immediately and lay siege in form." You certainly did not think at the time you wrote this of that paragraph in my letter wherein I mentioned to you my resolution of going to Britain. And to begin an affair of that kind now, and carry it on so long a time in form is by no means a proper plan. No, no, Page, whatever assurances I may give her in private of my esteem for her, or whatever assurances I may ask in return from her, depend on it they must be kept in private. Necessity will oblige me to proceed in a method which is not generally thought fair, that of treating with a ward before obtaining the approbation of her guardian. I say necessity will oblige me to it, because I never can bear to remain in suspense so long a time. If I am to succeed the sooner I know it the less uneasiness I shall have to go through: if I am to meet with a disappointment the sooner I know it the more of life I shall have to wear it off: and if I do meet with one, I hope in god and verily beleive it will be the last. I assure you that I almost envy you your present freedom; and if Belinda will not accept of my service it shall never be offered to another. That she may, I pray most sincerely, but that she will, she never gave me reason to hope. With regard to my not proceeding in form I do not know how she may like it: I am afraid not much: that her guardians would not, if they should know of it, is very certain. But I should think that if they were consulted after my return, it would be sufficient. The greatest inconvenience would be my not having the liberty of visiting so freely. This is a subject worth your talking over with her; and I wish you would, and would transmit me your whole confab at length. I should be scared to death at making her so unreasonable a proposal as that of waiting untill I returned from Britain, unless she could be first prepared for it. I am afraid it will make my chance of succeeding considerably worse. But the event at last must be this, that if she consents, I shall be happy; if she does not, I must endeavor to be as much so as possible. I have thought a good deal on your case, and as mine may perhaps be similar, I must endeavor to look on it in the same light in which I have often advised you to look on yours. Perfect happiness I believe was never intended by the deity to be the lot of any one of his creatures in this world; but that he has very much put in our power the nearness of our approaches to it, is what I as stedfastly beleive. The most fortunate of us all in our journey through life frequently meet with calamities and misfortunes which may greatly afflict us: and to fortify our minds against the attacks of these calamities and misfortunes should be one of the principal studies and endeavors of our lives. The only method of doing this is to assume a perfect resignation to the divine will, to consider that whatever does happen, must happen, and that by our uneasiness we cannot prevent the blow before it does fall, but we may add to it's force after it has fallen. These considerations and others such as these may enable us in some measure to surmount the difficulties thrown in our way, to bear up with a tolerable degree of patience under this burthen of life, and to proceed with a pious and unshaken resignation till we arrive at our journey's end, where we may deliver up our trust into the hands of him who gave it, and receive such reward as to him shall seem proportioned to our merit. Such dear Page, will be the language of the man who considers his situation in this life, and such should be the language of every man who would wish to render that situation as easy as the nature of it will admit. Few things will disturb him at all; nothing will disturb him much.

If this letter was to fall into the hands of some of our gay acquaintance, your correspondent and his solemn notions would probably be the subjects of a great deal of mirth and raillery, but to you I think I can venture to send it. It is in effect but a continuation of the many conversations we have had on subjects of this kind; and I heartily wish we could now continue these conversations face to face. The time will not be very long now before we may do it, as I expect to be in Williamsburg by the first of October if not sooner. I do not know that I shall have occasion to return if I can rent rooms in town to lodge in; and to prevent the inconvenience of moving my lodgings for the future, I think to build. No castle though I assure you, only a small house which shall contain a room for myself and another for you, and no more, unless Belinda should think proper to favor us with her company, in which case I will enlarge the plan as much as she pleases. Make my compliments to her particularly, as also to Suckey Potter, Judey Burwell and such others of my acquaintances as enquire after me. I am Dear Page your sincere friend,

My Strange Confusion

To John Page, October 7, 1763

The Rev. James Hurrox was master of the grammar school at William and Mary.

Dear Page,—In the most melancholy fit that ever any poor soul was, I sit down to write to you. Last night, as merry as agreeable company and dancing with Belinda in the Apollo could make me, I never could have thought the succeeding sun would have seen me so wretched as I now am! I was prepared to say a great deal: I had dressed up, in my own mind, such thoughts as occurred to me, in as moving a language as I knew how, and expected to have performed in a tolerably creditable manner. But, good God! When I had an opportunity of venting them, a few broken sentences, uttered in great disorder, and interrupted with pauses of uncommon length, were the too visible marks of my strange confusion! The whole confab I will tell you, word for word, if I can, when I see you, which God send may be soon. Affairs at W. and M. are in the greatest confusion. Walker, M'Clurg and Wat Jones are expelled *pro tempore*, or, as Horrox softens it, rusticated for a month. Lewis Burwell, Warner Lewis, and one Thompson, have fled to escape flagellation. I should have excepted Warner Lewis, who came off of his own accord. Jack Walker leaves town on Monday. The court is now at hand, which I must attend constantly, so that unless you come to town, there is little probability of my meeting with you anywhere else. For God sake come. I am, dear Page, your sincere friend.

I Do Not Like the Ups and Downs of a Country Life

To William Fleming [ca. October 1763]

A classmate of Jefferson's at William and Mary, Fleming was for some years his good friend and correspondent.

From a crowd of disagreeable [companions] among whom I have spent three or four of the most tedious hours of my life, I retire into Gunn's bedchamber to converse in black and white with an absent friend. I heartily wish you were here that I might converse with a Christian once more before I die: for die I must this night unless I should be releived by the arrival of some sociable fellow. But I will now endeavor to forget my present sufferings and think of what is more agreeable to both of us. Last Saturday I left Ned Carter's where I had been happy in other good company, but particularly that of Miss Jenny Taliaferro: and though I can view the beauties of this world with the most philosophical indifference, I could not but be sensible of the justice of the character you had given me of her. She has in my opinion a great resemblance of Nancy Wilton, but prettier. I was vastly pleased with her playing on the spinnette and singing, and could not help calling to mind those sublime verses of the Cumberland genius

> Oh! how I was charmed to see
> Orpheus' music all in thee.

When you see Patsy Dandridge, tell her 'god bless her.' I do not like the ups and downs of a country life: to day you are frolicking with a fine girl and tomorrow you are moping by yourself. Thank god! I shall shortly be where my happiness will be less interrupted. I shall salute all the girls below in your name, particularly S——y P——r. Dear Will I have thought of the cleverest plan of life that can be imagined. You exchange your land for Edgehill, or I mine for Fair-feilds, you marry S——y P——r, I marry R——a B——l,

[join] and get a pole chair and a pair of keen horses, practise the law in the same courts, and drive about to all the dances in the country together. How do you like it? Well I am sorry you are at such a distance I cannot hear your answer, however you must let me know it by the first opportunity, and all the other news in the world which you imagine will affect me. I am dear Will yours affectionately,

Many and Great Are the Comforts of a Single State

To William Fleming, March 20, 1764

Jefferson gives notice here of the headaches which were to bedevil him for the rest of his life. Despite his hard resolve to remain a bachelor, he married less than eight years later.

As the messenger who delivered me your letter, informs me that your boy is to leave town tomorrow morning I will endeavor to answer it as circumstantially as the hour of the night, and a violent head ache, with which I have been afflicted these two days, will permit. With regard to the scheme which I proposed to you some time since, I am sorry to tell you it is totally frustrated by Miss R. B.'s marriage with Jacquelin Ambler which the people here tell me they daily expect: I say, the people here tell me so, for (can you beleive it?) I have been so abominably indolent as not to have seen her since last October, wherefore I cannot affirm that I know it from herself, though am as well satisfied that it is true as if she had told me. Well the lord bless her I say! But S——y P——r is still left for you. I have given her a description of the gentleman who, as I told her, intended to make her an offer of his hand, and asked whether or not he might expect it would be accepted. She would not determine till she saw him or his picture. Now Will, as you are a piece of a limner I desire that you will seat yourself immediately before your lookingglass and draw such a picture of yourself as you think proper: and if it should be defective, blame yourself. (Mind that I mentioned no name to her.) You say you are determined to be married as soon as possible: and advise me to do the same. No, thank ye; I will consider of it first. Many and great are the comforts of a single state, and neither of the reasons you urge can have any influence with an inhabitant and a young inhabitant too of Wmsburgh. For St. Paul only says that it is better to be married than to burn. Now I presume that if that apostle had known that providence would at an after day be so kind to any particular set of people as to furnish them with other means of extinguishing their fire than those of matrimony, he would have earnestly recommended them to their practice. Who told you that I reported you was courting Miss Dandridge and Miss Dangerfeild? It might be worth your while to ask whether they were in earnest or not. So far was I from it that I frequently bantered Miss J——y T——o about you, and told her how feelingly you spoke of her. There is scarcely any thing new going on here. You have heard I suppose that J. Page is courting Fanny Burwell. W. Bland, and Betsy Yates are to be married thursday se'nnight. The Secretary's son is expected in shortly. Willis has left town intirely so that your commands to him cannot be executed immediately, but those to the ladies I shall do myself the pleasure of delivering tomorrow night at the ball. Tom: Randolph of Tuckahoe has a suit of Mecklenburgh Silk which he offered me for a suit of broadcloth. Tell him that if they can be altered to fit me, I will be glad to take them on them terms, and if they cannot, I make no doubt but I can dispose of them here to his advantage. Perhaps you will have room to bring them in your portmanteau, or can contrive them down by some other opportunity. Let him know this immediately. My head aches, my candle is just going out, and my boy asleep, so must bid you adieu.

Let Him Employ His Time for Himself Alone

To Thomas Turpin, February 5, 1769

Jefferson gives an extraordinarily astute and honest piece of advice here; John Adams, among others, made similar criticisms of the lawyer apprentice system then operative. This is the first instance of Jefferson's lifelong concern to improve the minds of younger friends, a concern invariably manifested by prescribing elaborate plans of study for them. Phillip Turpin was Jefferson's first cousin.

I am truly concerned that it is not in my power to undertake the superintendance of your son in his studies; but my situation both present and future render it utterly impossible. I do not expect to be here more than two months in the whole between this and November next, at which time I propose to remove to another habitation which I am about to erect, and on a plan so contracted as that I shall have but one spare bedchamber for whatever visitants I may have. Nor have I reason to expect at any future day to pass a greater proportion of my time at home. Thus situated it would even have been injustice to Phill to have undertaken to give him an assistance which will not be within my power; a task which I otherwise should with the greatest pleasure have taken on me, and would have desired no higher satisfaction than to see him hold that rank in the profession to which his genius and application must surely advance him. These however encourage me to hope that the presence of an assistant will be little necessary. I always was of opinion that the placing a youth to study with an attorney was rather a prejudice than a help. We are all too apt by shifting on them our business, to incroach on that time which should be devoted to their studies. The only help a youth wants is to be directed what books to read, and in what order to read them. I have accordingly recommended strongly to Phill to put himself into apprenticeship with no one, but to employ his time for himself alone. To enable him to do this to advantage I have laid down a plan of study which will afford him all the assistance a tutor could, without subjecting him to the inconvenience of expending his own time for the emolument of another. One difficulty only occurs, that is, the want of books. But this I am in hopes you will think less of remedying when it is considered that had he been placed under the care of another, a proper collection of books must have been provided for him before he engaged in the practice of his profession; for a lawyer without books would be like a workman without tools. The only difference then is that they must now be procured something earlier. Should you think it necessary, it would be better to consider the money laid out in books as a part of the provision made for him, and to deduct it from what you intended to give him, than that he should be without them. I have given him a catalogue of such as will be necessary, amounting in the whole to about £100. sterling, but divided into four invoices. Should Phill enter on the plan of study recommended, I shall endeavor as often as possible to take your house in my way to and from Williamsburgh as it will afford me the double satisfaction of observing his progress in science and of seeing yourself, my aunt, and the family. I am Dear Sir with great respect your most humble servant,

Happy Ruler of a Free and Happy People

Resolution for an Answer to Governor Botetourt's Speech, May 8, 1769

This is Jefferson's first public paper. Note its formal, ceremonial style which he was to eschew as his papers became republican in content.

Resolved, Nemine contradicente, That a most humble and dutiful Address be presented to his Excellency the Governor [Botetourt], returning Thanks for his very affectionate Speech at the Opening of the Session;

Expressing our firm Attachment to his Majesty's sacred Person and Government, and a lively Sense of his Royal Favour, manifested by frequent Approbations of our former Conduct; by extending his Paternal Regard to all his Subjects, however remote; and, by his gracious Purpose, that our Chief Governor shall, in future, reside among us;

Declaring, that we esteem, as a peculiar Mark of his Attention to our Happiness, the Appointment of his Lordship to preside over this Colony; and, that his Virtues and Abilities, manifested ever since his Arrival here, are to us the firmest Assurance, that Wisdom and Benevolence will distinguish his Administration;

Joining, in Congratulations on the Birth of another Princess, and the happy Restoration of her Majesty's Health;

Assuring his Excellency, that we shall, with Candour, proceed to the important Business on which we are met in General Assembly; and that, if in the Course of our Deliberations, any Matters shall arise, which may in any wise affect the Interests of *Great-Britain*, these shall ever be discussed on this ruling Principle, that her Interests, and ours, are inseparably the same; And finally, offering our Prayers, that Providence, and the Royal Pleasure, may long continue his Lordship the happy Ruler of a free and happy People.

PART II

REVOLUTIONIST: 1774–1778

Introduction

JEFFERSON WAS in the vanguard of the revolutionary up-surge against Great Britain after 1774. His thorough familiarity with Locke and with liberal philosophy generally, his weighty knowledge of the law, his wealth and social standing and his power as a writer carried him to the summit of leadership in his early thirties. It was given to him, as author of the Declaration of Independence, to express the quintessential ideals of revolutionary America.

In March 1773 Jefferson, Patrick Henry, Richard Henry Lee, Francis Lightfoot Lee and seven others formed the Virginia Committee of Correspondence in an act of solidarity with the patriots of Massachusetts. Great Britain, as a result of the *Gaspee* incident in June of the previous year, had threatened to try Americans abroad. Massachusetts governor Thomas Hutchinson had also announced that he and his retainers would henceforth be paid not by the legislature but by Great Britain, thus rendering the legislature impotent. In consequence, Massachusetts patriots, led by Sam Adams, had revised the old Committees of Correspondence in November 1772 and called for support from other colonies.

Matters came to a boil in early 1774 when Parliament, in retaliation for the Boston Tea Party, passed the Boston Port Bill, the Administration of Justice Act, the Massachusetts Government Act and the Quartering Act. The Massachusetts Government Act in particular threatened self-government in every Colony. Its worst provision stated that the governor alone was to determine whether or not town meetings could be held and what could be discussed in them. The call went out for colonial patriots to meet in Philadelphia in September 1774.

Jefferson was not one of the seven Virginia delegates to the First Continental Congress. But he wrote for their benefit his *Summary View of the Rights of British America*. It was his first ambitious venture in political theory, and it raised him from relative obscurity to notoriety well outside Virginia. In attempting to show that colonial legislatures owed no obedience to Parliament, only to the King, the *Summary View* expressed the sense of most patriots at the time. John

Adams' influential Novanglus letters, most of them published early in 1775, stated the same arguments.

Jefferson was himself chosen a delegate to the Continental Congress in June 1775. Before setting out for Philadelphia he drafted the Virginia legislature's rejection of Lord North's conciliatory proposal. Thanks to his "happy talent for composition" (as John Adams put it) Jefferson's main task, during his fifteen months in Philadelphia, was to draft official papers for Congress. His most notable writing was the *Declaration of the Causes and Necessity for Taking Up Arms* and, of course, the *Declaration of Independence*. The trenchancy and eloquence with which Jefferson expressed the arguments for independence attests to the power of his convictions. Expediency alone could not have made the Declaration possible. Not only did it announce the birth of a nation; it defined the principles by which the nation was expected to live. None of the delegates could have known that the chief author of the Declaration would himself someday oversee a triumphant vindication of those principles.

While fulfilling his duties for the Continental Congress, Jefferson was drafting a constitution for Virginia. It arrived too late, however, to be seriously considered by the Virginia Constitutional Convention. Nor, furthermore, were the delegates to that convention disposed to accept a body of laws as radical as Jefferson was proposing. But the convention did tack on to the constitution it ratified Jefferson's preamble, the language of which is nearly identical to that of the Declaration of Independence.

In September 1776 Jefferson returned to Virginia, where he was to be a political force and a reformer of the laws for the next five years. Less than two months after his return he succeeded in getting a bill passed abolishing entail. Jefferson was proud of this act, though its effect was modest. He considered it a first step in the attack upon aristocratic privilege.

Deal Out to All Equal and Impartial Right

Summary View of the Rights of British America, August 1774

Jefferson's Summary View *was not intended to be a polemic. Originally, he sent it untitled to Patrick Henry and Peyton Randolph upon their election as delegates to the First Continental Congress. He wrote it for them hoping to clarify the issues by a downright statement of principles and grievances. The* Summary View *was printed anonymously in Williamsburg without Jefferson's knowledge. It was reprinted in Philadelphia and London the same year. With it, Jefferson's talents as a writer came to the attention of patriots outside Virginia.*

Resolved that it be an instruction to the said deputies, when assembled in General Congress, with the deputies from the other states of British America, to propose to the said Congress, that an humble and dutiful address be presented to his Majesty, begging leave to lay before him, as Chief Magistrate of the British empire, the united complaints of his Majesty's subjects in America; complaints which are excited by many unwarrantable encroachments and usurpations, attempted to be made by the legislature of one part of the empire, upon the rights which God, and the laws, have given equally and independently to all. To represent to his Majesty that these, his States, have often individually made humble application to his imperial Throne, to obtain, through its intervention, some redress of their injured rights; to none of which, was ever even an answer condescended. Humbly to hope that this, their joint address, penned in the language of truth, and divested of those expressions of servility, which would persuade his Majesty that we are asking favors, and not rights, shall obtain from his Majesty a more respectful acceptance; and this his Majesty will think we have reason to expect, when he reflects that he is no more than the chief officer of the people, appointed by the laws, and circumscribed with definite powers, to assist in working the great machine of government, erected for their use, and, consequently, subject to their superintendence; and, in order that these, our rights, as well as the invasions of them, may be laid more fully before his Majesty, to take a view of them, from the origin and first settlement of these countries.

To remind him that our ancestors, before their emigration to America, were the free inhabitants of the British dominions in Europe, and possessesd a right, which nature has given to all men, of departing from the country in which chance, not choice, has placed them, of going in quest of new habitations, and of there establishing new societies, under such laws and regulations as, to them, shall seem most likely to promote public happiness. That their Saxon ancestors had, under this universal law, in like manner, left their native wilds and woods in the North of Europe, had possessed themselves of the Island of Britain, then less charged with inhabitants, and had established there that system of laws which has so long been the glory and protection of that country. Nor was ever any claim of superiority or dependence asserted over them, by that mother country from which they had migrated: and were such a claim made, it is believed his Majesty's subjects in Great Britain have too firm a feeling of the rights derived to them from their ancestors, to bow down the sovereignty of their state before such visionary pretensions. And it is thought that no circumstance has occurred to distinguish, materially, the British from the Saxon emigration. America was conquered, and her settlements made and firmly established, at the expense of individuals, and not of the British public. Their own blood was spilt in acquiring lands for their settlement, their own fortunes expended in making that settlement effectual. For themselves they fought, for themselves they conquered, and for themselves alone they have right to hold. No shilling was ever issued from the public treasures of his Majesty, or his ancestors, for their assistance, till of very late times, after the colonies had become established on a firm and permanent footing. That then, indeed, having become valuable to Great Britain for her commercial purposes, his Parliament was pleased to lend them assistance against an enemy who would fain have drawn to herself the benefits of their commerce, to the great aggrandisement of herself, and danger of Great Britain. Such assistance, and in such circumstances, they had often before given to Portugal and other allied states, with whom they carry on a commercial intercourse. Yet these states never supposed that by calling in her aid, they thereby submitted themselves to her sovereignty. Had such terms been proposed, they would have rejected them with disdain, and trusted for better, to the moderation of their enemies, or to a vigorous exertion of their own force. We do not, however, mean to underrate those aids, which, to us, were doubtless valuable, on whatever principles granted: but we would shew that they cannot give a title to that authority which the British Parliament would arrogate over us; and that may amply be repaid by our giving to the inhabitants of Great Britain such exclusive privileges in trade as may be advantageous to them, and, at the same time, not too restrictive to ourselves. That settlement having been thus effected in the wilds of America, the emigrants thought proper to adopt that system of laws, under which they had hitherto lived in the mother country, and to continue their union with her, by submitting themselves to the same common sovereign, who was thereby made the central link, connecting the several parts of the empire thus newly multiplied.

But that not long were they permitted, however far they thought themselves removed from the hand of oppression, to hold undisturbed the rights thus acquired at the hazard of their lives and loss of their fortunes. A family of Princes was then on the British throne, whose treasonable crimes against their people, brought on them, afterwards, the exertion of those sacred and sovereign rights of punishment, reserved in the hands of the people for cases of extreme necessity, and judged by the constitution unsafe to be delegated to any other judicature. While every day brought forth some new and unjustifiable exertion of power over their subjects on that side of the water, it was not to be expected that those here, much less able at that time to oppose the designs of despotism, should be exempted from injury. Accordingly, this country which had been acquired by the lives, the labors, and fortunes of individual adventurers, was by these Princes, several times, parted out and distributed among the favorites and followers of their fortunes; and, by an assumed right of the Crown alone, were erected into distinct and independent governments; a measure, which it is believed, his Majesty's prudence and understanding would prevent him from imitating at this day; as no exercise of such power, of dividing and dismembering a country, has ever occurred in his Majesty's realm of England, though now of very ancient standing; nor could it be justified or acquiesced under there, or in any part of his Majesty's empire.

That the exercise of a free trade with all parts of the world, possessed by the American colonists, as of natural right, and which no law of their own had taken away or abridged, was next the object of unjust encroachment. Some of the colonies having thought proper to continue the administration of their government in the name and under the authority of his Majesty, King Charles the first, whom, notwithstanding his late deposition by the Commonwealth of England, they continued in the sovereignty of their State, the Parliament, for the Commonwealth, took the same in high offence, and assumed upon themselves the power of prohibiting their trade with all other parts of the world, except the Island of Great Britain. This arbitrary act, however, they soon recalled, and by solemn treaty entered into on the 12th day of March, 1651, between the said Commonwealth, by their Commissioners, and the colony of Virginia by their House of Burgesses, it was expressly stipulated by the eighth article of the said treaty, that they should have 'free trade as the people of England do enjoy to all places and with all nations, according to the laws of that Commonwealth.' But that, upon the restoration of his Majesty, King Charles the second, their rights of free commerce fell once more a victim to arbitrary power; and by several acts of his reign, as well as of some of his successors, the trade of the colonies was laid under such restrictions, as show what hopes they might form from the justice of a British Parliament, were its uncontrolled power admitted over these States. History has informed us, that bodies of men as well as of individuals, are susceptible of the spirit of tyranny. A view of these acts of Parliament for regulation, as it has been affectedly called, of the American trade, if all other evidences were removed out of the case, would undeniably evince the truth of this observation. Besides the duties they impose on our articles of export and import, they prohibit our going to any markets Northward of Cape Finisterra, in the kingdom of Spain, for the sale of commodities which Great Britain will not take from us, and for the purchase of others, with which she cannot supply us; and that, for no other than the arbitrary purpose of purchasing for themselves, by a sacrifice of our rights and interests, certain privileges in their commerce with an allied state, who, in confidence, that their exclusive trade with America will be continued, while the principles and power of the British Parliament be the same, have indulged themselves in every exorbitance which their avarice could dictate or our necessity extort: have raised their commodities called for in America, to the double and treble of what they sold for, before such exclusive privileges were given them, and of what better commodities of the same kind would cost us elsewhere; and, at the same time, give us much less for what we carry thither, than might be had at more convenient ports. That these acts prohibit us from carrying, in quest of other purchasers, the surplus of our tobaccos, remaining after the consumption of Great Britain is supplied: so that we must leave them with the British merchant, for whatever he will please to allow us, to be by him re-shipped to foreign markets, where he will reap the benefits of making sale of them for full value. That, to heighten still the idea of Parliamentary justice, and to show with what moderation they are like to exercise power, where themselves are to feel no part of its weight, we take leave to mention to his Majesty, certain other acts of the British Parliament, by which they would prohibit us from manufacturing, for our own use, the articles we raise on our own lands, with our own labor. By an act passed in the fifth year of the reign of his late Majesty, King George the second, an American subject is forbidden to make a hat for himself, of the fur which he has taken, perhaps, on his own soil; an instance of despotism, to which no parallel can be produced in the most arbitrary ages of British history. By one other act, passed in the twenty-third year of the same reign, the iron which we make, we are forbidden to manufacture; and, heavy as that article is, and necessary in every branch of husbandry, besides commission and insurance, we are to pay freight for it to Great Britain, and freight for it back again, for the purpose of supporting, not men, but machines, in the island of Great Britain. In the same spirit of equal and impartial legislation, is to be viewed the act of Parliament, passed in the fifth year of the same reign, by which American lands are made subject to the demands of British creditors, while their own lands were still continued unanswerable for their debts; from which, one of these conclusions must necessarily follow, either that justice is not the same thing in America as in Britain, or else, that the British Parliament pay less regard to it here than there. But, that we do not point out to his

Majesty the injustice of these acts, with intent to rest on that principle the cause of their nullity; but to show that experience confirms the propriety of those political principles, which exempt us from the jurisdiction of the British Parliament. The true ground on which we declare these acts void, is, that the British Parliament has no right to exercise authority over us.

That these exercises of usurped power have not been confined to instances alone, in which themselves were interested; but they have also intermeddled with the regulation of the internal affairs of the colonies. The act of the 9th of Anne for establishing a post office in America, seems to have had little connection with British convenience, except that of accommodating his Majesty's ministers and favorites with the sale of a lucrative and easy office.

That thus have we hastened through the reigns which preceded his Majesty's, during which the violation of our rights were less alarming, because repeated at more distant intervals, than that rapid and bold succession of injuries, which is likely to distinguish the present from all other periods of American story. Scarcely have our minds been able to emerge from the astonishment into which one stroke of Parliamentary thunder has involved us, before another more heavy and more alarming is fallen on us. Single acts of tyranny may be ascribed to the accidental opinion of a day; but a series of oppressions, begun at a distinguished period, and pursued unalterably through every change of ministers, too plainly prove a deliberate, systematical plan of reducing us to slavery.

That the act, passed in the 4th year of his majesty's reign, entitled "An act [for granting certain duties in the British colonies and plantations in America, &c.]"[1]

One other act, passed in the 5th year of his reign, entitled "An act [for granting and applying certain stamp duties and other duties in the British colonies and plantations in America, &c.]"

One other act, passed in the 6th year of his reign, entitled "An act [for the better securing the dependency of his majesty's dominions in America upon the crown and parliament

---

[1] The bracketed areas indicate the insertions of Paul Leicester Ford, editor of the twelve volume *The Works of Thomas Jefferson* (Federal Edition. New York: G. P. Putnam's Sons, 1904–5.)

of Great Britain];" and one other act, passed in the 7th year of his reign, entitled "An act [for granting duties on paper, tea, &c.]" form that connected chain of parliamentary usurpation, which has already been the subject of frequent applications to his majesty, and the houses of lords and commons of Great Britain; and no answers having yet been condescended to any of these, we shall not trouble his majesty with a repetition of the matters they contained.

But that one other act, passed in the same 7th year of the reign, having been a peculiar attempt, must ever require peculiar mention; it is entitled "An act for suspending the legislature of New York."

One free and independent legislature, hereby takes upon itself to suspend the powers of another, free and independent as itself. Thus exhibiting a phenomenon unknown in nature, the creator, and creature of its own power. Not only the principles of common sense, but the common feelings of human nature must be surrendered up, before his Majesty's subjects here, can be persuaded to believe, that they hold their political existence at the will of a British Parliament. Shall these governments be dissolved, their property annihilated, and their people reduced to a state of nature, at the imperious breath of a body of men whom they never saw, in whom they never confided, and over whom they have no powers of punishment or removal, let their crimes against the American public be ever so great? Can any one reason be assigned, why one hundred and sixty thousand electors in the island of Great Britain, should give law to four millions in the States of America, every individual of whom is equal to every individual of them in virtue, in understanding, and in bodily strength? Were this to be admitted, instead of being a free people, as we have hitherto supposed, and mean to continue ourselves, we should suddenly be found the slaves, not of one, but of one hundred and sixty thousand tyrants; distinguished, too, from all others, by this singular circumstance, that they are removed from the reach of fear, the only restraining motive which may hold the hand of a tyrant.

That, by 'an act to discontinue in such manner, and for such time as are therein mentioned, the landing and discharging, lading or shipping of goods, wares and merchandize, at the town and within the harbor of Boston, in the province of Massachusetts bay, in North America,' which was passed at the last session of the British Parliament, a large and populous town, whose trade was their sole subsistence, was deprived of that trade, and involved in utter ruin. Let us for a while, suppose the question of right suspended, in order to examine this act on principles of justice. An act of Parliament had been passed, imposing duties on teas, to be paid in America, against which act the Americans had protested, as inauthoritative. The East India Company, who till that time, had never sent a pound of tea to America on their own account, step forth on that occasion, the asserters of Parliamentary right, and send hither many ship loads of that obnoxious commodity. The masters of their several vessels, however, on their arrival in America, wisely attended to admonition, and returned with their cargoes. In the province of New-England alone, the remonstrances of the people were disregarded, and a compliance, after being many days waited for, was flatly refused. Whether in this, the master of the vessel was governed by his obstinacy, or his instructions, let those who know, say. There are extraordinary situations which require extraordinary interposition. An exasperated people, who feel that they possess power, are not easily restrained within limits strictly regular. A number of them assembled in the town of Boston, threw the tea into the ocean, and dispersed without doing any other act of violence. If in this they did wrong, they were known, and were amenable to the laws of the land; against which, it could not be objected, that they had ever, in any instance, been obstructed or diverted from the regular course, in favor of popular offenders. They should, therefore, not have been distrusted on this occasion. But that ill-fated colony had formerly been bold in their enmities against the House of Stuart, and were now devoted to ruin, by that unseen hand which governs the momentous affairs of this great empire. On the partial representations of a few worthless ministerial dependants, whose constant office it has been to keep that government embroiled, and who, by their treacheries, hope to obtain the dignity of British knighthood, without calling for a party accused, without asking a proof, without attempting a distinction between the guilty and the innocent, the whole of that ancient and wealthy town, is in a moment reduced from opulence to beggary. Men who had spent their lives in extending the British commerce, who had invested, in that place, the wealth their honest endeavors had merited, found themselves and their families, thrown at once on the world, for subsistence by its charities. Not the hundredth part of the inhabitants of that town, had been concerned in the act complained of; many of them were in Great Britain, and in other parts beyond the sea; yet all were involved in one indiscriminate ruin, by a new executive power, unheard of till then, that of a British Parliament. A property of the value of many millions of money, was sacrificed to revenge, not repay, the loss of a few thousands. This is administering justice with a heavy hand indeed! And when is this tempest to be arrested in its course? Two wharves are to be opened again when his Majesty shall think proper: the residue, which lined the extensive shores of the bay of Boston, are forever interdicted the exercise of commerce. This little exception seems to have been thrown in for no other purpose, than that of setting a precedent for investing his Majesty with legislative powers. If the pulse of his people shall beat calmly under this experiment, another and another will be tried, till the measure of despotism be filled up. It would be an insult on common sense, to pretend that this exception was made, in order to restore its commerce to that great town. The trade, which cannot be received at two wharves alone, must of necessity be transferred to some other place; to which it will soon be followed by that of the two wharves. Considered in this light, it would be an insolent and cruel mockery at the annihilation of the town of Boston. By the act for the suppression of riots and tumults in the town of Boston, passed also in the last session of Parliament, a murder committed there, is, if the Governor pleases, to be tried in the court of King's bench, in the island of Great Britain, by a jury of Middlesex. The witnesses, too, on receipt of such a sum as the Governor shall think it reasonable for them to expend, are to enter into recognizance to appear at the trial. This is, in other words, taxing them to the amount of their recognizance; and that amount may be whatever a Governor pleases. For who does his Majesty think can be prevailed on to cross the Atlantic for the sole purpose of bearing evidence to a fact? His expenses are to be borne, indeed, as they shall be estimated by a Governor; but who are to feed the wife and children whom he leaves behind, and who have had no other subsistence but his daily labor? Those epidemical disorders, too, so terrible in a foreign climate, is the cure of them to be estimated among the articles of expense, and their danger to be warded off by the Almighty power of a Parliament? And the wretched criminal, if he happen to have offended on the American side, stripped of his privilege of trial by peers of his vicinage, removed from the place where alone full evidence could be obtained, without money, without counsel, without friends, without exculpatory proof, is tried before Judges predetermined to condemn. The cowards who would suffer a countryman to be torn from the bowels of their society, in order to be thus offered a sacrifice to Parliamentary tyranny, would merit that everlasting infamy now fixed on the authors of the act! A clause, for a similar purpose, had been introduced into an act passed in the twelfth year of his Majesty's reign, entitled, 'an act for the better securing and preserving his Majesty's Dockyards, Magazines, Ships, Ammunition and Stores;' against which, as meriting the same censures, the several colonies have already protested.

That these are the acts of power, assumed by a body of men foreign to our constitutions, and unacknowledged by our laws; against which we do, on behalf of the inhabitants of British America, enter this, our solemn and determined protest. And we do earnestly intreat his Majesty, as yet the only mediatory power between the several States of the British empire, to recommend to his Parliament of Great Britain, the total revocation of these acts, which, however nugatory they may be, may yet prove the cause of further discontents and jealousies among us.

That we next proceed to consider the conduct of his Majesty, as holding the Executive powers of the laws of these States, and mark out his deviations from the line of duty. By the Constitution of Great Britain, as well as of the several American States, his Majesty possesses the power of refusing to pass into a law, any bill which has already passed the other two branches of the legislature. His Majesty, however, and his ancestors, conscious of the impropriety of opposing their single opinion to the united wisdom of two Houses of Parliament, while their proceedings were unbiassed by interested principles, for several ages past, have modestly declined the exercise of this power, in that part of his empire called Great Britain. But, by change of circumstances, other principles than those of justice simply, have obtained an influence on their determinations. The addition of new States to the British empire has produced an addition of new, and, sometimes, opposite interests. It is now, therefore, the great office of his Majesty to resume the exercise of his negative power, and to prevent the passage of laws by any one legislature of the empire, which might bear injuriously on the rights and interests of another. Yet this will not excuse the wanton exercise of this power, which we have seen his Majesty practice on the laws of the American legislature. For the most trifling reasons, and, sometimes for no conceivable reason at all, his Majesty has rejected laws of the most salutary tendency. The abolition of domestic slavery is the great object of desire in those colonies, where it was, unhappily, introduced in their infant state. But previous to the enfranchisement of the slaves we have, it is necessary to exclude all further importations from Africa. Yet our repeated attempts to effect this, by prohibitions, and by imposing duties which might amount to a prohibition, having been hitherto defeated by his Majesty's negative: thus preferring the immediate advantages of a few British corsairs, to the lasting interests of the American States, and to the rights of human nature, deeply wounded by this infamous practice. Nay, the single interposition of an interested individual against a law was scarcely ever known to fail of success, though, in the opposite scale, were placed the interests of a whole country. That this is so shameful an abuse of a power, trusted with his Majesty for other purposes, as if, not reformed, would call for some legal restrictions.

With equal inattention to the necessities of his people here, has his Majesty permitted our laws to lie neglected, in England, for years, neither confirming them by his assent, nor annulling them by his negative: so, that such of them as have no suspending clause, we hold on the most precarious of all tenures, his Majesty's will; and such of them as suspend themselves till his Majesty's assent be obtained, we have feared might be called into existence at some future and distant period, when time and change of circumstances shall have rendered them destructive to his people here. And, to render this grievance still more oppressive, his Majesty, by his instructions, has laid his Governors under such restrictions, that they can pass no law, of any moment, unless it have such suspending clause: so that, however immediate may be the call for legislative interposition, the law cannot be executed, till it has twice crossed the Atlantic, by which time the evil may have spent its whole force.

But in what terms reconcilable to Majesty, and at the same time to truth, shall we speak of a late instruction to his

Majesty's Governor of the colony of Virginia, by which he is forbidden to assent to any law for the division of a county, unless the new county will consent to have no representative in Assembly? That colony has as yet affixed no boundary to the Westward. Their Western counties, therefore, are of an indefinite extent. Some of them are actually seated many hundred miles from their Eastern limits. Is it possible, then, that his Majesty can have bestowed a single thought on the situation of those people, who, in order to obtain justice for injuries, however great or small, must, by the laws of that colony, attend their county court at such a distance, with all their witnesses, monthly, till their litigation be determined? Or does his Majesy seriously wish, and publish it to the world, that his subjects should give up the glorious right of representation, with all the benefits derived from that, and submit themselves the absolute slaves of his sovereign will? Or is it rather meant to confine the legislative body to their present numbers, that they may be the cheaper bargain, whenever they shall become worth a purchase?

One of the articles of impeachment against Tresilian, and the other Judges of Westminster Hall, in the reign of Richard the Second, for which they suffered death, as traitors to their country, was, that they had advised the King, that he might dissolve his Parliament at any time; and succeeding kings have adopted the opinion of these unjust Judges. Since the establishment, however, of the British constitution, at the glorious Revolution, on its free and ancient principles, neither his Majesty, nor his ancestors, have exercised such a power of dissolution in the island of Great Britain; and when his Majesty was petitioned, by the united voice of his people there, to dissolve the present Parliament, who had become obnoxious to them, his Ministers were heard to declare, in open Parliament, that his Majesty possessed no such power by the constitution. But how different their language, and his practice, here! To declare, as their duty required, the known rights of their country, to oppose the usurpation of every foreign judicature, to disregard the imperious mandates of a Minister or Governor, have been the avowed causes of dissolving Houses of Representatives in America. But if such powers be really vested in his Majesty, can he suppose they are there placed to awe the members from such purposes as these? When the representative body have lost the confidence of their constituents, when they have notoriously made sale of their most valuable rights, when they have assumed to themselves powers which the people never put into their hands, then, indeed, their continuing in office becomes dangerous to the State, and calls for an exercise of the power of dissolution. Such being the cause for which the representative body should, and should not, be dissolved, will it not appear strange, to an unbiassed observer, that that of Great Britain was not dissolved, while those of the colonies have repeatedly incurred that sentence?

But your Majesty, or your Governors, have carried this power beyond every limit known or provided for by the laws. After dissolving one House of Representatives, they have refused to call another, so that, for a great length of time, the legislature provided by the laws, has been out of existence. From the nature of things, every society must, at all times, possess within itself the sovereign powers of legislation. The feelings of human nature revolt against the supposition of a State so situated, as that it may not, in any emergency, provide against dangers which, perhaps, threaten immediate ruin. While those bodies are in existence to whom the people have delegated the powers of legislation, they alone possess, and may exercise, those powers. But when they are dissolved, by the lopping off one or more of their branches, the power reverts to the people, who may use it to unlimited extent, either assembling together in person, sending deputies, or in any other way they may think proper. We forbear to trace consequences further; the dangers are conspicuous with which this practice is replete.

That we shall, at this time also, take notice of an error in the nature of our land holdings, which crept in at a very early period of our settlement. The introduction of the Feudal tenures into the kingdom of England, though ancient, is well enough understood to set this matter in a proper light. In the earlier ages of the Saxon settlement, feudal holdings were certainly altogether unknown, and very few, if any, had been introduced at the time of the Norman conquest. Our Saxon ancestors held their lands, as they did their personal property, in absolute dominion, disincumbered with any superior, answering nearly to the nature of those possessions which the Feudalist term Allodial. William the Norman, first introduced that system generally. The lands which had belonged to those who fell in the battle of Hastings, and in the subsequent insurrections of his reign, formed a considerable proportion of the lands of the whole kingdom. These he granted out, subject to feudal duties, as did he also those of a great number of his new subjects, who, by persuasions or threats, were induced to surrender them for that purpose. But still, much was left in the hands of his Saxon subjects, held of no superior, and not subject to feudal conditions. These, therefore, by express laws, enacted to render uniform the system of military defence, were made liable to the same military duties as if they had been feuds; and the Norman lawyers soon found means to saddle them, also, with the other feudal burthens. But still they had not been surrendered to the King, they were not derived from his grant, and therefore they were not holden of him. A general principle was introduced, that "all lands in England were held either mediately or immediately of the Crown;" but this was borrowed from those holdings which were truly feudal, and only applied to others for the purposes of illustration. Feudal holdings were, therefore, but exceptions out of the Saxon laws of possession, under which all lands were held in absolute right. These, therefore, still form the basis or groundwork of the Common law, to prevail wheresoever the exceptions have not taken place. America was not conquered by William the Norman, nor its lands surrendered to him or any of his successors. Possessions there are, undoubtedly, of the Allodial nature. Our ancestors, however, who migrated hither, were laborers, not lawyers. The fictitious principle, that all lands belong originally to the King, they were early persuaded to believe real, and accordingly took grants of their own lands from the Crown. And while the Crown continued to grant for small sums and on reasonable rents, there was no inducement to arrest the error, and lay it open to public view. But his Majesty has lately taken on him to advance the terms of purchase and of holding, to the double of what they were; by which means, the acquisition of lands being rendered difficult, the population of our country is likely to be checked. It is time, therefore, for us to lay this matter before his Majesty, and to declare, that he has no right to grant lands of himself. From the nature and purpose of civil institutions, all the lands within the limits, which any particular party has circumscribed around itself, are assumed by that society, and subject to their allotment; this may be done by themselves assembled collectively, or by their legislature, to whom they may have delegated sovereign authority; and, if they are allotted in neither of these ways, each individual of the society, may appropriate to himself such lands as he finds vacant, and occupancy will give him title.

That, in order to enforce the arbitrary measures before complained of, his Majesty has, from time to time, sent among us large bodies of armed forces, not made up of the people here, nor raised by the authority of our laws. Did his Majesty possess such a right as this, it might swallow up all our other rights, whenever he should think proper. But his Majesty has no right to land a single armed man on our shores; and those whom he sends here are liable to our laws, for the suppression and punishment of riots, routs, and unlawful assemblies, or are hostile bodies invading us in defiance of law. When, in the course of the late war, it became expedient that a body of Hanoverian troops should be brought over for the defence of Great Britain, his Majesty's grandfather, our late sovereign, did not pretend to introduce them under any authority he possessed. Such a measure would have given just alarm to his subjects of Great Britain, whose liberties would not be safe if armed men of another country, and of another spirit, might be brought into the realm at any time, without the consent of their legislature. He, therefore, applied to Parliament, who passed an act for that purpose, limiting the number to be brought in, and the time they were to continue. In like manner is his Majesty restrained in every part of the empire. He possesses indeed the executive power of the laws in every State; but they are the laws of the particular State, which he is to administer within that State, and not those of any one within the limits of another. Every State must judge for itself, the number of armed men which they may safely trust among them, of whom they are to consist, and under what restrictions they are to be laid. To render these proceedings still more criminal against our laws, instead of subjecting the military to the civil power, his majesty has expressly made the civil subordinate to the military. But can his Majesty thus put down all law under his feet? Can he erect a power superior to that which erected himself? He has done it indeed by force; but let him remember that force cannot give right.

That these are our grievances, which we have thus laid before his Majesty, with that freedom of language and sentiment which becomes a free people claiming their rights as derived from the laws of nature, and not as the gift of their

Chief Magistrate. Let those flatter, who fear: it is not an American art. To give praise where it is not due might be well from the venal, but would ill beseem those who are asserting the rights of human nature. They know, and will, therefore, say, that Kings are the servants, not the proprietors of the people. Open your breast, Sire, to liberal and expanded thought. Let not the name of George the Third, be a blot on the page of history. You are surrounded by British counsellors, but remember that they are parties. You have no ministers for American affairs, because you have none taken from among us, nor amenable to the laws on which they are to give you advice. It behooves you, therefore, to think and to act for yourself and your people. The great principles of right and wrong are legible to every reader; to pursue them, requires not the aid of many counsellors. The whole art of government consists in the art of being honest. Only aim to do your duty, and mankind will give you credit where you fail. No longer persevere in sacrificing the rights of one part of the empire to the inordinate desires of another; but deal out to all, equal and impartial right. Let no act be passed by any one legislature, which may infringe on the rights and liberties of another. This is the important post in which fortune has placed you, holding the balance of a great, if a well-poised empire. This, Sire, is the advice of your great American council, on the observance of which may perhaps depend your felicity and future fame, and the preservation of that harmony which alone can continue, both to Great Britain and America, the reciprocal advantages of their connection. It is neither our wish nor our interest to separate from her. We are willing, on our part, to sacrifice everything which reason can ask, to the restoration of that tranquillity for which all must wish. On their part, let them be ready to establish union on a generous plan. Let them name their terms, but let them be just. Accept of every commercial preference it is in our power to give, for such things as we can raise for their use, or they make for ours. But let them not think to exclude us from going to other markets to dispose of those commodities which they cannot use, nor to supply those wants which they cannot supply. Still less, let it be proposed, that our properties, within our own territories, shall be taxed or regulated by any power on earth, but our own. The God who gave us life, gave us liberty at the same time: the hand of force may destroy, but cannot disjoin them.

This, Sire, is our last, our determined resolution. And that you will be pleased to interpose, with that efficacy which your earnest endeavors may insure, to procure redress of these our great grievances, to quiet the minds of your subjects in British America against any apprehensions of future encroachment, to establish fraternal love and harmony through the whole empire, and that that may continue to the latest ages of time, is the fervent prayer of all British America.

A Phrensy of Revenge

To Dr. William Small, May 7, 1775

Dr. Small, an Englishman, had been Jefferson's teacher and friend at William and Mary. In this letter Jefferson implicitly answers Lord Dunmore, governor of Virginia, who had maintained that New Englanders provoked the action at Concord and Lexington in order to involve the other colonies.

Dear Sir,—Within this week we have received the unhappy news of an action of considerable magnitude, between the King's troops and our brethren of Boston, in which it is said 500 of the former, with the Earl of Percy, are slain. That such an action has occurred is undoubted, though perhaps the circumstances may not have reached us with truth. This accident has cut off our last hope of reconciliation, and a phrensy of revenge seems to have seized all ranks of people. It is a lamentable circumstance, that the only mediatory power, acknowledged by both parties, instead of leading to a reconciliation his divided people, should pursue the incendiary purpose of still blowing up the flames, as we find him constantly doing, in every speech and public declaration. This may, perhaps, be intended to intimidate into acquiescence, but the effect has been most unfortunately otherwise. A little knowledge of human nature, and attention to its ordinary workings, might have foreseen that the spirits of the people here were in a state, in which they were more likely to be provoked, than frightened, by haughty deportment. And to fill up the measure of irritation, a proscription of individuals has been substituted in the room of just trial. Can it be believed that a grateful people will suffer those to be consigned to execution, whose sole crime has been the developing and asserting their rights? Had the Parliament possessed the power of reflection, they would have avoided a measure as impotent, as it was inflammatory. When I saw Lord Chatham's bill, I entertained high hope that a reconciliation could have been brought about. The difference between his terms, and those offered by our Congress, might have been accommodated, if entered on, by both parties, with a disposition to accommodate. But the dignity of Parliament, it seems, can brook no opposition to its power. Strange, that a set of men, who have made sale of their virtue to the Minister, should yet talk of retaining dignity! But I am getting into politics, though I sat down only to ask your acceptance of the wine and express my constant wishes for your happiness. This however seems secured by your philosophy and peaceful vocation. I shall still hope that amidst public dissention private friendship may be preserved inviolate, and among the warmest you can ever possess is that of your obliged humble servt.,

For Us, Not for Them, Has Government Been Instituted Here

Virginia Resolutions on Lord North's Conciliation Proposal, June 10, 1775

Jefferson sat on a committee of the Virginia Assembly called to deliberate Lord North's "conciliatory propositions." In essence, Lord North had proposed that colonies which met their financial obligations to the Empire and to their governments—those obligations to be determined by Parliament— would be exempt from imperial taxation for revenue. Jefferson drafted the reply which, with a few changes, was adopted by the Assembly.

Resolved, that it is the opinion of this Committee that an Address be presented to his Excellency, the Governor, to inform him that we have taken into our consideration the joint Address of the two Houses of Parliament His Majesty's Answer, and the Resolution of the Commons, which your Lordship has been pleased to lay before us. Wishing nothing so sincerely as the perpetual continuance of that brotherly love which we bear to our fellow-subjects of Great Britain, and still continuing to hope and believe that they do not approve the measures which have so long oppressed their brethren in America, we were pleased to receive your Lordship's notification, that a benevolent tender had at length been made by the British House of Commons towards bringing to a good end our unhappy disputes with the Mother Country. Next to the possession of liberty, my Lord, we should consider such a reconciliation as the greatest of all human blessings. With these dispositions we entered into the consideration of that Resolution; we examined it minutely; we viewed it in every point of light in which we were able to place it; and, with pain and disappointment, we must ultimately declare it only changes the form of oppression, without lightening its burden. We cannot, my Lord, close with the terms of that Resolution, for these reasons:

Because the British Parliament has no right to intermeddle with the support of civil Government in the Colonies. For us, not for them, has Government been instituted here. Agreeable to our ideas, provision has been made for such officers as we think necessary for the administration of publick affairs; and we cannot conceive that any other legislature has a right to prescribe either the number or pecuniary appointments of our offices. As a proof that the claim of Parliament to interfere in the necessary provisions for the support of civil Government is novel, and of a late date, we take leave to refer to an Act of our Assembly, passed so long since as the thirty-second year of the reign of King Charles the Second, intituled, "An Act for raising a publick revenue, and for the better support of the Government of His Majesty's Colony of Virginia." This act was brought over by Lord Culpeper, then Governour, under the great seal of England, and was enacted in the name of the "King's most Excellent Majesty, by and with the consent of the General Assembly."

Because to render perpetual our exemption from an unjust taxation, we must saddle ourselves with a perpetual tax, adequate to the expectations, and subject to the disposal of Parliament alone; Whereas, we have a right to give our money, as the Parliament do theirs, without coercion, from time to time, as public exigencies may require. We conceive that we alone are the judges of the condition, circumstances, and situation of our people, as the Parliament are of theirs. It is not merely the mode of raising, but the freedom of granting our money, for which we have contended. Without this, we possess no check on the royal prerogative; and what must be lamented by dutiful and loyal subjects, we should be stripped of the only means, as well of recommending this Country to the favours of our most gracious Sovereign, as of strengthening those bands of amity with our fellow-subjects, which we would wish to remain indissoluble.

Because on our undertaking to grant money, as is proposed, the Commons only resolve to forbear levying pecuniary taxes on us, still leaving unrepealed their several Acts passed for the purposes of restraining the Trade, and altering the form of Government of the Eastern Colonies; extending the boundaries, and changing the Government and Religion of Quebeck; enlarging the jurisdiction of the Courts of Admiralty; taking from us the right of Trial by Jury, and transporting us into other countries to be tried for criminal offences. Standing Armies, too, are still to be kept among us, and the other numerous grievances, of which ourselves and sister Colonies, separately and by our Representatives in

General Congress, have so often complained, are still to continue without redress.

Because, at the very time of requiring from us grants of money, they are making disposition to invade us with large armaments by sea and land, which is a style of asking gifts not reconcilable to our freedom. They are also proceeding to a repetition of injury, by passing Acts for restraining the Commerce and Fisheries of the Provinces of New England, and for prohibiting the Trade of the other Colonies with all parts of the world, except the Island of Great Britain, Ireland, and the West Indies. This seems to bespeak no intention to discontinue the exercise of this usurped power over us in future.

Because on our agreeing to contribute our proportion towards the common defence, they do not propose to lay open to us a free trade with all the world: whereas, to us it appears just that those who bear equally the burdens of Government should equally participate of its benefits; either be contented with the monopoly of our trade, which brings greater loss to us and benefit to them than the amount of our proportional contributions to the common defence; or, if the latter be preferred, relinquish the former, and do not propose, by holding both, to exact from us double contributions. Yet we would remind Government, that on former emergencies, when called upon as a free people, however cramped by this monopoly in our resources of wealth, we have liberally contributed to the common defence. Be assured, then, that we shall be as generous in future as in past times, disclaiming the shackles of proportion when called to our free station in the general system of the Empire.

Because the proposition now made to us involves the interests of all the other Colonies. We are now represented in General Congress by members approved by this House, where the former union, it is hoped, will be so strongly cemented, that no partial applications can produce the slightest departure from the common cause. We consider ourselves as bound in honour, as well as interest, to share one general fate with our sister Colonies; and should hold ourselves base deserters of that union to which we have acceded, were we to agree on any measures distinct and apart from them.

There was, indeed, a plan of accommodation offered in Parliament, which, though not entirely equal to the terms we had a right to ask; yet differed but in few points from what the General Congress had held out. Had Parliament been disposed sincerely, as we are, to bring about a reconciliation, reasonable men had hoped, that by meeting us on this ground, something might have been done. Lord Chatham's Bill, on the one part, and the terms of Congress on the other, would have formed a basis for negotiations, which a spirit of accommodation on both sides might, perhaps, have reconciled. It came recommended, too, from one whose successful experience in the art of Government should have insured it some attention from those to whom it was intended. He had shown to the world, that Great Britain, with her Colonies united firmly under a just and honest Government, formed a power which might bid defiance to the most potent enemies. With a change of Ministers, however, a total change of measures took place. The component parts of the Empire have, from that moment, been falling asunder, and a total annihilation of its weight in the political scale of the world, seems justly to be apprehended.

These, my Lord, are our sentiments on this important subject, which we offer only as an individual part of the whole Empire. Final determination we leave to the General Congress, now sitting,[1] before whom we shall lay the papers your Lordship has communicated to us. To their wisdom we commit the improvement of this important advance; if it can be wrought into any good, we were assured they will do it. To them, also we refer the discovery of that proper method of representing our well-founded grievances, which your Lordship assures us will meet with the attention and regard so justly due to them. For ourselves, we have exhausted every mode of application which our invention could suggest as proper and promising. We have decently remonstrated with Parliament: they have added new injuries to the old. We have wearied our King with applications: he has not deigned to answer us. We have appealed to the native honour and justice of the British Nation. Their efforts in our favour have been hitherto ineffectual. What, then, remains to be done? That we commit our injuries to the evenhanded justice of the Being who doth no wrong, earnestly beseeching him to illuminate the counsels, and prosper the endeavours of those to whom America hath confided her hopes, that through their wise direction we may again see reunited the blessings of liberty, property, and harmony with Great Britain.

[1] Jefferson refers to the Second Continental Congress.

This Great Decision

Declaration of the Causes and Necessity for Taking Up Arms, July 6, 1775

Congress had turned down a Declaration for the Necessity of Taking up Arms *when, on June 26, Jefferson and John Dickinson of Pennsylvania joined the committee that had originally drawn it up. Jefferson wrote the draft of another declaration. The older and more conservative Dickinson, still hopeful of maintaining the imperial chord, toned it down while keeping much of Jefferson's content and style. Congress passed Dickinson's revision on July 6. Jefferson's draft, including the words Jefferson crossed out, is given below.*

A Declaration *of*[1] by *We* the representatives of the United colonies of America now sitting in General Congress, *to all nations send greeting of* setting forth the causes and necessity of their taking up arms.

The large strides of late taken by the *legislature of Great Britain* towards establishing over these colonies their absolute rule, and the hardiness of the present attempt to effect by force of arms what by law or right they could never effect, *render* it necessary for us also to change the ground of opposition, and to close with their last appeal from reason to arms. and it behoves those, *who are called to this great decision,* to be assured that their cause is approved before supreme reason; so is it of great avail that its justice be made known to the world, whose affections will ever take part with those encountering oppression. Our forefathers, inhabitants of the island of Great Britain, *having long endeavored to bear up against the evils of misrule* left their native lands to seek on these shores a residence for civil and religious freedom. At the expence of their blood, *with* to the ruin of their fortunes, with the relinquishment of everything quiet and comfortable in life, they effected settlements in the hospitable wilds of America; *they* and there established civil societies with various forms of constitution. *But possessing all, what is inherent in all, the full and perfect powers of

---

[1] Words enclosed in asterisks signify Jefferson's corrections.

legislation.* to continue their connection with the friends whom they had left, they arranged themselves by charters of compact under *one* the same common king, who thus completed their powers of full and perfect legislation and became the link of union between the several parts of the empire. some occasional assumptions of power by the parliament of Great Britain, however unacknowledged by the constitution of our governments, were finally acquiesced in thro' warmth of affection. proceeding thus in the fullness of mutual harmony and confidence, both parts of the empire increased in population and wealth with a rapidity unknown in the history of man. the political institutions of America, its various soils and climates opened a certain resource to the unfortunate and to the enterprising of every country, and ensured to them the acquisition and free possession of property. Great Britain too acquired a lustre and a weight among the powers of the earth which her internal resources could never have given her. to a communication of the wealth and power of *the whole* every part of the empire we may surely ascribe in some measure the illustrious character she sustained through her last European war, and its successful event. at the close of that war *however having subdued all her foes her successful and glorious Minister was discarded and successive* it pleased our sovereign to make a change in his counsels. The new ministry finding all the foes of Britain subdued she took up the unfortunate idea of subduing her friends also. by*their Influence* her parliament then for the first time *asserted a right were persuaded to assume and assert* assumed a power of unbounded legislation over the colonies of America and in the *space* course of ten years *during which they have proceeded to exercise this right,* have given such decisive specimens of the spirit of this new legislation, as leaves no room to doubt the consequence of acquiescence under it. By several acts of parliament passed within that *space of* time they have *attempted to take from us* undertaken to give and grant our money without our consent: a right of which we have ever had the exclusive exercise: they have interdicted all commerce to one of our principal towns, thereby annihilating its property in the hands of the holders; they have cut off the commercial intercourse of whole colonies with foreign countries; they have extended the jurisdiction of courts of admiralty beyond their ancient limits; *thereby* they have *depriving* deprived us of the inestimable *right* privilege of trial by a jury of the vicinage, in cases affecting both life and property; they have declared that American Subjects charged with certain offenses shall be transported beyond sea to be tried before the very persons against whose pretended sovereignty the offense is supposed to be committed; they have attempted fundamentally to alter the form of government in one of these colonies, a form *established* secured by charters on the part of the crown and confirmed by acts of its own legislature; *and further secured by charters on the part of the crown;* they have erected in a neighboring province acquired by the joint arms of Great Britain and America, a tyranny dangerous to the very existence of all these colonies. But why should we enumerate their injuries in the detail? by one act they have suspended the powers of one American legislature, and by another have declared they may legislate for us themselves in all cases whatsoever. these two acts alone form a basis broad enough whereon to erect a despotism of unlimited extent. and what is to secure us against this dreaded evil? the persons assuming these powers are not chosen by us, are not subject to our controul or influence, are exempted by their situation from the operation of these laws, and lighten their own burthens in proportion as they increase ours. these temptations might put to trial the severest characters of ancient virtue: with what new armour then shall a British parliament encounter the rude assault? towards these deadly injuries from the tender plant of liberty which we have brought over, and with so much affection fostered on these our own shores, we have pursued every temperate, every respectful measure. we have supplicated our king at various times, in terms almost disgraceful to freedom; we have reasoned, we have remonstrated with parliament in the most mild and decent language; we have even proceeded to break off our commercial intercourse with our fellow subjects, as the last peaceful admonition that our attachment to no nation on earth should supplant our attachment to liberty. and here we had well hoped was the ultimate step of the controversy. but subsequent events have shewn how vain was even this last remain of confidence in the moderation of the British ministry. during the course of the last year their troops in a hostile manner invested the town of Boston in the province of Massachusetts bay, and from that time have held the same beleaguered by sea and land. on the 19th day of April in the present year they made an unprovoked *attack* assault on the inhabitants of the said province at the town of Lexington, murdered eight of them on the spot and wounded many others. from thence they proceeded in *the* all the array of war to the town of Concord, where they set upon another party of the inhabitants of the same province, killing many of them also, burning houses, and laying waste property, until repressed by *the arms* the *country* people suddenly assembled to oppose this cruel aggression. hostilities thus commenced on the part of the ministerial army have been since by them pursued without regard to faith or to fame. The inhabitants of the town of Boston in order to procure their enlargement having entered into treaty with *a certain Thomas Gage, principal instigator of these enormities* General Gage, their Governor to procure their Enlargement, it was stipulated that the said inhabitants, *after* having first deposited their arms with their own magistrates *their arms and military stores* should have liberty to depart from out of the said town taking with them their other *goods and* effects. their arms *and military stores* they accordingly delivered in, and claimed the stipulated license of departing with their effects. but in open violation of plighted faith and honour, in defiance of the sacred obligations of treaty which even savage nations observe, their arms *and warlike stores* deposited with their own magistrates to be preserved as their property, were immediately seized by a body of armed men under orders from the said *Thomas Gage* General, the greater part of the inhabitants were detained in the town, and the few permitted to depart were compelled to leave their most valuable effects behind. we leave the world to *their* its own reflections on this atrocious perfidy. that we might no longer doubt the ultimate aim of these ministerial maneuvers *the same Thomas* General Gage, by proclamation bearing date the 12th day of June, after reciting the grossest falsehoods and calumnies against the good people of these colonies. proceeds to declare them all, either by name or description, to be rebels and traitors, to supersede *by his own authority* the exercise of the common law of the said province, and to proclaim and order instead thereof the use and exercise of the law martial. this bloody edict issued, he has proceeded to commit further ravages and murders in the same province, burning the town of Charlestown, attacking and killing great numbers of the people residing or assembled therein; and is now going on in an avowed course of murder and devastation, taking every occasion to destroy the lives and properties of the inhabitants *of the said province.* to oppose his arms we also have taken up arms. we should be wanting to ourselves, we should be perfidious to posterity, we should be unworthy that free ancestry from *whom which whom* which we derive our descent, should we submit with folded arms to military butchery and depredation, to gratify the lordly ambition, or sate the avarice of a British ministry. We do then most solemnly, before God and the world declare that, regardless of every consequence, at the risk of every distress, the arms we have been compelled to assume we will *wage* use with the perseverance, exerting to their utmost energies all those powers which our creator hath given us, to *guard* preserve that liberty which he committed to us in sacred deposit and to protect from every hostile hand our lives and our properties. But that this *our* declaration may not disquiet the minds of our *good* friends and fellow subjects *in Britain or other* in any parts of the empire, we do further assure them that we mean not in any wise to affect that union with them in which we have so long and so happily lived and which we wish so much to see again restored. that necessity must be hard indeed which may force upon us that desperate measure, or induce us to avail ourselves of any aid *which* their enemies might proffer. we did not embody a soldiery to commit aggression on them; we did not raise armies for glory or for conquest; we did not invade their island carrying death or slavery to its inhabitants. *we took arms* in defence of our persons and properties under actual violation. we *have taken* took up arms. when that violence shall be removed, when hostilities shall cease on the part of the aggressors, hostilities shall cease on our part also. *the moment they withdraw their armies, we will disband ours.* for the achievement of this happy event, we call for and confide in the good offices of our fellow subjects beyond the Atlantic. of their friendly dispositions we do not cease to hope; aware, as they must be, that they have nothing more to expect from the same common enemy, than the humble favour of being last devoured. and we devoutly implore assistance of Almighty God to conduct us happily thro' this great conflict, to dispose *the minds of* his majesty, his ministers, and parliament to *reasonable terms* reconciliation with us on reasonable terms and to deliver us from the evils of a civil war.

Our Real Determinations

To John Randolph, August 25, 1775

John Randolph, Attorney-General of Virginia, was the brother of Peyton and the father of Edmund, who were both patriots. The year before, John Randolph had written a pamphlet vigorously stating the British point of view. Now he was moving to Britain.

. . . I am sorry the situation of our country should render it not eligible to you to remain longer in it. I hope the returning wisdom of Great Britain will e'er long put an end to this unnatural contest. There may be people to whose tempers and dispositions Contention may be pleasing, and who may therefore wish a continuance of confusion. But to me it is of all states, but one, most horrid. My first wish is a restoration of our just rights; my second a return of the happy period when, consistently with duty, I may withdraw myself totally from the public stage and pass the rest of my days in domestic ease and tranquillity, banishing every desire of afterwards even hearing what passes in the world. Perhaps ardour for the latter may add considerably to the warmth of the former wish. Looking with fondness towards a reconciliation with Great Britain, I cannot help hoping you may be able to contribute towards expediting this good work. I think it must be evident to yourself that the ministry have been deceived by their officers on this side the water, who (for what purposes I cannot tell) have constantly represented the American opposition as that of a small faction, in which the body of the people took little part. This you can inform them of your own knolege to be untrue. They have taken it into their heads too that we are cowards and shall surrender at discretion to an armed force. The past and future operations of the war must confirm or undeceive them on that head. I wish they were thoroughly and minutely acquainted with every circumstance relative to America as it exists in truth. I am persuaded this would go far towards disposing them to reconciliation. Even those in parliament who are called friends to America seem to know nothing of our real determinations.

I observe they pronounced in the last parliament that the Congress of 1774 did not mean to insist rigorously on the terms they held out, but kept something in reserve to give up; and in fact that they would give up everything but the article of taxation. Now the truth is far from this, as I can affirm, and put my honor to the assertion; and their continuance in this error may perhaps have very ill consequences. The Congress stated the lowest terms they thought possible to be accepted in order to convince the world they were not unreasonable. They gave up the monopoly and regulation of trade, and all the acts of parliament prior to 1764, leaving to British generosity to render these at some future time as easy to America as the interest of Britain would admit. But this was before blood was spilt. I cannot affirm, but have reason to think, these terms would not now be accepted. I wish no false sense of honor, no ignorance of our real intentions, no vain hope that partial concessions of right will be accepted may induce the ministry to trifle with accomodation till it shall be put even out of our own power ever to accomodate. If indeed Great Britain, disjoined from her colonies, be a match for the most potent nations of Europe with the colonies thrown into their scale, they may go on securely. But if they are not assured of this, it would be certainly unwise, by trying the event of another campaign, to risque our accepting a foreign aid which perhaps may not be obtainable but on a condition of everlasting avulsion from Great Britain. This would be thought a hard condition to those who still wish for reunion with their parent country. I am sincerely one of those, and would rather be in dependance on Great Britain, properly limited, than on any nation upon earth, or than on no nation. But I am one of those too who rather than submit to the right of legislating for us assumed by the British parliament, and which late experience has shewn they will so cruelly exercise, would lend my hand to sink the whole island in the ocean.

If undeceiving the minister as to matters of fact may change his dispositions, it will perhaps be in your power by assisting to do this, to render service to the whole empire, at the most critical time certainly that it has ever seen. Whether Britain shall continue the head of the greatest empire on earth, or shall return to her original station in the political scale of Europe depends perhaps on the resolutions of the succeeding winter. God send they may be wise and salutary for us all!

I shall be glad to hear from you as often as you may be disposed to think of things here. You may be at liberty I expect to communicate some things consistently with your honor and the duties you will owe to a protecting nation. Such a communication among individuals may be mutually beneficial to the contending parties. On this or any future occasion if I affirm to you any facts, your knolege of me will enable you to decide on their credibility; if I hazard opinions on the dispositions of men, or other speculative points, you can only know they are my opinions. My best wishes for your felicity attend you wherever you go, and beleive me to be assuredly Your friend & servt.,

The Rights of Nations

Declaration on the Treatment of Ethan Allen, January 2, 1776

On learning that the British had taken Ethan Allen prisoner in Canada and were confining him "in irons on board a vessel," Congress asked Jefferson to write a public protest. It appeared before Congress on January 2, but nothing came of it.

To Majr. Genl. Howe.

When necessity compelled us to take up arms against Great Britain in defence of our just rights, we thought it a circumstance of comfort that our enemy was brave and civilized. It is the happiness of modern times that the evils of necessary war are softened by the refinement of manners and sentiment and that an enemy is an object of vengeance, in arms, and in the field only. It is with pain we hear that Mr. Allen and others taken with him while fighting bravely in their country's cause, are sent to Britain in irons, to be punished for pretended treason; treason too created by one of those very laws whose obligation we deny, and mean to contest by the sword. This question will not be decided by reeking vengeance on a few helpless captives but by achieving success in the fields of war, and gathering there those laurels which grow for the warrior brave. In this light we view the object between us, in this line we have hitherto conducted ourselves for its attainment. To those who bearing your arms have fallen into our hands we afforded every comfort for which captivity and misfortune call for. Enlargement and comfortable subsistence have been extended to both officers and men, and their restraint is a restraint of honor only. Should you think proper in these days to revive ancient barbarism and again disgrace our nature with the sacrifice the fortune of war has put it into our power subjects for multiplied retaliation. To them, to you, and to the world we declare they shall not be wretched unless their imprudence or your example shall oblige us to make them so; but we declare that their lives shall teach our enemies to respect the rights of nations. We have ordered Brigadier General Prescot to be bound in irons and to be confined in close jail, there to experience corresponding miseries to those which shall be inflicted on Mr. Allen. His life shall answer for that of Mr. Allen, and the lives of as many others of the brave men captivated with him. We deplore the event which shall oblige us to shed blood for blood, and shall resort to retaliation but as the means of stopping the progress of butchery. This it is a duty we owe to those engaged in the cause of their country, to assure them that if any unlucky circumstance baffling the efforts of their bravery shall put them in the power of their enemies, we will use the pledges in our hands to warrant their lives from sacrifice.

New-Modelling the Form of Government

The Virginia Constitution, before June 13, 1776

The Virginia Constitutional Convention met while Jefferson was in Philadelphia. He expressed to a friend his anxieties about the possibilities of republicanism in Virginia: "should a bad government be instituted for us, in future it had been as well to have accepted at first the bad one offered us from beyond the water without the risk and expense of contest." The constitution which Jefferson proposed (the text below is the third and last draft) came before the convention just as it was taking up, and for the most part adopting, George Mason's draft. The Virginia Constitution, as finally written, was conservative in comparison to Jefferson's. But it incorporated Jefferson's preamble, the language of which is remarkably similar to the language of the Declaration of Independence.

A Bill for new-modelling the form of Government and for establishing the Fundamental principles thereof in future.

Whereas George

Guelf[1] king of Great Britain and Ireland and Elector of Hanover, heretofore entrusted with the exercise of the kingly office in this government hath endeavored to pervert the same into a detestable and insupportable tyranny;

by putting his negative on laws the most wholesome and necessary for ye public good;

by denying to his governors permission to pass laws of immediate and pressing importance, unless suspended in their operations for his assent, and, when so suspended, neglecting to attend to them for many years;

by refusing to pass certain other laws, unless the person to be benefited by them would relinquish the inestimable right of representation in the legislature;

by dissolving legislative assemblies repeatedly and continually for opposing with manly firmness his invasions on the rights of the people;

---

[1] The Guelf party of Florence, opposed to the Ghibelline, stood against forming an alliance with the German emperors.

when dissolved, by refusing to call others for a long space of time, thereby leaving the political system without any legislative head;

by endeavoring to prevent the population of our country, and for that purpose obstructing the laws for the naturalization of foreigners and raising the conditions of new appropriations of lands;

by keeping among us, in times of peace, standing armies and ships of war;

by affecting to render the military independent of and superior to the civil power;

by combining with others to subject us to a foreign jurisdiction, giving his assent to their pretended acts of legislation.

for quartering large bodies of troops among us;

for cutting off our trade with all parts of the world;

for imposing taxes on us without our consent;

for depriving us of the benefits of trial by jury;

for transporting us beyond seas to be tried for pretended offences; and

for suspending our own legislatures and declaring themselves invested with power to legislate for us in all cases whatsoever;

by plundering our seas, ravaging our coasts, burning our towns and destroying the lives of our people;

by inciting insurrections of our fellow subjects with the allurements of forfeiture and confiscation;

by prompting our negroes to rise in arms among us; those very negroes whom *he hath from time to time*[2] by an inhuman use of his negative he hath refused permission to exclude by law;

by endeavoring to bring on the inhabitants of our frontiers the merciless Indian savages, whose known rule of warfare is an undistinguished destruction of all ages, sexes, and conditions of existence;

by transporting at this time a large army of foreign mercenaries to complete the works of death, desolation and tyranny already begun with circumstances of cruelty and perfidy so unworthy the head of a civilized nation;

by answering our repeated petitions for redress with a repetition of injuries;

[2] The words enclosed in asterisks signify Jefferson's corrections.

and finally by abandoning the helm of government and declaring us out of his allegiance and protection;

by which several acts of misrule the said George

Guelf has forfeited the kingly office and has rendered it necessary for the preservation of the people that he should be immediately deposed from the same, and divested of all its privileges, powers, and prerogatives:

And forasmuch as the public liberty may be more certainly secured by abolishing an office which all experience hath shewn to be inveterately inimical thereto *or which* and it will thereupon become further necessary to re-establish such ancient principles as are friendly to the rights of the people and to declare certain others which may cooperate with and fortify the same in future.

Be it therefore enacted by the authority of the people that the said, George—— Guelf be, and he hereby is deposed from the kingly office within this government and absolutely divested of all its rights, powers, and prerogatives: and that he and his descendants and all persons acting by or through him, and all other persons whatsoever shall be and forever remain incapable of the same: and that the said office shall henceforth cease and never more either in name or substance be re-established within this colony.

And be it further enacted by the authority aforesaid that the following fundamental laws and principles of government shall henceforth be established.

The Legislative, Executive and Judiciary offices shall be kept forever separate; no person exercising the one shall be capable of appointment to the others, or to either of them.

I. LEGISLATIVE.

Legislation shall be exercised by two separate houses, to wit a house of Representatives, and a house of Senators, which shall be called the General Assembly of Virginia.

The said house of Representatives shall be composed of persons chosen by the people annually on the [1st day of October][3] and shall meet in General assembly on the [1st day of November] following and so from time to time on their own adjournments, or at any time when summoned by the Administrator and shall continue sitting so long as they shall think the publick service requires.

---

[3] The brackets are Jefferson's.

Vacancies in the said house by death or disqualification shall be filled by the electors under a warrant from the Speaker of the said house.

All male persons of full age and sane mind having a freehold estate in [one fourth of an acre] of land in any town, or in [25] acres of land in the country, and all persons resident in the colony who shall have paid scot and lot to government the last [two years] shall have right to give their vote in the election of their respective representatives. And every person so qualified to elect shall be capable of being elected, provided he shall have given no bribe either directly or indirectly to any elector, and shall take an oath of fidelity to the state and of duty in his office, before he enters on the exercise thereof. During his continuance in the said office he shall hold no public pension nor post of profit, either himself, or by another for his use.

The number of Representatives for each county or borough shall be so proportioned to the numbers of its qualified electors that the whole number of representatives shall not exceed [300] nor be less than [125]; for the present there shall be one representative for every [ ] qualified electors in each county or borough; but whenever this or any future proportion shall be likely to exceed or fall short of the limits beforementioned, it shall be again adjusted by the house of representatives.

The house of Representatives when met shall be free to act according to their own judgment and conscience.

The Senate shall consist of not less than [15] nor more than [50] members who shall be appointed by the house of Representatives. One third of them shall be removed out of office by lot at the end of the first [three] years and their places be supplied by a new appointment; one other third shall be removed by lot in like manner at the end of the second [three] years and their places be supplied by a new appointment; after which one third shall be removed annually at the end of every [three] years according to seniority. When once removed, they shall be forever incapable of being reappointed to that house. Their qualifications shall be an oath of fidelity to the state, and of duty in their office, the being [31] years of age at the least, and the having given no bribe directly or indirectly to obtain their appointment. While in the senatorial office they shall be incapable of holding any public pension or post of profit either themselves, or by others for their use.

The judges of the General court and of the High court of Chancery shall have session and deliberative voice, but not suffrage in the house of Senators.

The Senate and the house of representatives shall each of them have power to originate and amend bills; save only that bills for levying money *bills* shall be originated and amended by the representatives only; the assent of both houses shall be requisite to pass a law.

The General assembly shall have no power to pass any law inflicting death for any crime, excepting murder, and *such* those offences in the military service for which they shall think punishment by death absolutely necessary: and all capital punishments in other cases are hereby abolished. Nor shall they have power to prescribe torture in any case whatever: nor shall there be power anywhere to pardon crimes or to remit fines or punishments: nor shall any law for levying money be in force longer than [ten years] from the time of its commencement.

[Two thirds] of the members of either house shall be a Quorum to proceed to business.

II. EXECUTIVE.

The executive powers shall be exercised in manner following.

One person to be called the [Administrator] shall be annually appointed by the house of Representatives on the second day of their first session, who after having acted [one] year shall be incapable of being again appointed to that office until he shall have been out of the same [three] years.

Under him shall be appointed by the same house and at the same time, a Deputy-Administrator to assist his principal in the discharge of his office, and to succeed, in case of his death before the year shall have expired, to the whole powers thereof during the residue of the year.

The administrator shall possess the power formerly held by the king: save only that, he shall be bound by acts of legislature though not expressly named.

he shall have no negative on the bills of the Legislature;

he shall be liable to action, though not to personal restraint for private duties or wrongs;

he shall not possess the prerogatives:

of dissolving, proroguing or adjourning either house of Assembly;

of declaring war or concluding peace;

of issuing letters of marque or reprisal;

of raising or introducing armed forces; building armed vessels, forts or strongholds;

of coining monies or regulating their values;

of regulating weights and measures;

of erecting courts, offices, boroughs, corporations, fairs, markets, ports, beacons, lighthouses, sea-marks.

of laying embargoes, or prohibiting the exportation of any commodity for a longer space than [40] days.

of retaining or recalling a member of the state but by legal process *pro delicto vel contractu.*

of making denizens.

of pardoning crimes, or remitting fines or punishments.

of creating dignities or granting rights or precedence.

but these powers shall be exercised by the legislature alone, and excepting also those powers which by these fundamentals are given to others, or abolished.

A Privy council shall be annually appointed by the house of representatives whose duties it shall be to give advice to the Administrator when called on by him. With them the Deputy Administrator shall have session and suffrage.

Delegates to represent this colony in the American Congress shall be appointed when necessary by the house of Representatives. After serving [one] year in that office they shall not be capable of being re-appointed to the same during an interval of [one] year.

A Treasurer shall be appointed by the house of Representatives who shall issue no money but by authority of both houses.

An Attorney general shall be appointed by the house of Representatives.

High Sheriffs and Coroners of counties shall be annually elected by those qualified to vote for representatives: and no person who shall have served as high sheriff [one] year shall be capable of being re-elected to the said office in the same county till he shall have been out of office [five] years.

All other Officers civil and military shall be appointed by the Administrator; but such appointment shall be subject to the negative of the Privy council, saving however to the Legislature a power of transferring to any other persons the appointment of such officers or any of them.

III. JUDICIARY.

The Judiciary powers shall be exercised

First, by County courts and other inferior jurisdictions:

Secondly, by a General court and a High court of Chancery:

Thirdly, by a Court of Appeals.

The judges of the county courts and other inferior jurisdictions shall be appointed by the Administrator, subject to the negative of the privy council. They shall not be fewer than [five] in number. Their jurisdictions shall be defined from time to time by the legislature: and they shall be removable for misbehavior by the court of Appeals.

The Judges of the General court and of the High court of Chancery shall be appointed by the Administrator and Privy council. If kept united they shall be [5] in number, if separate, there shall be [5] for the General court and [3] for the High court of Chancery. The appointment shall be made from the faculty of the law, and of such persons of that faculty as shall have actually exercised the same at the bar of some court or courts of record within this colony for [seven] years. They shall hold their commissions during good behavior, for breach of which they shall be removable by the court of Appeals. Their jurisdiction shall be defined from time to time by the Legislature.

The Court of Appeals shall consist of not less than [7] nor more than [11] members, to be appointed by the house of Representatives: they shall hold their offices during good behavior, for breach of which they shall be removable by an act of the legislature only. Their jurisdiction shall be to determine finally all causes removed before them from the General Court or High Court of Chancery, or of the county courts or other inferior jurisdictions for misbehavior: [to try] impeachments against high offenders lodged before them by the house of representatives for such crimes as shall hereafter be precisely defined by the Legislature, and for the punishment of which, the said legislature shall have previously prescribed certain and determinate pains]. In this court the judges of the General court and High court of Chancery shall have session and deliberative voice, but no suffrage.

All facts in causes whether of Chancery, Common, Ecclesiastical, or Marine law, shall be tried by a jury upon evidence given *viva voce,* in open court: but where witnesses are out of the colony or unable to attend through sickness or other invincible necessity, their deposition may be submitted to the credit of the jury.

All Fines or Amercements shall be assessed, and Terms of imprisonment for Contempts and Misdemeanors shall be fixed by the verdict of a Jury.

All Process Original and Judicial shall run in the name of the court from which it issues.

Two thirds of the members of the General court, High court of Chancery, or Court of Appeals shall be a Quorum to proceed to business.

IV. RIGHTS PRIVATE AND PUBLIC.

Unappropriated or Forfeited lands shall be appropriated by the Administrator with the consent of the Privy council.

Every person of full age neither owning nor having owned [50] acres of land, shall be entitled to an appropriation of [50] acres or to so much as shall make up what he owns or has owned [50] acres in full and absolute dominion. And no other person shall be capable of taking an appropriation.

Lands heretofore holden *in fee* of the crown in fee simple, and those hereafter to be appropriated shall be holden in full and absolute dominion, of no superior whatever.

No lands shall be appropriated until purchased of the Indian native proprietors; nor shall any purchases be made of them but on behalf of the public, by authority of acts of the General assembly to be passed for every purchase specially.

The territories contained within the charters erecting the colonies of Maryland, Pennsylvania, North and South Carolina, are hereby ceded, released, and forever confirmed to the people of those colonies respectively, with all the rights of property, jurisdiction and government and all other rights whatsoever which might at any time heretofore have been claimed by this colony. The Western and Northern extent of this country shall in all other respects stand as fixed by the charter of——until by act of the Legislature one or more territories shall be laid off Westward of the Alleghany mountains for new colonies, which colonies shall be established on the same fundamental laws contained in this instrument, and shall be free and independent of this colony and of all the world.

Descents shall go according to the laws Gavelkind, save only that females shall have equal rights with males.

No person hereafter coming into this county shall be held within the same in slavery under any pretext whatever.

All persons who by their own oath or affirmation, or by other testimony shall give satisfactory proof to any court of record in this colony that they propose to reside in the same [7] years at the least and who shall subscribe the fundamental laws, shall be considered as residents and entitled to all the rights of persons natural born.

All persons shall have full and free liberty of religious opinion; nor shall any be compelled to frequent or maintain any religious institution.

No freeman shall be debarred the use of arms [within his own lands].

There shall be no standing army but in time of actual war.

Printing presses shall be free, except so far as by commission of private injury cause may be given of private action.

All Forfeitures heretofore going to the king, shall go to the state; save only such as the legislature may hereafter abolish.

The royal claim to Wrecks, waifs, strays, treasure-trove, royal mines, royal fish, royal birds, are declared to have been usurpations on common right.

No Salaries or Perquisites shall be given to any officer but by some future act of the legislature. No salaries shall be given to the Administrator, members of the legislative houses, judges of the court of Appeals, judges of the County courts, or other inferior jurisdictions, Privy counsellors, or Delegates to the American Congress: but the reasonable expenses of the Administrator, members of the house of representatives, judges of the court of Appeals, Privy counsellors, and Delegates for subsistence while acting in the duties of their office, may be borne by the public, if the legislature shall so direct. No person shall be capable of acting in any office Civil, Military [or Ecclesiastical] *The Qualifications of all not otherwise directed, shall be an oath of fidelity to state and the having given no bribe to obtain their office* who shall have given any bribe to obtain such office, or who shall not previously take an oath of fidelity to the state.

None of these fundamental laws and principles of government shall be repealed or altered, but by the personal consent of the people on summons to meet in their respective counties on one and the same day by an act of Legislature to be passed for every special occasion: and if in such county meetings the people of two thirds of the counties shall give their suffrage for any particular alteration or repeal referred to them by the said act, the same shall be accordingly repealed or altered, and such repeal or alteration shall take its place among these fundamentals and stand on the same footing with them, in lieu of the article repealed or altered.

The laws heretofore in force in this colony shall remain in force, except so far as they are altered by the foregoing fundamental laws, or so far as they may be hereafter altered by acts of the Legislature.

These United Colonies Are Free and Independent States

Notes of Proceedings in the Continental Congress, June 7 to August 1, 1776

Thanks above all to Jefferson and to John Adams, posterity has a fair idea of what happened in Philadelphia between June and August 1776. But Jefferson's Notes of Proceedings has given rise to a slight controversy among historians. When were the Notes actually written and how accurate are they? Jefferson added his copy of the Notes to his "Autobiography," written in 1821, at a time when Federalists still questioned his authorship of the Declaration of Independence. Several misstatements in Jefferson's Notes tended to give some credence to the charge. His Notes err in stating that the Declaration was signed on July 4 (when it was signed on August 2) and that every member present signed except John Dickinson (when Dickinson was not even in Philadelphia). Nonetheless, there is no doubt that he wrote almost all of the Notes before June 1, 1783—for on that date Madison received a copy with interlineations similar to those found in the copy Jefferson inserted in his "Autobiography"—and that on the whole they are an incontestably accurate source for one of the great moments in human history.

Friday, June 7, 1776. The delegates from Virginia moved, in obedience to instructions from their constituents, that the Congress should declare that these United colonies are, and of right ought to be, free and independent states, that they are absolved from all allegiance to the British crown, and that all political connection between them and the state of Great Britain is, and ought to be, totally dissolved; that measures should be immediately taken for procuring the assistance of foreign powers, and a Confederation be formed to bind the colonies more closely together.

The House being obliged to attend at that time to some other business, the proposition was referred to the next day, when the members were ordered to attend punctually at ten o'clock.

Saturday, June 8. They proceeded to take it into consideration, and referred it to a committee of the whole, into which they immediately resolved themselves, and passed that day and Monday, the 10th, in debating on the subject.

It was argued by Wilson, Robert R. Livingston, E. Rutledge, Dickinson, and others:

That, though they were friends to the measures themselves, and saw the impossibility that we should ever again be united with Great Britain, yet they were against adopting them at this time:

That the conduct we had formerly observed was wise and proper now, of deferring to take any capital step till the voice of the people drove us into it:

That they were our power, and without them our declarations could not be carried into effect:

That the people of the middle colonies (Maryland, Delaware, Pennsylvania, the Jerseys and New York) were not yet ripe for bidding adieu to British connection, but that they were fast ripening, and, in a short time, would join in the general voice of America:

That the resolution, entered into by this House on the 15th of May, for suppressing the exercise of all powers derived from the crown, had shown, by the ferment into which it had thrown these middle colonies, that they had not yet accommodated their minds to a separation from the mother country:

That some of them had expressly forbidden their delegates to consent to such a declaration, and others had given no instructions, and consequently no powers to give such consent:

That if the delegates of any particular colony had no power to declare such colony independent, certain they were, the others could not declare it for them; the colonies being as yet perfectly independent of each other:

That the assembly of Pennsylvania was now sitting above stairs, their convention would sit within a few days, the convention of New York was now sitting, and those of the Jerseys and Delaware counties would meet on the Monday following, and it was probable these bodies would take up the question of Independence, and would declare to their delegates the voice of their state:

That if such a declaration should now be agreed to, these delegates must retire, and possibly their colonies might secede from the Union:

That such a secession would weaken us more than could be compensated by any foreign alliance:

That in the event of such a division, foreign powers would either refuse to join themselves to our fortunes, or, having us so much in their power as that desperate declaration would place us, they would insist on terms proportionably more hard and prejudicial:

That we had little reason to expect an alliance with those to whom alone, as yet, we had cast our eyes:

That France and Spain had reason to be jealous of that rising power, which would one day certainly strip them of all their American possessions:

That it was more likely they should form a connection with the British court, who, if they should find themselves unable otherwise to extricate themselves from their difficulties, would agree to a partition of our territories, restoring Canada to France, and the Floridas to Spain, to accomplish for themselves a recovery of these colonies:

That it would not be long before we should receive certain information of the disposition of the French court, from the agent whom we had sent to Paris for that purpose:

That if this disposition should be favorable, by waiting the event of the present campaign, which we all hoped would be successful, we should have reason to expect an alliance on better terms:

That this would in fact work no delay of any effectual aid from such ally, as from the advance of the season and distance of our situation, it was impossible we could receive any assistance during this campaign:

That it was prudent to fix among ourselves the terms on which we should form alliance, before we declared we would form one at all events:

And that if these were agreed on, and our Declaration of Independence ready by the time our Ambassador should be prepared to sail, it would be as well as to go into that Declaration at this day.

On the other side, it was urged by J. Adams, Lee, Wythe, and others, that no gentleman had argued against the policy or the right of separation from Britain, nor had supposed it possible we should ever renew our connection; that they had only opposed its being now declared:

That the question was not whether, by a Declaration of Independence, we should make ourselves what we are not;

but whether we should declare a fact which already exists:

That, as to the people or parliament of England, we had always been independent of them, their restraints on our trade deriving efficacy from our acquiescence only, and not from any rights they possessed of imposing them, and that so far, our connection had been federal only, and was now dissolved by the commencement of hostilities:

That, as to the King, we had been bound to him by allegiance, but that this bond was now dissolved by his assent to the last act of Parliament, by which he declares us out of his protection, and by his levying war on us, a fact which had long ago proved us out of his protection; it being a certain position in law, that allegiance and protection are reciprocal, the one ceasing when the other is withdrawn:

That James the Second never declared the people of England out of his protection, yet his actions proved it, and the Parliament declared it:

No delegates then can be denied, or ever want, a power of declaring an existing truth:

That the delegates from the Delaware counties having declared their constituents ready to join, there are only two colonies, Pennsylvania and Maryland, whose delegates are absolutely tied up, and that these had, by their instructions, only reserved a right of confirming or rejecting the measure:

That the instructions from Pennsylvania might be accounted for from the times in which they were drawn, near a twelve-month ago, since which the face of affairs has totally changed:

That within that time, it had become apparent that Britain was determined to accept nothing less than a *carte-blanche*, and that the King's answer to the Lord Mayor, Aldermen and Common Council of London, which had come to hand four days ago, must have satisfied every one of this point:

That the people wait for us to lead the way:

That *they* are in favor of the measure, though the instructions given by some of their *representatives* are not:

That the voice of the representatives is not always consonant with the voice of the people, and that this is remarkably the case in these middle colonies:

That the effect of the resolution of the 15th of May has proved this, which, raising the murmurs of some in the colonies of Pennsylvania and Maryland, called forth the opposing voice of the freer part of the people, and proved them to be the majority even in these colonies:

That the backwardness of these two colonies might be ascribed, partly to the influence of proprietary power and connections, and partly, to their having not yet been attacked by the enemy:

That these causes were not likely to be soon removed, as there seemed no probability that the enemy would make either of these the seat of this summer's war:

That it would be vain to wait either weeks or months for perfect unanimity, since it was impossible that all men should ever become of one sentiment on any question:

That the conduct of some colonies, from the beginning of this contest, had given reason to suspect it was their settled policy to keep in the rear of the confederacy, that their particular prospect might be better, even in the worst event:

That, therefore, it was necessary for those colonies who had thrown themselves forward and hazarded all from the beginning, to come forward now also, and put all again to their own hazard:

That the history of the Dutch Revolution, of whom three states only confederated at first, proved that a secession of some colonies would not be so dangerous as some apprehended:

That a Declaration of Independence alone could render it consistent with European delicacy, for European powers to treat with us, or even to receive an Ambassador from us:

That till this, they would not receive our vessels into their ports, nor acknowledge the adjudications of our courts of admiralty to be legitimate, in cases of capture of British vessels:

That though France and Spain may be jealous of our rising power, they must think it will be much more formidable with the addition of Great Britain; and will therefore see it their interest to prevent a coalition; but should they refuse, we shall be but where we are; whereas without trying, we shall never know whether they will aid us or not:

That the present campaign may be unsuccessful, and therefore we had better propose an alliance while our affairs wear a hopeful aspect:

That to wait the event of this campaign will certainly work delay, because, during the summer, France may assist us effectually, by cutting off those supplies of provisions from England and Ireland, on which the enemy's armies here are to depend; or by setting in motion the great power they have collected in the West Indies, and calling our enemy to the defence of the possessions they have there:

That it would be idle to lose time in settling the terms of alliance, till we had first determined we would enter into alliance:

That it is necessary to lose no time in opening a trade for our people, who will want clothes, and will want money too, for the payment of taxes:

And that the only misfortune is, that we did not enter into alliance with France six months sooner, as, besides opening her ports for the vent of our last year's produce, she might have marched an army into Germany, and prevented the petty princes there, from selling their unhappy subjects to subdue us.

It appearing in the course of these debates, that the colonies of New York, New Jersey, Pennsylvania, Delaware, Maryland, and South Carolina were not yet matured for falling from the parent stem, but that they were fast advancing to that state, it was thought most prudent to wait a while for them, and to postpone the final decision to July 1st; but, that this might occasion as little delay as possible, a committee was appointed to prepare a Declaration of Independence. The committee were John Adams, Dr. Franklin, Roger Sherman, Robert R. Livingston, and myself. Committees were also appointed, at the same time, to prepare a plan of confederation for the colonies, and to state the terms proper to be proposed for foreign alliance. The committee for drawing the Declaration of Independence, desired me to do it. It was accordingly done, and being approved by them, I reported it to the House on Friday, the 28th of June, when it was read, and ordered to lie on the table. On Monday, the 1st of July, the House resolved itself into a committee of the whole, and resumed the consideration of the original motion made by the delegates of Virginia, which, being again debated through the day, was carried in the affirmative by the votes of New Hampshire, Connecticut, Massachusetts, Rhode Island, New Jersey, Maryland, Virginia North Carolina and Georgia. South Carolina and Pennsylvania voted against it. Delaware had but two members present, and they were divided. The delegates from New York declared they were for it themselves, and were assured their constituents were for it; but that their instructions having been drawn near a twelvemonth before, when reconciliation was still the general object, they were enjoined by them to do nothing which should impede that object. They, therefore, thought themselves not justifiable in voting on either side, and asked leave to withdraw from the question; which was given them. The committee rose and reported their resolution to the House. Mr. Edward Rutledge, of South Carolina, then requested the determination might be put off to the next day, as he believed his colleagues, though they disapproved of the resolution, would then join in it for the sake of unanimity. The ultimate question, whether the House would agree to the resolution of the committee, was accordingly postponed to the next day, when it was again moved, and South Carolina concurred in voting for it. In the meantime, a third member had come post from the Delaware counties, and turned the vote of that colony in favor of the resolution. Members of a different sentiment attending that morning from Pennsylvania also, her vote was changed, so that the whole twelve colonies who were authorized to vote at all, gave their voices for it; and, within a few days, the convention of New York approved of it, and thus supplied the void occasioned by the withdrawing of her delegates from the vote.

Congress proceeded the same day to consider the Declaration of Independence, which had been reported and lain on the table the Friday preceding, and on Monday referred to a committee of the whole. The pusillanimous idea that we had friends in England worth keeping terms with, still haunted the minds of many. For this reason, those passages which conveyed censures on the people of England were struck out, lest they should give them offence. The clause too, reprobating the enslaving the inhabitants of Africa, was struck out in complaisance to South Carolina and Georgia, who had never attempted to restrain the importation of slaves, and who, on the contrary, still wished to continue it. Our northern brethren also, I believe, felt a little tender under those censures; for though their people had very few slaves themselves, yet they had been pretty considerable carriers of them to others. The debates, having taken up the greater parts of the 2d, 3d, and 4th days of July, were, on the evening of the last, closed; the Declaration was reported by the committee, agreed to by the House, and signed by every member present, except Mr. Dickinson. . . .

On Friday, July 12, the committee appointed to draw the articles of Confederation reported them, and, on the 22d, the

House resolved themselves into a committee to take them into consideration. On the 30th and 31st of that month, and 1st of the ensuing, those articles were debated which determined the proportion, or quota, of money which each state should furnish to the common treasury, and the manner of voting in Congress. The first of these articles was expressed in the original draught in these words. "Art. XI. All charges of war and all other expenses that shall be incurred for the common defence, or general welfare, and allowed by the United States assembled, shall be defrayed out of a common treasury, which shall be supplied by the several colonies in proportion to the number of inhabitants of every age, sex, and quality, except Indians not paying taxes, in each colony, a true account of which, distinguishing the white inhabitants, shall be triennially taken and transmitted to the Assembly of the United States."

Mr. Chase moved that the quotas should be fixed, not by the number of inhabitants of every condition, but by that of the "white inhabitants." He admitted that taxation should be always in proportion to property, that this was, in theory, the true rule; but that, from a variety of difficulties, it was a rule which could never be adopted in practice. The value of the property in every State, could never be estimated justly and equally. Some other measure for the wealth of the State must therefore be devised, some standard referred to, which would be more simple. He considered the number of inhabitants as a tolerably good criterion of property, and that this might always be obtained. He therefore thought it the best mode which we could adopt, with one exception only: he observed that negroes are property, and as such, cannot be distinguished from the lands or personalities held in those States where there are few slaves; that the surplus of profit which a Northern farmer is able to lay by, he invests in cattle, horses, &c., whereas a Southern farmer lays out the same surplus in slaves. There is no more reason, therefore, for taxing the Southern States on the farmer's head, and on his slave's head, than the Northern ones on their farmer's heads and the heads of their cattle; that the method proposed would, therefore, tax the Southern States according to their numbers and their wealth conjunctly, while the Northern would be taxed on numbers only: that negroes, in fact, should not be considered as members of the State, more than cattle, and that they have no more interest in it.

Mr. John Adams observed, that the numbers of people were taken by this article, as an index of the wealth of the State, and not as subjects of taxation; that, as to this matter, it was of no consequence by what name you called your people, whether by that of freemen or of slaves; that in some countries the laboring poor were called freemen, in others they were called slaves; but that the difference as to the state was imaginary only. What matters it whether a landlord, employing ten laborers on his farm, gives them annually as much money as will buy them the necessaries of life, or gives them those necessaries at short hand? The ten laborers add as much wealth annually to the State, increase its exports as much in the one case as the other. Certainly five hundred freemen produce no more profits, no greater surplus for the payment of taxes, than five hundred slaves. Therefore, the State in which are the laborers called freemen, should be taxed no more than that in which are those called slaves. Suppose, by an extraordinary operation of nature or of law, one-half the laborers of a State could in the course of one night be transformed into slaves; would the State be made the poorer or the less able to pay taxes? That the condition of the laboring poor in most countries, that of the fishermen particularly of the Northern States, is as abject as that of slaves. It is the number of laborers which produces the surplus for taxation, and numbers, therefore, indiscriminately, are the fair index of wealth; that it is the use of the word "property" here, and its application to some of the people of the State, which produces the fallacy. How does the Southern farmer procure slaves? Either by importation or by purchase from his neighbor. If he imports a slave, he adds one to the number of laborers in his country, and proportionably to its profits and abilities to pay taxes; if he buys from his neighbor, it is only a transfer of a laborer from one farm to another, which does not change the annual produce of the State, and therefore, should not change its tax: that if a Northern farmer works ten laborers on his farm, he can, it is true, invest the surplus of ten men's labor in cattle; but so may the Southern farmer, working ten slaves; that a State of one hundred thousand freemen can maintain no more cattle, than one of one hundred thousand slaves. Therefore, they have no more of that kind of property; that a slave may indeed, from the custom of speech, be more properly called the wealth of his master, than the free laborer might be called the wealth of his employer; but as to the State, both were equally its wealth, and should, therefore, equally add to the quota of its tax.

Mr. Harrison proposed, as a compromise, that two slaves should be counted as one freemen. He affirmed that slaves did not do as much work as freemen, and doubted if two effected more than one; that this was proved by the price of labor; the hire of a laborer in the Southern colonies being from £8 to £12, while in the Northern it was generally £24.

Mr. Wilson said, that if this amendment should take place, the Southern colonies would have all the benefit of slaves, whilst the Northern ones would bear the burthen: that slaves increase the profits of a State, which the Southern States mean to take to themselves; that they also increase the burthen of defence, which would of course fall so much the heavier on the Northern: that slaves occupy the places of freemen, and eat their food. Dismiss your slaves, and freemen will take their places. It is our duty to lay every discouragement on the importation of slaves; but this amendment would give the *jus trium liberorum*[1] to him who would import slaves: that other kinds of property were pretty equally distributed through all the colonies: there were as many cattle, horses and sheep, in the North as the South, and South as the North; but not so as to slaves: that experience has shown that those colonies have been always able to pay most, which have the most inhabitants, whether they be black or white; and the practice of the Southern colonies has always been to make every farmer pay poll taxes upon all his laborers, whether black or white. He acknowledges, indeed, that freemen work the most; but they consume the most also. They do not produce a greater surplus for taxation. The slave is neither fed nor clothed so expensively as a freeman. Again, white women are exempted from labor generally, but negro women are not. In this, then, the Southern States have an advantage as the article now stands. It has sometimes been said, that slavery is necessary, because the commodities they raise would be too dear for market if cultivated by freemen; but now it is said that the labor of the slave is the dearest.

Mr. Payne urged the original resolution of Congress, to proportion the quotas of the States to the number of souls.

Dr. Witherspoon was of opinion, that the value of lands

---

[1] Right of three freemen.

and houses was the best estimate of the wealth of a nation, and that it was practicable to obtain such a valuation. This is the true barometer of wealth. The one now proposed is imperfect in itself, and unequal between the States. It has been objected that negroes eat the food of freemen, and, therefore, should be taxed; horses also eat the food of freemen; therefore they also should be taxed. It has been said too, that in carrying slaves into the estimate of the taxes the State is to pay, we do no more than those States themselves do, who always take slaves into the estimate of the taxes the individual is to pay. But the cases are not parallel. In the Southern colonies slaves pervade the whole colony; but they do not pervade the whole continent. That as to the original resolution of Congress, to proportion the quotas according to the souls, it was temporary only, and related to the moneys heretofore emitted: whereas we are now entering into a new compact, and therefore stand on original ground.

August 1. The question being put, the amendment proposed was rejected by the votes of New Hampshire, Massachusetts, Rhode Island, Connecticut, New York, New Jersey, and Pennsylvania, against those of Delaware, Maryland, Virginia, North and South Carolina. Georgia was divided.

The other article was in these words. "Art. XVII. In determining questions, each colony shall have one vote."

July 30, 31, August 1. Present forty-one members. Mr. Chase observed this article was the most likely to divide us, of any one proposed in the draught then under consideration: that the larger colonies had threatened they would not confederate at all, if their weight in Congress should not be equal to the numbers of people they added to the confederacy; while the smaller ones declared against a union, if they did not retain an equal vote for the protection of their rights. That it was of the utmost consequence to bring the parties together, as, should we sever from each other, either no foreign power will ally with us at all, or the different States will form different alliances, and thus increase the horrors of those scenes of civil war and bloodshed, which in such a state of separation and independence, would render us a miserable people. That our importance, our interests, our peace required that we should confederate, and that mutual sacrifices should be made to effect a compromise of this difficult question. He was of opinion, the smaller colonies would lose their rights, if they were not in some instances allowed an equal vote; and, therefore, that a discrimination should take place among the questions which would come before Congress. That the smaller States should be secured in all questions concerning life or liberty, and the greater ones, in all respecting property. He, therefore, proposed, that in votes relating to money, the voice of each colony should be proportioned to the number of its inhabitants.

Dr. Franklin thought, that the votes should be so proportioned in all cases. He took notice that the Delaware counties had bound up their delegates to disagree to this article. He thought it a very extraordinary language to be held by any State, that they would not confederate with us, unless we would let them dispose of our money. Certainly, if we vote equally, we ought to pay equally; but the smaller States will hardly purchase the privilege at this price. That had he lived in a State where the representation, originally equal, had become unequal by time and accident, he might have submitted rather than disturb government; but that we should be very wrong to set out in this practice, when it is in our power to establish what is right. That at the time of the Union between England and Scotland, the latter had made the objection which the smaller States now do; but experience had proved that no unfairness had ever been shown them: that their advocates had prognosticated that it would again happen, as in times of old, that the whale would swallow Jonas [sic], but he thought the prediction reversed in event, and that Jonas had swallowed the whale; for the Scotch had in fact got possession of the government, and gave laws to the English. He reprobated the original agreement of Congress to vote by colonies, and, therefore, was for their voting, in all cases, according to the number of taxables.

Dr. Witherspoon opposed every alteration of the article. All men admit that a confederacy is necessary. Should the idea get abroad that there is likely to be no union among us, it will damp the minds of the people, diminish the glory of our struggle, and lessen its importance; because it will open to our view future prospects of war and dissension among ourselves. If an equal vote be refused, the smaller States will become vassals to the larger; and all experience has shown that the vassals and subjects of free States are the most enslaved. He instanced the Helots of Sparta, and the provinces of Rome. He observed that foreign powers, discovering this blemish, would make it a handle for disengaging the smaller

States from so unequal a confederacy. That the colonies should in fact be considered as individuals; and that, as such, in all disputes, they should have an equal vote; that they are now collected as individuals making a bargain with each other, and, of course, had a right to vote as individuals. That in the East India Company they voted by persons, and not by their proportion of stock. That the Belgic confederacy voted by provinces. That in questions of war the smaller States were as much interested as the larger, and, therefore, should vote equally; and indeed, that the larger States were more likely to bring war on the confederacy, in proportion as their frontier was more extensive. He admitted that equality of representation was an excellent principle, but then it must be of things which are co-ordinate; that is, of things similar, and of the same nature: that nothing relating to individuals could ever come before Congress; nothing but what would respect colonies. He distinguished between an incorporating and a federal union. The union of England was an incorporating one; yet Scotland had suffered by that union; for that its inhabitants were drawn from it by the hopes of places and employments: nor was it an instance of equality of representation; because, while Scotland was allowed nearly a thirteenth of representation they were to pay only one-fortieth of the land tax. He expressed his hopes, that in the present enlightened state of men's minds, we might expect a lasting confederacy, if it was founded on fair principles.

John Adams advocated the voting in proportion to numbers. He said that we stand here as the representatives of the people: that in some States the people are many, in others they are few; that therefore, their vote here should be proportioned to the numbers from whom it comes. Reason, justice and equity never had weight enough on the face of the earth, to govern the councils of men. It is interest alone which does it, and it is interest alone which can be trusted: that therefore the interests within doors, should be the mathematical representatives of the interests without doors: that the individuality of the colonies is a mere sound. Does the individuality of a colony increase its wealth or numbers? If it does, pay equally. If it does not add weight in the scale of the confederacy, it cannot add to their rights, nor weigh in argument. A. has £50, B. £500, C. £1000 in partnership. Is it just they should equally dispose of the moneys of the partnership? It has been said, we are independent individuals making a bargain together. The question is not what we are now, but what we ought to be when our bargain shall be made. The confederacy is to make us one individual only; it is to form us like separate parcels of metal, into one common mass. We shall no longer retain our separate individuality, but become a single individual as to all questions submitted to the confederacy. Therefore, all those reasons, which prove the justice and expediency of equal representation in other assemblies, hold good here. It has been objected that a proportional vote will endanger the smaller States. We answer that an equal vote will endanger the larger. Virginia, Pennsylvania, and Massachusetts, are the three greater colonies. Consider their distance, their difference of produce, of interests, and of manners, and it is apparent they can never have an interest or inclination to combine for the oppression of the smaller: that the smaller will naturally divide on all questions with the larger. Rhode Island, from its relation, similarity and intercourse, will generally pursue the same objects with Massachusetts; Jersey, Delaware, and Maryland, with Pennsylvania.

Dr. Rush took notice, that the decay of the liberties of the Dutch republic proceeded from three causes. I. The perfect unanimity requisite on all occasions. 2. Their obligation to consult their constituents. 3. Their voting by provinces. This last destroyed the equality of representation, and the liberties of Great Britain also are sinking from the same defect. That a part of our rights is deposited in the hands of our legislatures. There, it was admitted, there should be an equality of representation. Another part of our rights is deposited in the hands of Congress: why is it not equally necessary there should be an equal representation there? Were it possible to collect the whole body of the people together, they would determine the questions submitted to them by their majority. Why should not the same majority decide when voting here, by their representatives? The larger colonies are so providentially divided in situation, as to render every fear of their combining visionary. Their interests are different, and their circumstances dissimilar. It is more probable they will become rivals, and leave it in the power of the smaller States to give preponderance to any scale they please. The voting by the number of free inhabitants, will have one excellent effect, that of inducing the colonies to discourage slavery, and to encourage the increase of their free inhabitants.

Mr. Hopkins observed, there were four larger, four smaller,

and four middle-sized colonies. That the four largest would contain more than half the inhabitants of the confederated States, and therefore, would govern the others as they should please. That history affords no instance of such a thing as equal representation. The Germanic body votes by States. The Helvetic body does the same; and so does the Belgic confederacy. That too little is known of the ancient confederations, to say what was their practice.

Mr. Wilson thought, that taxation should be in proportion to wealth, but that representation should accord with the number of freemen. That government is a collection or result of the wills of all: that if any government could speak the will of all, it would be perfect; and that, so far as it departs from this, it becomes imperfect. It has been said that Congress is a representation of States, not of individuals. I say, that the objects of its care are all the individuals of the States. It is strange that annexing the name of "State" to ten thousand men, should give them an equal right with forty thousand. This must be the effect of magic, not of reason. As to those matters which are referred to Congress, we are not so many States; we are one large State. We lay aside our individuality, whenever we come here. The Germanic body is a burlesque on government; and their practice, on any point, is a sufficient authority and proof that it is wrong. The greatest imperfection in the constitution of the Belgic confederacy is their voting by provinces. The interest of the whole is constantly sacrificed to that of the small States. The history of the war in the reign of Queen Anne sufficiently proves this. It is asked, shall nine colonies put it into the power of four to govern them as they please? I invert the question, and ask, shall two millions of people put it in the power of one million to govern them as they please? It is pretended, too, that the smaller colonies will be in danger from the greater. Speak in honest language and say, the minority will be in danger from the majority. And is there an assembly on earth, where this danger may not be equally pretended? The truth is, that our proceedings will then be consentaneous with the interests of the majority, and so they ought to be. The probability is much greater, that the larger States will disagree, than that they will combine. I defy the wit of man to invent a possible case, or to suggest any one thing on earth, which shall be for the interests of Virginia, Pennsylvania and Massachusetts, and which will not also be for the interest of the other states.

To Assume Among the Powers of the Earth a Separate and Equal Station

Declaration of Independence, July 4, 1776

1. Jefferson's Rough Draft

On June 7, 1776 the Virginia delegates to the Continental Congress moved that the Colonies declare their independence of Great Britain. But because the Middle Colonies and South Carolina were, in Jefferson's words, "not yet matured for falling from the parent stem," Congress, on June 11, appointed a Committee of Five to prepare a Declaration to be considered at a later date. The Committee consisted of Jefferson, Franklin, John Adams, Roger Sherman and Robert R. Livingston. The task of drafting the Declaration fell to Jefferson who, at thirty-three, was already a writer of note. Nearly fifty years later Jefferson recalled his intention in writing it: "Neither aiming at originality of purpose or sentiment, nor yet copied from any particular and previous writing, it was intended to be an expression of the American mind, and to give that expression the proper tone and spirit called for by the occasion." It may be noted, however, that Jefferson himself had used similar language in the preamble to his draft of a constitution for Virginia.

On June 28 Jefferson's rough draft of the Declaration, containing changes made by the other members of the Committee, particularly by Adams and Franklin, went to Congress for further revisions.

A Declaration of the Representatives of the UNITED STATES OF AMERICA, in General Congress assembled.

When in the course of human events it becomes necessary for a people to advance from that subordination in which they have hitherto remained, & to assume among the powers of the earth the equal & independent station to which the laws of nature & of nature's god entitle them, a decent respect to the opinions of mankind requires that they should declare the causes which impel them to the change.

We hold these truths to be sacred & undeniable; that all men are created equal & independant, that from that equal creation they derive rights inherent & inalienable, among which are the preservation of life, & liberty, & the pursuit of happiness; that to secure these ends, governments are instituted among men, deriving their just powers from the consent of the governed; that whenever any form of government shall become destructive of these ends, it is the right of the people to alter or to abolish it, & to institute new government, laying it's foundation on such principles & organising it's powers in such form, as to them shall seem most likely to effect their safety & happiness. prudence indeed will dictate that governments long established should not be changed for light & transient causes: and accordingly all experience hath shewn that mankind are more disposed to suffer while evils are sufferable, than to right themselves by abolishing the forms to which they are accustomed. but when a long train of abuses & usurpations, begun at a distinguished period, & pursuing invariably the same object, evinces a design to subject them to arbitrary power, it is their right, it is their duty, to throw off such government & to provide new guards for their future security. such has been the patient sufferance of these colonies; & such is now the necessity which constrains them to expunge their former systems of government. the history of his present majesty, is a history of unremitting injuries and usurpations, among which no one fact stands single or solitary to contradict the uniform tenor of the rest, all of which have in direct object the establishment of an absolute tyranny over these states. to prove this, let facts be submitted to a candid world, for the truth of which we pledge a faith yet unsullied by falsehood.

he has refused his assent to laws the most wholesome and necessary for the public good:

he has forbidden his governors to pass laws of immediate & pressing importance, unless suspended in their operation till his assent should be obtained; and when so suspended, he has neglected utterly to attend to them.

he has refused to pass other laws for the accomodation of large districts of people unless those people would relinquish the right of representation, a right inestimable to them, & formidable to tyrants alone:

he has dissolved Representative houses repeatedly & continually, for opposing with manly firmness his invasions on the rights of the people:

he has refused for a long space of time to cause others to be elected, whereby the legislative powers, incapable of annihilation, have returned to the people at large for their exercise, the state remaining in the mean time exposed to all the dangers of invasion from without, & convulsions within:

he has endeavored to prevent the population of these states; for that purpose obstructing the laws for naturalization of foreigners; refusing to pass others to encourage their migrations hither; & raising the conditions of new appropriations of lands:

he has suffered the administration of justice totally to cease in some of these colonies, refusing his assent to laws for establishing judiciary powers:

he has made our judges dependant on his will alone, for the tenure of their offices, and amount of their salaries:

he has erected a multitude of new offices by a self-assumed power, & sent hither swarms of officers to harrass our people & eat out their substance:

he has kept among us in times of peace standing armies & ships of war:

he has affected to render the military, independant of & superior to the civil power:

he has combined with others to subject us to a jurisdiction foreign to our constitutions and unacknoleged by our laws; giving his assent to their pretended acts of legislation, for quartering large bodies of armed troops among us;

    for protecting them by a mock-trial from punishment for any murders they should commit on the inhabitants of these states;

    for cutting off our trade with all parts of the world;

    for imposing taxes on us without our consent;

    for depriving us of the benefits of trial by jury;

    for transporting us beyond seas to be tried for pretended offences:

    for taking away our charters, & altering fundamentally the forms of our governments;

    for suspending our own legislatures & declaring themselves invested with power to legislate for us in all cases whatsoever:

he has abdicated government here, withdrawing his governors, & declaring us out of his allegiance & protection:

he has plundered our seas, ravaged our coasts, burnt our towns & destroyed the lives of our people:

he is at this time transporting large armies of foreign mercenaries to compleat the works of death, desolation & tyranny, already begun with circumstances of cruelty & perfidy unworthy the head of a civilized nation:

he has endeavored to bring on the inhabitants of our frontiers the merciless Indian savages, whose known rule of warfare is an undistinguished destruction of all ages, sexes, & conditions of existence:

he has incited treasonable insurrections in our fellow-subjects, with the allurements of forfeiture & confiscation of our property:

he has waged cruel war against human nature itself, violating it's most sacred rights of life & liberty in the persons of a distant people who never offended him, captivating & carrying them into slavery in another hemisphere, or to incur miserable death in their transportation thither. this piratical warfare, the opprobrium of *infidel* powers, is the warfare of the CHRISTIAN king of Great Britain, determined to keep open a market where MEN should be bought & sold. he has prostituted his negative for suppressing every legislative attempt to prohibit or to restrain this execrable commerce: and that this assemblage of horrors might want no fact of distinguished die, he is now exciting those very people to rise in arms among us, and to purchase that liberty of which *he* has deprived them, by murdering the people upon whom *he* also obtruded them; thus paying off former crimes committed against the *liberties* of one people, with crimes which he urges them to commit against the *lives* of another.

in every stage of these oppressions we have petitioned for redress in the most humble terms; our repeated petitions have been answered by repeated injury. a prince whose character is thus marked by every act which may define a tyrant, is unfit to be the ruler of a people who mean to be free. future ages will scarce believe that the hardiness of one man, adventured within the short compass of 12 years only, on so many acts of tyranny without a mask, over a people fostered & fixed in principles of liberty.

Nor have we been wanting in attentions to our British brethren. we have warned them from time to time of attempts by their legislature to extend a jurisdiction over these our states. we have reminded them of the circumstances of our emigration & settlement here, no one of which could warrant so strange a pretension: that these were effected at the expence of our own blood & treasure, unassisted by the wealth or the strength of Great Britain: that in constituting indeed our several forms of government, we had adopted one common king, thereby laying a foundation for perpetual league & amity with them: but that submission to their parliament was no part of our constitution, nor ever in idea, if history may be credited: and we appealed to their native justice & magnanimity, as well as to the ties of our common kindred to disavow these usurpations which were likely to interrupt our correspondence & connection. they too have been deaf to the voice of justice & of consanguinity, & when occasions have been given them, by the regular course of their laws, of removing from their councils the disturbers of our harmony, they have by their free election re-established them in power. at this very time too they are permitting their chief magistrate to send over not only soldiers of our common blood, but Scotch & foreign mercenaries to invade & deluge us in blood. these facts have given the last stab to agonizing affection, and manly spirit bids us to renounce for ever these unfeeling brethren. we must endeavor to forget our former love for them, and to hold them as we hold the rest of mankind, enemies in war, in peace friends. we might have been a free & a great people together; but a communication of grandeur & of freedom it seems is below their dignity. be it so, since they will have it: the road to glory & happiness is open to us too; we will climb it in a separate state, and acquiesce in the necessity which pronounces our everlasting Adieu!

We therefore the representatives of the United States of America in General Congress assembled do, in the name & by authority of the good people of these states, reject and renounce all allegiance & subjection to the kings of Great Britain & all others who may hereafter claim by, through, or under them; we utterly dissolve & break off all political connection which may have heretofore subsisted between us & the people or parliament of Great Britain; and finally we do assert and declare these colonies to be free and independant states, and that as free & independant states they shall hereafter have power to levy war, conclude peace, contract alliances, establish commerce, & to do all other acts and things which independant states may of right do. And for the support of this declaration we mutually pledge to each other our lives, our fortunes, & our sacred honour.

2. Declaration of Independence

After adopting the resolution calling for independence Congress took up Jefferson's draft, made extensive changes in it and approved it on July 4. It was formally signed on August 2. The Declaration below follows the style of Jefferson's copy, inserted in his Autobiography. Words deleted by Congress are enclosed by brackets and italicized; words added by Congress are in capital letters.

A DECLARATION BY THE REPRESENTATIVES OF THE UNITED STATES OF AMERICA, IN *GENERAL* CONGRESS ASSEMBLED

When, in the course of human events, it becomes necessary for one people to dissolve the political bands which have connected them with another, and to assume among the powers of the earth the separate and equal station to which the laws of nature and of nature's God entitle them, a decent respect to the opinions of mankind requires that they should declare the causes which impel them to the separation.

We hold these truths to be self evident: that all men are created equal; that they are endowed by their Creator with CERTAIN [*inherent and*] inalienable rights; that among these are life, liberty, and the pursuit of happiness; that to secure these rights, governments are instituted among men, deriving their just powers from the consent of the governed; that whenever any form of government becomes destructive of these ends, it is the right of the people to alter or to abolish it, and to institute new government, laying its foundation on such principles, and organizing its powers in such form, as to them shall seem most likely to effect their safety and happiness. Prudence, indeed, will dictate that governments long established should not be changed for light and transient causes; and accordingly all experience hath shown that mankind are more disposed to suffer while evils are sufferable, than to right themselves by abolishing the forms to which they are accustomed. But when a long train of abuses and usurpations, [*begun at a distinguished period and*] pursuing invariably the same object, evinces a design to reduce them under absolute despotism, it is their right, it is their duty to throw off such government, and to provide new guards for their future security. Such has been the patient sufferance of these colonies; and such is now the necessity which constrains them to ALTER [*expunge*] their former systems of government. The history of the present king of Great Britain is a history of REPEATED [*unremitting*] injuries and usurpations, ALL HAVING [*among which appears no solitary fact to contradict the uniform tenor of the rest, but all have*] in direct object the establishment of an absolute tyranny over these states. To prove this, let facts be submitted to a candid world [*for the truth of which we pledge a faith yet unsullied by falsehood*].

He has refused his assent to laws the most wholesome and necessary for the public good.

He has forbidden his governors to pass laws of immediate and pressing importance, unless suspended in their operation till his assent should be obtained; and, when so suspended, he has utterly neglected to attend to them.

He has refused to pass other laws for the accommodation of large districts of people, unless those people would relinquish the right of representation in the legislature, a right inestimable to them, and formidable to tyrants only.

He has called together legislative bodies at places unusual, uncomfortable, and distant from the depository of their public records, for the sole purpose of fatiguing them into compliance with his measures.

He has dissolved representative houses repeatedly [*and continually*] for opposing with manly firmness his invasions on the rights of the people.

He has refused for a long time after such dissolutions to cause others to be elected, whereby the legislative powers, incapable of annihilation, have returned to the people at large for their exercise, the state remaining, in the meantime, exposed to all the dangers of invasion from without and convulsions within.

He has endeavored to prevent the population of these states; for that purpose obstructing the laws for naturalization of foreigners, refusing to pass others to encourage their migrations hither, and raising the conditions of new appropriations of lands.

He has OBSTRUCTED [*suffered*] the administration of

justice BY [*totally to cease in some of these states*] refusing his assent to laws for establishing judiciary powers.

He has made [*our*] judges dependent on his will alone for the tenure of their offices, and the amount and payment of their salaries.

He has erected a multitude of new offices, [*by a self-assumed power*] and sent hither swarms of new officers to harass our people and eat out their substance.

He has kept among us in times of peace standing armies [*and ships of war*] without the consent of our legislatures.

He has affected to render the military independent of, and superior to, the civil power.

He has combined with others to subject us to a jurisdiction foreign to our constitutions and unacknowledged by our laws, giving his assent to their acts of pretended legislation for quartering large bodies of armed troops among us; for protecting them by a mock trial from punishment for any murders which they should commit on the inhabitants of these states; for cutting off our trade with all parts of the world; for imposing taxes on us without our consent; for depriving us IN MANY CASES of the benefits of trial by jury; for transporting us beyond seas to be tried for pretended offences; for abolishing the free system of English laws in a neighboring province, establishing therein an arbitrary government, and enlarging its boundaries, so as to render it at once an example and fit instrument for introducing the same absolute rule into these COLONIES [*states*]; for taking away our charters, abolishing our most valuable laws, and altering fundamentally the forms of our governments; for suspending our own legislatures, and declaring themselves invested with power to legislate for us in all cases whatsoever.

He has abdicated government here BY DECLARING US OUT OF HIS PROTECTION, AND WAGING WAR AGAINST US [*withdrawing his governors, and declaring us out of his allegiance and protection*].

He has plundered our seas, ravaged our coasts, burnt our towns, and destroyed the lives of our people.

He is at this time transporting large armies of foreign mercenaries to complete the works of death, desolation and tyranny already begun with circumstances of cruelty and perfidy SCARCELY PARALLELED IN THE MOST BARBAROUS AGES, AND TOTALLY unworthy the head of a civilized nation.

He has constrained our fellow citizens taken captive on the high seas, to bear arms against their country, to become the executioners of their friends and brethren, or to fall themselves by their hands.

He has EXCITED DOMESTIC INSURRECTION AMONG US, AND HAS endeavored to bring on the inhabitants of our frontiers, the merciless Indian savages, whose known rule of warfare is an undistinguished destruction of all ages, sexes and conditions [*of existence*].

[*He has incited treasonable insurrections of our fellow citizens, with the allurements of forfeiture and confiscation of our property.*

He has waged cruel war against human nature itself; violating its most sacred rights of life and liberty in the persons of a distant people who never offended him, captivating and carrying them into slavery in another hemisphere, or to incur miserable death in their transportation hither. This piratical warfare, the opprobrium of INFIDEL powers, is the warfare of the CHRISTIAN king of Great Britain. Determined to keep open a market where MEN should be bought and sold, he has prostituted his negative for suppressing every legislative attempt to prohibit or to restrain this execrable commerce. And that this assemblage of horrors might want no fact of distinguished die, he is now exciting those very people to rise in arms among us, and to purchase that liberty of which he has deprived them, by murdering the people on whom he also obtruded them: thus paying off former crimes committed against the LIBERTIES of one people, with crimes which he urges them to commit against the LIVES of another.]

In every stage of these oppressions we have petitioned for redress in the most humble terms: our repeated petitions have been answered only by repeated injuries.

A prince whose character is thus marked by every act which may define a tyrant is unfit to be the ruler of a FREE people [*who mean to be·free. Future ages will scarcely believe that the hardiness of one man adventured, within the short compass of twelve years only, to lay a foundation so broad and so undisguised for tyranny over a people fostered and fixed in principles of freedom.*]

Nor have we been wanting in attentions to our British brethren. We have warned them from time to time of attempts by their legislature to extend AN UNWARRANTABLE [*a*] jurisdiction over US [*these our states*]. We have reminded them of the circumstances of our emigration and settlement here, [*no one of which could warrant so strange a pretension: that these were effected at the expense of our own blood and treasure, unassisted by the wealth or the strength of Great Britain; that in constituting indeed our several forms of government, we had adopted one common king, thereby laying a foundation for perpetual league and amity with them: but that submission to their parliament was no part of our constitution, nor ever in idea, if history may be credited: and,*] we HAVE appealed to their native justice and magnanimity AND WE HAVE CONJURED THEM BY [*as well as to*] the ties of our common kindred to disavow these usurpations which WOULD INEVITABLY [*were likely to*] interrupt our connection and correspondence. They too have been deaf to the voice of justice and of consanguinity. WE MUST THEREFORE [*and when occasions have been given them, by the regular course of their laws, of removing from their councils the disturbers of our harmony, they have, by their free election, re-established them in power. At this very time too, they are permitting their chief magistrate to send over not only soldiers of our common blood, but Scotch and foreign mercenaries to invade and destroy us. These facts have given the last stab to agonizing affection, and manly spirit bids us to renounce forever these unfeeling brethren. We must endeavor to forget our former love for them, and hold them as we hold the rest of mankind, enemies in war, in peace friends. We might have a free and a great people together; but a communication of grandeur and of freedom, it seems, is below their dignity. Be it so, since they will have it. The road to happiness and to glory is open to us, too. We will tread it apart from them, and*] acquiesce in the necessity which denounces our [*eternal*] separation AND HOLD THEM AS WE HOLD THE REST OF MANKIND, ENEMIES IN WAR, IN PEACE FRIENDS!

[1]We therefore the representatives of the United States of America in General Congress assembled, do in the name, and by the authority

We, therefore, the representatives of the United States of America in General Congress assembled, appealing to the supreme judge of the

---

[1] Jefferson divided the following section into two columns because of the numerous deletions that were made in it.

of the good people of these [*states reject and renounce all allegiance and subjection to the kings of Great Britain and all others who may hereafter claim by, through or under them; we utterly dissolve all political connection which may heretofore have subsisted between us and the people or parliament of Great Britain: and finally we do assert and declare these colonies to be free and independent states,*] and that as free and independent states, they have full power to levy war, conclude peace, contract alliances, establish commerce, and to do all other acts and things which independent states may of right do.

And for the support of this declaration, we mutually pledge to each other our lives, our fortunes, and our sacred honor.

world for the rectitude of our intentions, do in the name, and by the authority of the good people of these colonies, solemnly publish and declare, that these united colonies are, and of right ought to be free and independent states; that they are absolved from all allegiance to the British crown, and that all political connection between them and the state of Great Britain is, and ought to be, totally dissolved; and that as free and independent states, they have full power to levy war, conclude peace, contract alliances, establish commerce, and to do all other acts and things which independent states may of right do.

And for the support of this declaration, with a firm reliance on the protection of divine providence, we mutually pledge to each other our lives, our fortunes, and our sacred honor.

Shall Have Full Power to Pass, Convey or Use

A Bill to Enable Tenants in Fee tail to Convey Their Lands in Fee Simple, October 14, 1776

Jefferson introduced this bill to the Virginia House of Delegates on October 14. It passed less than three weeks later. Jefferson took particular pride in getting this legislation through. He always considered such a step necessary if the aristocracy of landed wealth was to be replaced by an aristocracy of virtue and talent.

Whereas the perpetuation of property in certain families by means of gifts made to them in fee tail is contrary to good policy, tends to deceive fair traders who give credit on the visible possession of such estates, discourages the holder thereof from taking care and improving the same, and sometimes does injury to the morals of youth by rendering them independent of, and disobedient to, their parents; and whereas the former method of docking such estates tail by special act of assembly formed for every particular case employed very much time of the legislature, was burthensome to the public, and also to the individual who made application for such acts:

Be it therefore enacted by the General Assembly of the Commonwealth of Virginia, and it is hereby enacted by authority of the same that any person who now hath, or hereafter may have any estate in fee tail general or special in any lands or slaves in possession, or who now is or hereafter may be entitled to any such estate tail in reversion or remainder after the determination of any estate for life or lives or of any lesser estate, whether such estate hath been or shall be created by deed, will, act of assembly, or any other ways or means shall have full power to pass, convey, or assure in fee simple or for any lesser estate the said lands or slaves, or use in lands or slaves or such reversion or remainder therein, or any part or parcel thereof, to any person or persons whatsoever by deed or deeds of feoffment, gift, grant, exchange, partition, lease, release, bargain, and sale, covenant to stand seized to uses, deed to lead uses, or by his last will and testament, or by any other mode or form of conveyance or assurance by which such lands or slaves, or use in lands or slaves, or such reversion or remainder therein might have been passed, conveyed or assured had the same been held in fee simple by the person so passing, conveying or assuring the same: and such deed, will or other conveyance shall be good and effectual to bar the issue in tail and those in remainder and revert as to such estate or estates so passed, conveyed, or assured by such deed, will, or other conveyance.

Provided nevertheless that such deed, will, or other conveyance shall be executed, acknowledged, or proved, and recorded in like manner as, and in all cases where, the same should have been done, had the person or persons so conveying or assuring held the said lands or slaves, or use of lands and slaves or such reversion or remainder in fee simple.

A Church Is a Voluntary Society of Men

Notes on Locke and Shaftesbury, 1776

Ratification in June 1776 of the Virginia Constitution, with its Declaration of Rights, inspired religious dissenters to press their claims for toleration, more concretely, for disestablishment of the Episcopal Church from the state. Jefferson, agreeing fully with their protests, sought to incorporate them in a bill for disestablishing the Church. But the bill reported out of committee and ultimately passed in November did not go nearly so far: it only exempted dissenters from having to support the Church. These Notes on Locke and Shaftesbury, mostly on Locke's A Letter Concerning Toleration, *were part of a much larger body of notes on religion which Jefferson wrote and kept in rough form some time before the drafting of the bill on dissenters.*

Why persecute for diffce. in religs. opinion?
1. for love to the person.
2. because of tendency of these opns. to dis[. . . .]
when I see them persecute their nearest connection & acquaintance for gross vices, I shall beleive it may proceed from love. till they do this, I appeal to their own conscences if they will examine, why they do nt. find some other principle. because of tendency. why not then level persecution at the crimes you fear will be introduced? burn or hang the adulterer, cheat &c. or exclude them from offices.
strange should be so zealous against things which tend to produce immorality & yet so indulgent to the immorality when produced. these moral vices all men acknolege to be diametrically against Xty. & obstructive of salvation of souls, but the fantastical points for which we generally persecute are often very questionable as we may be assured by the very different conclusions of people.
our Saviour chose not to propagate his religion by temporal punmts or civil incapacitation, if he had it was in his almighty power. but he chose to (*enforce*) extend it by it's influence on reason, thereby shewing to others how [they] should proceed.

Commonwealth is 'a society of men constituted for preser [ving] their *civil (rights) interests*.'

126

interests are 'life, health, indolency of body, liberty, property.'

the magistrate's jurisdn. extends only to civil rights and from these considns.:

the magistrate has no power but wt. ye. people gave hm.

the people hv. nt. givn. hm. (*powr.*) the care of souls bec. y cd. nt., y. cd. nt. because no man hs. *right* to abandon ye. care of his salvation to another.

no man has *power* to let another prescribe his faith. faith is not faith witht. believing. no man can conform his faith to the dictates of another.

the life & essence of religion consists in the internal persuasion or belief of the mind. external forms [of wor]ship, when against our belief, are hypocrisy [and im]piety. Rom. 14.23. 'he that doubteth is damned, if he eat, because he eateth not of faith: for whatsoever is not of faith is sin.

if it be said the magistrate may make use of a[rguments] and so draw the heterodox to truth: I [answer] every man has a commission to admonish, exhort, convince another of error.

[a church] is 'a *voluntary* society of men, joining [themselves] together of their own accord, in order to the [publick] worshipping of god in such a manner as they judge [accept]able to him & effectual to the salvation of their souls. [it is] *voluntary* because no man is *by nature* bound to any church. the hopes of salvation is the cause of his entering into it. if he find any thing wrong in it, he [sh]ould be as free to go out as he was to come in.

[w]hat is the power of that church &c.? as it is a society (*of voluntary*) it must have some laws for it's regulation. time & place of meeting, admitting & excluding members &c. must be regulated.

but as it was a spontaneous joining of members, it follows that it's laws extend to it's own members only, not to those of any other voluntary society: for then by the same rule some other voluntary society might usurp power (*of*) over them.

Christ has said 'wheresoever 2 or 3 are gatherd. togeth. in his name he will be in the midst of them.' this is his definition of a society. he does not make it essential that a bishop or presbyter govern them. without them it suffices for the salvation of souls.

from the dissensions among sects themselves arises necessarily a right of chusing & necessity of deliberating to which we will conform.

but if we chuse for ourselves, we must allow others to chuse also, & so reciprocally. this establishes religious liberty.

why require those things in order to ecclesiastical communion which Christ does not require in order to life eternal? how can that be the church of Christ which excludes such persons from it's communion as he will one day receive into the kingdom of heaven.

the arms of a religious society or church are exhortations admonitions & advice, & ultimately expulsion or excommunication. this last is the utmost limit of power.

how far does the duty of toleration extend? 1. no church is bound by the duty of toleration to retain within her bosom obstinate offenders against her laws. 2. we have no right to prejudice another in his civil enjoiments because he is of another church. if any man err from the right way, it is his own misfortune, no injury to thee, nor therefore art thou to punish him in the things of this life because thou supposest he will be miserable in that which is to come. on the contrary accdg to the spirit of the gospel, charity, bounty, liberality is due to him.

each church being free, no one can have jurisdiction over another; no not even when the civil magistrate joins it. it neither acquires the right of the sword by the magistrate's coming to it, nor does it lose the rights of instruction or excommunication by his going from it. it cannot by the accession of any new member acquire jurisdiction over those who do not accede. he brings only himself, having no power to bring others.

suppose for instance two churches one of Arminians another of (*Lutherans*) Calvinists in Constantinople. has either any right over the other? will it be said the orthodox one has? every church is to itself orthodox, to others erroneous or heretical.

no man complains of his neighbor for ill management of his affairs, for an error in sowing his land, or marrying his daughter, for consuming his substance in taverns, pulling down, building &c. in all these he has his liberty: but if he do not frequent the church, or there conform to ceremonies, there is an immediate uproar.

the care of every man's soul belongs to himself. but what if he neglect the care of it? well what if he neglect the care of his health or estate, which more nearly relate to the state. will the magistrate make a law that he shall not be poor or sick? laws provide against injury from others; but not from ourselves. God himself will not save men against their wills.

if I be marching on with my utmost vigour in that way which according to the sacred geography leads to Jerusalem streight, why am I beaten & ill used by others because my hair is not of the right cut; because I have not been kept right, bec. I eat flesh on the road, bec. I avoid certain by-ways which seem to lead into briars, bec. among several paths I take that which seems shortest & cleanest, bec. I avoid travellers less grave & keep company with others who are more sour & austere, or bec. I follow a guide crowned with a mitre & cloathed in white. yet these are the frivolous things which keep Xns. at war.

if the magistrate command me to [bring my commodity to a publick store house] I bring it because he can indemnify me if he erred & I thereby lose it; but what indemnification can he give me for the kdom. of heaven?

I cannot give up my guidance to the magistrate; because he knows no more of the way to heaven than I do & is less concerned to direct me right than I am to go right. if the jews had followed their kings, amongst so many, what number would have led them to idolatry? consider the vicissitudes among the emperors, Arians, Athans. or among our princes, H.8. E.6. Mary. Elizabeth.

[co]mpulsion in religion is distinguished peculiarly from compulsion in every other thing. I may grow rich by art I am compelled to follow, I may recover health by medicines I am compelled to take agt. my own judgmt., but I cannot be saved by a *worship* I disbelieve & abhor.

whatsoever is lawful in the Commonwealth, or permitted to the subject in the ordinary way, cannot be forbidden to him for religious uses; & whatsoever is prejudicial to the commonwealth in their ordinary uses & therefore prohibited by the laws, ought not to be permitted to churches in their sacred rites. for instance, it is unlawful in the ordinary course of things or in a private house to murder a child. it should not be permitted any sect then to sacrifice children: it is ordinarily lawful (or temporally lawful) to kill calves or lambs. they may therefore be religiously sacrificed. but if the good of the state required a temporary suspension of killing lambs (as during a siege); sacrifices of them may then be rightfully suspended also. this is the true extent of *toleration*.

[tr]uth will do well enough if left to shift for herself. she

seldom has received much aid from the power of great men to whom she is rarely known & seldom welcome. she has no need of force to procure entrance into the minds of men. error indeed has often prevailed by the assistance of power or force.

truth is the proper & sufficient antagonist to error.

[if] any thing pass in a religious meeting seditiously & contrary to the public peace, let it be punished in the same manner & no otherwise than as if it had happened in a fair or market. these meetings ought not to be sanctuaries for faction & flagitiousness.

[Lo]cke denies toleration to those who entertain opns. contrary to those moral rules necessary for the preservation of society; as for instance, that faith is not to be kept with those of another persuasion, that kings excommunicated forfeit their crowns, that dominion is founded in grace, or that obedience is due to some foreign prince, or who will not own & teach the duty of tolerating all men in matters of religion, or who deny the existence of a god. [It was a great thing to go so far (as he himself sais of the parl. who framed the act of tolern.) but where he stopped short, we may go on.]

[he] sais 'neither Pagan nor Mahamedan nor Jew ought to be excluded from the civil rights of the Commonwealth because of his religion.' shall we suffer a Pagan to deal with us and not suffer him to pray to his god?

[wh]y have Xns. been distinguished above all people who have ever lived for persecutions? is it because it is the genius of their religion? no, it's genius is the reverse. it is the refusing *toleration* to those of a different opn. which has produced all the bustles & wars on account of religion. it was the misfortune of mankind that during the darker centuries the Xn priests following their ambition & avarice & combining with the magistrates to divide the spoils of the people, could establish the notion that schismatics might be ousted of their possessions & destroyed. this notion we have not yet cleared ourselves from. in this case no wonder the oppressed should rebel, & they will continue to rebel & raise disturbance until their civil rights are fully restored to them & all partial distinctions, exclusions & incapacitations removed.

1. Shaftesbury. charact.

as the antients tolerated visionaries & enthusiasts of all kinds so they permitted a free scope to philosophy as a balance. as the Pythagoreans & latter Platonicks joined with the superstition of the times the Epicureans & Academicks were allowed all the use of wit & raillery against it. thus matters were balanced; reason had [full] play & science flourished. these contrarieties produced harmony. superstition & enthusiasm thus let alone never raged to bloodshed persecution &c. but now a new sort of policy, which considers the future lives & happiness of men rather than the present, has taught to distress one another, & raised an antipathy which no temporal interest could ever do, now *uniformity of opn.*, a hopeful project! is looked on as the only remedy agt. this evil & is made the very object of govmt itself. if magistracy should vouchsafe to interpose thus in other sciences we should [have] as bad logic, mathematics & philosophy as we have divinity in countries where the law settles orthodoxy.

[suppose the state should take into head that there should be an uniformity of countenance. men would be obliged to put an artificial bump or swelling here, a patch there &c. but this would be merely hypocritical.] or if the alternative was given of wearing a mask, $\frac{99}{100}$ ths must immediately mask. would this add to the beauty of nature? why otherwise in opinions. [in the middle ages of Xty. opposition to the state opns. was hushed. the consequence was, Xty. became loaded with all the Romish follies. nothing but free argument, raillery, & even ridicule will preserve the purity of religion.]

2. Cor. 1. 24. the apostles declare they had no dominion over the faith.

Locke's system of Christianity is this.

Adam was created happy & immortal: but his happiness was to have been *Earthly*, and *earthly* immortality. by *sin* he lost this, so that he became subject to total death (like that of brutes) & to the crosses & unhappinesses of this life. at the intercession however of the son of god this sentence was in part remitted. a life conformable to the law was to restore them again to immortality. and moreover to those who *believed* their *faith* was to be counted for righteousness. not that faith without works was to save them; St. James. c.2. sais expressly the contrary; & all make the fundamental pillars of Xty. to be faith & *repentance*. so that a reformation of life (included under *repentance*) was essential, & defects in this would be made up by their *faith*; i.e. their faith should be counted for righteousness. as to that part of mankind who never had the gospel preached to them, they are 1. Jews. 2. Pagans, or Gentiles. the Jews had the law of works revealed to them. by this therefore they were to be saved: & a *lively* faith in god's promises to send the Messiah would supply small defects. 2. the Gentiles St. Paul sais Rom.2.13. 'the Gentiles have the law written in their hearts' i.e. the law of nature: to which adding a *faith* in God, & his attributes that on their repentance he would pardon them, they also would be justified. this then explains the text 'there is no other *name* under heaven by which a man may be saved.' i.e. the defects in good works shall not be supplied by a faith in Mahomet, Foe, or any other except Christ.

The (*essentials*) fundamentals of Xty. as found in the gospels are 1. Faith. 2. Repentance. that faith is every[where?] explained to be a beleif that Jesus was the Messiah who had been promised. Repentance was to be proved sincere by good works. the advantages accruing to mankind from our Savior's mission are these: 1. the knolege of one god only. 2. a clear knolege of their duty, or system of morality, delivered on such authority as to give it sanction. 3. the outward forms of religious worship wanted to be purged of that farcical pomp & nonsense with which they were loaded. 4. an inducement to a pious life, by revealing clearly a future existence in bliss, & that it was to be the reward of the virtuous.

The Epistles were written (*occasionally*) to persons *already Christians*. a person might be a Xn. then before they were written. consequently the (*essentials*) fundamentals of Xty. were to be found in the preaching of our savior, which is related in the gospels. these fundamentals are to be found in the epistles dropped here & there & promiscuously mixed with other truths. but these other truths are not to be made fundamentals. they serve for edification indeed & explaining to us matters in worship & morality. but being written occasionally it will readily be seen that their explanations are adapted to the notions & customs of the people they were written to. but yet every sentence in them (tho the writers were inspired) must not be taken up & made a fundamental, without assent to which a man is not to be admitted a member of X's church here, or to his kingdom hereafter. the Apostles creed was by them taken to contain all things necessary to salvation, & consequently to a communion.

The Favorite Passion of My Soul

To Giovanni Fabbroni, June 8, 1778

A friend of Philip Mazzei, Jefferson's neighbor at Monticello, Fabbroni had written to Jefferson from Paris extolling liberty and asking if he could be of service to the United States. The two men carried on a sporadic correspondence for the next forty years.

. . . Tho' much of my time is employed in the councils of America I have yet a little leisure to indulge my fondness for philosophical studies. I could wish to correspond with you on subjects of that kind. It might not be unacceptable to you to be informed for instance of the true power of our climate as discoverable from the Thermometer, from the force and direction of the winds, the quantity of rain, the plants which grow without shelter in the winter &c. On the other hand we should be much pleased with contemporary observations on the same particulars in your country, which will give us a comparative view of the two climates. Farenheit's thermometer is the only one in use with us. I make my daily observations as early as possible in the morning and again about 4 o'clock in the afternoon, these generally showing the maxima of cold and heat in the course of 24 hours. I wish I could gratify your Botanical taste; but I am acquainted with nothing more than the first principles of that science, yet myself and my friends may furnish you with any Botanical subjects which this country affords, and are not to be had with you: and I shall take pleasure in procuring them when pointed out by you. The greatest difficulty will be the means of conveyance during the continuance of the war.

If there is a gratification, which I envy any people in this world, it is to your country its music. This is the favorite passion of my soul, and fortune has cast my lot in a country where it is in a state of deplorable barbarism. From the [line] of life in which we conjecture you to be, I have for some time lost the hope of seeing you here. Should the event prove so, I shall ask your assistance in procuring a substitute, who may be a proficient in singing, &, on the Harpsichord. I should be contented to receive such an one two or three years hence when it is hoped he may come more safely and find here a greater plenty of those useful things which commerce alone can furnish. The bounds of an American fortune will not admit the indulgence of a domestic band of musicians. Yet I have thought that a passion for music might be reconciled with that economy which we are obliged to observe. I retain among my domestic servants a gardener, *Ortolano*, a weaver, *Tessitore di lino e lano*, a cabinet maker, *Stipettaio*, and a stone-cutter, *Scalpettino, lavorante in piano*, to which I would add a *vigneron*. In a country where, like yours, music is cultivated and practiced by every class of men I suppose there might be found persons of these trades who could perform on the French horn, clarinet, or hautboy, and bassoon, so that one might have a band of two French horns, two clarinets, two hautboys, and a bassoon, without enlarging their domestic expenses. A certainty of employment for a half dozen years, and at [the] end of that time, to find them, if they chose, a conveyance to their own country, might induce [them] to come here on reasonable wages. Without meaning to give you trouble, perhaps it might be practicable for you in your ordinary intercourse with your people to find out such men disposed to come to America. Sobriety and good nature would be desirable parts of their characters. If you think such a plan practicable, and will be so kind as to inform me what will be necessary to be done on my part, I will take care that it shall be done. The necessary expenses, when informed of them, I can remit before they are wanting, to any port in France with which country alone we have safe correspondence. I am, Sir, with much esteem, your humble servant.

PART III

LEGISLATOR AND GOVERNOR: 1779–1781

Introduction

JEFFERSON HAD THE good luck to be a prophet armed. After 1776, he was in a position to provide legal sanction for his ideals of right and justice. The laws Jefferson wrote, conveying as they did the spirit of the Enlightenment, spread their influence far outside Virginia; they spread to the other states and to Europe as well.

On October 12, 1776 the Virginia House of Delegates moved to revise the laws. The task was assigned to a committee consisting of Jefferson, George Wythe and Edmund Pendleton. Jefferson was the most radical of the three. When they finished their work in the spring of 1779, they had assembled a roster of 126 bills. But because of the war with Britain and other exigencies, the legislature did not act on them until 1785 when Madison brought them forward. By 1787 nearly half of the bills were adopted in one form or another, by 1794 nearly all of them.

Of approximately fifty bills he himself drew up, Jefferson considered four supremely important: on citizenship, on crime, on religion, and on education. Of these the bills on citizenship and religion passed as he proposed them; the bill on crime failed; and the bill on education was emasculated beyond recognition. As a legislator, he took greatest pride in being author of the "Statute of Virginia for Religious Freedom." It was one of the three accomplishments of his life which he allowed to be recorded on his tombstone.

In June 1779 the Virginia legislature elected Jefferson governor to succeed Patrick Henry, who had served three one year terms. As Jefferson discovered in the next two years, the governor of Virginia, like the governors of every other state at this time, was too weak to meet the requirements of war.

Twice during Jefferson's administration British forces invaded Virginia. Benedict Arnold led a brief foray in December 1780, occupied the capital and then retired. In May 1781 a large expedition under Lord Cornwallis smashed into the capital and nearly captured Jefferson and the legislature. The government literally disintegrated under the blow. Despairing of politics, Jefferson gave up his office in June. This was the nadir of his public life.

137

When the legislature gathered again it inquired into Jefferson's conduct of office. In December 1781 he answered the charges effectively enough to convince the legislature of their falsity and of his "ability, rectitude and integrity" as governor. Satisfied that he had vindicated himself, Jefferson privately denounced his enemies, chief among them Patrick Henry, and vowed not to return to public life.

The Protection of the Law

A Bill Concerning Slaves (chapter 51), 1779

*The legislature adopted this bill in 1785 (deleting from it
the part enclosed by brackets). In his "Autobiography" Jefferson says that he intended to tack on to it an amendment proposing general emancipation. But there is no concrete evidence of such an amendment. Without question, Jefferson
hated slavery and favored its elimination—on condition,
however, that the manumitted Negroes quickly leave the
state. Despite his increasingly sympathetic and egalitarian
feelings towards Negroes, his belief in the fundamental in-
compatibility of the races remained fixed. The Bill Concerning Slaves and the others following it were published in
1785 as separate chapters under the title,* Report of the Committee of Revisions.

Be it enacted by the General Assembly, that no person
shall, henceforth, be slaves within this commonwealth, except such as were so on the first day of this present session
of Assembly, and the descendants of the females of them.

Negroes and mulattoes which shall hereafter be brought
into this commonwealth and kept therein one whole year,
together, or so long at different times as shall amount to one
year, shall be free. [But if they shall not depart the commonwealth within one year thereafter they shall be out of the
protection of the laws.

Those which shall come into this commonwealth of their
own accord shall be out of the protection of the laws; save
only such as being seafaring persons and navigating vessels
hither, shall not leave the same while here more than twenty
four hours together.

It shall not be lawful for any person to emancipate a slave
but by deed executed, proved and recorded as is required
by law in the case of a conveyance of goods and chattels, on
consideration not deemed valuable in law, or by last will and
testament, and with the free consent of such slave, expressed
in presence of the court of the county wherein he resides.
And if such slave, so emancipated, shall not within one year

thereafter, depart the commonwealth, he shall be out of the protection of the laws. All conditions, restrictions and limitations annexed to any act of emancipation shall be void from the time such emancipation is to take place.

If any white woman shall have a child by a Negro or mulatto, she and her child shall depart the commonwealth within one year thereafter. If they shall fail so to do, the woman shall be out of the protection of the laws, and the child shall be bound out by the Aldermen of the county, in like manner as poor orphans are by law directed to be, and within one year after its term of service expired shall depart the commonwealth, or on failure so to do, shall be out of the protection of the laws.

Where any of the persons before described shall be disabled from departing the commonwealth by grievous sickness, the protection of the law shall be continued to him until such disability be removed: And if the county shall in the meantime, incur any expense in taking care of him, as of other county poor, the Aldermen shall be entitled to recover the same from his master, if he had one, his heirs, executors and administrators.]

No Negro or mulatto shall be a witness except in pleas of the commonwealth against Negroes or mulattoes, or in civil pleas wherein Negroes or mulattoes alone shall be parties.

No slave shall go from the tenements of his master, or other person with whom he lives, without a pass, or some letter or token whereby it may appear that he is proceeding by authority from his master, employer, or overseer: If he does, it shall be lawful for any person to apprehend and carry him before a Justice of the Peace, to be by his order punished with stripes, or not in his direction.

No slaves shall keep any arms whatever, nor pass, unless with written orders from his master or employer, or in his company, with arms from one place to another. Arms in possession of a slave contrary to this prohibition shall be forfeited to him who will seize them.

Riots, routs, unlawful assemblies, trespasses and seditious speeches by a Negro or mulatto shall be punished with stripes at the discretion of a Justice of the Peace; and he who will may apprehend and carry him before such a Justice.

The Natural Right of Seeking Subsistence and Happiness

A Bill Declaring Who Shall Be Deemed Citizens (chapter 55), 1779

During his political conflicts much later, Jefferson took particular pride in this bill, for it represented to him precisely the free and liberal policy of granting citizenship which Federalists denied in the Naturalization Act of 1798.

Be it enacted by the General Assembly, that all white persons born within the territory of this Commonwealth and all who have resided therein two years next before the passing of this act, and all who shall hereafter migrate into the same; and shall before any court of record give satisfactory proof by their own oath or affirmation, that they intend to reside therein, and moreover shall give assurance of fidelity to the commonwealth; and all infants wheresoever born, whose father, if living, or otherwise, whose mother was, a citizen at the time of their birth, or who migrate hither, their father, if living, or otherwise their mother becoming a citizen, or who migrate hither without father or mother, shall be deemed citizens of this commonwealth, until they relinquish that character in manner as herein after expressed: And all others not being citizens of any of the United States of America, shall be deemed aliens. The clerk of the court shall enter such oath of record, and give the person taking the same a certificate thereof, for which he shall receive the fee of one dollar. And in order to preserve to the citizens of this commonwealth, that natural right, which all men have of relinquishing the country, in which birth, or other accident may have thrown them, and, seeking subsistence and happiness wheresoever they may be able, or may hope to find them: And to declare unequivocally what circumstances shall be deemed evidence of an intention in any citizen to exercise that right, it is enacted and declared, that whensoever any citizen of this commonwealth, shall by word of mouth in the presence of the court of the county, wherein he resides, or of the General Court, or by deed in writing, under his hand and seal, executed in the presence of three witnesses, and by them proved in either of the said courts, openly declare to the same court, that he relinquishes the character of a citizen, and shall depart the commonwealth; or whensoever he shall without such declaration depart the commonwealth and enter into the service of any other state, not in enmity with this, or any other of the United States of America, or do any act whereby he shall become a subject or citizen of such state, such person shall be considered as having exercised his natural right of expatriating himself, and shall be deemed no citizen of this commonwealth from the time of his departure. The free white inhabitants of every of the states, parties to the American confederation, paupers, vagabonds and fugitives from justice excepted, shall be intitled to all rights, privileges, and immunities of free citizens in this commonwealth, and shall have free egress and regress, to and from the same, and shall enjoy therein, all the privileges of trade, and commerce, subject to the same duties, impositions and restrictions as the citizens of this commonwealth. And if any person guilty of, or charged with treason, felony, or other high misdemeanor, in any of the said states, shall flee from justice and be found in this commonwealth, he shall, upon demand of the Governor, or Executive power of the state from which he fled, be delivered to be removed to the state having jurisdiction of his offence. Where any person holding property, within this commonwealth, shall be attainted within any of the said states, parties to the said confederation, of any of these crimes, which by the law of this commonwealth shall be punishable by forfeiture of such property, the said property shall be disposed of in the same manner as it would have been if the owner thereof had been attainted of the like crime in this commonwealth.

To Restrain Such Criminal Acts

A Bill for Proportioning Crimes and Punishments (chapter 64), 1779

Jefferson toiled long to draw up this bill. Annotated with erudite references (omitted here) from Old French, Anglo-Saxon, Latin and English texts, it was a model of scholarship and literary craftsmanship. The task of humanizing punishments was immense, and Jefferson could only go so far. This accounted for the harsh quality of the bill. He wrote to George Wythe (November 1, 1778): "I have strictly observed the scale of punishments settled by the Committee, without being entirely satisfied with it. The lex talionis, altho' *a restitution of the common law to the simplicity of which we have generally found it so advantageous to return will be revolting to the humanised feelings of modern times." It failed to pass by one vote in 1786.*

Whereas, it frequently happens that wicked and dissolute men, resigning themselves to the dominion of inordinate passions, commit violations on the lives, liberties, and property of others, and, the secure enjoyment of these having principally induced men to enter into society, goverment would be defective in its principal purpose, were it not to restrain such criminal acts, by inflicting due punishments on those who perpetrate them; but it appears, at the same time, equally deducible from the purposes of society, that a member thereof, committing an inferior injury, does not wholly forfeit the protection of his fellow citizens, but, after suffering a punishment in proportion to his offence, is entitled to their protection from all greater pain, so that it becomes a duty in the legislature to arrange, in a proper scale, the crimes which it may be necessary for them to repress, and to adjust thereto a corresponding gradation of punishments.

And whereas, the reformation of offenders, though an object worthy the attention of the laws, is not effected at all by capital punishments, which exterminate instead of reforming, and should be the last melancholy resource against those whose existence is become inconsistent with the safety of their fellow citizens, which also weaken the State, by cutting off so many who, if reformed, might be restored sound members to society, who, even under a course of correction, might be rendered useful in various labors for the public, and would be living and long-continued spectacles to deter others from committing the like offences.

And forasmuch as the experience of all ages and countries hath shown, that cruel and sanguinary laws defeat their own purpose, by engaging the benevolence of mankind to withhold prosecutions, to smother testimony, or to listen to it with bias, when, if the punishment were only proportioned to the injury, men would feel it their inclination, as well as their duty, to see the laws observed.

For rendering crimes and punishments, therefore, more proportionate to each other:

Be it enacted by the General Assembly, that no crime shall be henceforth punished by the deprivation of life or limb, except those hereinafter ordained to be so punished.

If a man do levy war against the Commonwealth [*in the same*], or be adherent to the enemies of the Commonwealth [*within the same*], giving to them aid or comfort in the Commonwealth, or elsewhere, and thereof be convicted of open deed, by the evidence of two sufficient witnesses, or his own voluntary confession, the said cases, and no others, shall be adjudged treasons which extend to the Commonwealth, and the person so convicted shall suffer death, by hanging, and shall forfeit his lands and goods to the Commonwealth.

If any person commit petty treason, or a husband murder his wife, a parent his child, or a child his parent, he shall suffer death by hanging, and his body be delivered to anatomists to be dissected.

Whosoever committeth murder by poisoning shall suffer death by poison.

Whosoever committeth murder by way of duel shall suffer death by hanging; and if he were the challenger, his body, after death, shall be gibbetted. He who removeth it from the gibbet shall be guilty of a misdemeanor; and the officer shall see that it be replaced.

Whosoever shall commit murder in any other way shall suffer death by hanging.

And in all cases of petty treason and murder, one half of the lands and goods of the offender, shall be forfeited to the next of kin to the person killed, and the other half descend and go to his own representatives. Save only, where one shall slay the challenger in a duel, in which case, no part of his lands or goods shall be forfeited to the kindred of the party slain, but, instead thereof, a moiety shall go to the Commonwealth.

The same evidence shall suffice, and order and course of trial be observed in cases of petty treason, as in those of other murders.

Whosoever shall be guilty of manslaughter, shall, for the first offence, be condemned to hard labor for seven years in the public works, shall forfeit one half of his lands and goods to the next of kin to the person slain; the other half to be sequestered during such term, in the hands and to the use of the Commonwealth, allowing a reasonable part of the profits for the support of his family. The second offence shall be deemed murder.

And where persons, meaning to commit a trespass only, or larceny, or other unlawful deed, and doing an act from which involuntary homicide hath ensued, have heretofore been adjudged guilty of manslaughter, or of murder, by transferring such their unlawful intention to an act, much more penal than they could have in probable contemplation; no such case shall hereafter be deemed manslaughter, unless manslaughter was intended, nor murder, unless murder was intended.

In other cases of homicide, the law will not add to the miseries of the party, by punishments and forfeitures.

Whenever sentence of death shall have been pronounced against any person for treason or murder, execution shall be done on the next day but one after such sentence, unless it be Sunday, and then on the Monday following.

Whosoever shall be guilty of rape, polygamy, or sodomy with man or woman, shall be punished, if a man, by castration, if a woman, by cutting through the cartilage of her nose a hole of one half inch in diameter at the least.

But no one shall be punished for polygamy, who shall have married after probable information of the death of his or her husband or wife, or after his or her husband or wife, hath absented him or herself, so that no notice of his or her being alive hath reached such person for seven years together, or hath suffered the punishments before prescribed for rape, polygamy, or sodomy.

Whosoever on purpose, and of malice forethought, shall

maim another, or shall disfigure him, by cutting out or disabling the tongue, slitting or cutting off a nose, lip, or ear, branding, or otherwise, shall be maimed, or disfigured in like sort: or if that cannot be, for want of the same part, then as nearly as may be, in some other part of at least equal value and estimation, in the opinion of a jury, and moreover, shall forfeit one half of his lands and goods to the sufferer.

Whosoever shall counterfeit any coin, current by law within this Commonwealth, or any paper bills issued in the nature of money, or of certificates of loan on the credit of this Commonwealth, or of all or any of the United States of America, or any Inspectors' notes for tobacco, or shall pass any such counterfeit coin, paper, bills, or notes, knowing them to be counterfeit; or, for the sake of lucre, shall diminish, case, or wash any such coin, shall be condemned to hard labor six years in the public works, and shall forfeit all his lands and goods to the Commonwealth.

Whosoever committeth arson, shall be condemned to hard labor five years in the public works, and shall make good the loss of the sufferers threefold.

If any person shall, within this Commonwealth, or being a citizen thereof, shall without the same, wilfully destroy, or run away with any sea-vessel, or goods laden on board thereof, or plunder or pilfer any wreck, he shall be condemned to hard labor five years in the public works, and shall make good the loss of the sufferers threefold.

Whosoever committeth Robbery, shall be condemned to hard labor four years in the public works, and shall make double reparation to the persons injured.

Whatsoever act, if committed on any Mansion house, would be deemed Burglary, shall be Burglary, if committed on any other house; and he, who is guilty of Burglary, shall be condemned to hard labor four years in the public works, and shall make double reparation to the persons injured.

Whatsoever act, if committed in the night time, shall constitute the crime of Burglary, shall, if committed in the day, be deemed House-breaking; and whosoever is guilty thereof, shall be condemned to hard labor three years in the public works, and shall make reparation to the persons injured.

Whosoever shall be guilty of Horse-stealing, shall be condemned to hard labor three years in the public works, and shall make reparation to the person injured.

Grand Larceny shall be where the goods stolen are of the

value of five dollars; and whosoever shall be guilty thereof, shall be forthwith put in the pillory for one half hour, shall be condemned to hard labor two years in the public works, and shall make reparation to the person injured.

Petty Larceny shall be, where the goods stolen are of less value than five dollars; and whosoever shall be guilty thereof, shall be forthwith put in the pillory for a quarter of an hour, shall be condemned to hard labor one year in the public works, and shall make reparation to the person injured.

Robbery or larceny of bonds, bills obligatory, bills of exchange, or promissory notes for the payment of money or tobacco, lottery tickets, paper bills issued in the nature of money, or of certificates of loan on the credit of this Commonwealth, or of all or any of the United States of America, or Inspectors' notes for tobacco, shall be punished in the same manner as robbery or larceny of the money or tobacco due on, or represented by such papers.

Buyers and receivers of goods taken by way of robbery or larceny, knowing them to have been so taken, shall be deemed accessaries to such robbery or larceny after the fact.

Prison-breakers, also, shall be deemed accessaries after the fact, to traitors or felons whom they enlarge from prison.

All attempts to delude the people, or to abuse their understanding by exercise of the pretended arts of witchcraft, conjuration, enchantment, or sorcery, or by pretended prophecies, shall be punished by ducking and whipping, at the discretion of a jury, not exceeding fifteen stripes.

If the principal offenders be fled, or secreted from justice, in any case not touching life or member, the accessaries may, notwithstanding, be prosecuted as if their principal were convicted.

If any offender stand mute of obstinacy, or challenge peremptorily more of the jurors than by law he may, being first warned of the consequence thereof, the court shall proceed as if he had confessed the charge.

Pardon and Privilege of clergy, shall henceforth be abolished, that none may be induced to injure through hope of impunity. But if the verdict be against the defendant, and the court before whom the offence is heard and determined, shall doubt that it may be untrue for defect of testimony, or other cause, they may direct a new trial to be had.

No attainder shall work corruption of blood in any case.

In all cases of forfeiture, the widow's dower shall be saved to her, during her title thereto; after which it shall be disposed of as if no such saving had been.

The aid of Counsel, and examination of their witnesses on oath, shall be allowed to defendants in criminal prosecutions.

Slaves guilty of any offence punishable in others by labor in the public works, shall be transported to such parts in the West Indies, South America or Africa, as the Governor shall direct, there to be continued in slavery.

To Illuminate the Minds of the People at Large

A Bill for the More General Diffusion of Knowledge (chapter 79), 1779

Jefferson considered no bill more important than this one. Education was for him the bedrock of liberty. His bill would have set up an elaborate system of education, from primary schools to college, through which gifted students, poor and rich alike, would have passed. But the legislature delayed action on an education bill until 1796. The act of that year concerned only primary schools, leaving the matter entirely with local communities.

Whereas it appeareth that however certain forms of government are better calculated than others to protect individuals in the free exercise of their natural rights, and are at the same time themselves better guarded against degeneracy, yet experience hath shewn, that even under the best forms, those entrusted with power have, in time, and by slow operations, perverted it into tyranny; and it is believed that the most effectual means of preventing this would be, to illuminate, as far as practicable, the minds of the people at large, and more especially to give them knowledge of those facts, which history exhibiteth, that, possessed thereby of the experience of other ages and countries, they may be enabled to know ambition under all its shapes, and prompt to exert their natural powers to defeat its purposes; And whereas it is generally true that that people will be happiest whose laws are best, and are best administered, and that laws will be wisely formed, and honestly administered, in proportion as those who form and administer them are wise and honest; whence it becomes expedient for promoting the public happiness that those persons, whom nature hath endowed with genius and virtue, should be rendered by liberal education worthy to receive, and able to guard the sacred deposit of the rights and liberties of their fellow citizens, and that they should be called to that charge without regard to wealth, birth or other accidental condition or circumstance; but the indigence of the greater number disabling them from so educating, at their own expence, those of their children whom nature hath fitly formed and disposed to become useful instruments for the public, it is better that such should be sought for and educated at the common expence of all, than that the happiness of all should be confined to the weak or wicked:

Be it therefore enacted by the General Assembly, that in every county within this commonwealth, there shall be chosen annually, by the electors qualified to vote for Delegates, three of the most honest and able men of their county, to be called the Aldermen of the county; and that the election of the said Aldermen shall be held at the same time and place, before the same persons, and notified and conducted in the same manner as by law is directed, for the annual election of Delegates for the county.

The person before whom such election is holden shall certify to the court of the said county the names of the Aldermen chosen, in order that the same may be entered of record, and shall give notice of their election to the said Aldermen within a fortnight after such election.

The said Aldermen on the first Monday in October, if it be fair, and if not, then on the next fair day, excluding Sunday, shall meet at the court-house of their county, and proceed to divide their said county into hundreds, bounding the same by water courses, mountains, or limits, to be run and marked, if they think necessary, by the county surveyor, and at the county expence, regulating the size of the said hundreds, according to the best of their discretion, so as that they may contain a convenient number of children to make up a school, and be of such convenient size that all the children within each hundred may daily attend the school to be established therein, and distinguishing each hundred by a particular name; which division, with the names of the several hundreds, shall be returned to the court of the county and be entered of record, and shall remain unaltered until the increase or decrease of inhabitants shall render an alteration necessary, in the opinion of any succeeding Alderman, and also in the opinion of the court of the county.

The electors aforesaid residing within every hundred shall meet on the third Monday in October after the first election of Aldermen, at such place, within their hundred, as the said Aldermen shall direct, notice thereof being previously given to them by such person residing within the hundred as the said Aldermen shall require who is hereby enjoined to obey such requisition, on pain of being punished by amercement and imprisonment. The electors being so assembled shall choose the most convenient place within their hundred for building a school-house. If two or more places, having a greater number of votes than any others, shall yet be equal between themselves, the Aldermen, or such of them as are not of the same hundred, on information thereof, shall decide between them. The said Aldermen shall forthwith proceed to have a school-house built at the said place, and shall see that the same shall be kept in repair, and, when necessary, that it be rebuilt; but whenever they shall think necessary that it be rebuilt, they shall give notice as before directed, to the electors of the hundred to meet at the said school-house, on such a day as they shall appoint, to determine by vote, in the manner before directed, whether it shall be rebuilt at the same, or what other place in the hundred.

At every of those schools shall be taught reading, writing, and common arithmetick, and the books which shall be used therein for instructing the children to read shall be such as will at the same time make them acquainted with Graecian, Roman, English, and American history. At these schools all the free children, male and female, resident within the respective hundred, shall be intitled to receive tuition gratis, for the term of three years, and as much longer, at their private expence, as their parents, guardians, or friends shall think proper.

Over every ten of these schools (or such other number nearest thereto, as the number of hundreds in the county will admit, without fractional divisions) an overseer shall be appointed annually by the Aldermen at their first meeting, eminent for his learning, integrity, and fidelity to the commonwealth, whose business and duty it shall be, from time to time, to appoint a teacher to each school, who shall give assurance of fidelity to the commonwealth, and to remove him as he shall see cause; to visit every school once in every half year at the least; to examine the scholars; see that any general plan of reading and instruction recommended by the visiters of William and Mary College shall be observed; and to superintend the conduct of the teacher in everything relative to his school.

Every teacher shall receive a salary of——by the year, which, with the expences of building and repairing the school-houses, shall be provided in such manner as other county expences are by law directed to be provided and shall also have his diet, lodging, and washing found him, to be levied in like manner, save only that such levy shall be on the inhabitants of each hundred for the board of their own teacher only. . . .

The said overseers having determined the place at which the grammar school for their district shall be built, shall forthwith (unless they can otherwise agree with the proprietors of the circumjacent lands as to location and price) make application to the clerk of the county in which the said house is to be situated, who shall thereupon issue a writ, in the nature of a writ of ad quod damnum, directed to the sheriff of the said county commanding him to summon and impanel twelve fit persons to meet at the place, so destined for the grammer school-house, on a certain day, to be named in the said writ, not less than five, nor more than ten, days from the date thereof; and also to give notice of the same to the proprietors and tenants of the lands to be viewed if they be found within the county, and if not, then to their agents therein if any they have. Which freeholders shall be charged by the said sheriff impartially, and to the best of their skill and judgment to view the lands round about the said place, and to locate and circumscribe, by certain meets and bounds, one hundred acres thereof, having regard therein principally to the benefit and convenience of the said school, but respecting in some measure also the convenience of the said proprietors, and to value and appraise the same in so many several and distinct parcels as shall be owned or held by several and distinct owners or tenants, and according to their respective interests and estates therein. And after such location and appraisement so made, the said sheriff shall forthwith return the same under the hands and seals of the said jurors, together with the writ, to the clerk's office of the said county and the right and property of the said proprietors and tenants in the said lands so circumscribed shall be immediately devested and be transferred to the commonwealth for the use of the said grammar school, in full and absolute dominion, any want of consent or disability to consent in the said owners or tenants notwithstanding. But it shall not be lawful for the said overseers so to situate the grammer school-house, nor to the said jurors so to locate the said lands, as to include the mansion-house of the proprietor of the lands, nor the offices, curtilage, or garden, thereunto immediately belonging.

The said overseers shall forthwith proceed to have a house of brick or stone, for the said grammar school, with necessary offices, built on the said lands, which grammar school-house shall contain a room for the school, a hall to dine in, four rooms for a master and usher, and ten or twelve lodging rooms for the scholars.

To each of the said grammar schools shall be allowed out of the public treasury, the sum of——pounds, out of which shall be paid by the Treasurer, on warrant from the Auditors, to the proprietors or tenants of the lands located, the value of their several interests as fixed by the jury, and the balance thereof shall be delivered to the said overseers to defray the expense of the said buildings.

In either of these grammar schools shall be taught the Latin and Greek languages, English Grammar, geography, and the higher part of numerical arithmetick, to wit, vulgar and decimal fractions, and the extrication of the square and cube roots.

A visiter from each county constituting the district shall be appointed, by the overseers, for the county, in the month of October annually, either from their own body or from their county at large, which visiters, or the greater part of them, meeting together at the said grammar school on the first Monday in November, if fair, and if not, then on the next fair day, excluding Sunday, shall have power to choose their own Rector, who shall call and preside at future meetings, to employ from time to time a master, and if necessary, an usher, for the said school, to remove them at their will, and to settle the price of tuition to be paid by the scholars. They shall also visit the school twice in every year at the least, either together or separately at their discretion, examine the scholars, and see that any general plan of instruction recommended by the visiters, of William and Mary College shall be observed. The said masters and ushers, before they enter on the execution of their office, shall give assurance of fidelity to the commonwealth.

A steward shall be employed, and removed at will by the master, on such wages as the visiters shall direct; which steward shall see to the procuring provisions, fuels, servants for cooking, waiting, house cleaning, washing, mending, and gardening on the most reasonable terms; the expence of which, together with the steward's wages, shall be divided equally among all the scholars boarding either on the public or private expence. And the part of those who are on private expence, and also the price of their tuitions due to the master or usher, shall be paid quarterly by the respective scholars, their parents, or guardians, and shall be recoverable, if withheld, together with costs, on motion in any Court of Record, ten days' notice thereof being previously given to the party, and a jury impanelled to try the issue joined, or enquire of the damages. The said steward shall also, under the direction of the visiters, see that the houses be kept in repair, and necessary enclosures be made and repaired, the accounts for which, shall, from time to time, be submitted to the Auditors, and on their warrant paid by the Treasurer.

Every overseer of the hundred schools shall, in the month of September annually, after the most diligent and impartial examination and inquiry, appoint from among the boys who shall have been two years at the least at some one of the schools under his superintendence, and whose parents are too poor to give them farther education, someone of the best and most promising genius and disposition, to proceed to the grammer school of his district; which appointment shall be made in the court-house of the county, and on the court day for that month if fair, and if not, then on the next fair day, excluding Sunday, in the presence of the Aldermen, or two of them at the least, assembled on the bench for that purpose, the said overseer being previously sworn by them to make such appointment, without favor or affection, according to the best of his skill and judgment, and being interrogated by the Aldermen, either on their own motion, or on suggestions from the parents, guardians, friends, or teachers of the children, competitors for such appointment; which teachers the parents shall attend for the information of the Aldermen. On which interrogatories the said Aldermen, if they be not satisfied with the appointment proposed, shall have right to negative it; whereupon the said visiter may proceed to make a new appointment, and the said Aldermen again to interrogate and negative, and so toties quoties until an appointment be approved.

Every boy so appointed shall be authorized to proceed to the grammar school of his district, there to be educated and boarded during such time as is hereafter limited; and his quota of the expenses of the house together with a compensation to the master or usher for his tuition, at the rate of twenty dollars by the year, shall be paid by the Treasurer quarterly on warrant from the Auditors.

A visitation shall be held, for the purpose of probation, annually at the said grammar school on the last Monday in September, if fair, and if not, then on the next fair day, excluding Sunday, at which one third of the boys sent thither by appointment of the said overseers, and who shall have been there one year only, shall be discontinued as public foundationers, being those who, on the most diligent examination and enquiry, shall be thought to be the least promising genius and disposition; and of those who shall have been there two years, all shall be discontinued save one only the best in genius and disposition, who shall be at liberty to continue there four years longer on the public foundation, and shall thence forward be deemed a senior.

The visiters for the districts which, or any part of which, be southward and westward of James river, as known by that name, or by the names of Fluvanna and Jackson's river, in every other year, to wit, at the probation meetings held in the years, distinguished in the Christian computation by odd numbers, and the visitors for all the other districts at their said meetings to be held in those years, distinguished by even numbers, after diligent examination and enquiry as before directed, shall chuse one among the said seniors, of the best learning and most hopeful genius and disposition, who shall be authorized by them to proceed to William and Mary College; there to be educated, boarded, and clothed, three years; the expence of which annually shall be paid by the Treasurer on warrant from the Auditors.

By Indulging the Researches of the Learned and Curious

A Bill for Establishing a Public Library (chapter 81), 1779

In his Notes on Virginia *Jefferson made it clear that the purpose of a "public library" was not to serve the general public but rather, as stated in the bill, "the learned and curious." Madison introduced this bill along with the others in 1785. Though brought up again the following year, nothing came of it.*

Be it enacted by the General Assembly, that on the first day of January, in every year, there shall be paid out of the treasury the sum of two thousand pounds, to be laid out in such books and maps as may be proper to be preserved in a public library, and in defraying the expences necessary for the care and preservation thereof; which library shall be established at the town of Richmond.

The two houses of Assembly shall appoint three persons of learning and attention to literary matters, to be visiters of the said library, and shall remove them, and fill any vacancies from time to time, as they shall think fit; which visiters shall have power to receive the annual sums before mentioned, and therewith to procure such books and maps as aforesaid, and shall superintend the preservation thereof. Whensoever a keeper shall be found necessary they shall appoint such keeper, from time to time, at their will, on such annual salary (not exceeding one hundred pounds) as they shall think reasonable.

If during the time of war the importation of books and maps shall be hazardous, or if the rate of exchange between this commonwealth and any state from which such articles are wanted, shall from any cause be such that they cannot be imported to such advantage as may be hoped at a future day, the visiters shall place the annual sums, as they become due, in the public loan office, if any there be, for the benefit of interest, or otherwise shall suffer them to remain in the treasury until fit occasions shall occur of employing them.

It shall not be lawful for the said keeper, or the visiters themselves, or any other person to remove any book or map out of the said library, unless it be for the necessary repair thereof; but the same be made useful by indulging the researches of the learned and curious, within the said library, without fee or reward, and under such rules for preserving them safe and in good order and condition as the visiters shall constitute.

The visiters shall annually settle their accounts with the Auditors and leave with them the vouchers for the expenditure of the monies put into their hands.

The Opinions of Men Are Not the Objects of Civil Government

A Bill for Establishing Religious Freedom
(chapter 82), 1779

Jefferson framed this great bill to complete the task begun in 1776. He considered it, after the Declaration of Independence, his most important contribution to liberty. It became the basis in all subsequent constitutions, state and federal, for determining the relation between church and state. Madison perceived what its effect would be when he wrote Jefferson soon after its adoption in Januray 1786: "This country [has] extinguished for ever the ambitious hope of making laws for the human mind." In the text below, deletions from the original bill are bracketed and italicized; additions are in capital letters.

[*Well aware that the opinions and belief of men depend not on their own will, but follow involuntarily the evidence proposed to their minds; that*] WHEREAS Almighty God hath created the mind free; [*and manifested his supreme will that free it shall remain by making it altogether insusceptible of restraint;*] that all attempts to influence it by temporal punishments, or burthens, or by civil incapacitations, tend only to beget habits of hypocrisy and meanness, and are a departure from the plan of the holy author of our religion, who being lord both of body and mind, yet choose not to propagate it by coercions on either, as was in his Almighty power to do; [*but to extend it by its influence on reason alone;*] that the impious presumption of legislature and ruler, civil as well as ecclesiastical, who, being themselves but fallible and uninspired men, have assumed dominion over the faith of others, setting up their own opinions and modes of thinking as the only true and infallible, and as such endeavoring to impose them on others, hath established and maintained false religions over the greatest part of the world and through all time: That to compel a man to furnish contributions of money for the propagation of opinions which he disbelieves [*and abhors,*] is sinful and tyrannical; that even the forcing him to support this or that teacher of his own religious persuasion, is depriving him of the comfortable liberty of giving his contributions to the particular pastor whose morals he would make his pattern, and whose powers he feels most persuasive to righteousness; and is withdrawing from the ministry those temporary rewards, which proceeding from an approbation of their personal conduct, are an additional incitement to earnest and unremitting labours for the instruction of mankind; that our civil rights have no dependence on our religious opinions, any more than our opinions in physics or geometry; and therefore the proscribing any citizen as unworthy the public confidence by laying upon him an incapacity of being called to offices of trust or emolument, unless he profess or renounce this or that religious opinion, is depriving him injudiciously of those privileges and advantages to which, in common with his fellow-citizens, he has a natural right; that it tends also to corrupt the principles of that [very] religion it is meant to encourage, by bribing with a monopoly of worldly honours and emoluments, those who will externally profess and conform to it; that though indeed these are criminals who do not withstand such temptation, yet neither are those innocent who lay the bait in their way; [that the opinions of men are not the object of civil government, nor under its jurisdiction;] that to suffer the civil magistrate to intrude his powers into the field of opinion and to restrain the profession or propagation of principles on supposition of their ill tendency is a dangerous fallacy, which at once destroys all religious liberty, because he being of course judge of that tendency will make his opinions the rule of judgment, and approve or condemn the sentiments of others only as they shall square with or suffer from his own; that it is time enough for the rightful purposes of civil government for its officers to interfere when principles break out into overt acts against peace and good order; and finally, that truth is great and will prevail if left to herself; that she is the proper and sufficient antagonist to error, and has nothing to fear from the conflict unless by human interposition disarmed of her natural weapons, free argument and debate; errors ceasing to be dangerous when it is permitted freely to contradict them.

[We the General Assembly of Virginia do enact] BE IT ENACTED BY THE GENERAL ASSEMBLY that no man shall be compelled to frequent or support any religious worship, place, or ministry whatsoever, nor shall be enforced, restrained, molested, or burthened in his body or goods, or shall otherwise suffer, on account of his religious opinions or belief; but that all men shall be free to profess, and by argument to maintain, their opinions in matters of religion, and that the same shall in no wise diminish, enlarge, or affect their civil capacities.

And though we well know that this Assembly, elected by the people for their ordinary purposes of legislation only, have no power to restrain the acts of succeeding Assemblies, constituted with powers equal to our own, and that therefore to declare this act to be irrevocable would be of no effect in law; yet we are free to declare, and do declare, that the rights hereby asserted are of the natural rights of mankind, and that if any act shall be hereafter passed to repeal the present or to narrow its operations, such act will be an infringement of natural right.

Such a One May Keep Us Above Water

To Richard Henry Lee, September 13, 1780

Within a year of his election as governor Jefferson was weary. The problems resulting from inflation, administrative inefficiency and military defeat seemed insurmountable. He wanted nothing more than to return to his family and farm and books. As this letter indicates he thought of resigning. But Lee and others dissuaded him from it.

. . . The application requisite to the duties of the office I hold is so excessive, and the execution of them after all so imperfect, that I have determined to retire from it at the close of the present campaign. I wish a successor to be thought of in time who, to sound whiggism, can join perseverence in business, and an extensive knowledge of the various subjects he must superintend. Such a one may keep us above water even in our present moneyless situation. . . .

This Shameful Desertion

To George Washington, with a Narrative of the Battle of Camden, September 3, 1780

The defeat at the battle of Camden was a bitter one. The Virginia militia turned and fled in the heat of conflict. The way was open for the British to advance into Virginia. Following is Jefferson's very precise description of the battle.

On the 13th. of August Genl. Gates with the Maryland line the Artillery and North Carolina Militia arrived at Ridgeley thirteen miles from Cambden and took post there and was the Next day joined by Genl. Stevens with Seven hundred of the Virginia Militia. Col. Sumpter was then at the Waxsaws with four hundred South Carolina Militia, and had on the Sunday before killed and taken near three hundred of the enemy who were posted at the hanging rock. This and other strokes on their advanced post Occasioned their Calling in all their out post to Cambden. The 15th. at day light Genl. Gates reinforced Col. Sumpter with three hundred North Carolina Militia one hundred of the Maryland line and two three pounders. Col. Sumpter took possession of all the passes on the Wateree from Elkins's ford to Whiticars farm five Miles below Campden. At one of these he supprised the enemy's Guard killed Seven and took about thirty a mong which was Colo. Cary their Commanding officer with thirty eight waggons loaded with Corn rum &c. also a Number of horses; and afterwards on the Same day he took about Seventy prisoners, British, Six waggons, baggage &c. on their way from Ninety Six. At ten OClock Genl. Gates's Army Marched intending to take post on an advantageous Situation where was a deep Creek in front about seven Miles from Cambden, the heavy baggage being ordered to proceed by the waxaw road; the March was in the following order, Col. Armand's legion in front supported on both flanks by Colo. Porterfield Commanding officer of Virginia regulars and the light infantry of the Militia, the advanced Guard of infantry, the Maryland line with their Artillery in front of the brigades, the N. C. Militia, the Virga. Militia, the Artillery &c. and the rear guard. Between 12. and 1 oClock after Marching About Five Miles they Met with the enemy, under the Command of Lord Cornwallis who had Marched out from Cambden about Nine OClock of the Same Night intending to attack our Camp by supprise about day break. This Meeting was equally unexpected on both Sides and Occationed a halt of both Armies. The enemy's Cavalry then charged Col. Armands legion which was well supported on the flanks by Col. Porterfield's Corps who repulsed the Assailants, but Unfortunately Col. Porterfield himself had his leg broke in the first fire. The enemy's infantry then advancing with a heavy fire, the troops in front gave way to the front of the 1st. Maryland brigade and a Confusion ensued which took Some time to regulate. At length the Army was ranged in line of battle in the following order, General Gist's brigade on the right with his right close to a swamp, the N. C. Militia in Close Order two deep in the Center, and the Virginia Militia in like order with the Light infantry and Porterfield's Corps on the left, the Artillery divided to the brigades and the first Maryland brigade as a Corps de reserve and to Cover the Cannon in the road at a proper distance in the rear. Col. Armands Corps was ordered to the left to Support the left flank and oppose the enemy's Cavalry. Their infantry from a defect in Numbers were only a Single file five feet apart. In this Situation they remained till day break of the 16th. when our troops advanced in a line a few hundred yards. The enemy attacked and drove in our light party in front; and after the first fire charged the Militia with bayonets where upon the whole gave way, except Col. Dixon's regiment of N. C. Militia, and their cavalry continuing to harrass the rear. Such was the panic diffused through the whole that the utmost and unremitting exertions of the Generals Gates Stevens Caswell and others assisted by a Number of Officers to rally them even in small parties, at the several advantageous posts at which it was Occasionally attempted, proved ineffectual. They ran like a torrent and bore all before them. This shamefull d[e]sertion of the Militia gave the enemy an opportunity of bending their whole force against the Maryland troops and Dixons Regiment of N C. Militia. The Conflict was obstinate and bloody and lasted fifteen Minutes, Dixons Militia standing firm with their regular brethren and pushing bayonets to the last. Superior bravery was at length obliged to give way to superior Numbers, and this gallant Corps Compelled to retreat from the ground. They were then furisly charged by a party of British horse (their Numbers Not known) whom they Compleatly Vanquished, insomuch that not more than two of the party are said to have got off. These brave men suffered greatly, having lost as is believed one half of their number, and to their immortal honour made their retreat good. The waggons were some distance behind. The Waggoners cut loose the horses on which they were, the flying militia the rest, and left the waggons. How many they were is not yet known nor what numbers of them were lost. An account of no light authority sais they were all taken to the number of 400; an officer in the engagement sais that not more than 20 were taken, that the enemy never pursued so far as to the place where the waggons were posted; that the cavalry indeed did pursue beyond them, but as the waggons stood without horses, they were unable to carry them off; and that teams were afterwards collected at Charlotte which were sent and brought them away safely. We lost 8 pieces of cannon, all the ammunition which was with the army, tents, baggage, military chests papers and nearly the whole muskets which were in the hands of the militia who basely threw them away. The numbers of the enemy are not certainly known; prisoners say they were 3500 regulars; Colo. Sumpter's intelligence on the 15th. made them 1200 regulars 1000 militia and a reinforcement of 500 regulars on their way, but whether these had joined or not is unknown. It is believed their loss was full 500 killed and wounded. They retreated immediately to campden; but sent a party of horse against Colo. Sumpter, who after he had withdrawn up the Wateree 40 miles came on him by surprize, cut him off from his arms which they took retook the prisoners waggons and other things he had captured. Few of his men were lost as they flew to the woods. Generals Gates, Gist, Smallwood, Huger, Stevens, Butler and Gregory are safe. Generals DeKalb and Rutherford are missing, the latter a prisoner certainly, the former a prisoner and some accounts say mortally wounded, others that he is unhurt. Colo. Porterfield an inestimable officer, is said, we fear too truly to be dead of his wounds. About one third of his corps was lost. On this defeat the yeomanry of N. Carolina immediately turned out unsollicited. An army is collecting which when our last advices came away, viz August 23d. already consisted of between four and 5000 men.

Oppressed with the Labors of My Office

To Washington, May 28, 1781

The British invasion now overwhelmed Virginia. Jefferson and his government were rendered hopeless by it. Worst of all, the possibility became real that Virginia farmers might acquiesce to British rule. Thus Jefferson's entreaty for the presence of "their beloved Countryman."

. . . I make no doubt you will have heard, before this shall have the honour of being presented to Your Excellency, of the junction of Lord Cornwallis with the force at Petersburg under Arnold who had succeeded to the command on the death of Major General Philips. I am now advised that they have evacuated Petersburg, joined at Westover a Reinforcement of 2000 Men just arrived from New York, crossed James River, and on the 26th. Instant were three Miles advanced on their way towards Richmond; at which place Majr. General the Marquiss Fayette lay with 3000 men, regulars and militia, that being the whole number we could Arm till the arrival of the 1100 Arms from Rhode Island which are about this time getting to the place where our public Stores are deposited. The whole force of the Enemy within this State from the best intelligence I have been able to get, I think, is about 7000 Men, Infantry and Cavalry, including also the small Garrison left at Portsmouth. A number of Privateers and small Vessels which are constantly ravaging the Shores of our Rivers prevent us from receiving any aid from the Counties lying on Navigable Waters; [and powerful Operations meditated against our Western Frontier by a joint force of British and Indian savages have, as your Excellency before knew, obliged us to embody between two and three thousand Men in that quarter. Your Excellency will judge from this state of things and from what you know of your own Country what it may probably suffer during the present Campaign. Should the Enemy be able to produce no opportunity of annihilating the Marquis's Army a small proportion of their force may yet restrain his movements effectually while the greater part is employed in detachment to waste an unarmed Country and to lead the minds of the people to acquiesence under those events which they see no human power prepared to ward off. We are too far removed from the other scenes of war, to say whether the main force of the Enemy be within this State, but I suppose they cannot any where spare so great an Army for the operations of the field: Were it possible for this Circumstance to justify in Your Excellency a determination to lend us Your personal aid, it is evident from the universal voice that the presence of their beloved Countryman, whose talents have been so long successfully employed in establishing the freedom of kindred States, to whose person they have still flattered themselves they retained some right, and have ever looked up as their dernier resort in distress, that your appearance among them I say would restore full confidence of salvation, and would render them equal to whatever is not impossible. I cannot undertake to foresee and obviate the difficulties which stand in the way of such a resolution: the whole Subject is before you of which I see only detached parts; and your judgment will be formed on view of the whole. Should the danger of this State and its consequence to the Union be such as to render it best for the whole that you should repair to it's assistance, the difficulty would then be how to keep men out of the field. I have undertaken to hint this matter to your Excellency not only on my own sense of its importance to us, but at the sollicitations of many members of weight in our legislature which is not yet assembled to speak their own desires. A few days will bring to me that period of relief which the Constitution has prepared for those oppressed with the labours of my office, and a long declared resolution of relinquishing it to abler hands has prepared my way for retirement to a private station: still however as an individual citizen I should feel the comfortable effects of your presence, and have (what I thought could not have been), an additional motive for that gratitude, esteem & respect with which] I have the honour to be Your Excellency's Most obedient & Most humble servant,

I Have Taken My Final Leave of Every Thing

To Edmund Randolph, September 16, 1781

Jefferson's friends tried to dissuade him from his decision to retire from public life. He refused to accept the post of peace commissioner which would have taken him to France. His resolution to return to the state legislature for only as long as it would be necessary to clear his name disturbed Randolph. The latter replied to Jefferson on October 9: "If you can justify this resolution to yourself, I am confident that you cannot to the world."

. . . When I received the first letter fr[om the President of C]ongress inclosing their resolution, and mentioning [the necessity of an] expeditious departure, my determination to attend at the [next session of] assembly offered a ready and insuperable obstacle to my acceptance of that appointment and left me under no necessity of deliberating with myself whether that objection being removed, any other considerations might prevent my undertaking it. I find these are many and must therefore decline it altogether. Were it possible for me to determine again to enter into public business there is no appointment whatever which would have been so agreeable to me. But I have taken my final leave of every thing of that nature, have retired to my farm, my family and books from which I think nothing will evermore tempt me. A desire to leave public office with a reputation not more blotted than it has deserved will oblige me to emerge at the next session of our assembly and perhaps to accept of a seat in it, but as I go with a single object, I shall withdraw when that shall be accomplished. . . .

These Intimations Hanging over Our Head

Charges by George Nicholas with Jefferson's Answers, [after July 31, 1781]

On June 12, 1781, the Virginia House of Delegates, dominated by Patrick Henry, resolved to inquire into "the Conduct of the Executive for the last twelve months." One George Nicholas drew up the charges. The following are Jefferson's answers to them delivered before the legislature sometime in the fall of 1781. On December 12, the legislature acquitted Jefferson and voted him a "resolution of thanks."

OBJ. That Genl. Washington's information was that an embarkation was taking place destined for *this state*.

ANS. His information was, that it was destined for the Southward as was *given out* in N. York. Had similar informations from Genl. Washington and Congress been considered as sufficient ground at all times for calling the militia into the feild there would have been a standing army of militia kept up; because there has never been a time since the invasion expected in Dec. 1779, but what we have had those intimations hanging over our heads. The truth is that Genl. Washington always considered it as his duty to convey every rumor of an embarkation: but we (for some time past at least) never thought any thing but actual invasion should induce us to the expence of calling the militia into the feild; except in the case of Dec. 1779 when it was thought proper to do this in order to convince the French of our disposition to protect their ships. Inattention to this necessary œconomy in the beginning went far towards that ruin of our finances which followed.

Where were the post riders established last summer?

ANS. They were established at Continental expence to convey speedy information to Congress of the arrival of the French fleet then expected here. When that arrived at Rhode island these expresses were discontinued. They were again established on the invasion of October, and discontinued when that ceased, and again on the first intimation of the invasion of Dec. But it will be asked, why were they not established on Genl. Washington's letters? Because those letters were no more than we had received upon many former occasions, and would have led to a perpetual establishment of post riders.

OBJ. If a proper number of men had been put into motion on Monday for the relief of the lower country and ordered to march to Wmsburg. that they would at least have been in the neighborhood of Richmond on Thursday.

ANS. The order could not be till Tuesday because we then received our first certain inform[ation]. Half the militia of the counties round about Richmond were then ordered out, and the whole of them on the 4th, and ordered not to wait to come in a body but in detachments as they could assemble. Yet were there not on Friday more than 200 collected, and they were principally of the town of Richmond.

OBJ. That we had not signals.

ANS. This tho' a favorite plan of some gentlemen and perhaps a practicable one, has hitherto been thought too difficult.

OBJ. That we had not look-outs.

ANS. There had been no cause to order lookouts more than has been ever existing. This is only in fact asking why we do not always keep lookouts.

OBJ. That we had not heavy artillery on travelling carriages.

ANS. The gentlemen who acted as members of the B. of W. [Board of War] a twelvemonth can answer this question by giving the character of the artificers whom during that time they could never get to mount the heavy artillery. The same reason prevented their being mounted from May 1780 to December. We have even been unable to get those heavy cannon moved from Cumberland by the whole energy of government. A like difficulty which occurred in the removal of those at S. Quay in their day, will convince them of the possibility of this.

OBJ. That there was not a body of militia thrown into Portsmouth, the Great bridge, Suffolk.

ANS. In the Summer of 1780, we asked the favor of Genl. Nelson to call together the County Lieutenants of the lower counties and concert the general measures which should be taken for instant opposition on any invasion until aid could be ordered by the Executive, and these county Lieutenants were ordered to obey his call. He did so. The first moment to wit on Sat. Dec. 31. 8. o'clock A.M. of our receiving information of the appearance of a fleet in the bay, we asked the favor of Genl. Nelson to go down, which he did, with full powers to call together the militia of any counties he thought proper, to call on the keepers of any public arms or stores, and to adopt for the instant such measures as exigencies required till we could be better informed.

Qu. Why were not Genl. Nelson and the brave officers with him particularly mentioned?

Ans. What should have been said of them? The enemy did not land nor give them an opportunity of doing what nobody doubts they would have done, that is, somewhat worthy of being minutely recited.

Qu. Why publish Arnold's letter without Genl. Nelson's answer?

Ans. Ask the printer. He got neither from the Executive.

'As to the calling out a few militia and that not till late.'

Ans. It is denied that they were few or late. 4700 men (the number required by Baron Steuben) were called out the moment an invasion was known to have taken place; that is on Tuesday Jan. 2.

Obj. The abandonment of York and Portsmouth fortifications.

Ans. How can they be kept without regulars on the large scale on which they were formed? Would it be approved of to harrass the militia with garrisoning them?

The Tool Worked with by Another Hand

To Isaac Zane, December 24, 1781

This is an uncommonly acerbic letter for Jefferson. The "tool" referred to is George Nicholas, the "whale" undoubtedly Patrick Henry.

. . . You have heard probably of the vote of the H. of Delegates at the last session of assembly. I came here in consequence of it, and found neither accuser nor accusation. They have acknowledged by express vote that the former was founded on *rumours* only, for which no foundation can be discovered: they have thanked &c. The trifling body who moved this matter was below contempt; he was more an object of pity. His natural ill-temper was the tool worked with by another hand. He was like the minners that go in and out of the fundament of the whale. But the whale himself was discoverable enough by the turbulence of the water under which he moved. But enough of this. . . .

PART IV

NOTES ON VIRGINIA: 1781-1782

Introduction

AFTER FRANCE joined the American side in the Revolutionary War, the Secretary of the French Legation in Philadelphia, the Marquis de Barbé-Marbois, at the behest of his government, solicited information from prominent Americans on the nature and laws of the thirteen United States. Learning of Marbois' inquiry in October 1780, Jefferson set about at once to write on Virginia. He completed the *Notes* while recuperating from a fall off his horse in the summer of 1781. Though Marbois received the manuscript the following April, Jefferson, for the next two years, corrected and improved it, thanks in large part to the help of his Virginia friends.

In May 1785, while minister to France, Jefferson privately published the *Notes* in Paris. He saw to it that the limited printing of two hundred copies went only to his friends—he wanted no public controversy over such matters as slavery and the meaning of republicanism. Two years later, however, it appeared in (what Jefferson thought a bad) French translation. This compelled him to bring out the *Notes* the same year (1787) in an English edition for the general public. For unless he did so it was probable that an unauthorized English retranslation from the French would be published.

Jefferson's *Notes on Virginia* contains a rich vein of ore which may be mined both for itself and for what it discloses of its author. One point will be briefly taken up here: the dissonance between the *Notes* and the Declaration of Independence. The Declaration held aloft the revolutionary standard of natural rights. Life, liberty and happiness were the inheritance of all men, everywhere, and governments alone stood in the way of their possessing it. But in the *Notes* Jefferson maintains that liberty in Virginia or America arises from a unique environment. If American liberty justifies the special praise which Jefferson confers upon it in the *Notes,* what becomes of the universal ideals expressed in the Declaration?

In what is probably the best known section of the *Notes*— Query XIX: "The present state of manufactures, commerce, interior and exterior trade?"—Jefferson refers to those "who labor in the earth" as "the chosen people of God." America, he holds, is fortunate in being able to support such a race of chosen people, in providing a habitat for the cultivation of virtue. "While we have land to labor then, let us never wish to see our citizens occupied at a workbench, or twirling a distaff. . . . The mob of great cities add just so much to the support of pure government, as sores do to the strength of the human body. It is the manners and spirit of a people which preserve a republican vigor." Jefferson knew that what America possessed was not available to the masses of humanity crowded into cities and infertile farms throughout the world. Logically, they were condemned by the same force of circumstances which liberated Americans. Did this mean that republicanism was possible only in America or some similar environment?

In the *Notes,* Indians and Negroes also fall from the uniformly high estate to which Jefferson raised all men in the Declaration. His description of Indians and Negroes attempts to be scientific in the tradition of 18th century taxonomy. Jefferson deplores slavery but denies that Negroes are the equal of whites. He admires and sympathizes with Indians but finds their way of life untenable compared to that of the whites. As against the undifferentiated equalitarianism of the Declaration, the *Notes on Virginia* posits a natural hierarchy, the summit of which is occupied by white American yoemen farmers. In this context the French Revolution was to be an event in Jefferson's life. It was to revivify his radical faith in the possibility of republicanism for all men.

In Answer to Certain Queries

Notes on Virginia, 1781–1782

The title page of the first edition reads: NOTES *on the state of* VIRGINIA; *written in the year 1781, somewhat corrected and enlarged in the winter of 1782, for the use of a Foreigner of distinction, in answer to certain queries proposed by him respecting 1. Its boundaries—2. Rivers—3. Sea ports—4. Mountains—5. Cascades and caverns—6. Productions mineral, vegetable and animal—7. Climate—8. Population—9. Military force—10. Marine force—11. Aborigines—12. Counties and towns—13. Constitution—14. Laws—15. Colleges, buildings and roads—16. Proceedings as to tories—17. Religion—18. Manners—19. Manufactures—20. Subjects of commerce—21. Weights, measures and money—22. Public revenue and expenses—23. Histories, memorials and statepapers.*

QUERY IV

A notice of its Mountains?

For the particular geography of our mountains I must refer to Fry and Jefferson's map of Virginia; and to Evans' analysis of this map of America, for a more philosophical view of them than is to be found in any other work. It is worthy of notice, that our mountains are not solitary and scattered confusedly over the face of the country; but that they commence at about one hundred and fifty miles from the sea-coast, are disposed in ridges, one behind another, running nearly parallel with the sea-coast, though rather approaching it as they advance northeastwardly. To the south-west, as the tract of country between the sea-coast and the Mississippi becomes narrower, the mountains converge into a single ridge which, as it approaches the Gulf of Mexico, subsides into plain country, and gives rise to some of the waters of that gulf, and particularly to a river called the Apalachiocola, probably from the Apalachies, an Indian nation formerly residing on it. Hence, the mountains giving rise to that river, and seen from its various parts, were called the Apalachian mountains, being in fact the end or termination only of the great ridges passing through the continent. European geographers, however, extended the name northwardly as far as the mountains extended; some giving it, after their separation into different ridges, to the Blue Ridge, others to the North Mountain, others to the Alleghany, others to the Laurel Ridge, as may be seen by their different maps. But the fact I believe is, that none of these ridges were ever known by that name to the inhabitants, either native or emigrant, but as they saw them so called in European maps. In the same direction, generally, are the veins of limestone, coal, and other minerals hitherto discovered; and so range the falls of our great rivers. But the courses of the great rivers are at right angles with these. James and Potomac penetrate through all the ridges of mountains eastward of the Alleghany; that is, broken by no water course. It is in fact the spine of the country between the Atlantic on one side, and the Mississippi and St. Lawrence on the other. The passage of the Potomac through the Blue Ridge is, perhaps, one of the most stupendous scenes in nature. You stand on a very high point of land. On your right comes up the Shenandoah, having ranged along the foot of the mountain an hundred miles to seek a vent. On your left approaches the Potomac, in quest of a passage also. In the moment of their junction, they rush together against the mountain, rend it asunder, and pass off to the sea. The first glance of this scene hurries our senses into the opinion, that this earth has been created in time, that the mountains were formed first, that the rivers began to flow afterwards, that in this place, particularly, they have been dammed up by the Blue Ridge of mountains, and have formed an ocean which filled the whole valley; that continuing to rise they have at length broken over at this spot, and have torn the mountain down from its summit to its base. The piles of rock on each hand, but particularly on the Shenandoah, the evident marks of their disrupture and avulsion from their beds by the most powerful agents of nature, corroborate the impression. But the distant finishing which nature has given to the picture, is of a very different character. It is a true contrast to the foreground. It is as placid and delightful as that is wild and tremendous. For the mountain being cloven asunder, she presents to your eye, through the cleft, a small catch of smooth blue horizon, at an infinite distance in the plain country, inviting you, as it were, from the riot and tumult roaring around, to pass through the breach and participate of the calm below. Here the eye ultimately composes itself; and that way, too, the road happens actually to lead. You cross the Potomac above the junction, pass along its side through the base of the mountain for three miles, its terrible precipices hanging in fragments over you, and within about twenty miles reach Fredericktown, and the fine country round that. This scene is worth a voyage across the Atlantic. Yet here, as in the neighborhood of the Natural Bridge, are people who have passed their lives within half a dozen miles, and have never been to survey these monuments of a war between rivers and mountains, which must have shaken the earth itself to its centre. . . .

QUERY V

Its Cascades and Caverns?

In the lime-stone country there are many caverns of very considerable extent. The most noted is called Madison's Cave, and is on the north side of the Blue Ridge, near the intersection of the Rockingham and Augusta line with the south fork of the southern river of Shenandoah. It is in a hill of about two hundred feet perpendicular height, the ascent of which, on one side, is so steep that you may pitch a biscuit from its summit into the river which washes its base. The entrance of the cave is, in this side, about two-thirds of the way up. It extends into the earth about three hundred feet, branching into subordinate caverns, sometimes ascending a little, but more generally descending, and at length terminates, in two different places, at basins of water of unknown extent, and which I should judge to be nearly on a level with the water of the river; however, I do not think they are formed by refluent water from that, because they are never turbid; because they do not rise and fall in correspondence with that in times of flood or of drought; and because the water is always cool. It is probably one of the many reservoirs with which the interior parts of the earth are supposed to abound, and yield supplies to the fountains of water, distinguished from others only by being accessible. The vault of this cave is of solid lime-stone, from twenty to forty or fifty feet high; through which water is continually percolating. This, trickling down the sides of the cave, has incrusted them over in the form of elegant drapery; and dripping from the top of the vault generates on that and on the base below, stalactites of a conical form, some of which have met and formed massive columns.

Another of these caves is near the North Mountain, in the county of Frederic, on the lands of Mr. Zane. The entrance into this is on the top of an extensive ridge. You descend thirty or forty feet, as into a well, from whence the cave extends, nearly horizontally, four hundred feet into the earth, preserving a breadth of from twenty to fifty feet, and a height of from five to twelve feet. After entering this cave a few feet, the mercury, which in the open air was 50°, rose to 57° of Fahrenheit's thermometer, answering to 11° of Reaumur's, and it continued at that to the remotest parts of the cave. The uniform temperature of the cellars of the observatory of Paris, which are ninety feet deep, and of all subterraneous cavities of any depth, where no chemical agencies may be supposed to produce a factitious heat, has been found to be 10° of Reaumur, equal to 54½° of Fahrenheit. The temperature of the cave above mentioned so nearly corresponds with this, that the difference may be ascribed to a difference of instruments.

At the Panther gap, in the ridge which divides the waters of the Cow and the Calf pasture, is what is called the *Blowing Cave.* It is in the side of a hill, is of about one hundred feet diameter, and emits constantly a current of air of such force as to keep the weeds prostrate to the distance of twenty yards before it. This current is strongest in dry, frosty weather, and in long spells of rain weakest. Regular inspirations and expirations of air, by caverns and fissures, have been probably enough accounted for by supposing them combined with intermitting fountains; as they must of course inhale air while their reservoirs are emptying themselves, and again emit it while they are filling. But a constant issue of air, only varying in its force as the weather is drier or damper, will require a new hypothesis. There is another blowing cave in the Cumberland mountain, about a mile from where it crosses the Carolina line. All we know of this is, that it is not constant, and that a fountain of water issues from it.

The *Natural Bridge,* the most sublime of nature's works, though not comprehended under the present head, must not be pretermitted. It is on the ascent of a hill, which seems to have been cloven through its length by some great convulsion. The fissure, just at the bridge, is, by some admeasurements, two hundred and seventy feet deep, by others only two hundred and five. It is about forty-five feet wide at the bottom and ninety feet at the top; this of course determines the length of the bridge, and its height from the water. Its breadth in the middle is about sixty feet, but more at the ends, and the thickness of the mass, at the summit of the arch, about forty feet. A part of this thickness is constituted by a coat of earth, which gives growth to many large trees. The residue, with the hill on both sides, is one solid rock of lime-stone. The arch approaches the semi-elliptical form; but the larger axis of the ellipsis, which would be the cord of the arch, is many times longer than the transverse. Though the sides of this bridge are provided in some parts with a parapet of fixed rocks, yet few men have resolution to walk to them, and look over into the abyss. You involuntarily fall on your hands and feet, creep to the parapet, and peep over it. Looking down from this height about a minute, gave me a violent headache. If the view from the top be painful and intolerable, that from below is delightful in an equal extreme. It is impossible for the emotions arising from the sublime to be felt beyond what they are here; so beautiful an arch, so elevated, so light, and springing as it were up to heaven! The rapture of the spectator is really indescribable! The fissure continuing narrow, deep, and straight, for a considerable distance above and below the bridge, opens a short but very pleasing view of the North mountain on one side and the Blue Ridge on the other, at the distance each of them of about five miles. This bridge is in the county of Rockbridge, to which it has given name, and affords a public and commodious passage over a valley which cannot be crossed elsewhere for a considerable distance. The stream passing under it is called Cedar creek. It is a water of James' river, and sufficient in the driest seasons to turn a grist-mill, though its fountain is not more than two miles above. . . .

QUERY VI

A notice of the mines and other subterraneous riches; its trees, plants, fruits, etc.

Our quadrupeds have been mostly described by Linnæus and Mons. de Buffon. Of these the mammoth, or big buffalo, as called by the Indians, must certainly have been the largest. Their tradition is, that he was carnivorous, and still exists in the northern parts of America. A delegation of warriors from the Delaware tribe having visited the Governor of Virginia, during the revolution, on matters of business, after these had been discussed and settled in council, the Governor asked them some questions relative to their country, and among others, what they knew or had heard of the animal whose bones were found at the Saltlicks on the Ohio. Their chief speaker immediately put himself into an attitude of oratory, and with a pomp suited to what he conceived the elevation of his subject, informed him that it was a tradition handed down from their fathers, "That in ancient times a herd of these tremendous animals came to the Big-bone licks, and began an universal destruction of the bear, deer, elks, buffaloes, and other animals which had been created for the use of the Indians; that the Great Man above, looking down and seeing this, was so enraged that he seized his lightning, descended on the earth, seated himself on a neighboring mountain, on a rock of which his seat and the print of his feet are still to be seen, and hurled his bolts among them till the whole were slaughtered, except the big bull, who presenting his forehead to the shafts, shook them off as they fell; but missing one at length, it wounded him in the side; whereon, springing round, he bounded over the Ohio, over the Wabash, the Illinois, and finally over the great lakes, where he is living at this day." It is well known, that on the Ohio, and in many parts of America further north, tusks, grinders, and skeletons of unparalleled magnitude, are found in great numbers, some lying on the surface of the earth, and some a little below it. A Mr. Stanley, taken prisoner near the mouth of the Tennessee, relates, that after being transferred through several tribes, from one to another, he was at length carried over the mountains west of the Missouri to a river which runs westwardly; that these bones abounded there, and that the natives described to him the animal to which they belonged as still existing in the northern parts of their country; from which description he judged it to be an elephant. Bones of the same kind have been lately found, some feet below the surface of the earth, in salines opened on the North Holston, a branch of the Tennessee, about the latitude of 36½ ° north. From the accounts published in Europe, I suppose it to be decided that these are of the same kind with those found in Siberia. Instances are mentioned of like animal remains found in the more southern climates of both hemispheres; but they are either so loosely mentioned as to leave a doubt of the fact, so inaccurately described as not to authorize the classing

them with the great northern bones, or so rare as to found a
suspicion that they have been carried thither as curiosities
from the northern regions. So that, on the whole, there seem
to be no certain vestiges of the existence of this animal farther south than the salines just mentioned. It is remarkable
that the tusks and skeletons have been ascribed by the natu-
ralists of Europe to the elephant, while the grinders have been
given to the hippopotamus, or river horse. Yet it is acknowledged, that the tusks and skeletons are much larger than
those of the elephant, and the grinders many times greater
than those of the hippopotamus, and essentially different in
form. Wherever these grinders are found, there also we find
the tusks and skelton; but no skeleton of the hippopotamus
nor grinders of the elephant. It will not be said that the
hippopotamus and elephant came always to the same spot,
the former to deposit his grinders, and the latter his tusks and
skeleton. For what became of the parts not deposited there?
We must agree then, that these remains belong to each other,
that they are of one and the same animal, that this was not
a hippopotamus, because the hippopotamus had no tusks, nor
such a frame, and because the grinders differ in their size as
well as in the number and form of their points. That this was
not an elephant, I think ascertained by proofs equally decisive. I will not avail myself of the authority of the celebrated[1]
anatomist, who, from an examination of the form and structure of the tusks, has declared they were essentially different
from those of the elephant; because another[2] anatomist,
equally celebrated, has declared, on a like examination, that
they are precisely the same. Between two such authorities I
will suppose this circumstance equivocal. But, 1. The skeleton
of the mammoth (for so the incognitum has been called) bespeaks an animal of five or six times the cubic volume of
the elephant, as Mons. de Buffon has admitted. 2. The
grinders are five times as large, are square, and the grinding
surface studded with four or five rows of blunt points;
whereas those of the elephant are broad and thin, and their
grinding surface flat. 3. I have never heard an instance, and
suppose there has been none, of the grinder of an elephant
being found in America. 4. From the known temperature
and constitution of the elephant, he could never have existed
in those regions where the remains of the mammoth have

[1] Hunter [Jefferson].
[2] D'Aubenton [Jefferson].

been found. The elephant is a native only of the torrid zone and its vicinities; if, with the assistance of warm apartments and warm clothing, he has been preserved in the temperate climates of Europe, it has only been for a small portion of what would have been his natural period, and no instance of his multiplication in them has ever been known. But no bones of the mammoth, as I have before observed, have been ever found further south than the salines of Holston, and they have been found as far north as the Arctic circle. Those, therefore, who are of opinion that the elephant and mammoth are the same, must believe, 1. That the elephant known to us can exist and multiply in the frozen zone; or, 2. That an eternal fire may once have warmed those regions, and since abandoned them, of which, however, the globe exhibits no unequivocal indications; or, 3. That the obliquity of the ecliptic, when these elephants lived, was so great as to include within the tropics all those regions in which the bones are found; the tropics being, as is before observed, the natural limits of habitation for the elephant. But if it be admitted that this obliquity has really decreased, and we adopt the highest rate of decrease yet pretended, that is, of one minute in a century, to transfer the northern tropic to the Arctic circle, would carry the existence of these supposed elephants two hundred and fifty thousand years back; a period far beyond our conception of the duration of animal bones less exposed to the open air than these are in many instances. Besides, though these regions would then be supposed within the tropics, yet their winters would have been too severe for the sensibility of the elephant. They would have had, too, but one day and one night in the year, a circumstance to which we have no reason to suppose the nature of the elephant fitted. However, it has been demonstrated, that, if a variation of obliquity in the ecliptic takes place at all, it is vibratory, and never exceeds the limits of nine degrees, which is not sufficient to bring these bones within the tropics.

One of these hypotheses, or some other equally voluntary and inadmissible to cautious philosophy, must be adopted to support the opinion that these are the bones of the elephant. For my own part, I find it easier to believe that an animal may have existed, resembling the elephant in his tusks, and general anatomy, while his nature was in other respects extremely different. From the 30th degree of south latitude to the 30th degree of north, are nearly the limits which nature has fixed for the existence and multiplication of the elephant known to us. Proceeding thence northwardly to 36½ degrees, we enter those assigned to the mammoth. The farther we advance north, the more their vestiges multiply as far as the earth has been explored in that direction; and it is as probable as otherwise, that this progression continues to the pole itself, if land extends so far. The centre of the frozen zone, then, may be the acmé of their vigor, as that of the torrid is of the elephant. Thus nature seems to have drawn a belt of separation between these two tremendous animals, whose breadth, indeed, is not precisely known, though at present we may suppose it about 6½ degrees of latitude; to have assigned to the elephant the regions south of these confines, and those north to the mammoth, founding the constitution of the one in her extreme of heat, and that of the other in the extreme of cold. When the Creator has therefore separated their nature as far as the extent of the scale of animal life allowed to this planet would permit, it seems perverse to declare it the same, from a partial resemblance of their tusks and bones. But to whatever animal we ascribe these remains, it is certain such a one has existed in America, and that it has been the largest of all terrestrial beings. It should have sufficed to have rescued the earth it inhabited, and the atmosphere it breathed, from the imputation of impotence in the conception and nourishment of animal life on a large scale; to have stifled, in its birth, the opinion of a writer, the most learned, too, of all others in the science of animal history, that in the new world, *"La nature vivante est beaucoup moins agissante, beaucoup moins forte:"*[3] that nature is less active, less energetic on one side of the globe than she is on the other. As if both sides were not warmed by the same genial sun; as if a soil of the same chemical composition was less capable of elaboration into animal nutriment; as if the fruits and grains from that soil and sun yielded a less rich chyle, gave less extension to the solids and fluids of the body, or produced sooner in the cartilages, membranes, and fibres, that rigidity which restrains all further extension, and terminates animal growth. The truth is, that a pigmy and a Patagonian, a mouse and a mammoth, derive their dimensions from the same nutritive juices. The difference of increment depends on circumstances unsearchable to beings with our capacities.

[3] Buffon, xviii, 112 edit. Paris, 1764 [Jefferson].

Every race of animals seems to have received from their Maker certain laws of extension at the time of their formation. Their elaborate organs were formed to produce this, while proper obstacles were opposed to its further progress. Below these limits they cannot fall, nor rise above them. What intermediate station they shall take may depend on soil, on climate, on food, on a careful choice of breeders. But all the manna of heaven would never raise the mouse to the bulk of the mammoth.

The opinion advanced by the Count de Buffon,[4] is 1. That the animals common both to the old and new world are smaller in the latter. 2. That those peculiar to the new are on a smaller scale. 3. That those which have been domesticated in both have degenerated in America; and 4. That on the whole it exhibits fewer species. And the reason he thinks is, that the heats of America are less; that more waters are spread over its surface by nature, and fewer of these drained off by the hand of man. In other words, that *heat* is friendly, and *moisture* adverse to the production and development of large quadrupeds. I will not meet this hypothesis on its first doubtful ground, whether the climate of America be comparatively more humid? Because we are not furnished with observations sufficient to decide this question. And though, till it be decided, we are as free to deny as others are to affirm the fact, yet for a moment let it be supposed. The hypothesis, after this supposition, proceeds to another; that *moisture* is unfriendly to animal growth. The truth of this is inscrutable to us by reasonings *à priori*. Nature has hidden from us her *modus agendi*. Our only appeal on such questions is to experience; and I think that experience is against the supposition. It is by the assistance of *heat* and *moisture* that vegetables are elaborated from the elements of earth, air, water, and fire. We accordingly see the more humid climates produce the greater quantity of vegetables. Vegetables are mediately or immediately the food of every animal; and in proportion to the quantity of food, we see animals not only multiplied in their numbers, but improved in their bulk, as far as the laws of their nature will admit. Of this opinion is the Count de Buffon himself in another part of his work; *"en general il paroit ques les pays un peu* froids *conviennent mieux á nos boeufs que les pays chauds, et qu'ils sont d'autant*

[4] Buffon, xviii, 100, 156 [Jefferson].

plus gross et plus grands que le climat est plus humide *et plus abondans en paturages. Les boeufs de Danemarck, de la Podolie, de l'Ulkraine et de la Tartarie qu habitent les Calmouques sont les plus grands de tous."*[5] Here then a race of animals, and one of the largest too, has been increased in its dimensions by *cold* and *moisture*, in direct opposition to the hypothesis, which supposes that these two circumstances diminish animal bulk, and that it is their contraries *heat* and *dryness* which enlarge it. But when we appeal to experience we are not to rest satisfied with a single fact. Let us, therefore, try our question on more general ground. Let us take two portions of the earth, Europe and America for instance, sufficiently extensive to give operation to general causes; let us consider the circumstances peculiar to each, and observe their effect on animal nature. America, running through the torrid as well as temperate zone, has more *heat* collectively taken, than Europe. But Europe, according to our hypothesis, is the *dryest*. They are equally adapted then to animal productions; each being endowed with one of those causes which befriends animal growth, and with one which opposes it. If it be thought unequal to compare Europe with America, which is so much larger, I answer, not more so than to compare America with the whole world. Besides, the purpose of the comparison is to try an hypothesis, which makes the size of animals depend on the *heat* and *moisture* of climate. If, therefore, we take a region so extensive as to comprehend a sensible distinction of climate, and so extensive, too, as that local accidents, or the intercourse of animals on its borders, may not materially affect the size of those in its interior parts, we shall comply with those conditions which the hypothesis may reasonably demand. The objection would be the weaker in the present case, because any intercourse of animals which may take place on the confines of Europe and Asia, is to the advantage of the former, Asia producing certainly larger animals than Europe. Let us then take a comparative view of the quadrupeds of Europe and America, presenting them to the eye in three different tables, in one of which shall be

[5] viii, 134 [Jefferson]. "Generally, it appears that countries tending to be cold better suit our oxen than countries tending to be warm, and that they become bigger and fatter in proportion to the humidity of the climate and the abundance of pasturage. The oxen of Denmark, of Podoly, of the Ukraine and of the Tartary inhabited by the Calmuks are the biggest of all."

enumerated those found in both countries; in a second, those found in one only; in a third, those which have been domesticated in both. To facilitate the comparison, let those of each table be arranged in gradation according to their sizes, from the greatest to the smallest, so far as their sizes can be conjectured. The weights of the large animals shall be expressed in the English avoirdupois and its decimals; those of the smaller, in the same ounce and its decimals. . . .

The white bear of America is as large as that of Europe. The bones of the mammoth which has been found in America, are as large as those found in the old world. It may be asked, why I insert the mammoth, as if it still existed? I ask in return, why I should omit it, as if it did not exist? Such is the economy of nature, that no instance can be produced, of her having permitted any one race of her animals to become extinct; of her having formed any link in her great work so weak as to be broken. To add to this, the traditionary testimony of the Indians, that this animal still exists in the northern and western parts of America, would be adding the light of a taper to that of the meridian sun. Those parts still remain in their aboriginal state, unexplored and undisturbed by us, or by others for us. He may as well exist there now, as he did formerly where we find his bones. If he be a carnivorous animal, as some anatomists have conjectured, and the Indians affirm, his early retirement may be accounted for from the general destruction of the wild game by the Indians, which commences in the first instant of their connection with us, for the purpose of purchasing match-coats, hatchets, and fire-locks, with their skins. There remain then the buffalo, red deer, fallow deer, wolf, roe, glutton, wild cat, monax, bison, hedgehog, marten, and water-rat, of the comparative sizes of which we have not sufficient testimony. It does not appear that Messieurs de Buffon and D'Aubenton have measured, weighed, or seen those of America. It is said of some of them, by some travellers, that they are smaller than the European. But who were these travellers? Have they not been men of a very different description from those who have laid open to us the other three quarters of the world? Was natural history the object of their travels? Did they measure or weigh the animals they speak of? or did they not judge of them by sight, or perhaps even from report only? Were they acquainted with the animals of their own country, with which they undertake to compare them? Have they not been so ignorant as often to mistake the species? A true answer to these questions would probably lighten their authority, so as to render it insufficient for the foundation of an hypothesis. How unripe we yet are, for an accurate comparison of the animals of the two countries, will appear from the work of Monsieur de Buffon. The ideas we should have formed of the sizes of some animals, from the formation he had received at his first publications concerning them, are very different from what his subsequent communications give us. . . .

An afflicting picture, indeed, which for the honor of human nature, I am glad to believe has no original. Of the Indian of South America I know nothing; for I would not honor with the appellation of knowledge, what I derive from the fables published of them. These I believe to be just as true as the fables of Æsop. This belief is founded on what I have seen of man, white, red, and black, and what has been written of him by authors, enlightened themselves, and writing among an enlightened people. The Indian of North America being more within our reach, I can speak of him somewhat from my own knowledge, but more from the information of others better acquainted with him, and on whose truth and judgment I can rely. From these sources I am able to say, in contradiction to this representation, that he is neither more defective in ardor, nor more impotent with his female, than the white reduced to the same diet and exercise; that he is brave, when an enterprise depends on bravery; education with him making the point of honor consists in the destruction of an enemy by stratagem, and in the preservation of his own person free from injury; or, perhaps, this is nature, while it is education which teaches us to honor force more than finesse; that he will defend himself against a host of enemies, always choosing to be killed, rather than to surrender, though it be to the whites, who he knows will treat him well; that in other situations, also, he meets death with more deliberation, and endures tortures with a firmness unknown almost to religious enthusiasm with us; that he is affectionate to his children, careful of them, and indulgent in the extreme; that his affections comprehend his other connections, weakening, as with us, from circle to circle, as they recede from the centre; that his friendships are strong and faithful to the uttermost extremity; that his sensibility is keen, even the warriors weeping most bitterly on the loss of their children, though in general they endeavor to appear superior to human events; that his vivacity and activity of mind is equal to ours in the same situation; hence his eagerness for hunting, and for games of chance. The women are submitted to unjust drudgery. This I believe is the case with every barbarous people. With such, force is law. The stronger sex imposes on the weaker. It is civilization alone which replaces women in the enjoyment of their natural equality. That first teaches us to subdue the selfish passions, and to respect those rights in others which we value in ourselves. Were we in equal barbarism, our females would be equal drudges. The man with them is less strong than with us, but their women stronger than ours; and both for the same obvious reason; because our man and their woman is habituated to labor, and formed by it. With both races the sex which is indulged with ease is the least athletic. An Indian man is small in the hand and wrist, for the same reason for which a sailor is large and strong in the arms and shoulders, and a porter in the legs and thighs. They raise fewer children than we do. The causes of this are to be found, not in a difference of nature, but of circumstance. The women very frequently attending the men in their parties of war and of hunting, child-bearing becomes extremely inconvenient to them. It is said, therefore, that they have learned the practice of procuring abortion by the use of some vegetable; and that it even extends to prevent conception for a considerable time after. During these parties they are exposed to numerous hazards, to excessive exertions, to the greatest extremities of hunger. Even at their homes the nation depends for food, through a certain part of every year, on the gleanings of the forest; that is, they experience a famine once in every year. With all animals, if the female be badly fed, or not fed at all, her young perish; and if both male and female be reduced to like want, generation becomes less active, less productive. To the obstacles, then, of want and hazard, which nature has opposed to the multiplication of wild animals, for the purpose of restraining their numbers within certain bounds, those of labor and of voluntary abortion are added with the Indian. No wonder, then, if they multiply less than we do. Where food is regularly supplied, a single farm will show more of cattle, than a whole country of forests can of buffaloes. The same Indian women, when married to white traders, who feed them and their children plentifully and regularly, who exempt them from excessive

drudgery, who keep them stationary and unexposed to accident, produce and raise as many children as the white women. Instances are known, under these circumstances, of their
rearing a dozen children. An inhuman practice once prevailed
in this country, of making slaves of the Indians. It is a fact
well known with us, that the Indian women so enslaved produced and raised as numerous families as either the whites or
blacks among whom they lived. It has been said that Indians
have less hair than the whites, except on the head. But this is
a fact of which fair proof can scarcely be had. With them it
is disgraceful to be hairy on the body. They say it likens
them to hogs. They therefore pluck the hair as fast as it
appears. But the traders who marry their women, and prevail
on them to discontinue this practice, say, that nature is the
same with them as with the whites. Nor, if the fact be true,
is the consequence necessary which has been drawn from it.
Negroes have notoriously less hair than the whites; yet they
are more ardent. . . .

Before we condemn the Indians of this continent as wanting genius, we must consider that letters have not yet been
introduced among them. Were we to compare them in their
present state with the Europeans, north of the Alps, when
the Roman arms and arts first crossed those mountains, the
comparison would be unequal, because, at that time, those
parts of Europe were swarming with numbers; because numbers produce emulation, and multiply the chances of improvement, and one improvement begets another. Yet I may
safely ask, how many good poets, how many able mathe-
maticians, how many great inventors in arts or sciences, had
Europe, north of the Alps, then produced? And it was sixteen
centuries after this before a Newton could be formed. I do
not mean to deny that there are varieties in the race of man,
distinguished by their powers both of body and mind. I believe there are, as I see to be the case in the races of other
animals. I only mean to suggest a doubt, whether the bulk
and faculties of animals depend on the side of the Atlantic
on which their food happens to grow, or which furnishes the
elements of which they are compounded? Whether nature has
enlisted herself as a Cis or Trans-Atlantic partisan? I am
induced to suspect there has been more eloquence than sound
reasoning displayed in support of this theory; that it is one
of those cases where the judgment has been seduced by a
glowing pen; and whilst I render every tribute of honor and

esteem to the celebrated zoologist, who has added, and is still adding, so many precious things to the treasures of science, I must doubt whether in this instance he has not cherished error also, by lending her for a moment his vivid imagination and bewitching language.

So far the Count de Buffon has carried this new theory of the tendency of nature to belittle her productions on this side the Atlantic. Its application to the race of whites transplanted from Europe, remained for the Abbé Raynal. *"On doit etre etonné* (he says) *que l'Amerique n'ait pas encore produit un bon poëte, un habile mathematicien, un homme de genie dans un seul art, ou seule science."*[6] "America has not yet produced one good poet." When we shall have existed as a people as long as the Greeks did before they produced a Homer, the Romans a Virgil, the French a Racine and Voltaire, the English a Shakespeare and Milton, should this reproach be still true, we will inquire from what unfriendly causes it has proceeded, that the other countries of Europe and quarters of the earth shall not have inscribed any name in the roll of poets.[7] But neither has America produced "one able mathematician, one man of genius in a single art or a single science." In war we have produced a Washington, whose memory will be adored while liberty shall have votaries, whose name shall triumph over time, and will in future ages assume its just station among the most celebrated worthies of the world, when that wretched philosophy shall be forgotten which would have arranged him among the degeneracies of nature. In physics we have produced a Franklin, than whom no one of the present age has made more important discoveries, nor has enriched philosophy with more, or more ingenious solutions of the phenomena of nature. We have supposed Mr. Rittenhouse second to no astronomer living; that in genius he must be the first, because he is self-

---

[6] "One cannot help but be astonished that America has not yet produced a good poet, an able mathematician, a man of genius in a single art or science." Hist. Philos. p. 92, ed. Maestricht, 1774.

[7] Has the world as yet produced more than two poets, acknowledged to be such by all nations? An Englishman only reads Milton with delight, an Italian, Tasso, a Frenchman the Henriade; a Portuguese, Camoens; but Homer and Virgil have been the rapture of every age and nation; they are read with enthusiasm in their originals by those who can read the originals, and in translations by those who cannot. [Jefferson].

taught. As an artist he has exhibited as great a proof of mechanical genius as the world has ever produced. He has not indeed made a world; but he has by imitation approached nearer its Maker than any man who has lived from the creation to this day.[8]

As in philosophy and war, so in government, in oratory, in painting, in the plastic art, we might show that America, though but a child of yesterday, has already given hopeful proofs of genius, as well as of the nobler kinds, which arouse the best feelings of man, which call him into action, which substantiate his freedom, and conduct him to happiness, as of the subordinate, which serve to amuse him only. We therefore suppose, that this reproach is as unjust as it is unkind: and that, of the geniuses which adorn the present age, America contributes its full share. For comparing it with those countries where genius is most cultivated, where are the most excellent models for art, and scaffoldings for the attainment of science, as France and England for instance, we calculate thus: The United States contains three millions of inhabitants; France twenty millions; and the British islands ten. We produce a Washington, a Franklin, a Rittenhouse. France then should have half a dozen in each of these lines, and Great Britain half that number, equally eminent. It may be true that France has; we are but just becoming acquainted with her, and our acquaintance so far gives us high ideas of the genius of her inhabitants. It would be injuring too many of them to name particularly a Voltaire, a Buffon, the constellation of Encyclopedists, the Abbé Raynal himself, &c. &c. We, therefore, have reason to believe she can produce her full quota of genius. The present war having so long cut off all communication with Great Britain, we are not able to make a fair estimate of the state of science in that country. The spirit in which she wages war, is the only sample before our eyes, and that does not seem the legitimate offspring either of science or of civilization. The sun of her glory is fast descending to the horizon. Her philosophy has crossed the channel, her freedom the Atlantic, and herself seems

---

[8] There are various ways of keeping truth out of sight. Mr. Rittenhouse's model of the planetary system has the plagiary application of an Orrery; and the quadrant invented by Godfrey, an American also, and with the aid of which the European nations traverse the globe, is called Hadley's quadrant. [Jefferson].

passing to that awful dissolution whose issue is not given human foresight to scan. . . .

QUERY XIII

The constitution of the state and its several charters?

[Following their break with Britain the colonies] declared themselves independent states. They confederated together into one great republic; thus securing to every State the benefit of an union of their whole force. In each State separately a new form of government was established. Of ours particularly the following are the outlines: The executive powers are lodged in the hands of a governor, chosen annually, and incapable of acting more than three years in seven. He is assisted by a council of eight members. The judiciary powers are divided among several courts, as will be hereafter explained. Legislation is exercised by two houses of assembly, the one called the house of Delegates, composed of two members from each county, chosen annually by the citizens, possessing an estate for life in one hundred acres of uninhabited land, or twenty-five acres with a house on it, or in a house or lot in some town: the other called the Senate, consisting of twenty-four members, chosen quadrenially by the same electors, who for this purpose are distributed into twenty-four districts. The concurrence of both houses is necessary to the passage of a law. They have the appointment of the governor and council, the judges of the superior courts, auditors, attorney-general, treasurer, register of the land office, and delegates to Congress. As the dismemberment of the State had never had its confirmation, but, on the contrary, had always been the subject of protestation and complaint, that it might never be in our own power to raise scruples on that subject, or to disturb the harmony of our new confederacy, the grants to Maryland, Pennsylvania, and the two Carolinas, were ratified.

This constitution was formed when we were new and unexperienced in the science of government. It was the first, too, which was formed in the whole United States. No wonder then that time and trial have discovered very capital defects in it.

1. The majority of the men in the State, who pay and fight for its support, are unrepresented in the legislature, the roll of freeholders entitled to vote not including generally the half of those on the role of the militia, or of the tax-gatherers.

2. Among those who share the representation, the shares are very unequal. Thus the county of Warwick, with only one hundred fighting men, has an equal representation with the county of Loudon, which has one thousand seven hundred and forty-six. So that every man in Warwick has as much influence in the government as seventeen men in Loudon. . . .

3. The senate is, by its constitution, too homogeneous with the house of delegates. Being chosen by the same electors, at the same time, and out of the same subjects, the choice falls of course on men of the same description. The purpose of establishing different houses of legislation is to introduce the influence of different interests or different principles. Thus in Great Britain it is said their constitution relies on the house of commons for honesty, and the lords for wisdom; which would be a rational reliance, if honesty were to be bought with money, and if wisdom were hereditary. In some of the American States, the delegates and senators are so chosen, as that the first represent the persons, and the second the property of the State. But with us, wealth and wisdom have equal chance for admission into both houses. We do not, therefore, derive from the separation of our legislature into two houses, those benefits which a proper complication of principles are capable of producing, and those which alone can compensate the evils which may be produced by their dissensions.

4. All the powers of government, legislative, executive, and judiciary, result to the legislative body. The concentrating these in the same hands is precisely the definition of despotic government. It will be no alleviation that these powers will be exercised by a plurality of hands, and not by a single one. One hundred and seventy-three despots would surely be as oppressive as one. Let those who doubt it turn their eyes on the republic of Venice. As little will it avail us that they are chosen by ourselves. An *elective despotism* was not the government we fought for, but one which should not only be founded on free principles, but in which the powers of government should be so divided and balanced among several bodies of magistracy, as that no one could transcend their legal limits, without being effectually checked and restrained by the others. For this reason that convention which passed the ordinance of government, laid its foundation on this basis, that the legislative, executive, and judiciary departments should be separate and distinct, so that no person should exercise the powers of more than one of them at the same

time. But no barrier was provided between these several powers. The judiciary and executive members were left dependent on the legislative, for their subsistence in office, and some of them for their continuance in it. If, therefore, the legislature assumes executive and judiciary powers, no opposition is likely to be made; nor, if made, can it be effectual; because in that case they may put their proceedings into the form of an act of assembly, which will render them obligatory on the other branches. They have, accordingly, in many instances, decided rights which should have been left to judiciary controversy; and the direction of the executive, during the whole time of their session, is becoming habitual and familiar. And this is done with no ill intention. The views of the present members are perfectly upright. When they are led out of their regular province, it is by art in others, and inadvertance in themselves. And this will probably be the case for some time to come. But it will not be a very long time. Mankind soon learn to make interested uses of every right and power which they possess, or may assume. The public money and public liberty, intended to have been deposited with three branches of magistracy, but found inadvertently to be in the hands of one only, will soon be discovered to be sources of wealth and dominion to those who hold them; distinguished, too, by this tempting circumstance, that they are the instrument, as well as the object of acquisition. With money we will get men, said Cæsar, and with men we will get money. Nor should our assembly be deluded by the integrity of their own purposes, and conclude that these unlimited powers will never be abused, because themselves are not disposed to abuse them. They should look forward to a time, and that not a distant one, when a corruption in this, as in the country from which we derive our origin, will have seized the head of government, and be spread by them through the body of the people; when they will purchase the voices of the people, and make them pay the price. Human nature is the same on every side of the Atlantic and will be alike influenced by the same causes. The time to guard against corruption and tyranny, is before they shall have gotten hold of us. It is better to keep the wolf out of the fold, than to trust to drawing his teeth and claws after he shall have entered. . . .

When, therefore, it is considered, that there is no legal obstacle to the assumption by the assembly of all the powers legislative, executive, and judiciary, and that these may come to the hands of the smallest rag of delegation, surely the people will say, and their representatives, while yet they have honest representatives, will advise them to say, that they will not acknowledge as laws any acts not considered and assented to by the major part of their delegates.

In enumerating the defects of the Constitution, it would be wrong to count among them what is only the error of particular persons. In December 1776, our circumstances being much distressed, it was proposed in the house of delegates to create a *dictator*, invested with every power legislative, executive, and judiciary, civil and military, of life and of death, over our persons and over our properties; and in June 1781, again under calamity, the same proposition was repeated, and wanted a few votes only of being passed. One who entered into this contest from a pure love of liberty, and a sense of injured rights, who determined to make every sacrifice, and to meet every danger, for the re-establishment of those rights on a firm basis, who did not mean to expend his blood and substance for the wretched purpose of changing this matter for that, but to place the powers of governing him in a plurality of hands of his own choice, so that the corrupt will of no one man might in future oppress him, must stand confounded and dismayed when he is told, that a considerable portion of that plurality had mediated the surrender of them into a single hand, and, in lieu of a limited monarchy, to deliver him over to a despotic one! How must we find his efforts and sacrifices abused and baffled, if he may still, by a single vote, be laid prostrate at the feet of one man! In God's name, from whence have they derived this power? Is it from our ancient laws? None such can be produced. Is it from any principle in our new Constitution expressed or implied? Every lineament expressed or implied, is in full opposition to it. Its fundamental principle is, that the State shall be governed as a commonwealth. It provides a republican organization, proscribes under the name of *prerogative* the exercise of all powers undefined by the laws; places on this basis the whole system of our laws; and by consolidating them together, chooses that they should be left to stand or fall together, never providing for any circumstances, nor admitting that such could arise, wherein either should be suspended; no, not for a moment. Our ancient laws expressly declare, that those who are but delegates themselves shall not delegate to others powers which require judgment and integrity in their exercise.

Or was this proposition moved on a supposed right in the movers, of abandoning their posts in a moment of distress? The same laws forbid the abandonment of that post, even on ordinary occasions; and much more a transfer of their powers into other hands and other forms, without consulting the people. They never admit the idea that these, like sheep or cattle, may be given from hand to hand without an appeal to their own will. Was it from the necessity of the case? Necessities which dissolve a government, do not convey its authority to an oligarchy or a monarchy. They throw back, into the hands of the people, the powers they had delegated, and leave them as individuals to shift for themselves. A leader may offer, but not impose himself, nor be imposed on them. Much less can their necks be submitted to his sword, their breath to be held at his will or caprice.

The necessity which should operate these tremendous effects should at least be palpable and irresistible. Yet in both instances, where it was feared, or pretended with us, it was belied by the event. It was belied, too, by the preceding experience of our sister States, several of whom had grappled through greater difficulties without abandoning their forms of government. When the proposition was first made, Massachusetts had found even the government of committees sufficient to carry them through an invasion. But we at the time of that proposition, were under no invasion. When the second was made, there had been added to this example those of Rhode Island, New York, New Jersey, and Pennsylvania, in all of which the republican form had been found equal to the task of carrying them through the severest trials. In this State alone did there exist so little virtue, that fear was to be fixed in the hearts of the people, and to become the motive of their exertions, and principle of their government? The very thought alone was treason against the people; was treason against mankind in general; as riveting forever the chains which bow down their necks, by giving to their oppressors a proof, which they would have trumpeted through the universe, of the imbecility of republican government, in times of pressing danger, to shield them from harm. Those who assume the right of giving away the reins of government in any case, must be sure that the herd, whom they hand on to the rods and hatchet of the dictator, will lay their necks on the block when they shall nod to them. But if our assemblies supposed such a recognition in the people, I hope they mistook their character.

I am of opinion, that the government, instead of being braced and invigorated for greater exertions under their difficulties, would have been thrown back upon the bungling machinery of county committees for administration, till a convention could have been called, and its wheels again set into regular motion. What a cruel moment was this for creating such an embarrassment, for putting to the proof the attachment of our countrymen to republican government! Those who meant well, of the advocates of this measure, (and most of them meant well, for I know them personally, had been their fellow-laborer in the common cause, and had often proved the purity of their principles,) had been seduced in their judgment by the example of an ancient republic, whose constitution and circumstances were fundamentally different. They had sought this precedent in the history of Rome, where alone it was to be found, and where at length, too, it had proved fatal. They had taken it from a republic rent by the most bitter factions and tumults, where the government was of a heavy-handed unfeeling aristocracy, over a people ferocious, and rendered desperate by poverty and wretchedness; tumults which could not be allayed under the most trying circumstances, but by the omnipotent hand of a single despot. Their constitution, therefore, allowed a temporary tyrant to be erected, under the name of a dictator; and that temporary tyrant, after a few examples, became perpetual. They misapplied this precedent to a people mild in their dispositions, patient under their trial, united for the public liberty, and affectionate to their leaders. But if from the constitution of the Roman government there resulted to their senate a power of submitting all their rights to the will of one man, does it follow that the assembly of Virginia have the same authority? What clause in our constitution has substituted that of Rome, by way of residuary provision, for all cases not otherwise provided for? Or if they may step *ad libitum* into any other form of government for precedents to rule us by, for what oppression may not a precedent be found in this world of the *ballum omnium in omnia?* Searching for the foundations of this proposition, I can find none which may pretend a color of right or reason, but the defect before developed, that there being no barrier between the legislative,

executive, and judiciary departments, the legislature may seize
the whole; that having seized it, and possessing a right to fix
their own quorum, they may reduce that quorum to one,
whom they may call a chairman, speaker, dictator, or by any
other name they please. Our situation is indeed perilous, and
I hope my countrymen will be sensible of it, and will apply,
at a proper season, the proper remedy; which is a convention
to fix the constitution, to amend its defects, to bind up the
several branches of government by certain laws, which, when
they transgress, their acts shall become nullities; to render
unnecessary an appeal to the people, or in other words a
rebellion, on every infraction of their rights, on the peril that
their acquiescence shall be construed into an intention to surrender those rights.

QUERY XIV

The administration of justice and the description of the laws?

. . . Many of the laws which were in force during the
monarchy being relative merely to that form of government,
or inculcating principles inconsistent with republicanism, the
first assembly which met after the establishment of the commonwealth appointed a committee to revise the whole code, to
reduce it into proper form and volume, and report it to the
assembly. This work has been executed by three gentlemen,
and reported;[9] but probably will not be taken up till a restoration of peace shall leave to the legislature leisure to go
through such a work.

The plan of the revisal was this. The common law of England, by which is meant, that part of the English law which
was anterior to the date of the oldest statues extant, is made
the basis of the work. It was thought dangerous to attempt
to reduce it to a text; it was therefore left to be collected
from the usual monuments of it. Necessary alterations in that,
and so much of the whole body of the British statutes, and of
acts of assembly, as were thought proper to be retained, were
digested into one hundred and twenty-six new acts, in which
simplicity of style was aimed at, as far as was safe. The following are the most remarkable alterations proposed:

To change the rules of descent, so as that the lands of any

[9] See Part III, Documents 1–6, for the revisal of the laws of
Virginia.

person dying intestate shall be divisible equally among all his children, or other representatives, in equal degree.

To make slaves distributable among the next of kin, as other movables.

To have all public expenses, whether of the general treasury, or of a parish or county, (as for the maintenance of the poor, building bridges, courthouses, &c.,) supplied by assessment on the citizens, in proportion to their property.

To hire undertakers for keeping the public roads in repair, and indemnify individuals through whose lands new roads shall be opened.

To define with precision the rules whereby aliens should become citizens, and citizens make themselves aliens.

To establish religious freedom on the broadest bottom.

To emancipate all slaves born after the passing the act. The bill reported by the revisers does not itself contain this proposition; but an amendment containing it was prepared, to be offered to the legislature whenever the bill should be taken up, and farther directing, that they should continue with their parents to a certain age, then to be brought up, at the public expense, to tillage, arts, or sciences, according to their geniuses, till the females should be eighteen, and the males twenty-one years of age, when they should be colonized to such place as the circumstances of the time should render most proper, sending them out with arms, implements of household and of the handicraft arts, seeds, pairs of the useful domestic animals, &c., to declare them a free and independent people, and extend to them our alliance and protection, till they have acquired strength; and to send vessels at the same time to other parts of the world for an equal number of white inhabitants; to induce them to migrate hither proper encouragements were to be proposed. It will probably be asked, Why not retain and incorporate the blacks into the State, and thus save the expense of supplying by importation of white settlers, the vacancies they will leave? Deep-rooted prejudices entertained by the whites; ten thousand recollections, by the blacks, of the injuries they have sustained; new provocations; the real distinctions which nature has made; and many other circumstances, will divide us into parties, and produce convulsions, which will probably never end but in the extermination of the one or the other race. To these objections, which are political, may be added others, which are physical and moral. The first difference which strikes us is that of color. Whether the black of the negro resides in the reticular membrane between the skin and scarf-skin, or in the scarf-skin itself; whether it proceeds from the color of the blood, the color of the bile, or from that of some other secretion, the difference is fixed in nature, and is as real as if its seat and cause were better known to us. And is this difference of no importance? Is it not the foundation of a greater or less share of beauty in the two races? Are not the fine mixtures of red and white, the expressions of every passion by greater or less suffusions of color in the one, preferable to that eternal monotony, which reigns in the countenances, that immovable veil of black which covers the emotions of the other race? Add to these, flowing hair, a more elegant symmetry of form, their own judgment in favor of the whites, declared by their preference of them, as uniformly as is the preference of the Oran-utan for the black woman over those of his own species. The circumstance of superior beauty, is thought worthy attention in the propagation of our horses, dogs, and other domestic animals; why not in that of man? Besides those of color, figure, and hair, there are other physical distinctions proving a difference of race. They have less hair on the face and body. They secrete less by the kidneys, and more by the glands of the skin, which gives them a very strong and disagreeable odor. This greater degree of transpiration, renders them more tolerant of heat, and less so of cold than the whites. Perhaps, too, a difference of structure in the pulmonary apparatus, which a late ingenious experimentalist has discovered to be the principal regulator of animal heat, may have disabled them from extricating, in the act of inspiration, so much of that fluid from the outer air, or obliged them in expiration, to part with more of it. They seem to require less sleep. A black after hard labor through the day, will be induced by the slightest amusements to sit up till midnight, or later, though knowing he must be out with first dawn of the morning. They are at least as brave, and more adventuresome. But this may perhaps proceed from a want of forethought, which prevents their seeing a danger till it be present. When present, they do not go through it with more coolness or steadiness than the whites. They are more ardent after their female; but love seems with them to be more an eager desire, than a tender delicate mixture of sentiment and sensation. Their griefs are transient. Those numberless afflictions, which render it doubtful whether heaven has given life to us in mercy or in wrath, are less felt, and sooner forgotten with them. In general, their existence appears to participate more of sensation than reflection.

To this must be ascribed their disposition to sleep when abstracted from their diversions, and unemployed in labor. An animal whose body is at rest, and who does not reflect must be disposed to sleep of course. Comparing them by their faculties of memory, reason, and imagination, it appears to me that in memory they are equal to the whites; in reason much inferior, as I think one could scarcely be found capable of tracing and comprehending the investigations of Euclid; and that in imagination they are dull, tasteless, and anomalous. It would be unfair to follow them to Africa for this investigation. We will consider them here, on the same stage with the whites, and where the facts are not apocryphal on which a judgment is to be formed. It will be right to make great allowances for the difference of condition, of education, of conversation, of the sphere in which they move. Many millions of them have been brought to, and born in America. Most of them, indeed, have been confined to tillage, to their own homes, and their own society; yet many have been so situated, that they might have availed themselves of the conversation of their masters; many have been brought up to the handicraft arts, and from that circumstance have always been associated with the whites. Some have been liberally educated, and all have lived in countries where the arts and sciences are cultivated to a considerable degree, and all have had before their eyes samples of the best works from abroad. The Indians, with no advantages of this kind, will often carve figures on their pages not destitute of design and merit. They will crayon out an animal, a plant, or a country, so as to prove the existence of a germ in their minds which only wants cultivation. They astonish you with strokes of the most sublime oratory; such as prove their reason and sentiment strong, their imagination glowing and elevated.

But never yet could I find that a black had uttered a thought above the level of plain narration; never saw even an elementary trait of painting or sculpture. In music they are more generally gifted than the whites with accurate ears for tune and time, and they have been found capable of imagining a small catch.[10] Whether they will be equal to the composition of a more extensive run of melody, or of complicated harmony, is yet to be proved. Misery is often the parent of the most affecting touches in poetry. Among the blacks is misery enough, God knows, but no poetry. Love is the peculiar oestrum of the poet. Their love is ardent, but it kindles the senses only, not the imagination. Religion, indeed, has produced a Phyllis Whately;[11] but it could not produce a poet. The compositions published under her name are below the dignity of criticism. The heroes of the Dunciad are to her, as Hercules to the author of that poem.

Ignatius Sancho[12] has approached nearer to merit in composition; yet his letters do more honor to the heart than the head. They breathe the purest effusions of friendship and general philanthropy, and show how great a degree of the latter may be compounded with strong religious zeal. He is often happy in the turn of his compliments, and his style is easy and familiar, except when he affects a Shandean fabrication of words. But his imagination is wild and extravagant, and escapes incessantly from every restraint of reason and taste, and, in the course of its vagaries, leaves a tract of thought as incoherent and eccentric, as is the course of a meteor through the sky. His subjects should often have led him to a process of sober reasoning; yet we find him always substituting sentiment for demonstration. Upon the whole, though we admit him to the first place among those of his own color who have presented themselves to the public judgment, yet when we compare him with the writers of the race among whom he lived and particularly with the epistolary class in which he has taken his own stand, we are compelled to enrol him at the bottom of the column. This criticism supposes the letters published under his name to be genuine, and to have received amendment from no other hand; points which would not be of easy investigation.

The improvement of the blacks in body and mind, in the

[10] The instrument proper to them is the Banjar, which they brought hither from Africa, and which is the original of the guitar, it's chords being precisely the four lower chords of the guitar [Jefferson].

[11] Her name was Wheatley. In 1773 she brought out a volume of poetry.

[12] Sancho's *Letters, with Memoirs of his Life* was published in London in 1782.

first instance of their mixture with the whites, has been observed by every one, and proves that their inferiority is not the effect merely of their condition of life. We know that among the Romans, about the Augustan age especially, the condition of their slaves was much more deplorable than that of the blacks on the continent of America. The two sexes were confined in separate apartments, because to raise a child cost the master more than to buy one. Cato, for a very restricted indulgence to his slaves in this particular, took from them a certain price. But in this country the slaves multiply as fast as the free inhabitants. Their situation and manners place the commerce between the two sexes almost without restraint. The same Cato, on a principle of economy, always sold his sick and superannuated slaves. He gives it as a standing precept to a master visiting his farm, to sell his old oxen, old wagons, old tools, old and diseased servants, and everything else become useless. . . . The American slaves cannot enumerate this among the injuries and insults they receive. It was the common practice to expose in the island Aesculapius, in the Tyber, diseased slaves whose cure was like to become tedious. The emperor Claudius by an edict, gave freedom to such of them as should recover, and first declared that if any person chose to kill rather than to expose them, it should not be deemed homicide. The exposing them is a crime of which no instance has existed with us; and were it to be followed by death, it would be punished capitally. We are told of a certain Vedius Pollio, who, in the presence of Augustus, would have given a slave as food to his fish, for having broken a glass. With the Roman, the regular method of taking the evidence of their slaves was under torture. Here it has been thought better never to resort to their evidence. When a master was murdered, all his slaves, in the same house, or within hearing, were condemned to death. Here punishment falls on the guilty only, and as precise proof is required against him as against a freeman.

Yet notwithstanding these and other discouraging circumstances among the Romans, their slaves were often their rarest artists. They excelled too in science, insomuch as to be usually employed as tutors to their master's children. Epictetus, Terence, and Phaedrus, were slaves. But they were of the race of whites. It is not their condition then, but nature, which has produced the distinction. Whether further observation will or will not verify the conjecture, that nature has been less bountiful to them in the endowments of the head, I believe that in those of the heart she will be found to have done them justice. That disposition to theft with which they have been branded, must be ascribed to their situation, and not to any depravity of the moral sense. The man in whose favor no laws of property exist, probably feels himself less bound to respect those made in favor of others. When arguing for ourselves, we lay it down as a fundamental, that laws, to be just, must give a reciprocation of right; that, without this, they are mere arbitrary rules of conduct, founded in force, and not in conscience; and it is a problem which I give to the master to solve, whether the religious precepts against the violation of property were not framed for him as well as his slave? And whether the slave may not as justifiably take a little from one who has taken all from him, as he may slay one who would slay him? That a change in the relations in which a man is placed should change his ideas of moral right or wrong, is neither new, nor peculiar to the color of the blacks. Homer tells us it was so two thousand six hundred years ago.

> Jove fix'd it certain, take whatever day
> Makes man a slave, takes half his worth away.

But the slaves of which Homer speaks were whites. Notwithstanding these considerations which must weaken their respect for the laws of property, we find among them numerous instances of the most rigid integrity, and as many as among their better instructed masters, of benevolence, gratitude, and unshaken fidelity. The opinion that they are inferior in the faculties of reason and imagination, must be hazarded with great diffidence. To justify a general conclusion, requires many observations, even where the subject may be submitted to the anatomical knife, to optical glasses, to analysis by fire or by solvents. How much more then where it is a faculty, not a substance, we are examining; where it eludes the research of all the senses; where the conditions of its existence are various and variously combined; where the effects of those which are present or absent bid defiance to calculation; let me add too, as a circumstance of great tenderness, where our conclusion would degrade a whole race of men from the rank in the scale of beings which their Creator may perhaps have given them.

To our reproach it must be said, that though for a century and a half we have had under our eyes the races of black and of red men, they have never yet been viewed by us as subjects of natural history. I advance it, therefore, as a suspicion only, that the blacks, whether originally a distinct race, or made distinct by time and circumstances, are inferior to the whites in the endowments both of body and mind. It is not against experience to suppose that different species of the same genus, or varieties of the same species, may possess different qualifications. Will not a lover of natural history then, one who views the gradations in all the races of animals with the eye of philosophy, excuse an effort to keep those in the department of man as distinct as nature has formed them? This unfortunate difference of color, and perhaps of faculty, is a powerful obstacle to the emancipation of these people. Many of their advocates, while they wish to vindicate the liberty of human nature, are anxious also to preserve its dignity and beauty. Some of these, embarrassed by the question, "What further is to be done with them?" join themselves in opposition with those who are actuated by sordid avarice only. Among the Romans emancipation required but one effort. The slave, when made free, might mix with, without staining the blood of his master. But with us a second is necessary, unknown to history. When freed, he is to be removed beyond the reach of mixture. . . .

Another object of the revisal is to diffuse knowledge more generally through the mass of the people. This bill proposes to lay off every county into small districts of five or six miles square, called hundreds, and in each of them to establish a school for teaching, reading, writing, and arithmetic. The tutor to be supported by the hundred, and every person in it entitled to send their children three years gratis, and as much longer as they please, paying for it. These schools to be under a visitor who is annually to choose the boy of best genius in the school, of those whose parents are too poor to give them further education, and to send him forward to one of the grammar schools, of which twenty are proposed to be erected in different parts of the country, for teaching Greek, Latin, Geography, and the higher branches of numerical arithmetic. Of the boys thus sent in one year, trial is to be made at the grammar schools one or two years, and the best genius of the whole selected, and continued six years, and the residue dismissed. By this means twenty of the best geniuses will be raked from the rubbish annually, and be instructed, at the public expense, so far as the grammar schools go. At the end of six years' instruction, one half are to be discontinued (from among whom the grammar schools will probably be supplied with future masters); and the other half, who are to be chosen for the superiority of their parts and disposition, are to be sent and continued three years in the study of such sciences as they shall choose, at William and Mary College, the plan of which is proposed to be enlarged, as will be hereafter explained, and extended to all the useful sciences. The ultimate result of the whole scheme of education would be the teaching all the children of the State reading, writing, and common arithmetic; turning out ten annually, of superior genius, well taught in Greek, Latin, Geography, and the higher branches of arithmetic; turning out ten others annually, of still superior parts, who, to those branches of learning, shall have added such of the sciences as their genius shall have led them to; the furnishing to the wealthier part of the people convenient schools at which their children may be educated at their own expense. The general objects of this law are to provide an education adapted to the years, to the capacity, and the condition of every one, and directed to their freedom and happiness.

Specific details were not proper for the law. These must be the business of the visitors entrusted with its execution. The first stage of this education being the schools of the hundreds, wherein the great mass of the people will receive their instruction, the principal foundations of future order will be laid here. Instead, therefore, of putting the Bible and Testament into the hands of the children at an age when their judgments are not sufficiently matured for religious inquiries, their memories may here be stored with the most useful facts from Grecian, Roman, European and American history. The first elements of morality too may be instilled into their minds; such as, when further developed as their judgments advance in strength, may teach them how to work out their own greatest happiness, by showing them that it does not depend on the condition of life in which chance has placed them, but is always the result of a good conscience, good health, occupation, and freedom in all just pursuits. Those whom either the wealth of their parents or the adoption of the State shall destine to higher degrees of learning, will go on to the grammar schools, which constitute the next stage, there to be instructed in the languages. The learning Greek and Latin, I am told, is going into disuse in Europe. I know not what their manners and occupations may call for; but it would be very ill-judged in us to follow their example in this instance. There is a certain period of life, say from eight to fifteen or sixteen years of age, when the mind like the body is not yet firm enough for laborious and close operations. If applied to such, it falls an early victim to premature exertion; exhibiting, indeed, at first, in these young and tender subjects, the flattering appearance of their being men while they are yet children, but ending in reducing them to be children when they should be men. The memory is then most susceptible and tenacious of impressions; and the learning of languages being chiefly a work of memory, it seems precisely fitted to the powers of this period, which is long enough, too, for acquiring the most useful languages, ancient and modern.

I do not pretend that language is science. It is only an instrument for the attainment of science. But that time is not lost which is employed in providing tools for future operation; more especially as in this case the books put into the hands of the youth for this purpose may be such as will at the same time impress their minds with useful facts and good principles. If this period be suffered to pass in idleness, the mind becomes lethargic and impotent, as would the body it inhabits if unexercised during the same time. The sympathy between body and mind during their rise, progress and decline, is too strict and obvious to endanger our being missed while we reason from the one to the other. As soon as they are of sufficient age, it is supposed they will be sent on from grammar schools to the university, which constitutes our third and last stage, there to study those sciences which may be adapted to their views. By that part of our plan which prescribes the selection of the youths of genius from among the classes of the poor, we hope to avail the State of those talents which nature has sown as liberally among the poor as the rich, but which perish without use, if not sought for and cultivated. But of the views of this law none is more important, none more legitimate, than that of rendering the people the safe, as they are the ultimate, guardians of their own liberty. For this purpose the reading in the first stage, where *they* will receive their whole education, is proposed, as has been said, to be chiefly historical. History, by apprizing them of the past, will enable them to judge of the future; it will avail them of the experience of other times and other nations; it will qualify them as judges of the actions and designs of men; it will enable them to know ambition under every disguise it may assume; and knowing it, to defeat its views. In every government on earth is some trace of human weakness, some germ of corruption and degeneracy, which cunning will discover, and wickedness insensibly open, cultivate and improve. Every government degenerates when trusted to the rulers of the people alone. The people themselves therefore are its only safe depositories. And to render even them safe, their minds must be improved to a certain degree. This indeed is not all that is necessary, though it be essentially necessary. An amendment of our constitution must here come in aid of the public education. The influence over government must be shared among all the people. If every individual which composes their mass participates of the ultimate authority, the government will be safe; because the corrupting the whole mass will exceed any private resources of wealth; and public ones cannot be provided but by levies on the people. In this case every man would have to pay his own price. The government of Great Britain has been corrupted, because but one man in ten has a right to vote for members of parliament. The sellers of the government, therefore, get ninetenths of their price clear. It has been thought that corruption is restrained by confining the right of suffrage to a few of the wealthier of the people; but it would be more effectually restrained by an extension of that right to such members as would bid defiance to the means of corruption.

Lastly, it is proposed, by a bill in this revisal, to begin a public library and gallery, by laying out a certain sum annually in books, paintings, and statues. . . .

QUERY XVII

The different religions received into that State?

The first settlers in this country were emigrants from England, of the English Church, just at a point of time when it was flushed with complete victory over the religious of all other persuasions. Possessed, as they became, of the powers of making, administering, and executing the laws, they showed equal intolerance in this country with their Presbyterian brethren, who had emigrated to the northern government. The poor Quakers were flying from persecution in England.

They cast their eyes on these new countries as asylums of civil and religious freedom; but they found them free only for the reigning sect. Several acts of the Virginia assembly of 1659, 1662, and 1693, had made it penal in parents to refuse to have their children baptized; had prohibited the unlawful assembling of Quakers; had made it penal for any master of a vessel to bring a Quaker into the State; had ordered those already here, and such as should come thereafter, to be imprisoned till they should abjure the country; provided a milder punishment for their first and second return, but death for their third; had inhibited all persons from suffering their meetings in or near their houses, entertaining them individually, or disposing of books which supported their tenets. If no execution took place here, as did in New England, it was not owing to the moderation of the church, or spirit of the legislature, as may be inferred from the law itself; but to historical circumstances which have not been handed down to us. The Anglicans retained full possession of the country about a century. Other opinions began then to creep in, and the great care of the government to support their own church, having begotten an equal degree of indolence in its clergy, two-thirds of the people had become dissenters at the commencement of the present revolution. The laws, indeed, were still oppressive on them, but the spirit of the one party had subsided into moderation, and of the other had risen to a degree of determination which commanded respect.

The present state of our laws on the subject of religion is this. The convention of May, 1776, in their declaration of rights, declared it to be a truth, and a natural right, that the exercise of religion should be free; but when they proceeded to form on that declaration the ordinance of government, instead of taking up every principle declared in the bill of rights, and guarding it by legislative sanction, they passed over that which asserted our religious rights, leaving them as they found them. The same convention, however, when they met as a member of the general assembly in October, 1776, repealed all *acts of Parliament* which had rendered criminal the maintaining any opinions in matters of religion, the forbearing to repair to church, and the exercising any mode of worship; and suspended the laws giving salaries to the clergy, which suspension was made perpetual in October, 1779.

Statutory oppressions in religion being thus wiped away,

we remain at present under those only imposed by the common law, or by our own acts of assembly. At the common law, *heresy* was a capital offence, punishable by burning. Its definition was left to the ecclesiastical judges, before whom the conviction was, till the statute of the I. El. c. I circumscribed it, by declaring, that nothing should be deemed heresy, but what had been so determined by authority of the canonical scriptures, or by one of the four first general councils, or by other council, having for the grounds of their declaration the express and plain words of the scriptures. Heresy, thus circumscribed, being an offence against the common law, our act of assembly of October 1777, c. 17, gives cognizance of it to the general court, by declaring that the jurisdiction of that court shall be general in all matters at the common law. The execution is by the writ *De haeretico comburendo*. By our own act of assembly of 1705, c. 30, if a person brought up in the Christian religion denies the being of a God, or the Trinity, or asserts there are more gods than one, or denies the Christian religion to be true, or the scriptures to be of divine authority, he is punishable on the first offence by incapacity to hold any office or employment ecclesiastical, civil, or military; on the second by disability to sue, to take any gift or legacy, to be guardian, executor, or administrator, and by three years imprisonment without bail. A father's right to the custody of his own children being founded in law on his right of guardianship, this being taken away, they may of course be severed from him, and put by the authority of a court into more orthodox hands. This is a summary view of that religious slavery under which a people have been willing to remain, who have lavished their lives and fortunes for the establishment of their civil freedom. The error seems not sufficiently eradicated, that the operations of the mind, as well as the acts of the body, are subject to the coercion of the laws. But our rulers can have no authority over such natural rights, only as we have submitted to them. The rights of conscience we never submitted, we could not submit. We are answerable for them to our God. The legitimate powers of government extend to such acts only as are injurious to others. But it does me no injury for my neighbor to say there are twenty gods, or no God. It neither picks my pocket nor breaks my leg. If it be said, his testimony in a court of justice cannot be relied on, reject it then, and be the stigma on him. Constraint may make him worse by making him a hypocrite, but it will never make him a truer man. It may fix him obstinately in his errors, but will not cure them.

Reason and free inquiry are the only effectual agents against error. Give a loose to them, they will support the true religion by bringing every false one to their tribunal, to the test of their investigation. They are the natural enemies of error, and of error only. Had not the Roman government permitted free inquiry, Christianity could never have been introduced. Had not free inquiry been indulged at the era of the Reformation, the corruptions of Christianity could not have been purged away. If it be restrained now, the present corruptions will be protected, and new ones encouraged. Was the government to prescribe to us our medicine and diet, our bodies would be in such keeping as our souls are now. Thus in France the emetic was once forbidden as a medicine, the potato as an article of food. Government is just as infallible, too, when it fixes systems in physics. Galileo was sent to the Inquisition for affirming that the earth was a sphere; the government had declared it to be as flat as a trencher, and Galileo was obliged to abjure his error. This error, however, at length prevailed, the earth became a globe, and Descartes declared it was whirled round its axis by a vortex. The government in which he lived was wise enough to see that this was no question of civil jurisdiction, or we should all have been involved by authority in vortices. In fact, the vortices have been exploded, and the Newtonian principle of gravitation is now more firmly established, on the basis of reason, than it would be were the government to step in, and to make it an article of necessary faith. Reason and experiment have been indulged, and error has fled before them. It is error alone which needs the support of government. Truth can stand by itself. Subject opinion to coercion: whom will you make your inquisitors? Fallible men; men governed by bad passions, by private as well as public reasons. And why subject it to coercion? To produce uniformity.

But is uniformity of opinion desirable? No more than of face and stature. Introduce the bed of Procrustes then, and as there is danger that the large men may beat the small, make us all of a size, by lopping the former and stretching the latter. Difference of opinion is advantageous in religion. The several sects perform the office of a *censor morum* over such other. Is uniformity attainable? Millions of innocent men, women, and children, since the introduction of Christianity, have been burnt, tortured, fined, imprisoned; yet we have not advanced one inch towards uniformity. What has been the effect of coercion? To make one half the world fools, and the other half hypocrites. To support roguery and error all over the earth. Let us reflect that it is inhabited by a thousand millions of people. That these profess probably a thousand different systems of religion. That ours is but one of that thousand. That if there be but one right, and ours that one, we should wish to see the nine hundred and ninety-nine wandering sects gathered into the fold of truth. But against such a majority we cannot effect this by force. Reason and persuasion are the only practicable instruments. To make way for these, free inquiry must be indulged; and how can we wish others to indulge it while we refuse it ourselves?

But every State, says an inquisitor, has established some religion. No two, say I, have established the same. Is this a proof of the infallibility of establishments? Our sister States of Pennsylvania and New York, however, have long subsisted without any establishment at all. The experiment was new and doubtful when they made it. It has answered beyond conception. They flourish infinitely. Religion is well supported; of various kinds, indeed, but all good enough; all sufficient to preserve peace and order; or if a sect arises, whose tenets would subvert morals, good sense has fair play, and reasons and laughs it out of doors, without suffering the State to be troubled with it. They do not hang more malefactors than we do. They are not more disturbed with religious dissensions. On the contrary, their harmony is unparalleled, and can be ascribed to nothing but their unbounded tolerance, because there is no other circumstance in which they differ from every nation on earth. They have made the happy discovery, that the way to silence religious disputes, is to take no notice of them. Let us too give this experiment fair play, and get rid, while we may, of those tyrannical laws. It is true, we are as yet secured against them by the spirit of the times. I doubt whether the people of this country would suffer an execution for heresy, or a three years' imprisonment for not comprehending the mysteries of the Trinity. But is the spirit of the people an infallible, a permanent reliance? Is it government? Is this the kind of protection we receive in return for the rights we give up? Besides, the spirit of the times may alter, will alter. Our rulers will become corrupt, our people careless. A single zealot may commence persecutor, and better men be his victims. It can never be too often repeated, that the time for fixing every essential right on a legal basis is while our rulers are honest, and ourselves united. From the conclusion of this war we shall be going down hill. It will not then be necessary to resort every moment to the people for support. They will be forgotten, therefore, and their rights disregarded. They will forget themselves, but in the sole faculty of making money, and will never think of uniting to effect a due respect for their rights. The shackles, therefore, which shall not be knocked off at the conclusion of this war, will remain on us long, will be made heavier and heavier, till our rights shall revive or expire in a convulsion.

QUERY XVIII

The particular customs and manners that may happen to be received in that State?

It is difficult to determine on the standard by which the manners of a nation may be tried, whether *catholic* or *particular*. It is more difficult for a native to bring to that standard the manners of his own nation, familiarized to him by habit. There must doubtless be an unhappy influence on the manners of our people produced by the existence of slavery among us. The whole commerce between master and slave is a perpetual exercise of the most boisterous passions, the most unremitting despotism on the one part, and degrading submissions on the other. Our children see this, and learn to imitate it; for man is an imitative animal. This quality is the germ of all education in him. From his cradle to his grave he is learning to do what he sees others do. If a parent could find no motive either in his philanthropy or his self-love, for restraining the intemperance of passion towards his slave, it should always be a sufficient one that his child is present. But generally it is not sufficient. The parent storms, the child looks on, catches the lineaments of wrath, puts on the same airs in the circle of smaller slaves, gives a loose to the worst of passions, and thus nursed, educated, and daily exercised in tyranny, cannot but be stamped by it with odious peculiarities.

The man must be a prodigy who can retain his manners and morals undepraved by such circumstances. And with what execration should the statesman be loaded, who, permitting one half the citizens thus to trample on the rights of the other, transforms those into despots, and these into enemies, destroys the morals of the one part, and the *amor patriae* of the other. For if a slave can have a country in this world, it must be any other in preference to that in which he is born to live and labor for another; in which he must lock up the faculties of his nature, contribute as far as depends on his individual endeavors to the evanishment of the human race, or entail his own miserable condition on the endless generations proceeding from him. With the morals of the people, their industry also is destroyed. For in a warm climate, no man will labor for himself who can make another labor for him. This is so true, that of the proprietors of slaves a very small proportion indeed are ever seen to labor. And can the liberties of a nation be thought secure when we have removed their only firm basis, a conviction in the minds of the people that these liberties are of the gift of God? That they are not to be violated but with His wrath? Indeed I tremble for my country when I reflect that God is just; that his justice cannot sleep forever; that considering numbers, nature and natural means only, a revolution of the wheel of fortune, an exchange of situation is among possible events; that it may become probably by supernatural interference! The Almighty has no attribute which can take side with us in such a contest. But it is impossible to be temperate and to pursue this subject through the various considerations of policy, of morals, of history natural and civil. We must be contented to hope they will force their way into every one's mind. I think a change already perceptible, since the origin of the present revolution. The spirit of the master is abating, that of the slave rising from the dust, his condition mollifying, the way I hope preparing, under the auspices of heaven, for a total emancipation, and that this is disposed, in the order of events, to be with the consent of the masters, rather than by their extirpation.

QUERY XIX

The present state of manufactures, commerce, interior and exterior trade?

We never had an interior trade of any importance. Our exterior commerce has suffered very much from the beginning of the present contest. During this time we have manufactured within our families the most necessary articles of clothing. Those of cotton will bear some comparison with the same kinds of manufacture in Europe; but those of wool, flax and hemp are very coarse, unsightly, and unpleasant; and such is our attachment to agriculture, and such our preference for foreign manufactures, that be it wise or unwise, our people will certainly return as soon as they can, to the raising raw materials, and exchanging them for finer manufactures than they are able to execute themselves.

The political economists of Europe have established it as a principle, that every State should endeavor to manufacture for itself; and this principle, like many others, we transfer to America, without calculating the difference of circumstance which should often produce a difference of result. In Europe the lands are either cultivated, or locked up against the cultivator. Manufacture must therefore be resorted to of necessity not of choice, to support the surplus of their people. But we have an immensity of land courting the industry of the husbandman. Is it best then that all our citizens should be employed in its improvement, or that one half should be called off from that to exercise manufactures and handicraft arts for the other? Those who labor in the earth are the chosen people of God, if ever He had a chosen people, whose breasts He has made His peculiar deposit for substantial and genuine virtue. It is the focus in which he keeps alive that sacred fire, which otherwise might escape from the face of the earth. Corruption of morals in the mass of cultivators is a phenomenon of which no age nor nation has furnished an example. It is the mark set on those, who, not looking up to heaven, to their own soil and industry, as does the husbandman, for their subsistence, depend for it on casualties and caprice of customers.

Dependence begets subservience and venality, suffocates the germ of virtue, and prepares fit tools for the designs of ambition. This, the natural progress and consequence of the arts, has sometimes perhaps been retarded by accidental circumstances; but, generally speaking, the proportion which the aggregate of the other classes of citizens bears in any State to that of its husbandmen, is the proportion of its unsound to its healthy parts, and is a good enough barometer whereby to measure its degree of corruption. While we have land to labor then, let us never wish to see our citizens occupied at a workbench, or twirling a distaff. Carpenters, masons, smiths, are wanting in husbandry; but, for the general operations of manufacture, let our workshops remain in Europe. It is better to carry provisions and materials to workmen there, than bring them to the provisions and materials, and with them their manners and principles. The loss by the transportation of commodities across the Atlantic will be made up in happiness and permanence of government. The mobs of great cities add just so much to the support of pure government, as sores do to the strength of the human body. It is the manners and spirit of a people which preserve a republic in vigor. A degeneracy in these is a canker which soon eats to the heart of its laws and constitution. . . .

PART V

DELEGATE AND MINISTER: 1783—1789

Introduction

SEVERAL MONTHS after his wife died, Jefferson consented to return to public life. His duties proved to be especially congenial to him. First as commissioner in France, then as minister replacing Franklin, he was able to participate in public affairs while pursuing his private interests without restriction. He indulged in philosophy, science, travel, even love, in the five years he spent abroad. His observations on the corruption of French political life hardened his radical convictions. The imminence of a new revolution caught him up in its fervor. For Jefferson, the fates of the French Revolution and of American republicanism were inseparably joined. Nothing less than human progress hung in the balance.

Before embarking for France, Jefferson spent six months as a member of the post-war Continental Congress. Impotent as that Congress was, it dealt successfully with one important matter in which Jefferson again—and for the last time—acted as a legislator. When Virginia finally ceded her territory to Congress, it fell to a committee headed by Jefferson to draw up a plan of government for it. The result was Jefferson's great Ordinance of 1784, with its liberal terms for entry into the Confederacy and its prohibition of slavery—principles incorporated into the Northwest Ordinance of 1787.

In France Jefferson, on the whole, accomplished little in his function as commissioner and minister. The efforts of Jefferson, John Adams and Franklin in 1784 to secure trade rights with European powers proved fruitless even with France. Later, Jefferson did sign some trade agreements with France. He found the whole idea of trying to promote the trade of manufactured goods personally and philosophically unpalatable. America, he emphasized, should, for moral as well as economic reasons, devote herself exclusively to agriculture.

Two political events of transcendant importance occupied his attention in France: the drawing up of a federal Constitution for the United States and the launching of the French Revolution. Jefferson conducted a stimulating correspondence with Madison on the new Constitution. He at once recognized its necessity and shortcomings. Its failure to include a bill of rights particularly distressed him. For the next thirty years Jefferson remained remarkably consistent in his attitude toward the Constitution and the power it granted the federal government.

Jefferson foresaw the coming of the French Revolution. How was it possible, he asked, for so rich and sophisticated a people to endure a form of government as abominable as theirs? When the crisis erupted in May 1789, Jefferson went so far as to offer advice to the King on how to cope with it. Jefferson's extensive report of events from May through August is shrewd and penetrating; it compares to the best written by other foreigners at the time. (Regrettably, our limited space does not permit us to present Jefferson's account of the Revolution; it deserves a book of its own.)

Jefferson utilized his personal time to excellent advantage. In his inner circle of French friends he counted, among other notables, Lafayette and Condorcet—both of whose ideals were so akin to his own. He continued his polite controversies with Buffon on American zoology, going to parlous expense to prove his contentions. He traveled much and recorded with the eye of an artist and scientist his impressions of France, England, Holland and Italy. His idyl with the talented Maria Cosway in the summer of 1786 aroused deep passions which he disclosed in a famous letter to her. But as the letter further disclosed, he did not allow himself to stray too far from the measured, rational tones of the enlightenment philosopher; he was no Benjamin Constant. Jefferson would always recall his years in France—years when he was free of politics, when he was free to read and converse and travel—as among the happiest of his life.

On An Equal Footing

The Western Territory, March 1784

For three years Congress had been expostulating with Virginia to cede her lands beyond the Ohio River on terms more favorable than she had been willing to grant. Finally, on March 1, 1784, Virginia laid before Congress her deed of cession. As chairman of the committee for planning a temporary government in the territories, Jefferson drew up the report of March 1. Congress, to Jefferson's pique, eliminated the clauses prohibiting the existence of slavery and the granting of hereditary titles. Congress did well, however, to do away with the names Jefferson suggested for the projected new states—an awkward amalgam of Indian and classical terms. The great Northwest Ordinance of 1787, which did prohibit slavery from its territory, derived from Jefferson's revised plan as adopted by Congress on April 23, 1784.

PLAN FOR THE TEMPORARY GOVERNMENT OF THE WESTERN TERRITORY

March 1, 1784

The Committee appointed to prepare a plan for the temporary government of the Western Territory, have agreed to the following resolutions:

Resolved, That the territory ceded or to be ceded by individual States to the United States, whensoever the same shall have been purchased of the Indian inhabitants, and offered for sale by the United States, shall be formed into distinct States, bounded in the following manner, as nearly as such cessions will admit—that is to say: northwardly and southwardly by parallels of latitude, so that each State shall comprehend, from south to north, two degrees of latitude, beginning to count from the completion of thirty-one degrees north of the equator; but any territory northwardly of the forty-seventh degree shall make part of the State next below; and eastwardly and westwardly they shall be bounded, those on the Mississippi by that river on one side, and the meridian of the lowest point of the rapids of Ohio on the other; and those adjoining on the east by the same meridian on their western side, and on their eastern by the meridian of the western cape of the mouth of the Great Kanawha and the territory eastward of this last meridian, between the Ohio, Lake Erie, and Pennsylvania, shall be one State.

That the settlers within the territory so to be purchased and offered for sale, shall, either on their own petition, or on the order of Congress, receive authority from them, with appointments of time and place for their free males, of full age, to meet together for the purpose of establishing a temporary government, to adopt the constitution and laws of any one of these States, so that such laws nevertheless shall be subject to alteration by their ordinary legislature; and to erect, subject to a like alteration, counties or townships for the election of members for their legislature.

That such temporary government shall only continue in force in any State until it shall have acquired twenty thousand free inhabitants; when, giving due proof thereof to Congress, they shall receive from them authority, with appointments of time and place, to call a convention of representatives to establish a permanent constitution and government for themselves.

Provided, That both the temporary and permanent governments be established on these principles as their basis: 1. That they shall forever remain a part of the United States of America. 2. That, in their persons, property, and territory, they shall be subject to the Government of the United States in Congress assembled, and to the Articles of Confederation in all those cases in which the original States shall be so subject. 3. That they shall be subject to pay a part of the federal debts contracted or to be contracted, to be apportioned on them by Congress according to the same common rule and measure by which apportionments thereof shall be made on the other States. 4. That their respective governments shall be in republican forms, and shall admit no person to be a citizen who holds any hereditary title. 5. That after the year 1800 of the Christian era there shall be neither slavery nor involuntary servitude in any of the said States, otherwise than in punishment of crimes, whereof the party shall have been duly convicted to have been personally guilty.

That whensoever any of the said States shall have, of free inhabitants, as many as shall then be in any one of the least numerous of the thirteen original States, such State shall be admitted by its delegates into the Congress of the United States on an equal footing with the said original States; after which the assent of two-thirds of the United States in Congress assembled shall be requisite in all those cases wherein, by the Confederation, the assent of nine States is now required: Provided, The consent of nine States to such admission may be obtained according to the eleventh of the Articles of Confederation. Until such admission by their delegates into Congress, any of the said States, after the establishment of their temporary government, shall have authority to keep a sitting member in Congress, with right of debating but not of voting.

That the territory northward of the forty-fifth degree, that is to say, of the completion of forty-five degrees from the equator, and extending to the Lake of the Woods, shall be called SYLVANIA.

That of the territory under the forty-fifth and forty-fourth degrees, that which lies westward of Lake Michigan, shall be called MICHIGANIA; and that which is eastward thereof, within the peninsula formed by the lakes and waters of Michigan, Huron, St. Clair, and Erie, shall be called CHERRONESUS, and shall include any part of the peninsula which may extend above the forty-fifth degree.

Of the territory under the forty-third and forty-second degrees, that to the westward, through which the Assenisipi or Rock River runs, shall be called ASSENISIPIA; and that to the eastward, in which are the fountains of the Muskingum, the two Miamies of the Ohio, the Wabash, the Illinois, the Miami of the Lake, and Sandusky rivers, shall be called METROPOTAMIA.

Of the territory which lies under the forty-first and fortieth degrees, the western, through which the river Illinois runs, shall be called ILLINOIA; that next adjoining to the eastward, SARATOGA; and that between this last and Pennsylvania, and extending from the Ohio to Lake Erie, shall be called WASHINGTON.

Of the territory which lies under the thirty-ninth and thirty-eighth degrees, to which shall be added so much of the point of land within the fork of the Ohio and Mississippi as lies under the thirty-seventh degree, that to the westward, within and adjacent to which are the confluences of the rivers Wabash, Shawanee, Tanissee, Ohio, Illinois, Mississippi, and Missouri, shall be called POLYPOTAMIA; and that to the eastward further up the Ohio, otherwise called the Pelisipi, shall be called PELISIPIA.

That the preceding articles shall be formed into a charter of compact, shall be duly executed by the President of the United States in Congress assembled, under his hand and the seal of the United States, shall be promulgated, and shall stand as fundamental constitutions between the thirteen original States and those newly described, unalterable but by the joint consent of the United States in Congress assembled, and of the particular State within which such alteration is proposed to be made.

GOVERNMENT FOR THE WESTERN TERRITORY

March 22, 1784

The Committee to whom was recommitted the report of a plan for a temporary government of the Western territory have agreed to the following resolutions.

Resolved, that so much of the territory ceded or to be ceded by individual states to the United States as is already purchased or shall be purchased of the Indian inhabitants and offered for sale by Congress, shall be divided into distinct states, in the following manner, as nearly as such cessions will admit; that is to say, by parallels of latitude, so that each state shall comprehend from South to North two degrees of latitude beginning to count from the completion of thirty-one degrees North of the Equator; and by meridians of longitude, one of which shall pass through the lowest point of the rapids of Ohio, and the other through the Western Cape of the mouth of the Great Kanhaway, but the territory Eastward of this last meridian, between the Ohio, Lake Erie, and Pennsylvania shall be one state, whatsoever may be its comprehension of latitude. That which may lie beyond the completion of the 45th degree between the said meridians shall make part of the state adjoining it on the South, and that part of the Ohio which is between the same meridians coinciding nearly with the parallel of 39° shall be substituted so far in lieu of that parallel as a boundary line.

That the settlers on any territory so purchased and offered for sale shall, either on their own petition, or on the order of Congress, receive authority from them with appointments of time and place for their free males of full age, within the limits of their state to meet together for the purpose of establishing a temporary government, to adopt the constitution and laws of any one of the original states, so that such laws nevertheless shall be subject to alteration by their ordinary legislature; and to erect, subject to a like alteration, counties or townships for the election of members for their legislature.

That such temporary government shall only continue in force in any state until it shall have acquired 20,000 free inhabitants, when giving due proof thereof to Congress, they shall receive from them authority with appointment of time and place to call a convention of representatives to establish a permanent Constitution and Government for themselves. Provided that both the temporary and permanent governments be established on these principles as their basis. 1. That they shall forever remain a part of this confederacy of the United States of America. 2. That in their persons, property and territory they shall be subject to the Government of the United States in Congress assembled, and to the articles of Confederation in all those cases in which the original states shall be so subject. 3. That they shall be subject to pay a part of the federal debts contracted or to be contracted, to be apportioned on them by Congress, according to the same common rule and measure, by which apportionments thereof shall be made on the other states. 4. That their respective Governments shall be in republican forms and shall admit no person to be a citizen who holds any hereditary title. 5. That after the year 1800 of the Christian era, there shall be neither slavery nor involuntary servitude in any of the said states, otherwise than in punishment of crimes whereof the party shall have been convicted to have been personally guilty.

That whensoever any of the said states shall have, of free inhabitants, as many as shall then be in any one the least numerous, of the thirteen original states, such state shall be admitted by its delegates into the Congress of the United States on an equal footing with the said original states: provided nine States agree to such admission according to the reservation of the 11th of the articles of Confederation, and in order to adopt the said articles of Confederation to the state of Congress when its numbers shall be thus increased, it shall be proposed to the legislatures of the states originally parties thereto, to require the assent of two thirds of the United States in Congress assembled in all those cases wherein by the said articles the assent of nine states is now required;

which being agreed to by them shall be binding on the new states. Until such admission by their delegates into Congress, any of the said states after the establishment of their temporary government shall have authority to keep a sitting member in Congress, with a right of debating, but not of voting.

That the preceding articles shall be formed into a charter of compact, shall be duly executed by the president of the United States in Congress assembled, under his hand and the seal of the United States, shall be promulgated and shall stand as fundamental constitutions between the thirteen original states and each of the several states now newly described, unalterable but by the joint consent of the United States in Congress assembled, and of the particular state within which such alteration is proposed to be made.

That measures not inconsistent with the principles of the Confederation and necessary for the preservation of peace and good order among the settlers in any of the said new states until they shall assume a temporary Government as aforesaid, may from time to time be taken by the United States in Congress assembled.

The Most Easy Ratio Is by Ten

Notes on the Establishment of a Money Unit, and of a Coinage for the United States, April 1784

Robert Morris, "Financier" of the Confederation, had delivered a report to Congress designed to rationalize the inchoate monetary system in America. Morris had proposed adoption of a monetary unit ultimately reducible to 1/1440. While Morris' proposals on the whole "were sound," according to Jefferson, the unit he proposed "was too minute for ordinary use, too laborious for computation, either by the head or in figures." Before a committee called to act on Morris' report, Jefferson laid the following "Notes" which provided the basis for establishing the dollar as the monetary unit of the United States.

In fixing the Unit of Money, these circumstances are of principal importance.

I. That it be of *convenient size* to be applied as a measure to the common money transactions of life.

II. That its parts and multiples be in an *easy proportion* to each other, so as to facilitate the money arithmetic.

III. That the Unit and its parts, or divisions, *be so nearly of the value of some of the known coins,* as that they may be of easy adoption for the people.

The Spanish Dollar seems to fulfil all these conditions.

I. Taking into our view all money transactions, great and small, I question if a common measure of more *convenient size* than the Dollar could be proposed. The value of 100, 1000, 10,000 dollars is well estimated by the mind; so is that of the tenth or the hundredth of a dollar. Few transactions are above or below these limits. The expediency of attending to the size of the money Unit will be evident, to anyone who will consider how inconvenient it would be to a manufacturer or merchant, if, instead of the yard for measuring cloth, either the inch or the mile had been made the Unit of Measure.

II. The most *easy ratio* of multiplication and division, is that by ten. Everyone knows the facility of Decimal Arithmetic. Everyone remembers, that, when learning Money-Arithmetic, he used to be puzzled with adding the farthings, taking out the fours and carrying them on; adding the pence, taking out the twelves and carrying them on; adding the shillings, taking out the twenties and carrying them on; but when he came to the pounds, where he had only tens to carry forward, it was easy and free from error. The bulk of mankind are school-boys through life. These little perplexities are always great to them. And even mathematical heads feel the relief of an easier, substituted for a more difficult process. Foreigners, too, who trade and travel among us will find a great facility in understanding our coins and accounts from this ratio of subdivision. Those who have had occasion to convert the livres, sols, and deniers of the French; the gilders, stivers, and frenings of the Dutch; the pounds, shillings, pence, and farthings of these several States, into each other, can judge how much they would have been aided, had their several subdivisions been in a decimal ratio. Certainly, in all cases, where we are free to choose between easy and difficult modes of operation, it is most rational to choose the easy. The Financier, therefore, in his report, well proposes that our Coins should be in decimal proportions to one another. If we adopt the Dollar for our Unit, we should strike four coins, one of gold, two of silver, and one of copper, *viz.:*

1. A golden piece, equal in value to ten dollars:
2. The Unit or Dollar itself, of silver:
3. The tenth of a Dollar, of silver also:
4. The hundreth of a Dollar, of copper. . . .

III. The third condition required is, that the Unit, its multiples, and subdivisions, coincide in value with some of the known coins so nearly, that the people may, by a quick reference in the mind, estimate their value. If this be not attended to, they will be very long in adopting the innovation, if ever they adopt it. . . .

That this subject may be properly prepared, and in readiness for Congress to take up at their meeting in November, something must now be done. The present session drawing to a close, they probably would not choose to enter far into this undertaking themselves. The Committee of the States, however, during the recess, will have time to digest it thoroughly, if Congress will fix some general principles for their government. Suppose they be instructed,

To appoint proper persons to assay and examine, with the

utmost accuracy practicable, the Spanish milled dollars of different dates, in circulation with us.

To assay and examine, in like manner, the fineness of all the other coins which may be found in circulation within these States.

To report to the Committee the result of these assays, by them to be laid before Congress.

To appoint, also, proper persons to enquire what are the proportions between the values of fine gold, and fine silver, at the markets of the several countries with which we are, or probably may be, connected in commerce; and what would be a proper proportion here, having regard to the average of their values at those markets, and to other circumstances, and to report the same to the Committee, by them to be laid before Congress.

To prepare an Ordinance for esablishing the Unit of Money within these States; for subdividing it; and for striking coins of gold, silver, and copper, on the following principles:

That the Money Unit of these States shall be equal in value to a Spanish milled dollar containing so much fine silver as the assay, before directed, shall show to be contained, on an average, in dollars of the several dates in circulation with us.

That this Unit shall be divided into tenths and hundredths; that there shall be a coin of silver of the value of a Unit; one other of the same metal, of the value of one-tenth of a Unit; one other of copper, of the value of the hundredth of a Unit.

That there shall be a coin of gold of the value of ten Units, according to the report before directed, and the judgment of the Committee thereon.

That the alloy of the said coins of gold and silver, shall be equal in weight to one-eleventh part of the fine metal.

That there be proper devices for these coins.

That measures be proposed for preventing their diminution, and also their currency, and that of any others, when diminished.

That the several foreign coins be described and classed in the said Ordinance, the fineness of each class stated, and its value by weight estimated in Units and decimal parts of Units.

And that the said draught of an Ordinance be reported to Congress at their next meeting, for their consideration and determination.

Encourage All Your Virtuous Dispositions

To Peter Carr, August 19, 1785

Jefferson's concern for public education was matched by his concern for the education of young friends and relatives. Peter Carr was his nephew, the son of Dabney and Martha Jefferson Carr. For young men who, like Carr, were expected to enter "the public stage," Jefferson laid down a severe regimen for building character and intellect. Often Jefferson's counsel had more than a touch of sententiousness. Whether the counsel was followed is not known.

. . . I am much mortified to hear that you have lost so much time; and that, when you arrived in Williamsburg, you were not at all advanced from what you were when you left Monticello. Time now begins to be precious to you. Every day you lose will retard a day your entrance on that public stage whereon you may begin to be useful to yourself. However, the way to repair the loss is to improve the future time. I trust, that with your dispositions, even the acquisition of science is a pleasing employment. I can assure you, that the possession of it is, what (next to an honest heart) will above all things render you dear to your friends, and give you fame and promotion in your own country. When your mind shall be well improved with science, nothing will be necessary to place you in the highest points of view, but to pursue the interests of your country, the interests of your friends, and your own interests also, with the purest integrity, the most chaste honor. The defect of these virtues can never be made up by all the other acquirements of body and mind.

Make these, then, your first object. Give up money, give up fame, give up science, give up the earth itself and all it contains, rather than do an immoral act. And never suppose, that in any possible situation, or under any circumstances, it is best for you to do a dishonorable thing, however slightly so it may appear to you. Whenever you are to do a thing, though it can never be known but to yourself, ask yourself how you would act were all the world looking at you, and act accordingly. Encourage all your virtuous dispositions, and exercise them whenever an opportunity arises; being assured that they will gain strength by exercise, as a limb of the body does, and that exercise will make them habitual. From the practice of the purest virtue, you may be assured you will derive the most sublime comforts in every moment of life, and in the moment of death. If ever you find yourself environed with difficulties and perplexing circumstances, out of which you are at a loss how to extricate yourself, do what is right, and be assured that that will extricate you the best out of the worst situations. Though you cannot see, when you take one step, what will be the next, yet follow truth, justice, and plain dealing, and never fear their leading you out of the labyrinth, in the easiest manner possible. The knot which you thought a Gordian one, will untie itself before you.

Nothing is so mistaken as the supposition, that a person is to extricate himself from a difficulty, by intrigue, by chicanery, by dissimulation, by trimming, by an untruth, by an injustice. This increases the difficulties tenfold; and those, who pursue these methods, get themselves so involved at length, that they can turn no way but their infamy becomes more exposed. It is of great importance to set a resolution, not to be shaken, never to tell an untruth. There is no vice so mean, so pitiful, so contemptible; and he who permits himself to tell a lie once, finds it much easier to do it a second and third time, till at length it becomes habitual; he tells lies without attending to it, and truths without the world's believing him. This falsehood of the tongue leads to that of the heart, and in time depraves all its good dispositions.

An honest heart being the first blessing, a knowing head is the second. It is time for you now to begin to be choice in your reading; to begin to pursue a regular course in it; and not to suffer yourself to be turned to the right or left by reading anything out of that course. I have long ago digested a plan for you, suited to the circumstances in which you will be placed. This I will detail to you, from time to time, as you advance. For the present, I advise you to begin a course of ancient history, reading everything in the original and not in translations. First read Goldsmith's history of Greece. This will give you a digested view of that field. Then take up ancient history in the detail, reading the following books, in the following order: Herodotus, Thucydides, Xenophontis Anabasis, Arrian, Quintus, Curtius, Diodorus Siculus, Justin. This shall form the first stage of your historical reading, and is all I need mention to you now. The next will be of Roman history.[1] From that, we will come down to modern history. In Greek and Latin poetry, you have read or will read at school, Virgil, Terence, Horace, Anacreon, Theocritus, Homer, Euripides, Sophocles. Read also Milton's "Paradise Lost," Shakespeare, Ossian, Pope's and Swift's works, in order to form your style in your own language. In morality, read Epictetus, Xenophontis Memorabilia, Plato's Socratic dialogues, Cicero's philosophies, Antoninus, and Seneca. In order to assure a certain progress in this reading, consider what hours you have free from the school and the exercises of the school. Give about two of them, every day, to exercise; for health must not be sacrificed to learning. A strong body makes the mind strong. As to the species of exercise, I advise the gun. While this gives a moderate exercise to the body, it gives boldness, enterprise, and independence to the mind. Games played with the ball, and others of that nature, are too violent for the body, and stamp no character on the mind. Let your gun, therefore, be the constant companion of your walks. Never think of taking a book with you. The object of walking is to relax the mind. You should therefore not permit yourself even to think while you walk; but divert yourself by the objects surrounding you. Walking is the best possible exercise. Habituate yourself to walk very far. The Europeans value themselves on having subdued the horse to the uses of man; but I doubt whether we have not lost more than we have gained, by the use of this animal. No one has occasioned so much the degeneracy of the human body. An Indian goes on foot nearly as far in a day, for a long journey, as an enfeebled white does on his horse; and he will tire the best horses. There is no habit you will value so much as that of walking far without fatigue. I would advise you to take your exercise in the afternoon: not because it is the best time for exercise, for certainly it is not; but because it is the best time to spare from your studies; and habit will soon reconcile it to health, and render it nearly as useful as if you gave to that the more precious hours of the day.

A little walk of half an hour, in the morning, when you first rise, is advisable also. It shakes off sleep, and produces other good effects in the animal economy. Rise at a fixed and an early hour, and go to bed at a fixed and early hour also.

[1] Livy, Sallust, Caesar, Cicero's epistles, Suetonius, Tacitus, Gibbon [Jefferson].

Sitting up late at night is injurious to the health, and not useful to the mind. Having ascribed proper hours to exercise, divide what remain (I mean of your vacant hours) into three portions. Give the principal to History, the other two, which should be shorter, to Philosophy and Poetry. Write to me once every month or two, and let me know the progress you make. Tell me in what manner you employ every hour in the day. The plan I have proposed for you is adapted to your present situation only. When that is changed, I shall propose a corresponding change of plan. I have ordered the following books to be sent to you from London, to the care of Mr. Madison: Herodotus, Thucydides, Xenophon's Hellenics, Anabasis and Memorabilia, Cicero's works, Baretti's Spanish and English Dictionary, Martin's Philosophical Grammar, and Martin's Philosophia Britannica. I will send you the following from hence: Bezout's Mathematics, De la Lande's Astronomy, Muschenbrock's Physics, Quintus Curtius, Justin, a Spanish Grammar, and some Spanish books. You will observe that Martin, Bezout, De la Lande, and Muschenbrock, are not in the preceding plan. They are not to be opened till you go to the University. You are now, I expect, learning French. You must push this; because the books which will be put into your hands when you advance into Mathematics, Natural philosophy, Natural history, &c., will be mostly French, these sciences being better treated by the French than the English writers. Our future connection with Spain renders that the most necessary of the modern languages, after the French. When you become a public man, you may have occasion for it, and the circumstance of your possessing that language, may give you a preference over other candidates. I have nothing further to add for the present, but husband well your time, cherish your instructors, strive to make everybody your friend; and be assured that nothing will be so pleasing as your success to, Dear Peter, Yours affectionately.

The Most Valuable Citizens

To John Jay, August 23, 1785

As ambassador, Jefferson attempted to secure concrete trade agreements with France. Like his predecessor Franklin, he was unsuccessful. What he thought of his task is recorded in this letter to John Jay, Secretary of State.

I shall sometimes ask your permission to write you letters, not official but private. The present is of this kind, and is occasioned by the question proposed in yours of June 14 'Whether it would be useful to us to carry all our own productions, or none?' Were we perfectly free to decide this question, I should reason as follows. We have now lands enough to employ an infinite number of people in their cultivation. Cultivators of the earth are the most valuable citizens. They are the most vigorous, the most independant, the most virtuous, and they are tied to their country and wedded to it's liberty and interests by the most lasting bands. As long therefore as they can find emploiment in this line, I would not convert them into mariners, artisans, or any thing else. But our citizens will find emploiment in this line till their numbers, and of course their productions, become too great for the demand both internal and foreign. This is not the case as yet, and probably will not be for a considerable time. As soon as it is, the surplus of hands must be turned to something else. I should then perhaps wish to turn them to the sea in preference to manufactures, because comparing the characters of the two classes I find the former the most valuable citizens. I consider the class of artificers as the panders of vice and the instruments by which the liberties of a country are generally overturned. However we are not free to decide this question on principles of theory only. Our people are decided in the opinion that it is necessary for us to take a share in the occupation of the ocean, and their established habits induce them to require that the sea be kept open to them, and that that line of policy be pursued which will render the use of that element as great as possible to them. I think it a duty in those entrusted with the administration of their affairs to conform themselves to the decided choice of their constituents: and that therefore we should in every instance preserve an equality of right to them in the transportation of commodities, in the right of fishing, and in the other uses of the sea. But what will be the consequence? Frequent wars without a doubt. Their property will be violated on the sea, and in foreign ports, their persons will be insulted, emprisoned &c. for pretended debts, contracts, crimes, contraband &c. &c. These insults must be resented, even if we had no feelings, yet to prevent their eternal repetition. Or in other words, our commerce on the ocean and in other countries must be paid for by frequent war. The justest dispositions possible in ourselves will not secure us against it. It would be necessary that all other nations were just also. Justice indeed on our part will save us from those wars which would have been produced by a contrary disposition. But how to prevent those produced by the wrongs of other nations? By putting ourselves in a condition to punish them. Weakness provokes insult and injury, while a condition to punish it often prevents it. This reasoning leads to the necessity of some naval force, that being the only weapo[n] with which we can reach an enemy. I think it to our interest to punis[h] the first insult: because an insult unpunished is the parent of many oth[ers]. We are not at this moment in a condition to do it, but we should put ourselv[es] into it as soon as possible. If a war with England should take place it see[ms] to me that the first thing necessary would be a resolution to abandon the carrying trade because we cannot protect it. Foreign nations must in that case be invited to bring us what we want and to take our productions in their own bottoms. . . .

The Laboring People Began to Be Alarmed at This New Institution

The Society of Cincinnati, June 22, 1786

Information about America was as inaccurate as the desire for it was voracious. Jefferson sought where possible to correct the falsehoods, many of them originating in Britain. His most notable contribution to an understanding of America at this time—the Notes on Virginia *excepted—consisted of his corrections of Jean-Nicholas Démeunier's articles* on les Etats-Unis *for the* Encyclopédie Méthodique. *Démeunier had not done justice to the Society of Cincinnati. Jefferson, though he saw in the Society a demonstrable threat to American freedom and though his point of view was radical enough, presents a fair and balanced account. Démeunier used it in place of his own.*

. . . Page 240. *"Les Officiers Américains,"* &c., to page 264, *"qui le méritoient."*[1] I would propose to new model this section, in the following manner. 1. Give a succinct history of the origin and establishment of the Cincinnati. 2. Examine whether, in its present form, it threatens any dangers to the State. 3. Propose the most practicable method of preventing them.

Having been in America, during the period in which this institution was formed, and being then in a situation which gave me opportunities of seeing it, in all its stages, I may venture to give M. de Meusnier materials for the first branch of the preceding distribution of the subject. The second and third, he will best execute himself. I should write its history in the following form:

When, on the close of that war, which established the independence of America, its army was about to be disbanded, the officers, who, during the course of it, had gone through the most trying scenes together, who, by mutual aids and good offices, had become dear to one another, felt with great oppression of mind, the approach of that moment which was to

---

[1] "The American officers . . . who deserve it."

separate them, never, perhaps, to meet again. They were from different States, and from distant parts of the same State. Hazard alone could, therefore, give them but rare and partial occasions of seeing each other. They were, of course, to abandon altogether the hope of ever meeting again, or to devise some occasion which might bring them together. And why not come together on purpose, at stated times? Would not the trouble of such a journey be greatly overpaid, by the pleasure of seeing each other again, by the sweetest of all consolations, the talking over the scenes of difficulty and of endearment they had gone through? This, too, would enable them to know who of them should succeed in the world, who should be unsuccessful, and to open the purses of all to every laboring brother. This idea was too soothing, not to be cherished in conversation. It was improved into that of a regular association, with an organized administration, with periodical meetings, general and particular, fixed contributions for those who should be in distress, and a badge, by which, not only those who had not had occasion to become personally known, should be able to recognize one another, but which should be worn by their descendants, to perpetuate among them the friendships which had bound their ancestors together.

General Washington was, at that moment, oppressed with the operation of disbanding an army which was not paid, and the difficulty of this operation was increased, by some two or three States having expressed sentiments, which did not indicate a sufficient attention to their payment. He was sometimes present, when his officers were fashioning in their conversations, their newly proposed society. He saw, the innocence of its origin, and foresaw no effects less innocent. He was, at that time, writing his valedictory letter to the States, which has been so deservedly applauded by the world. Far from thinking it a moment to multiply the causes of irritation, by thwarting a proposition which had absolutely no other basis but that of benevolence and friendship, he was rather satisfied to find himself aided in his difficulties by this new incident, which occupied, and, at the same time, soothed the minds of the officers. He thought, too, that this institution would be one instrument the more for strengthening the federal bond, and for promoting federal ideas. The institution was formed. They incorporated into it the officers of the French army and navy, by whose sides they had fought, and with whose aid they had finally prevailed, extending it to such grades as they were told might be permitted to enter into it. They sent an officer to France, to make the proposition to them, and to procure the badges which they had devised for their order. The moment of disbanding the army having come, before they could have a full meeting to appoint their President, the General was prayed to act in that office till their first general meeting, which was to be held at Philadelphia, in the month of May following.

The laws of the society were published. Men who read them in their closets, unwarmed by those sentiments of friendship which had produced them, inattentive to those pains which an approaching separation had excited in the minds of the institutors, politicians, who see in everything only the dangers with which it threatens civil society, in fine, the laboring people, who, shielded by equal laws, had never seen any difference between man and man, but had read of terrible oppressions, which people of their description experience in other countries, from those who are distinguished by titles and badges, began to be alarmed at this new institution. A remarkable silence, however, was observed. Their solicitudes were long confined within the circles of private conversation. At length, however, a Mr. Burke, Chief Justice of South Carolina, broke that silence. He wrote against the new institution, foreboding its dangers, very imperfectly indeed, because he had nothing but his imagination to aid him. An American could do no more; for to detail the real evils of aristocracy, they must be seen in Europe. Burke's fears were thought exaggerations in America; while in Europe, it is known that even Mirabeau has but faintly sketched the curses of hereditary aristocracy as they are experienced here, and as they would have followed in America, had this institution remained. The epigraph of Burke's pamphlet, was, "Blow ye the trumpet in Zion." Its effect corresponded with its epigraph. This institution became, first, the subject of general conversation. Next, it was made the subject of deliberation in the legislative Assemblies of some of the States. The Governor of South Carolina censured it, in an address to the Assembly of that State. The Assemblies of Massachusetts, Rhode Island, and Pennsylvania, condemned its principles. No circumstance, indeed, brought the consideration of it expressly before Congress; yet it had sunk deep into their minds. An offer having been made to them, on the part of the Polish order of Divine Providence, to receive some of their distinguished citizens into that order, they made that an occasion to declare, that these distinctions were contrary to the principles of their Confederation.

The uneasiness excited by this institution, had very early caught the notice of General Washington. Still recollecting all the purity of the motives which gave it birth, he became sensible that it might produce political evils, which the warmth of those motives had masked. Add to this, that it was disapproved by the mass of citizens of the Union. This, alone, was reason strong enough, in a country where the will of the majority is the law, and ought to be the law. He saw that the objects of the institution were too light, to be opposed to considerations as serious as these; and that it was become necessary to annihilate it absolutely. On this, therefore, he was decided. The first annual meeting at Philadelphia was now at hand; he went to that, determined to exert all his influence for its suppression. He proposed it to his fellow officers, and urged it with all his powers. It met an opposition which was observed to cloud his face with an anxiety, that the most distressful scenes of the war had scarcely ever produced. It was canvassed for several days, and, at length, it was no more a doubt what would be its ultimate fate. The order was on the point of receiving its annihilation, by the vote of a great majority of its members. In this moment, their envoy arrived from France, charged with letters from the French officers, accepting with cordiality the proposed badges of union, with solicitations from others to be received into the order, and with notice that their respectable Sovereign had been pleased to recognize it, and permit his officers to wear its badges. The prospect now changed. The question assumed a new form. After the offer made by them, and accepted by their friends, in what words could they clothe a proposition to retract it, which would not cover themselves with the reproaches of levity and ingratitude? which would not appear an insult to those whom they loved? Federal principles, popular discontent, were considerations whose weight was known and felt by themselves. But would foreigners know and feel them equally? Would they so far acknowledge their cogency, as to permit without any indignation, the eagle and ribbon to be torn from their breasts, by the very hands which had placed them there? The idea revolted the whole society. They found it necessary, then, to preserve so much of their institution as might continue to support this foreign branch, while they should prune off every other, which would give offence to their fellow citizens: thus sacrificing, on each hand, to their friends and to their country.

The society was to retain its existence, its name, its meetings, and its charitable funds: but these last were to be deposited with their respective legislatures. The order was to be no longer hereditary, a reformation, which had been pressed even from this side of the Atlantic; it was to be communicated to no new members; the general meetings, instead of annual, were to be triennial only. The eagle and ribbon, indeed, were retained; because they were worn, and they wished them to be worn by their friends who were in a country where they would not be objects of offence; but themselves never wore them. They laid them up in their bureaus with the medals of American Independence, with those of the trophies they had taken, and the battles they had won. But through all the United States, no officer is seen to offend the public eye, with the display of this badge. These changes have tranquillized the American States. Their citizens feel too much interest in the reputation of their officers, and value too much, whatever may serve to recall to the memory of their allies, the moments wherein they formed but one people, not to do justice to the circumstance which prevented a total annihilation of the order. Though they are obliged by a prudent foresight to keep out everything from among themselves, which might pretend to divide them into orders, and to degrade one description of men below another, yet they hear with pleasure, that their allies, whom circumstances have already placed under these distinctions, are willing to consider it as one, to have aided them in the establishment of their liberties, and to wear a badge which may recall them to their remembrance; and it would be an extreme affliction to them, if the domestic reformation which has been found necessary, if the censures of individual writers, or if any other circumstance should discourage the wearing their badge or lessen its reputation.

This short but true history of the order of the Cincinnati, taken from the mouths of persons on the spot, who were privy to its origin and progress, and who knew its present state, is the best apology which can be made for an insinuation, which appeared to be, and was really, so heterogeneous to the governments in which it was erected.

It should be further considered, that in America no other

distinction between man and man had ever been known, but that of persons in office, exercising powers by authority of the laws, and private individuals. Among these last, the poorest laborer stood on equal ground with the wealthiest millionnaire, and generally on a more favored one, whenever their rights seemed to jar. It has been seen that a shoemaker or other artisan, removed by the voice of his country from his work bench into a chair of office, has instantly commanded all the respect and obedience which the laws ascribe to his office. But of distinction by birth or badge, they had no more idea than they had of the mode of existence in the moon or planets. They had heard only that there were such, and knew that they must be wrong. A due horror of the evils which flow from these distinctions, could be excited in Europe only, where the dignity of man is lost in arbitrary distinctions, where the human species is classed into several stages of degradation, where the many are crushed under the weight of the few, and where the order established, can present to the contemplation of a thinking being, no other picture than that of God Almighty and his angels, trampling under foot the host of the damned. No wonder, then, that the institution of the Cincinnati should be innocently conceived by one order of American citizens, should raise in the other orders, only a slow, temperate, and rational opposition, and should be viewed in Europe as a detestable parricide.

The second and third branches of this subject, no body can better execute than M. de Meusnier. Perhaps it may be curious to him to see how they strike an American mind at present. He shall, therefore, have the ideas of one who was an enemy to the institution from the first moment of its conception, but who was always sensible that the officers neither foresaw nor intended the injury they were doing to their country.

As to the question, then, whether any evil can proceed from the institution as it stands at present, I am of the opinion there may. 1. From the meetings. These will keep the officers formed into a body; will continue a distinction between the civil and military, which it would be for the good of the whole to obliterate, as soon as possible; and the military assemblies will not only keep alive the jealousies and fears of the civil government, but give ground for these fears and jealousies. For when men meet together, they will make business if they have none; they will collate their grievances, some real, some imaginary, all highly painted; they will communicate to each other the sparks of discontent; and these may engender a flame which will consume their particular, as well as the general happiness. 2. The charitable part of the institution is still more likely to do mischief, as it perpetuates the dangers apprehended in the preceding clause. For here is a fund provided of permanent existence. To whom will it belong? To the descendants of American officers of a certain description. These descendants, then, will form a body, having sufficient interest to keep up an attention to their description, to continue meetings, and perhaps, in some moment, when the political eye shall be slumbering, or the firmness of their fellow citizens relaxed, to replace the insignia of the order and revive all its pretensions. What good can the officers propose which may weigh against these possible evils? The securing their descendants against want? Why afraid to trust them to the same fertile soil, and the same genial climate, which will secure from want the descendants or their other fellow citizens? Are they afraid they will be reduced to labor the earth for their sustenance? They will be rendered thereby both more honest and happy. An industrious farmer occupies a more dignified place in the scale of beings, whether moral or political, than a lazy lounger, valuing himself on his family, too proud to work, and drawing out a miserable existence, by eating on that surplus of other men's labor, which is the sacred fund of the helpless poor. A pitiful annuity will only prevent them from exerting that industry and those talents which would soon lead them to better fortune.

How are these evils to be prevented? 1. At their first general meeting, let them distribute the funds on hand to the existing objects of their destination, and discontinue all further contributions. 2. Let them declare, at the same time, that their meetings, general and particular, shall thenceforth cease. 3. Let them melt up their eagles and add the mass to the distributable fund, that their descendants may have no temptation to hang them in their button holes. . . .

The People Alone Can Protect Us Against These Evils

To George Wythe, August 13, 1786

The condition of the French people proved to Jefferson what he had always believed: that, no matter what their potential resources, a people will be happy only when they govern themselves.

. . . If anybody thinks that kings, nobles, or priests are good conservators of the public happiness, send him here. It is the best school in the universe to cure him of that folly. He will see here, with his own eyes, that these descriptions of men are an abandoned confederacy against the happiness of the mass of the people. The omnipotence of their effect cannot be better proved, than in this country particularly, where, notwithstanding the finest soil upon earth, the finest climate under heaven and a people of the most benevolent, the most gay and amiable character of which the human form is susceptible; where such a people, I say, surrounded by so many blessings from nature, are loaded with misery, by kings, nobles, and priests, and by them alone. Preach, my dear Sir, a crusade against ignorance; establish and improve the law for educating the common people. Let our countrymen know, that the people alone can protect us against these evils, and that the tax which will be paid for this purpose, is not more than the thousandth part of what will be paid to kings, priests and nobles, who will rise up among us if we leave the people in ignorance. The people of England, I think, are less oppressed than here. But it needs but half an eye to see, when among them, that the foundation is laid in their dispositions for the establishment of a despotism. Nobility, wealth, and pomp are the objects of their admiration. They are by no means the free-minded people we suppose them in America. Their learned men, too, are few in number, and are less learned, and infinitely less emancipated from prejudice, than those of this country. . . .

The Paroxysm Can Never Return

To Maria Cosway, October 12, 1786

This is Jefferson's only love letter—or rather love treatise. He had abandoned himself to the wiles and charms of young Maria Cosway. The affair was now over. It was time to put his "paroxysm" in its proper place, and to give it an accounting. He wrote this long letter with his left hand. He had dislocated his right wrist on September 18 as a result of trying to jump a fence while walking with Maria Cosway along the Seine. He continued to correspond with her as a friend for another thirty-five years.

My Dear Madam,—Having performed the last sad office of handing you into your carriage, at the pavillon de St. Denis, and seen the wheels get actually into motion, I turned on my heel and walked, more dead than alive, to the opposite door, where my own was awaiting me. Mr. Danquerville was missing. He was sought for, found, and dragged down stairs. We were crammed into the carriage, like recruits for the Bastille, and not having soul enough to give orders to the coachman, he presumed Paris our destination, and drove off. After a considerable interval, silence was broke, with a *Je suis vraiment affligé du départ de ces bons gens.*[1] This was a signal for a mutual confession of distress. We began immediately to talk of Mr. and Mrs. Cosway, of their goodness, their talents, their amiability; and, though we spoke of nothing else, we seemed hardly to have entered into the matter, when the coachman announced the rue St. Denis, and that we were opposite Mr. Danquerville's. He insisted on descending there, and traversing a short passage to his lodgings. I was carried home. Seated by my fireside, solitary and sad, the following dialogue took place between my Head and my Heart.

HEAD Well, friend, you seem to be in a pretty trim.

HEART I am indeed the most wretched of all earthly beings. Overwhelmed with grief, every fibre of my frame distended

---

[1] "I am truly grieved because of the departure of these good people."

beyond its natural powers to bear, I would willingly meet whatever catastrophe should leave me no more to feel, or to fear.

HEAD These are the eternal consequences of your warmth and precipitation. This is one of the scrapes into which you are ever leading us. You confess your follies, indeed; but still you hug and cherish them; and no reformation can be hoped where there is no repentance.

HEART Oh, my friend! this is no moment to upbraid my foibles. I am rent into fragments by the force of my grief! If you have any balm, pour it into my wounds; if none, do not harrow them by new torments. Spare me in this awful moment! At any other, I will attend with patience to your admonitions.

HEAD On the contrary, I never found that the moment of triumph, with you, was the moment of attention to my admonitions. While suffering under your follies, you may perhaps be made sensible of them, but the paroxysm over, you fancy it can never return. Harsh, therefore, as the medicine may be, it is my office to administer it. You will be pleased to remember, that when our friend Trumbull used to be telling us of the merits and talents of these good people, I never ceased whispering to you that we had no occasion for new acquaintances; that the greater their merits and talents, the more dangerous their friendship to our tranquillity, because the regret at parting would be greater.

HEART Accordingly, Sir, this acquaintance was not the consequence of my doings. It was one of your projects, which threw us in the way of it. It was you, remember, and not I, who desired the meeting at Legrand and Motinos. I never trouble myself with domes nor arches. The Halle aux bleds might have rotted down, before I should have gone to see it. But you, forsooth, who are eternally getting us to sleep with your diagrams and crotchets, must go and examine this wonderful piece of architecture; and when you had seen it, oh! it was the most superb thing on earth! What you had seen there was worth all you had yet seen in Paris! I thought so too. But I meant it of the lady and gentleman to whom we had been presented; and not of a parcel of sticks and chips put together in pens. You, then, Sir, and not I, have been the cause of the present distress.

HEAD It would have been happy for you if my diagrams and crotchets had gotten you to sleep on that day, as you are pleased to say they eternally do. My visit to Legrand and Motinos had public utility for its object. A market is to be built in Richmond. What a commodious plan is that of Legrand and Motinos; especially, if we put on it the noble dome of the Halle aux bleds. If such a bridge as they showed us can be thrown across the Schuylkill, at Philadelphia, the floating bridges taken up, and the navigation of that river opened, what a copious resource will be added, of wood and provisions, to warm and feed the poor of that city? While I was occupied with these objects, you were dilating with your new acquaintances, and contriving how to prevent a separation from them. Every soul of you had an engagement for the day. Yet all these were to be sacrificed, that you might dine together. Lying messengers were to be despatched into every quarter of the city, with apologies for your breach of engagement. You, particularly, had the effrontery to send word to the Duchess Danville, that on the moment we were setting out to dine with her, despatches came to hand, which required immediate attention. You wanted me to invent a more ingenious excuse; but I knew you were getting into a scrape, and I would have nothing to do with it. Well; after dinner to St. Cloud, from St. Cloud to Ruggieri's, from Ruggieri's to Krumholtz; and if the day had been as long as a Lapland summer day, you would still have contrived means among you to have filled it.

HEART Oh! my dear friend, how you have revived me by recalling to my mind the transactions of that day! How well I remember them all, and that, when I came home at night, and looked back to the morning, it seemed to have been a month agone. Go on, then, like a kind comforter, and paint to me the day we went to St. Germains. How beautiful was every object! the Port de Reuilly, the hills along the Seine, the rainbows of the machine of Marly, the terrace of St. Germains, the châteaux, the gardens, the statues of Marly, the pavillon of Lucienne. Recollect, too, Madrid, Bagatelle, the King's garden, the Dessert. How grand the idea excited by the remains of such a column. The spiral staircase, too, was beautiful. Every moment was filled with something agreeable. The wheels of time moved on with a rapidity, of which those of our carriage gave but a faint idea. And yet, in the evening, when one took a retrospect of the day, what a mass of happiness had we travelled over! Retrace all those scenes to me, my good companion, and I will forgive the unkindness with which you were chiding me. The day we went to St. Germains was a little too warm, I think; was it not?

HEAD Thou art the most incorrigible of all the beings that ever sinned! I reminded you of the follies of the first day, intending to deduce from thence some useful lessons for you; but instead of listening to them, you kindle at the recollection, you retrace the whole series with a fondness, which shows you want nothing, but the opportunity, to act it over again. I often told you, during its course, that you were imprudently engaging your affections, under circumstances that must have cost you a great deal of pain; that the persons, indeed, were of the greatest merit, possessing good sense, good humor, honest hearts, honest manners, and eminence in a lovely art; that the lady had, moreover, qualities and accomplishments belonging to her sex, which might form a chapter apart for her; such as music, modesty, beauty, and that softness of disposition, which is the ornament of her sex and charm of ours; but that all these considerations would increase the pang of separation; that their stay here was to be short; that you rack our whole system when you are parted from those you love, complaining that such a separation is worse than death, inasmuch as this ends our sufferings, whereas that only begins them; and that the separation would, in this instance, be the more severe, as you would probably never see them again.

HEART But they told me they would come back again, the next year.

HEAD But, in the meantime, see what you suffer; and their return, too, depends on so many circumstances, that if you had a grain of prudence, you would not count upon it. Upon the whole, it is improbable, and therefore you should abandon the idea of ever seeing them again.

HEART May heaven abandon me if I do!

HEAD Very well. Suppose, then, they come back. They are to stay two months, and, when these are expired, what is to follow? Perhaps you flatter yourself they may come to America?

HEART God only knows what is to happen. I see nothing impossible in that supposition; and I see things wonderfully contrived sometimes, to make us happy. Where could they find such objects as in America, for the exercise of their enchanting art? especially the lady, who paints landscapes so inimitably. She wants only subjects worthy of immortality, to render her pencil immortal. The Falling Spring, the Cascade of Niagara, the passage of the Potomac through the Blue Mountains, the Natural Bridge; it is worth a voyage across the Atlantic to see these objects; much more to paint, and make them, and thereby ourselves, known to all ages. And our own dear Monticello; where has nature spread so rich a mantle under the eye? mountains, forests, rocks, river. With what majesty do we there ride above the storms! How sublime to look down into the workhouse of nature, to see her clouds, hail, snow, rain, thunder, all fabricated at our feet! and the glorious sun, when rising as if out of a distant water, just gilding the tops of the mountains, and giving life to all nature! I hope in God, no circumstance may ever make either seek an asylum from grief! With what sincere sympathy I would open every cell of my composition, to receive the effusion of their woes! I would pour my tears into their wounds; and if a drop of balm could be found on the top of the Cordilleras, or at the remotest sources of the Missouri, I would go thither myself to seek and to bring it. Deeply practised in the school of affliction, the human heart knows no joy which I have not lost, no sorrow of which I have not drunk! Fortune can present no grief of unknown form to me! Who, then, can so softly bind up the wound of another, as he who has felt the same wound himself? But heaven forbid they should ever know a sorrow! Let us turn over another leaf, for this has distracted me.

HEAD Well. Let us put this possibility to trial then, on another point. When you consider the character which is given of our country, by the lying newspapers of London, and their credulous copiers in other countries; when you reflect that all Europe is made to believe we are a lawless banditti, in a state of absolute anarchy, cutting one another's throats, and plundering without distinction, how could you expect that any reasonable creature would venture among us?

HEART But you and I know that all this is false: that there is not a country on earth, where there is greater tranquillity; where the laws are milder, or better obeyed; where everyone is more attentive to his own business, or meddles less with that of others; where strangers are better received, more hospitably treated, and with a more sacred respect.

HEAD True, you and I know this, but your friends do not know it.

HEART But they are sensible people, who think for themselves. They will ask of impartial foreigners, who have been among us, whether they saw or heard on the spot, any instance of anarchy. They will judge, too, that a people, occupied as we are, in opening rivers, digging navigable canals, making roads, building public schools, establishing academies, erecting busts and statues to our great men, protecting religious freedom, abolishing sanguinary punishments, reforming and improving our laws in general; they will judge, I say, for themselves, whether these are not the occupations of a people at their ease; whether this is not better evidence of our true state, than a London newspaper, hired to lie, and from which no truth can ever be extracted but by reversing everything it says.

HEAD I did not begin this lecture, my friend, with a view to learn from you what America is doing. Let us return, then, to our point. I wish to make you sensible how imprudent it is to place your affections, without reserve, on objects you must so soon lose, and whose loss, when it comes, must cost you such severe pangs. Remember the last night. You knew your friends were to leave Paris today. This was enough to throw you into agonies. All night you tossed us from one side of the bed to the other; no sleep, no rest. The poor crippled wrist, too, never left one moment in the same position; now up, now down, now here, now there; was it to be wondered at, if its pains returned? The surgeon then was to be called, and to be rated as an ignoramus, because he could not divine the cause of this extraordinary change. In fine, my friend, you must mend your manners. This is not a world to live at random in, as you do. To avoid those eternal distresses, to which you are forever exposing us, you must learn to look forward, before you take a step which may interest our peace. Everything in this world is matter of calculation. Advance then with caution, the balance in your hand. Put into one scale the pleasures which any object may offer; but put fairly into the other, the pains which are to follow, and see which preponderates. The making an acquaintance, is not a matter of indifference. When a new one is proposed to you, view it all round. Consider what advantages it presents, and to what inconveniences it may expose you. Do not bite at the bait of pleasure, till you know there is no hook beneath it. The art of life is the art of avoiding pain; and he is the best pilot, who steers clearest of the rocks and shoals with which it is beset. Pleasure is always before us; but misfortune is at our side: while running after that, this arrests us. The most effectual means of being secure against pain, is to retire within ourselves, and to suffice for our own happiness. Those which depend on ourselves, are the only pleasures a wise man will count on: for nothing is ours, which another may deprive us of. Hence the inestimable value of intellectual pleasures. Ever in our power, always leading us to something new, never cloying, we ride serene and sublime above the concerns of this mortal world, contemplating truth and nature, matter and motion, the laws which bind up their existence, and that Eternal Being who made and bound them up by those laws. Let this be our employ. Leave the bustle and tumult of society to those who have not talents to occupy themselves without them. Friendship is but another name for an alliance with the follies and the misfortunes of others. Our own share of miseries is sufficient: why enter then as volunteers into those of another? Is there so little gall poured into our cup, that we must need help to drink that of our neighbor? A friend dies, or leaves us: we feel as if a limb was cut off. He is sick: we must watch over him, and participate of his pains. His fortune is shipwrecked: ours must be laid under contribution. He loses a child, a parent, or a partner: we must mourn the loss as if it were our own.

HEART And what more sublime delight than to mingle tears with one whom the hand of heaven hath smitten! to watch over the bed of sickness, and to beguile its tedious and its painful moments! to share our bread with one to whom misfortune has left none! This world abounds indeed with misery; to lighten its burthen, we must divide it with one another. But let us now try the virtue of your mathematical balance, and as you have put into one scale the burthens of friendship, let me put its comforts into the other. When languishing then under disease, how grateful is the solace of our friends! how are we penetrated with their assiduities and attentions! how much are we supported by their encouragements and kind offices! When heaven has taken from us some object of our love, how sweet is it to have a bosom whereon to recline our heads, and into which we may pour the torrent of our tears! Grief, with such a comfort, is almost a luxury! In a life, where we are perpetually exposed to want and accident, yours is a wonderful proposition, to insulate ourselves, to retire from all aid, and to wrap ourselves in the mantle of self-sufficiency! For, assuredly, nobody will care for him who cares for nobody. But friendship is precious, not only in the shade, but in the sunshine of life; and thanks to a benevolent arrangement of things, the greater part of life is sunshine. I will recur for proof to the days we have lately passed. On these, indeed, the sun shone brightly. How gay did the face of nature appear! Hills, valleys, châteaux, gardens, rivers, every object wore its liveliest hue! Whence did they borrow it? From the presence of our charming companion. They were pleasing, because she seemed pleased. Alone, the scene would have been dull and insipid: the participation of it with her gave it relish. Let the gloomy monk, sequestered from the world, seek unsocial pleasures in the bottom of his cell! Let the sublimated philosopher grasp visionary happiness, while pursuing phantoms dressed in the garb of truth! Their supreme wisdom is supreme folly; and they mistake for happiness the mere absence of pain. Had they ever felt the solid pleasure of one generous spasm of the heart, they would exchange for it all the frigid speculations of their lives, which you have been vaunting in such elevated terms. Believe me, then, my friend, that that is a miserable arithmetic which could estimate friendship at nothing, or at less than nothing. Respect for you has induced me to enter into this discussion, and to hear principles uttered which I detest and abjure. Respect for myself now obliges me to recall you into the proper limits of your office. When nature assigned us the same habitation, she gave us over it a divided empire. To you, she allotted the field of science; to me, that of morals. When the circle is to be squared, or the orbit of a comet to be traced; when the arch of greatest strength, or the solid of least resistance, is to be investigated, take up the problem; it is yours; nature has given me no cognizance of it. In like manner, in denying to you the feelings of sympathy, of benevolence, of gratitude, of justice, of love, of friendship, she has excluded you from their control. To these, she has adapted the mechanism of the heart. Morals were too essential to the happiness of man, to be risked on the uncertain combinations of the head. She laid their foundation, therefore, in sentiment, not in science. That she gave to all, as necessary to all; this to a few only, as sufficing with a few. I know, indeed, that you pretend authority to the sovereign control of our conduct, in all its parts; and a respect for your grave saws and maxims, a desire to do what is right, has sometimes induced me to conform to your counsels. A few facts, however, which I can readily recall to your memory, will suffice to prove to you, that nature has not organized you for our moral direction. When the poor, wearied soldier whom we overtook at Chickahomony, with his pack on his back, begged us to let him get up behind our chariot, you began to calculate that the road was full of soldiers, and that if all should be taken up, our horses would fail in their journey. We drove on therefore. But, soon becoming sensible you had made me do wrong, that, though we cannot relieve all the distressed, we should relieve as many as we can, I turned about to take up the soldier; but he had entered a bye-path, and was no more to be found; and from that moment to this, I could never find him out, to ask his forgiveness. Again, when the poor woman came to ask a charity in Philadelphia, you whispered that she looked like a drunkard, and that half a dollar was enough to give her for the ale-house. Those who want the dispositions to give, easily find reasons why they ought not to give. When I sought her out afterwards, and did what I should have done at first, you know that she employed the money immediately towards placing her child at school. If our country, when pressed with wrongs at the point of the bayonet, had been governed by its heads instead of its hearts, where should we have been now? Hanging on a gallows as high as Haman's. You began to calculate, and to compare wealth and numbers: we threw up a few pulsations of our blood; we supplied enthusiasm against wealth and numbers; we put our existence to the hazard, when the hazard seemed against us, and we saved our country: justifying, at the same time, the ways of Providence, whose precept is, to do always what is right, and leave the issue to him. In short, my friend, as far as my recollection serves me, I do not know that I ever did a good thing on your suggestion, or a dirty one without it. I do forever, then, disclaim your interference in my province. Fill paper as you please with triangles and squares: try how many ways you can hang and combine them together. I shall never envy nor control your sublime delights. But leave me to decide, when and where friendships are to be contracted. You say, I contract them at random. So you said the woman at Philadelphia was a drunkard. I receive none into my esteem, till I know they are worthy of it. Wealth, title, office, are no recommendations to my friendship. On the contrary, great good qualities are requisite to make amends for their having wealth, title, and office. You confess, that, in the present case, I could not have made a worthier choice. You only object, that I was so soon to lose them. We are not immortal ourselves, my friend; how can we expect our enjoyments to be so? We have no rose without its thorn; no pleasure without alloy. It is the law of our existence; and we must acquiesce. It is the condition annexed to all our pleasures, not by us who receive, but by him who gives them. True, this condition is pressing cruelly on me at this moment. I feel more fit for death than life. But, when I look back on the pleasures of which it is the consequence, I am conscious they were worth the price I am paying. Notwithstanding your endeavors, too, to damp my hopes, I comfort myself with expectations of their promised return. Hope is sweeter than despair; and they were too good to mean to deceive me. "In the summer," said the gentleman; but "in the spring," said the lady; and I should love her forever, were it only for that! Know, then, my friend, that I have taken these good people into my bosom; that I have lodged them in the warmest cell I could find; that I love them, and will continue to love them through life; that if fortune should dispose them on one side the globe, and me on the other, my affections shall pervade its whole mass to reach them. Knowing then my determination, attempt not to disturb it. If you can, at any time, furnish matter for their amusement, it will be the office of a good neighbor to do it. I will, in like manner, seize any occasion which may offer, to do the like good turn for you with Condorcet, Rittenhouse, Madison, La Cretelle, or any other of those worthy sons of science, whom you so justly prize.

I thought this a favorable proposition whereon to rest the issue of the dialogue. So I put an end to it by calling for my nightcap. Methinks, I hear you wish to heaven I had called a little sooner, and so spared you the ennui of such a sermon. I did not interrupt them sooner, because I was in a mood for hearing sermons. You too were the subject; and on such a thesis, I never think the theme long; not even if I am to write it, and that slowly and awkwardly, as now, with the left hand. But, that you may not be discouraged from a correspondence which begins so formidably, I will promise you, on my honor, that my future letters shall be of a reasonable length. I will even agree to express but half my esteem for you, for fear of cloying you with too full a dose. But, on your part, no curtailing. If your letters are as long as the Bible, they will appear short to me. Only let them be brimful of affection. I shall read them with the dispositions with which Arlequin, in *Les deux billets,* spelt the words *"je t'aime,"* and wished that the whole alphabet had entered into their composition.

We have had incessant rains since your departure. These make me fear for your health, as well as that you had an uncomfortable journey. The same cause has prevented me from being able to give you any account of your friends here. This voyage to Fontainebleau will probably send the Count de Moutier and the Marquis de Brehan, to America. Danquerville promised to visit me, but has not done it as yet. De la Tude comes sometimes to take family soup with me, and entertains me with anecdotes of his five and thirty years' imprisonment. How fertile is the mind of man, which can make the Bastile and dungeon of Vincennes yield interesting anecdotes! You know this was for making four verses on Madame de Pompadour. But I think you told me you did not know the verses. They were these: *"Sans esprit, sans sentiment, Sans etre belle, ni neuve, En France on peut avoir le premier amant: Pompadour en est l' épreuve."*[2] I have read the memoir of his three escapes. As to myself, my health is good, except my wrist which mends slowly, and my mind which mends not at all, but broods constantly over your departure. The lateness of the season obliges me to decline my journey into the south of France. Present me in the most friendly terms to Mr. Cosway, and receive me into your own recollection with a partiality and warmth, proportioned not to my own poor merit, but to the sentiments of sincere affection and esteem, with which I have the honor to be, my dear Madam, your most obedient humble servant.

---

[2] "Without spirit, without feelings, without being beautiful, or new, in France one can have the first lover: Pompadour is the proof of this."

It Is a Medicine Necessary for the Sound Health of Government

To James Madison, January 30, 1787

Jefferson was one of the few important politicians to judge Shay's Rebellion leniently when it took place. He was able to do so only because he sympathized with "little rebellions." Owing in part to Shay's Rebellion his political friend Madison came to favor a federal government.

. . . I am impatient to learn your sentiments on the late troubles in the Eastern States. So far as I have yet seen, they do not appear to threaten serious consequences. Those States have suffered by the stoppage of the channels of their commerce, which have not yet found other issues. This must render money scarce, and make the people uneasy. This uneasiness has produced acts absolutely unjustifiable; but I hope they will provoke no severities from their governments. A consciousness of those in power that their administration of the public affairs has been honest, may, perhaps, produce too great a degree of indignation; and those characters, wherein fear predominates over hope, may apprehend too much from these instances of irregularity. They may conclude too hastily, that nature has formed man insusceptible of any other government than that of force, a conclusion not founded in truth nor experience. Societies exist under three forms, sufficiently distinguishable. 1. Without government, as among our Indians. 2. Under governments, wherein the will of every one has a just influence; as is the case in England, in a slight degree, and in our States, in a great one. 3. Under governments of force; as is the case in all other monarchies, and in most of the other republics. To have an idea of the curse of existence under these last, they must be seen. It is a government of wolves over sheep. It is a problem, not clear in my mind, that the first condition is not the best. But I believe it to be inconsistent with any great degree of population. The second state has a great deal of good in it. The mass of mankind under that, enjoys a precious degree of liberty and happiness. It has its evils, too; the principal of which is the turbulence to which it is subject. But weigh this against the oppressions of monarchy, and it becomes nothing. *Malo periculosam libertatem quam quietam servitutem.*[1] Even this evil is productive of good. It prevents the degeneracy of government, and nourishes a general attention to the public affairs. I hold it, that a little rebellion, now and then, is a good thing, and as necessary in the political world as storms in the physical. Unsuccessful rebellions, indeed, generally establish the encroachments on the rights of the people, which have produced them. An observation of this truth should render honest republican governors so mild in their punishment of rebellions, as not to discourage them too much. It is a medicine necessary for the sound health of government. . . .

[1] I prefer dangerous liberty to tranquil servitude.

They Are Like Pure Metal

To Madison, June 20, 1787

In letters of March 18 and 19 and April 13, Madison in-
formed Jefferson of the progress made toward holding a
Federal Convention in the course of which he enunciated his
conservative philosophy on the need for restraints upon the
majority.

. . . The idea of separating the executive business of the
confederacy from Congress, as the judiciary is already, in
some degree, is just and necessary. I had frequently pressed
on the members individually, while in Congress, the doing
this by a resolution of Congress for appointing an executive
committee, to act during the sessions of Congress, as the
committee of the States was to act during their vacations.
But the referring to this committee all executive business, as
it should present itself, would require a more persevering
self-denial than I suppose Congress to possess. It will be much
better to make that separation by a federal act. The negative,
proposed to be given them on all the acts of the several
legislatures, is now, for the first time, suggested to my mind.
Prima facie, I do not like it. It fails in an essential character;
that the hole and the patch should be commensurate. But
this proposes to mend a small hole by covering the whole
garment. Not more than 1. out of 100. State acts concern
the confederacy. This proposition, then, in order to give
them 1. degree of power, which they ought to have, gives
them 99. more, which they ought not to have, upon a presumption that they will not exercise the 99. But upon every
act, there will be a preliminary question, Does this act concern the confederacy? And was there ever a proposition so
plain, as to pass Congress without a debate? Their decisions
are almost always wise; they are like pure metal. But you
know of how much dross this is the result. Would not an
appeal from the State judicature to a federal court, in all
cases where the act of Confederation controlled the question,
be as effectual a remedy, and exactly commensurate to the
defect? A British creditor, for example, sues for his debt in

Virginia; the defendant pleads an act of the State, excluding him from their courts; the plaintiff urges the Confederation, and the treaty made under that, as controlling the State law; the judges are weak enough to decide according to the views of their legislature. An appeal to a federal court sets all to rights. It will be said, that this court may encroach on the jurisdiction of the State courts. It may. But there will be a power, to wit, Congress, to watch and restrain them. But place the same authority in Congress itself, and there will be no power above them, to perform the same office. They will restrain within due bounds, a jurisdiction exercised by others, much more rigorously than if exercised by themselves. . . .

They Have It by the Law of Nature

To Edward Carrington, August 4, 1787

Jefferson's defense of the Confederacy is based, ironically enough, on its implied powers. He was to spend a good portion of the next three decades denying such powers to the Federal Constitution. Carrington was a Virginia conservative, later an avowed enemy of Jefferson's.

Dear Sir,—Since mine of the 16th of January, I have been honored by your favors of April the 24th and June the 9th. I am happy to find that the States have come so generally into the schemes of the federal convention, from which, I am sure, we shall see wise propositions. I confess, I do not go as far in the reforms thought necessary, as some of my correspondents in America; but if the convention should adopt such propositions, I shall suppose them necessary. My general plan would be, to make the States one as to everything connected with foreign nations, and several as to everything purely domestic. But with all the imperfections of our present government, it is without comparison the best existing, or that ever did exist. Its greatest defect is the imperfect manner in which matters of commerce have been provided for. It has been so often said, as to be generally believed, that Congress have no power by the Confederation to enforce anything; for example, contributions of money. It was not necessary to give them that power expressly; they have it by the law of nature. When two parties make a compact, there results to each a power of compelling the other to execute it. Compulsion was never so easy as in our case, where a single frigate would soon levy on the commerce of any State the deficiency of its contributions; nor more safe than in the hands of Congress, which has always shown that it would wait, as it ought to do, to the last extremities, before it would execute any of its powers which are disagreeable. I think it very material, to separate, in the hands of Congress, the executive and legislative powers, as the judiciary already are, in some degree. This, I hope, will be done. The want of it has been the source of more evil than we have experienced from any other cause. Nothing is so embarrassing nor so mischievous, in a great assembly, as the details of execution. The smallest trifle of that kind occupies as long as the most important act of legislation, and takes place of everything else. Let any man recollect, or look over, the files of Congress; he will observe the most important propositions hanging over, from week to week, and month to month, till the occasions have passed them, and the things never done. I have ever viewed the executive details as the greatest cause of evil to us, because they in fact place us as if we had no federal head, by diverting the attention of that head from great to small subjects; and should this division of power not be recommended by the convention, it is my opinion Congress should make it itself, by establishing an executive committee. . . .

The Tree of Liberty Must Be Refreshed with the Blood of Patriots and Tyrants

To William Stephen Smith, November 13, 1787

In this famous, often quoted letter, Jefferson once again addresses himself to the issues raised by Shay's Rebellion. Smith was John Adams' son-in-law.

. . . I do not know whether it is to yourself or Mr. Adams I am to give my thanks for the copy of the new constitution. I beg leave through you to place them where due. It will be yet three weeks before I shall receive them from America. There are very good articles in it: and very bad. I do not know which preponderate. What we have lately read in the history of Holland, in the chapter on the Stadtholder, would have sufficed to set me against a Chief magistrate eligible for a long duration, if I had ever been disposed towards one: and what we have always read of the elections of Polish kings should have forever excluded the idea of one continuable for life. Wonderful is the effect of impudent and persevering lying. The British ministry have so long hired their gazetteers to repeat and model into every form lies about our being in anarchy, that the world has at length believed them, the English nation has believed them, the ministers themselves have come to believe them, and what is more wonderful, we have believed them ourselves. Yet where does this anarchy exist? Where did it ever exist, except in the single instance of Massachusetts? And can history produce an instance of a rebellion so honourably conducted? I say nothing of it's motives. They were founded in ignorance, not wickedness. God forbid we should ever be 20. years without such a rebellion. The people can not be all, and always, well informed. The part which is wrong will be discontented in proportion to the importance of the facts they misconceive. If they remain quiet under such misconceptions it is a lethargy, the forerunner of death to the public liberty. We have had 13. states independant 11. years. There has been one rebellion. That comes to one rebellion in a century and a half for each state. What country before ever existed a century and half without a rebellion? And what country can preserve it's liberties if their rulers are not warned from time to time that their people preserve the spirit of resistance? Let them take arms. The remedy is to set them right as to facts, pardon and pacify them. What signify a few lives lost in a century or two? The tree of liberty must be refreshed from time to time with the blood of patriots and tyrants. It is it's natural manure. Our Convention has been too much impressed by the insurrection of Massachusetts: and in the spur of the moment they are setting up a kite to keep the hen yard in order. . . .

The Will of the Majority Should Prevail

To James Madison, December 20, 1787

Showing less combativeness, less hostility than before, Jefferson here gives his most detailed commentary on the new Constitution.

. . . I like much the general idea of framing a government, which should go on of itself, peaceably, without needing continual recurrence to the State legislatures. I like the organization of the government into legislative, judiciary and executive. I like the power given the legislature to levy taxes, and for that reason solely, I approve of the greater House being chosen by the people directly. For though I think a House so chosen, will be very far inferior to the present Congress, will be very illy qualified to legislate for the Union, for foreign nations, etc., yet this evil does not weigh against the good, of preserving inviolate the fundamental principle, that the people are not to be taxed but by representatives chosen immediately by themselves. I am captivated by the compromise of the opposite claims of the great and little States, of the latter to equal, and the former to proportional influence. I am much pleased, too, with the substitution of the method of voting by person, instead of that of voting by States; and I like the negative given to the Executive, conjointly with a third of either House; though I should have liked it better, had the judiciary been associated for that purpose, or invested separately with a similar power. There are other good things of less moment. I will now tell you what I do not like. First, the omission of a bill of rights, providing clearly, and without the aid of sophism, for freedom of religion, freedom of the press, protection against standing armies, restriction of monopolies, the eternal and unremitting force of the habeas corpus laws, and trials by jury in all matters of fact triable by the laws of the land, and not by the laws of nations. To say, as Mr. Wilson does, that a bill of rights was not necessary, because all is reserved in the case of the general government which is not given, while in the particular ones, all is given which is not reserved, might do for the audience to which it was addressed; but it is surely a *gratis dictum,* the reverse of which might just as well be said; and it is opposed by strong inferences from the body of the instrument, as well as from the omission of the cause of our present Confederation, which had made the reservation in express terms. It was hard to conclude, because there has been a want of uniformity among the States as to the cases triable by jury, because some have been so incautious as to dispense with this mode of trial in certain cases, therefore, the more prudent States shall be reduced to the same level of calamity. It would have been much more just and wise to have concluded the other way, that as most of the States had preserved with jealousy this sacred palladium of liberty, those who had wandered, should be brought back to it; and to have established general right rather than general wrong. For I consider all the ill as established, which may be established. I have a right to nothing, which another has a right to take away; and Congress will have a right to take away trials by jury in all civil cases. Let me add, that a bill of rights is what the people are entitled to against every government on earth, general or particular; and what no just government should refuse, or rest on inference.

The second feature I dislike, and strongly dislike, is the abandonment, in every instance, of the principle of rotation in office, and most particularly in the case of the President. Reason and experience tell us, that the first magistrate will always be re-elected if he may be re-elected. He is then an officer for life. This once observed, it becomes of so much consequence to certain nations to have a friend or a foe at the head of our affairs, that they will interfere with money and with arms. A Galloman, or an Angloman, will be supported by the nation he befriends. If once elected, and at a second or third election outvoted by one or two votes, he will pretend false votes, foul play, hold possession of the reins of government, be supported by the States voting for him, especially if they be the central ones, lying in a compact body themselves, and separating their opponents; and they will be aided by one nation in Europe, while the majority are aided by another. The election of a President of America, some years hence, will be much more interesting to certain nations of Europe, than ever the election of a King of Poland was. Reflect on all the instances in history, ancient and modern, of elective monarchies, and say if they do not give foundation for my fears; the Roman Emperors, the Popes while they were of any importance, the German Emperors till they became hereditary in practice, the Kings of Poland, the Deys of the Ottoman dependencies.

It may be said, that if elections are to be attended with these disorders, the less frequently they are repeated the better. But experience says, that to free them from disorder, they must be rendered less interesting by a necessity of change. No foreign power, nor domestic party, will waste their blood and money to elect a person, who must go out at the end of a short period. The power of removing every fourth year by the vote of the people, is a power which they will not exercise, and if they were disposed to exercise it, they would not be permitted. The King of Poland is removable every day by the diet. But they never remove him. Nor would Russia, the Emperor, etc., permit them to do it. Smaller objections are, the appeals on matters of fact as well as laws; and the binding all persons, legislative, executive, and judiciary by oath, to maintain that constitution. I do not pretend to decide, what would be the best method of procuring the establishment of the manifold good things in this constitution, and of getting rid of the bad. Whether by adopting it, in hopes of future amendment; or after it shall have been duly weighed and canvassed by the people, after seeing the parts they generally dislike, and those they generally approve, to say to them, "We see now what you wish. You are willing to give to your federal government such and such powers; but you wish, at the same time, to have such and such fundamental rights secured to you, and certain sources of convulsion taken away. Be it so. Send together deputies again. Let them establish your fundamental rights by a sacrosanct declaration, and let them pass the parts of the Constitution you have approved. These will give powers to your federal goverment sufficient for your happiness."

This is what might be said, and would probably produce a speedy, more perfect and more permanent form of government. At all events, I hope you will not be discouraged from making other trials, if the present one should fail. We are never permitted to despair of the commonwealth.

I have thus told you freely what I like, and what I dislike, merely as a matter of curiosity; for I know it is not in my power to offer matter of information to your judgment, which has been formed after hearing and weighing everything which the wisdom of man could offer on these subjects. I own, I am not a friend to a very energetic government. It is always oppressive. It places the governors indeed more at their ease, at the expense of the people. The late rebellion in Massachusetts has given more alarm, than I think it should have done. Calculate that one rebellion in thirteen States in the course of eleven years, is but one for each State in a century and a half. No country should be so long without one. Nor will any degree of power in the hands of government, prevent insurrections. In England, where the hand of power is heavier than with us, there are seldom half a dozen years without an insurrection. In France, where it is still heavier, but less despotic, as Montesquieu supposes, than in some other countries, and where there are always two or three hundred thousand men ready to crush insurrections, there have been three in the course of the three years I have been here, in every one of which greater numbers were engaged than in Massachusetts, and a great deal more blood was spilt. In Turkey, where the sole nod of the despot is death, insurrections are the events of every day. Compare again the ferocious depredations of their insurgents, with the order, the moderation and the almost self-extinguishment of ours. And say, finally, whether peace is best preserved by giving energy to the government, or information to the people. This last is the most certain, and the most legitimate engine of government. Educate and inform the whole mass of the people. Enable them to see that it is their interest to preserve peace and order, and they will preserve them. And it requires no very high degree of education to convince them of this. They are the only sure reliance for the preservation of our liberty. After all, it is my principle that the will of the majority should prevail. If they approve the proposed constitution in all its parts, I shall concur in it cheerfully, in hopes they will amend it, whenever they shall find it works wrong. This reliance cannot deceive us, as long as we remain virtuous; and I think we shall be so, as long as agriculture is our principal object, which will be the case, while there remains vacant lands in any part of America. When we get piled upon one another in large cities, as in Europe, we shall become corrupt as in Europe, and go to eating one another as they do there. I have tired you by this time with disquisitions which you have already heard repeated by others a thousand and a thousand times; and therefore, shall only add assurances of the esteem and attachment with which I have the honor to be, dear Sir, your affectionate friend and servant.

P. S. The instability of our laws is really an immense evil. I think it would be well to provide in our constitutions, that there shall always be a twelvemonth between the engrossing a bill and passing it; that it should then be offered to its passage without changing a word; and that if circumstances should be thought to require a speedier passage, it should take two-thirds of both Houses, instead of a bare majority.

There Is a Great Deal of Good in It

To Washington, May 3, 1788

Jefferson here repeats his objections to the Constitution.

. . . I had intended to have written a word to your Excellency on the subject of the new constitution, but I have already spun out my letter to an immoderate length. I will just observe therefore that according to my ideas there is a great deal of good in it. There are two things however which I dislike strongly. 1. The want of a declaration of rights. I am in hopes the opposition of Virginia will remedy this, and produce such a declaration. 2. The perpetual re-eligibility of the President. This I fear will make that an office for life first, and then hereditary. I was much an enemy to monarchy before I came to Europe. I am ten thousand times more so since I have seen what they are. There is scarcely an evil known in these countries which may not be traced to their king as it's source, nor a good which is not derived from the small fibres of republicanism existing among them. I can further say with safety there is not a crowned head in Europe whose talents or merit would entitle him to be elected a vestryman by the people of any parish in America. However I shall hope that before there is danger of this change taking place in the office of President, the good sense and free spirit of our countrymen will make the changes necessary to prevent it. Under this hope I look forward to the general adoption of the new constitution with anxiety, as necessary for us under our present circumstances. . . .

By Way of Supplement

To James Madison, March 15, 1789

Madison disagreed with Jefferson about rotating the Presidents, and he had reservations about a declaration of rights. Jefferson, for his part, would compromise with the first but not the second.

. . . I am happy to find that, on the whole, you are a friend to this amendment. The declaration of rights is, like all other human blessings, alloyed with some inconveniences, and not accomplishing fully its object. But the good in this instance, vastly overweighs the evil. I cannot refrain from making short answers to the objections which your letter states to have been raised. 1. That the rights in question are reserved, by the manner in which the federal powers are granted. Answer. A constitutive act may, certainly, be so formed, as to need no declaration of rights. The act itself has the force of a declaration, as far as it goes, and if it goes to all material points, nothing more is wanting. In the draught of a constitution which I had once a thought of proposing in Virginia, and printed afterwards, I endeavored to reach all the great objects of public liberty, and did not mean to add a declaration of rights. Probably the object was imperfectly executed; but the deficiencies would have been supplied by others, in the course of discussion. But in a constitutive act which leaves some precious articles unnoticed, and raises implications against others, a declaration of rights becomes necessary, by way of supplement. This is the case of our new federal Constitution. This instrument forms us into one State, as to certain objects, and gives us a legislative and executive body for these objects. It should, therefore, guard us against their abuses of power, within the field submitted to them. 2. A positive declaration of some essential rights could not be obtained in the requisite latitude. Answer. Half a loaf is better than no bread. If we cannot secure all our rights, let us secure what we can. 3. The limited powers of the federal government, and jealousy of the subordinate governments, afford a security which exists in no other instance. Answer. The first member of this seems resolvable into the first objection before stated. The jealousy of the subordinate governments is a precious reliance. But observe that those governments are only agents. They must have principles furnished them, whereon to found their opposition. The declaration of rights will be the text, whereby they will try all the acts of the federal government. In this view, it is necessary to the federal government also; as by the same text, they may try the opposition of the subordinate governments. 4. Experience proves the inefficacy of a bill of rights. True. But though it is not absolutely efficacious under all circumstances, it is of great potency always, and rarely inefficacious. A brace the more will often keep up the building which would have fallen, with that brace the less. There is a remarkable difference between the characters of the inconveniences which attend a declaration of rights, and those which attend the want of it. The inconveniences of the declaration are, that it may cramp government in its useful exertions. But the evil of this is short-lived, moderate and reparable. The inconveniences of the want of a declaration are permanent, afflicting and irreparable. They are in constant progression from bad to worse. The executive, in our governments, is not the sole, it is scarcely the principal object of my jealousy. The tyranny of the legislatures is the most formidable dread at present, and will be for many years. That of the executive will come in its turn; but it will be at a remote period. I know there are some among us, who would now establish a monarchy. But they are inconsiderable in number and weight of character. The rising race are all republicans. We were educated in royalism; no wonder, if some of us retain that idolatry still. Our young people are educated in republicanism; an apostasy from that to royalism, is unprecedented and impossible. I am much pleased with the prospect that a declaration of rights will be added; and I hope it will be done in that way, which will not endanger the whole frame of government, or any essential part of it. . . .

To Avoid the Ill Which Seems to Threaten

To Rabaut Saint-Étienne, June 3, 1789

Jefferson's friendship with Lafayette involved him directly in the opening phases of the French Revolution. Jefferson greeted the convention of the Estates-General on May 4, 1789 as a first step toward reforms. Ultimately, he hoped, France would become a constitutional monarchy on the model of Great Britain. In the dispute between Estates—the First and Second, representing church and nobility, insisted that each Estate as a whole should vote; the Third, representing the people, and containing as many deputies as the other two combined, insisted that each deputy should vote—in their dispute Jefferson sided with the Third Estate. Negotiations were held between the 23 and 27 of May and failed. The King on the following day proposed resumption of talks. Under these ominous conditions, Jefferson outlined his suggestions, which he hoped would reach the King, for breaking the impasse. But events moved too swiftly. The King, moreover, chose to support the nobility over the people. Rabaut Saint-Étienne was a deputy of the Third Estate, well-known for his defense of religious freedom.

Sir,—After you quitted us yesterday evening, we continued our conversation (Monsieur de La Fayette, Mr. Short and myself) on the subject of the difficulties which environ you. The desirable object being, to secure the good which the King has offered, and to avoid the ill which seems to threaten, an idea was suggested, which appearing to make an impression on Monsieur de La Fayette, I was encouraged to pursue it on my return to Paris, to put it into form, and now to send it to you and him. It is this; that the King, in a *séance royale* should come forward with a Charter of Rights in his hand, to be signed by himself and by every member of the three orders. This charter to contain the five great points which the Resultat of December offered, on the part of the King, the abolition of pecuniary privileges offered by the privileged orders, and the adoption of the national debt, and a grant of the sum of money asked from the nation. This last will be a cheap price for the preceding articles; and let the same act declare your immediate separation till the next anniversary meeting. You will carry back to your constituents more good than ever was effected before without violence, and you will stop exactly at the point where violence would otherwise begin. Time will be gained, the public mind will continue to ripen and to be informed, a basis of support may be prepared with the people themselves, and expedients occur for gaining still something further at your next meeting, and for stopping again at the point of force. I have ventured to send to yourself and Monsieur de La Fayette a sketch of my ideas of what this act might contain, without endangering any dispute. But it is offered merely as a canvas for you to work on, if it be fit to work on at all. I know too little of the subject, and you know too much of it, to justify me in offering anything but a hint. I have done it, too, in a hurry; insomuch, that since committing it to writing, it occurs to me that the fifth article may give alarm; that it is in a good degree included in the fourth, and is, therefore, useless. But after all, what excuse can I make, Sir, for this presumption. I have none but an unmeasurable love for your nation, and a painful anxiety lest despotism, after an unaccepted offer to bind its own hands, should seize you again with tenfold fury. Permit me to add to these, very sincere assurances of the sentiments of esteem and respect, with which I have the honor to be, Sir, your most obedient, and most humble servant.

[Following is the charter Jefferson sent to Saint-Étienne.]

A CHARTER OF RIGHTS, SOLEMNLY ESTABLISHED BY THE KING AND NATION

1. The States General shall assemble, uncalled, on the first day of November, annually, and shall remain together so long as they shall see cause. They shall regulate their own elections and proceedings, and until they shall ordain otherwise, their elections shall be in the forms observed in the present year, and shall be triennial.

2. The States General alone shall levy money on the nation, and shall appropriate it.

3. Laws shall be made by the States General only, with the consent of the King.

4. No person shall be restrained of his liberty, but by

regular process from a court of justice, authorized by a general law. (Except that a Noble may be imprisoned by order of a court of justice, on the prayer of twelve of his nearest relations.) On complaint of an unlawful imprisonment, to any judge whatever, he shall have the prisoner immediately brought before him, and shall discharge him, if his imprisonment be unlawful. The officer in whose custody the prisoner is, shall obey the orders of the judge; and both judge and officer shall be responsible, civilly and criminally, for a failure of duty herein.

5. The military shall be subordinate to the civil authority.

6. Printers shall be liable to legal prosecution for printing and publishing false facts, injurious to the party prosecuting; but they shall be under no other restraint.

7. All pecuniary privileges and exemptions, enjoyed by any description of persons, are abolished.

8. All debts already contracted by the King, are hereby made the debts of the nation; and the faith thereof is pledged for their payment in due time.

9. Eighty millions of livres are now granted to the King, to be raised by loan, and reimbursed by the nation; and the taxes heretofore paid, shall continue to be paid to the end of the present year, and no longer.

10. The States General shall now separate, and meet again on the 1st day of November next.

Done, on behalf of the whole nation, by the King and their representatives in the States General, at Versailles, this —— day of June, 1789.

Signed by the King, and by every member individually, and in his presence.

The Earth Belongs in Usufruct to the Living

To James Madison, September 6, 1789

While ill and in bed, Jefferson wrote this famous letter in which his radical philosophy assumes the aspect of a social law. The ideas were suggested to him by the remarkable Dr. Richard Gem, his physician. Gem, an atheist and republican well known to his contemporaries, submitted several propositions to Jefferson on which the letter below is based. But Jefferson, it is worth pointing out, never as a moderate political leader, nor later, as President, sought to apply directly the revolutionary principle enunciated in his letter. Very likely, he had in mind France, where the Revolution was then getting under way.

Dear Sir,—I sit down to write to you without knowing by what occasion I shall send my letter. I do it, because a subject comes into my head, which I would wish to develop a little more than is practicable in the hurry of the moment of making up general despatches.

The question, whether one generation of men has a right to bind another, seems never to have been started either on this or our side of the water. Yet it is a question of such consequences as not only to merit decision, but place also among the fundamental principles of every government. The course of reflection in which we are immersed here, on the elementary principles of society, has presented this question to my mind; and that no such obligation can be transmitted, I think very capable of proof. I set out on this ground, which I suppose to be self-evident, that the *earth belongs in usufruct to the living;* that the dead have neither powers nor rights over it. The portion occupied by any individual ceases to be his when himself ceases to be, and reverts to the society. If the society has formed no rules for the appropriation of its lands in severalty, it will be taken by the first occupants, and these will generally be the wife and children of the decedent. If they have formed rules of appropriation, those rules may give it to the wife and children, or to some one of them, or to the legatee of the deceased. So they may give it to its creditor.

But the child, the legatee or creditor, takes it, not by natural right, but by a law of the society of which he is a member, and to which he is subject. Then, no man can, by *natural right,* oblige the lands he occupied, or the persons who succeed him in that occupation, to the payment of debts contracted by him. For if he could, he might during his own life, eat up the usufruct of the lands for several generations to come; and then the lands would belong to the dead, and not to the living, which is the reverse of our principle.

What is true of every member of the society, individually, is true of them all collectively; since the rights of the whole can be no more than the sum of the rights of the individuals. To keep our ideas clear when applying them to a multitude, let us suppose a whole generation of men to be born on the same day, to attain mature age on the same day, and to die on the same day, leaving a succeeding generation in the moment of attaining their mature age, all together. Let the ripe age be supposed of twenty-one years, and their period of life thirty-four years more, that being the average term given by the bills of mortality to persons of twenty-one years of age. Each successive generation would, in this way, come and go off the stage at a fixed moment, as individuals do now. Then I say, the earth belongs to each of these generations during its course, fully and in its own right. The second generation receives it clear of the debts and incumbrances of the first, the third of the second, and so on. For if the first could charge it with a debt, then the earth would belong to the dead and not to the living generation. Then, no generation can contract debts greater than may be paid during the course of its own existence. At twenty-one years of age, they may bind themselves and their lands for thirty-four years to come; at twenty-two, for thirty-three; at twenty-three, for thirty-two; and at fifty-four, for one year only; because these are the terms of life which remain to them at the respective epochs. But a material difference must be noted, between the succession of an individual and that of a whole generation. Individuals are parts only of a society, subject to the laws of a whole. These laws may appropriate the portion of land occupied by a decedent, to his creditor, rather than to any other, or to his child, on condition he satisfies the creditor. But when a whole generation, that is, the whole society, dies, as in the case we have supposed, and another generation or society succeeds, this forms a whole, and there is no superior who can give their territory to a third society, who may have lent money to their predecessors, beyond their faculties of paying.

What is true of generations succeeding one another at fixed epochs, as has been supposed for clearer conception, is true for those renewed daily, as in the actual course of nature. As a majority of the contracting generation will continue in being thirty-four years, and a new majority will then come into possession, the former may extend their engagement to that term, and no longer. The conclusion then, is, that neither the representatives of a nation, nor the whole nation itself assembled, can validly engage debts beyond what they may pay in their own time, that is to say, within thirty-four years of the date of the engagement.

To render this conclusion palpable, suppose that Louis the XIV. and XV. had contracted debts in the name of the French nation, to the amount of ten thousand milliards, and that the whole had been contracted in Holland. The interest of this sum would be five hundred milliards, which is the whole rent-roll or net proceeds of the territory of France. Must the present generation of men have retired from the territory in which nature produces them, and ceded it to the Dutch creditors? No; they have the same rights over the soil on which they were produced, as the preceding generations had. They derive these rights not from them, but from nature. They, then, and their soil are, by nature, clear of the debts of their predecessors. To present this in another point of view, suppose Louis XV. and his contemporary generation, had said to the money lenders of Holland, give us money, that we may eat, drink, and be merry in our day; and on condition you will demand no interest till the end of thirty-four years, you shall then, forever after, receive an annual interest of fifteen per cent. The money is lent on these conditions, is divided among the people, eaten, drunk, and squandered. Would the present generation be obliged to apply the produce of the earth and of their labor, to replace their dissipations? Not at all.

I suppose that the received opinion, that the public debts of one generation devolve on the next, has been suggested by our seeing, habitually, in private life, that he who succeeds to lands is required to pay the debts of his predecessor; without considering that this requisition is municipal only, not moral, flowing from the will of the society, which has found it convenient to appropriate the lands of a decedent on the condition of a payment of his debts; but that between society and society, or generation and generation, there is no municipal obligation, no umpire but the law of nature.

The interest of the national debt of France being, in fact, but a two thousandth part of its rent-roll, the payment of it is practicable enough; and so becomes a question merely of honor or of expediency. But with respect to future debts, would it not be wise and just for that nation to declare in the constitution they are forming, that neither the legislature nor the nation itself, can validly contract more debt than they may pay within their own age, or within the term of thirty-four years? And that all future contracts shall be deemed void, as to what shall remain unpaid at the end of thirty-four years from their date? This would put the lenders, and the borrowers also, on their guard. By reducing, too, the faculty of borrowing within its natural limits, it would bridle the spirit of war, to which too free a course has been procured by the inattention of money lenders to this law of nature, that succeeding generations are not responsible for the preceding.

On similar ground it may be proved, that no society can make a perpetual constitution, or even a perpetual law. The earth belongs always to the living generation: they may manage it, then, and what proceeds from it, as they please, during their usufruct. They are masters, too, of their own persons, and consequently may govern them as they please. But persons and property make the sum of the objects of government. The constitution and the laws of their predecessors are extinguished then, in their natural course, with those whose will gave them being. This could preserve that being, till it ceased to be itself, and no longer. Every constitution, then, and every law, naturally expires at the end of thirty-four years. If it be enforced longer, it is an act of force, and not of right. It may be said, that the succeeding generation exercising, in fact, the power of repeal, this leaves them as free as if the constitution or law had been expressly limited to thirty-four years only. In the first place, this objection admits the right, in proposing an equivalent. But the power of repeal is not an equivalent. It might be, indeed, if every form of government were so perfectly contrived, that the will of the majority could always be obtained, fairly and without impediment. But this is true of no form. The people cannot assemble themselves; their representation is unequal and vicious. Various checks are opposed to every legislative proposition.

Factions get possession of the public councils, bribery corrupts them, personal interests lead them astray from the general interests of their constituents; and other impediments arise, so as to prove to every practical man, that a law of limited duration is much more manageable than one which needs a repeal.

This principle, that the earth belongs to the living and not to the dead, is of very extensive application and consequences in every country, and most especially in France. It enters into the resolution of the questions, whether the nation may change the descent of lands holden in tail; whether they may change the appropriation of lands given anciently to the church, to hospitals, colleges, orders of chivalry, and otherwise in perpetuity; whether they may abolish the charges and privileges attached on lands, including the whole catalogue, ecclesiastical and feudal; it goes to hereditary offices, authorities and jurisdictions, to hereditary orders, distinctions and appellations, to perpetual monopolies in commerce, the arts or sciences, with a long train of *et ceteras;* renders the question of reimbursement, a question of generosity and not of right. In all these cases, the legislature of the day could authorize such appropriations and establishments for their own time, but no longer; and the present holders, even where they or their ancestors have purchased, are in the case of *bona fide* purchasers of what the seller had no right to convey.

Turn this subject in your mind, my dear Sir, and particularly as to the power of contracting debts, and develop it with that cogent logic which is so peculiarly yours. Your station in the councils of our country gives you an opportunity of producing it to public consideration, of forcing it into discussion. At first blush it may be laughed at, as the dream of a theorist; but examination will prove it to be solid and salutary. It would furnish matter for a fine preamble to our first law for appropriating the public revenue; and it will exclude, at the threshold of our new government, the ruinous and contagious errors of this quarter of the globe, which have armed despots with means which nature does not sanction, for binding in chains their fellow-men. We have already given, for example, one effectual check to the dog of war, by transferring the power of declaring war from the executive to the legislative body, from those who are to spend, to those who are to pay. I should be pleased to see this second obstacle held out by us also, in the first instance. No nation can make a declaration against the validity of long-contracted debts, so disinterestedly as we, since we do not owe a shilling which will not be paid, principal and interest, by the measures you have taken, within the time of our own lives. I write you no news, because when an occasion occurs, I shall write a separate letter for that.

I am always, with great and sincere esteem, dear Sir, your affectionate friend and servant.

PART VI

SECRETARY OF STATE: 1790–1793

Introduction

JEFFERSONIANISM, IF IT meant anything, meant the concrete realization of Jefferson's abstract political philosophy. In the decade after his arrival from France, Jefferson adopted an anti-Federalist constitutional position, formed an opposition party out of very disparate elements and, as the coping stone of his public career, defeated the incumbent Federalist Party to become President of the United States.

Jefferson was still a political innocent when he reported to President Washington on May 21, 1790 to assume his duties as Secretary of State. It did not take him long, however, to be drawn into the controversy over Secretary of the Treasury Hamilton's assumption scheme. Early in 1790 Hamilton had proposed to Congress that the federal government assume state debts incurred during the Revolution. James Madison, then a Congressman, led the fight against it on the grounds that it penalized states (like Virginia) which, having conscientiously paid their debts, would now have to help those states which had not paid them. Near defeat, Hamilton implored Jefferson to throw his weight on the side of assumption. Should it be turned down, Hamilton argued, Northern states might secede. Jefferson, desiring that the seat of government be nearer the South, agreed to support assumption if Hamilton would agree to make Georgetown on the Potomac the future capital of the nation. This turned the trick. Hamilton's scheme barely passed in the House. Many years later Jefferson bitterly recalled the deal he had made with Hamilton. Rarely again, never on any important matter, did these two great adversaries come to terms.

Essentially, Jefferson contended with Hamilton over two large issues: over the power and responsibility of the federal government in domestic affairs, and over the position to be taken toward Britain and France in foreign affairs. Lines of distinction between different departments of the government were vague during this formative period, and each secretary easily encroached upon the province of the others. Hamilton was chief offender in this sort of administrative imperialism, first, because he was a bold federalist and an aggressive man and, second, because he headed a department that was, by 1791, larger than the other three departments combined. In the nearly three years that they served in the same cabinet, Hamilton won most of his skirmishes with Jefferson.

Their conflicting interpretations of the Constitution symbolized differences between them that cut to the heart of American political and social life. Hamilton, in his proposal to fund and assume the debt, in his legal justification for establishing a Bank of the United States, and in his Report on Manufactures, presented a consistent public philosophy: for the nation to grow, he held, a strong federal government must act in behalf of commercial, banking and industrial interests. To Jefferson, on the contrary, the nation, to retain its republican virtue, must remain a nation of yeomen farmers. This was possible only if the power of the federal government were strictly limited by the Constitution. Hamilton thought that Jefferson was a dissembler and a demagogue. Jefferson thought that Hamilton wanted to restore "monocratic" rule in America.

Their views on America's relations with Britain and France were inseparable from their political and social philosophies. The French Revolution produced conflicts in foreign policy that corresponded to—or rather intensified—conflicts at home. Hamilton was hostile to France after 1789. Jefferson regarded revolutionary France along with republican America as the hope of mankind. Differences between them crystallized fully when France—ten days after executing Louis XVI—declared war on Britain, Spain and Holland. In 1778 the United States and France had signed treaties of mutual aid. What was to be done now that France was at war? Hamilton advised a policy of strict neutrality and the recision of the treaties with France on the ground that they had been concluded with a royal, not a republican, government. Jefferson counseled against a declaration of neutrality, so that concessions might be won from Britain, and protested against a recision of the treaties, as they had been concluded with a nation, not with any government. Washington, in effect, took Hamilton's side in his Neutrality Proclamation of April 22, 1793, though he acknowledged that treaties are binding on nations.

While Jefferson was insisting that the United States could not be indifferent to the fate of a sister republic and an old ally, the Genêt affair came along to embarrass him and the cause of anti-Federalism. Citizen Edmund Charles Genêt, minister of revolutionary France, having arrived in the United States in early April 1793 to great popular acclaim, decided that he would hold the government, including Jefferson, in contempt, and appeal directly to the people. He took the liberty of outfitting privateers in American ports. The President told Genêt that war vessels could not prey in American waters and that their prizes could not be brought to American ports. After promising to obey, Genêt ordered the *Little Sarah* outfitted for service. And after promising Jefferson that the *Little Sarah* would be kept in port, Genêt ordered her to sneak out to sea. Washington then ordered Genêt's recall. Meanwhile the Jacobins had taken power and marked Genêt, a Girondist, for the guillotine. Valuing his life more than the Revolution, he asked for, and received, asylum, and settled down to a happy and quiet life. The Genêt affair made it easier for Washington to sustain his policy of neutrality (which, in practice, meant favoring Britain).

Jefferson came to feel toward the State Department as he once felt toward the governorship of Virginia. Weary and discontented, he wanted to return to his family and farm. Although he asked to resign at the end of 1792 he waited another full year at Washington's request. With Jefferson gone, the Washington administration turned more sharply to the right. At the same time Jefferson and his friends looked to the day when another party, representing different principles, would take power.

The Only Sure Guardian of the Rights of Man

Response to the Address of the Citizens, February 12, 1790

Early in the year, thirteen of Jefferson's friends and neighbors in Albemarle County, on learning of his pending arrival, drew up a letter of welcome and congratulations. Obviously moved by it, Jefferson carefully composed his reply, given below.

Gentlemen,—The testimony of esteem with which you are pleased to honour my return to my native county fills me with gratitude and pleasure. While it shews that my absence has not lost me your friendly recollection, it holds out the comfortable hope that when the hour of retirement shall come, I shall again find myself amidst those with whom I have long lived, with whom I wish to live, and whose affection is the source of my purest happiness. Their favor was the door thro' which I was ushered on the stage of public life; and while I have been led on thro' it's varying scenes, I could not be unmindful of those who assigned me my first part.

My feeble and obscure exertions in their service, and in the holy cause of freedom, have had no other merit than that they were my best. We have all the same. We have been fellow-labourers and fellow-sufferers, and heaven has rewarded us with a happy issue from our struggles. It rests now with ourselves alone to enjoy in peace and concord the blessings of self-government, so long denied to mankind: to shew by example the sufficiency of human reason for the care of human affairs and that the will of the majority, the Natural law of every society, is the only sure guardian of the rights of man. Perhaps even this may sometimes err. But it's errors are honest, solitary and short-lived.—Let us then, my dear friends, for ever bow down to the general reason of the society. We are safe with that, even in it's deviations, for it soon returns again to the right way. These are lessons we have learnt together. We have prospered in their practice, and the liberality with which you are pleased to approve my

attachment to the general rights of mankind assures me we
are still together in these it's kindred sentiments.

Wherever I may be stationed, by the will of my country, it
will be my delight to see, in the general tide of happiness,
that yours too flows on in just place and measure. That it may
flow thro' all times, gathering strength as it goes, and spread-
ing the happy influence of reason and liberty over the face
of the earth, is my fervent prayer to heaven.

A Puzzle and a Machine

Anas, February 4, 1818

Jefferson kept notes of his public life from 1791 to 1809. Written with brio and force from a partisan point of view, these Anas, as he called them, comprise an invaluable record of men and events during those years. He later revised the Anas to remove from them what he thought "incorrect or doubtful." Rather than present them consecutively, we have broken them up and placed them in the company of the events they describe. The particular note below, which Jefferson wrote long after the event occurred, will serve to introduce his sustained conflict with Hamilton and the Federalists.

. . . [I] landed in Virginia in December, 1789, and proceeded to New York in March, 1790, to enter on the office of Secretary of State. Here, certainly, I found a state of things which, of all I had ever contemplated, I the least expected. I had left France in the first year of her revolution, in the fervor of natural rights, and zeal for reformation. My conscientious devotion to these rights could not be heightened, but it had been aroused and excited by daily exercise. The President received me cordially, and my colleagues and the circle of principal citizens apparently with welcome. The courtesies of dinner parties given me, as a stranger newly arrived among them, placed me at once in their familiar society. But I cannot describe the wonder and mortification with which the table conversations filled me. Politics were the chief topic, and a preference of kingly over republican government was evidently the favorite sentiment. An apostate I could not be, nor yet a hypocrite; and I found myself, for the most part, the only advocate on the republican side of the question, unless among the guests there chanced to be some member of that party from the legislative Houses. Hamilton's financial system had then passed. It had two objects; 1st, as a puzzle, to exclude popular understanding and inquiry; 2d, as a machine for the corruption of the legislature; for he avowed the opinion, that man could be governed by one of two motives only, force or interest; force, he observed, in this country was out of the question, and the interests, therefore, of the members must be laid hold of, to keep the legislative in unison with the executive. And with grief and shame it must be acknowledged that his machine was not without effect; that even in this, the birth of our government, some members were found sordid enough to bend their duty to their interests, and to look after personal rather than public good.

It is well known that during the war the greatest difficulty we encountered was the want of money or means to pay our soldiers who fought, or our farmers, manufacturers and merchants, who furnished the necessary supplies of food and clothing for them. After the expedient of paper money had exhausted itself, certificates of debt were given to the individual creditors, with assurance of payment so soon as the United States should be able. But the distresses of these people often obliged them to part with these for the half, the fifth, and even a tenth of their value; and speculators had made a trade of cozening them from the holders by the most fraudulent practices, and persuasions that they would never be paid. In the bill for funding and paying these, Hamilton made no difference between the original holders and the fraudulent purchasers of this paper. Great and just repugnance arose at putting these two classes of creditors on the same footing, and great exertions were used to pay the former the full value, and to the latter, the price only which they had paid, with interest. But this would have prevented the game which was to be played, and for which the minds of greedy members were already tutored and prepared. When the trial of strength on these several efforts had indicated the form in which the bill would finally pass, this being known within doors sooner than without, and especially, than to those who were in distant parts of the Union, the base scramble began. Couriers and relay horses by land, and swift sailing pilot boats by sea, were flying in all directions. Active partners and agents were associated and employed in every State, town, and country neighborhood, and this paper was bought up at five shillings, and even as low as two shillings in the pound, before the holder knew that Congress had already provided for its redemption at par. Immense sums were thus filched from the poor and ignorant, and fortunes accumulated by those who had themselves been poor enough before. Men thus enriched by the dexterity of a leader, would follow of course the chief who was leading them to fortune, and become the zealous instruments of all his enterprises.

This game was over, and another was on the carpet at the moment of my arrival; and to this I was most ignorantly and innocently made to hold the candle. This fiscal maneuvre is well known by the name of the Assumption.

Independently of the debts of Congress, the States had during the war contracted separate and heavy debts; and Massachusetts particularly, in an absurd attempt, absurdly conducted, on the British post of Penobscott: and the more debt Hamilton could rake up, the more plunder for his mercenaries. This money, whether wisely or foolishly spent, was pretended to have been spent for general purposes, and ought, therefore, to be paid from the general purse. But it was objected, that nobody knew what these debts were, what their amount, or what their proofs. No matter; we will guess them to be twenty millions. But of these twenty millions, we do not know how much should be reimbursed to one State, or how much to another. No matter; we will guess. And so another scramble was set on foot among the several States, and some got much, some little, some nothing. But the main object was obtained, the phalanx of the Treasury was reinforced by additional recruits.

This measure produced the most bitter and angry contest ever known in Congress, before or since the Union of the States. I arrived in the midst of it. But a stranger to the ground, a stranger to the actors on it, so long absent as to have lost all familiarity with the subject, and as yet unaware of its object, I took no concern in it. The great and trying question, however, was lost in the House of Representatives. So high were the feuds excited by this subject, that on its rejection business was suspended. Congress met and adjourned from day to day without doing any thing, the parties being too much out of temper to do business together. The eastern members particularly, who, with Smith from South Carolina, were the principal gamblers in these scenes, threatened a secession and dissolution. Hamilton was in despair. As I was going to the President's one day, I met him in the street. He walked me backwards and forwards before the President's door for half an hour. He painted pathetically the temper into which the legislature had been wrought; the disgust of those who were called the creditor States; the danger of the *secession* of their members, and the separation of the States. He observed that the members of the administration ought to act in concert; that though this question was not of my department, yet a common duty should make it a common concern; that the President was the centre on which all administrative questions ultimately rested, and that all of us should rally around him, and support, with joint efforts, measures approved by him; and that the question having been lost by a small majority only, it was probable that an appeal from me to the judgment and discretion of some of my friends, might effect a change in the vote, and the machine of government, now suspended, might be again set into motion. I told him that I was really a stranger to the whole subject; that not having yet informed myself of the system of finances adopted, I knew not how far this was a necessary sequence; that undoubtedly, if its rejection endangered a dissolution of our Union at this incipient stage, I should deem that the most unfortunate of all consequences, to avert which all partial and temporary evils should be yielded. I proposed to him, however, to dine with me the next day, and I would invite another friend or two, bring them into conference together, and I thought it impossible that reasonable men, consulting together coolly, could fail, by some mutual sacrifices of opinion, to form a compromise which was to save the Union.

The discussion took place. I could take no part in it but an exhortatory one, because I was a stranger to the circumstances which should govern it. But it was finally agreed, that whatever importance had been attached to the rejection of this proposition, the preservation of the Union and of concord among the States was more important, and that therefore it would be better that the vote of rejection should be rescinded, to effect which, some members should change their votes. But it was observed that this pill would be peculiarly bitter to the southern States, and that some concomitant measure should be adopted, to sweeten it a little to them. There had before been propositions to fix the seat of government either at Philadelphia, or at Georgetown on the Potomac; and it was thought that by giving it to Philadelphia for ten years, and to Georgetown permanently afterwards, this might, as an anodyne, calm in some degree the ferment which might be excited by the other measure alone. So two of the Potomac members (White and Lee, but White with a revulsion of stomach almost convulsive), agreed to change their votes, and Hamilton undertook to carry the other point. In doing this, the influence he had established over the eastern members, with the agency of Robert Morris with those of the middle States, effected his side of the engagement; and so the Assumption was passed, and twenty millions of stock divided among favored States, and thrown in as a pabulum to the stock-jobbing herd. This added to the number of votaries to the Treasury, and made its chief the master of every vote in the legislature, which might give to the government the direction suited to his political views.

I know well, and so must be understood, that nothing like a majority in Congress had yielded to this corruption. Far from it. But a division, not very unequal, had already taken place in the honest part of that body, between the parties styled republican and federal. The latter being monarchists in principle, adhered to Hamilton of course, as their leader in that principle, and this mercenary phalanx added to them, insured him always a majority in both Houses: so that the whole action of legislature was now under the direction of the Treasury. Still the machine was not complete. The effect of the funding system, and of the Assumption, would be temporary; it would be lost with the loss of the individual members whom it has enriched, and some engine of influence more permanent must be contrived, while these myrmidons were yet in place to carry it through all opposition. This engine was the Bank of the United States. All that history is known, so I shall say nothing about it. While the government remained at Philadelphia, a selection of members of both Houses were constantly kept as directors who, on every question interesting to that institution, or to the views of the federal head, voted at the will of that head; and, together with the stockholding members, could always make the federal vote that of the majority. By this combination, legislative expositions were given to the constitution, and all the administrative laws were shaped on the model of England, and so passed. And from this influence we were not relieved, until the removal from the precincts of the bank, to Washington.

Here then was the real ground of the opposition which was made to the course of administration. Its object was to preserve the legislature pure and independent of the executive, to restrain the administration to republican forms and principles, and not permit the constitution to be construed into a monarchy, and to be warped, in practice, into all the principles and polutions of their favorite English model. Nor was this an opposition to General Washington. He was true to the republican charge confided to him; and has solemnly and repeatedly protested to me, in our conversations, that he would lose the last drop of his blood in support of it; and he did this the oftener and with the more earnestness, because he knew my suspicions of Hamilton's designs against it, and wished to quiet them. For he was not aware of the drift, or of the effect of Hamilton's schemes. Unversed in financal projects and calculations and budgets, his approbation of them was bottomed on his confidence in the man.

But Hamilton was not only a monarchist, but for a monarchy bottomed on corruption. In proof of this, I will relate an anecdote, for the truth of which I attest the God who made me. Before the President set out on his southern tour in April, 1791, he addressed a letter of the fourth of that month, from Mount Vernon, to the Secretaries of State, Treasury and War, desiring that if any serious and important cases should arise during his absence, they would consult and act on them. And he requested that the Vice President should also be consulted. This was the only occasion on which that officer was ever requested to take part in a cabinet question. Some occasion for consultation arising, I invited those gentlemen (and the Attorney General, as well as I remember), to dine with me, in order to confer on the subject. After the cloth was removed, and our question agreed and dismissed, conversation began on other matters, and by some circumstance, was led to the British constitution, on which Mr. Adams observed, "Purge that constitution of its corruption, and give to its popular branch equality of representation, and it would be the most perfect constitution ever devised by the wit of man." Hamilton paused and said, "Purge it of its corruption, and give to its popular branch equality of representation, and it would become an *impracticable* government: as it stands at present, with all its supposed defects, it is the most perfect government which ever existed." And this was assuredly the exact line which separated the political creeds of these two gentlemen. The one was for two hereditary branches and an honest elective one: the other, for an hereditary King, with a House of Lords and Commons corrupted to his will, and standing between him and the people.

Hamilton was, indeed, a singular character. Of acute understanding, disinterested, honest, and honorable in all private transactions, amiable in society, and duly valuing virtue in private life, yet so bewitched and perverted by the British example, as to be under thorough conviction that corruption was essential to the government of a nation. Mr. Adams had originally been a republican. The glare of royalty and nobility, during his mission to England, had made him believe their fascination a necessary ingredient in government; and Shay's rebellion, not sufficiently understood where he then was, seemed to prove that the absence of want and oppression was not a sufficient guarantee of order. . . .

Mr. Adams, I am sure, has been long since convinced of the treacheries with which he was surrounded during his administration. He has since thoroughly seen, that his constituents were devoted to republican government, and whether his judgment is re-settled on its ancient basis, or not, he is conformed as a good citizen to the will of the majority, and would now, I am persuaded, maintain its republican structure with the zeal and fidelity belonging to his character. For even an enemy has said, "He is always an honest man, and often a great one." . . .

Convenience Cannot Constitute Necessity

Opinion on the Constitutionality of a National Bank, February 15, 1791

The bank bill precipitated an ideological conflict between Hamilton and Jefferson that did not abate until their death. In early February 1791 Hamilton laid before Congress his bill proposing that the federal government charter a private bank, a fifth of whose shares it would own and whose notes it would honor as legal tender, redeemable in specie. Thus the country was to buttress the financial transactions of a private corporation. Washington asked Jefferson to comment on the bill's constitutionality. Washington then showed Jefferson's opinion to Hamilton who wrote a strong rebuttal. On the strength of Hamilton's defense, Washington decided to approve the bill even though he had asked Madison to draft a veto message.

The bill for establishing a National Bank undertakes among other things:

1. To form the subscribers into a corporation.

2. To enable them in their corporate capacities to receive grants of land; and so far is against the laws of *mortmain*.[1]

3. To make alien subscribers capable of holding lands; and so far is against the laws of *alienage*.

4. To transmit these lands, on the death of a proprietor, to a certain line of successors; and so far changes the course of *descents*.

5. To put the lands out of the reach of forfeiture or escheat; and so far is against the laws of *forfeiture and escheat*.

6. To transmit personal chattels to successors in a certain line; and so far is against the laws of *distribution*.

7. To give them the sole and exclusive right of banking under the national authority; and so far is against the laws of *monopoly*.

---

[1] Though the Constitution controls the laws of mortmain so far as to permit Congress itself to hold lands for certain purposes, yet not so far as to permit them to communicate a similar right to other corporate bodies. [Jefferson].

8. To communicate to them a power to make laws paramount to the laws of the States; for so they must be construed, to protect the institution from the control of the State legislatures; and so, probably, they will be construed.

I consider the foundation of the Constitution as laid on this ground: That "all powers not delegated to the United States, by the Constitution, nor prohibited by it to the States, are reserved to the States or to the people." [XII amendment.] To take a single step beyond the boundaries thus specially drawn around the powers of Congress, is to take possession of a boundless field of power, no longer susceptible of any definition.

The incorporation of a bank, and the powers assumed by this bill, have not, in my opinion, been delegated to the United States, by the Constitution.

I. They are not among the powers specially enumerated: for these are: 1. A power to lay taxes for the purpose of paying the debts of the United States; but no debt is paid by this bill, nor any tax laid. Were it a bill to raise money, its origination in the Senate would condemn it by the Constitution.

2. "To borrow money." But this bill neither borrows money nor ensures the borrowing it. The proprietors of the bank will be just as free as any other money holders, to lend or not to lend their money to the public. The operation proposed in the bill, first, to lend them two millions, and then to borrow them back again, cannot change the nature of the latter act, which will still be a payment, and not a loan, call it by what name you please.

3. To "regulate commerce with foreign nations, and among the States, and with the Indian tribes." To erect a bank, and to regulate commerce, are very different acts. He who erects a bank, creates a subject of commerce in its bills; so does he who makes a bushel of wheat, or digs a dollar out of the mines; yet neither of these persons regulates commerce thereby. To make a thing which may be bought and sold, is not to prescribe regulations for buying and selling. Besides, if this was an exercise of the power of regulating commerce, it would be void, as extending as much to the internal commerce of every State, as to its external. For the power given to Congress by the Constitution does not extend to the internal regulation of the commerce of a State (that is to say of the commerce between citizen and citizen), which remain ex-

clusively with its own legislature; but to its external commerce only, that is to say, its commerce with another State, or with foreign nations, or with the Indian tribes. Accordingly the bill does not propose the measure as a regulation of trade, but as "productive of considerable advantages to trade." Still less are these powers covered by any other of the special enumerations.

II. Nor are they within either of the general phrases, which are the two following:

1. To lay taxes to provide for the general welfare of the United States, that is to say, "to lay taxes for *the purpose* of providing for the general welfare." For the laying of taxes is the *power,* and the general welfare the *purpose* for which the power is to be exercised. They are not to lay taxes *ad libitum for any purpose they please;* but only *to pay the debts or provide for the welfare of the Union.* In like manner, they are not *to do anything they please* to provide for the general welfare, but only to *lay taxes* for that purpose. To consider the latter phrase, not as describing the purpose of the first, but as giving a distinct and independent power to do any act they please, which might be for the good of the Union, would render all the preceding and subsequent enumerations of power completely useless.

It would reduce the whole instrument to a single phrase, that of instituting a Congress with power to do whatever would be for the good of the United States; and, as they would be the sole judges of the good or evil, it would be also a power to do whatever evil they please.

It is an established rule of construction where a phrase will bear either of two meanings, to give it that which will allow some meaning to the other parts of the instrument, and not that which would render all the others useless. Certainly no such universal power was meant to be given them. It was intended to lace them up straitly within the enumerated powers, and those without which, as means, these powers could not be carried into effect. It is known that the very power now proposed *as a means* was rejected as *an end* by the Convention which formed the Constitution. A proposition was made to them to authorize Congress to open canals, and an amendatory one to empower them to incorporate. But the whole was rejected, and one of the reasons for rejection urged in debate was, that then they would have a power to erect a bank, which would render the great cities, where there were prejudices and jealousies on the subject, adverse to the reception of the Constitution.

2. The second general phrase is, "to make all laws *necessary* and proper for carrying into execution the enumerated powers." But they can all be carried into execution without a bank. A bank therefore is not *necessary*, and consequently not authorized by this phrase.

It has been urged that a bank will give great facility or convenience in the collection of taxes. Suppose this were true: yet the Constitution allows only the means which are *"necessary,"* not those which are merely "convenient" for effecting the enumerated powers. If such a latitude of construction be allowed to this phrase as to give any non-enumerated power, it will go to everyone, for there is not one which ingenuity may not torture into a *convenience* in some instance *or other*, to *someone* of so long a list of enumerated powers. It would swallow up all the delegated powers, and reduce the whole to one power, as before observed. Therefore it was that the Constitution restrained them to the *necessary* means, that is to say, to those means without which the grant of power would be nugatory.

But let us examine this convenience and see what it is. The report on this subject, states the only *general* convenience to be, the preventing the transportation and re-transportation of money between the States and the treasury, (for I pass over the increase of circulating medium, ascribed to it as a want, and which, according to my ideas of paper money, is clearly a demerit.) Every State will have to pay a sum of tax money into the treasury; and the treasury will have to pay, in every State, a part of the interest on the public debt, and salaries to the officers of government resident in that State. In most of the States there will still be a surplus of tax money to come up to the seat of government for the officers residing there. The payments of interest and salary in each State may be made by treasury orders on the State collector. This will take up the great export of the money he has collected in his State, and consequently prevent the great mass of it from being drawn out of the State. If there be a balance of commerce in favor of that State against the one in which the government resides, the surplus of taxes will be remitted by the bills of exchange drawn for that commercial balance. And so it must be if there was a bank. But if there be no balance of commerce, either direct or circuitous, all the banks in the world could not bring up the surplus of taxes, but in the form of money. Treasury orders then, and bills of exchange may prevent the displacement of the main mass of the money collected, without the aid of any bank; and where these fail, it cannot be prevented even with that aid.

Perhaps, indeed, bank bills may be a more *convenient* vehicle than treasury orders. But a little *difference* in the degree of *convenience,* cannot constitute the necessity which the constitution makes the ground for assuming any non-enumerated power.

Besides, the existing banks will, without a doubt, enter into arrangements for lending their agency, and the more favorable, as there will be a competition among them for it; whereas the bill delivers us up bound to the National Bank, who are free to refuse all arrangement, but on their own terms, and the public not free, on such refusal, to employ any other bank. That of Philadelphia, I believe, now does this business, by their post-notes, which, by an arrangement with the treasury, are paid by any State collector to whom they are presented. This expedient alone suffices to prevent the existence of that *necessity* which may justify the assumption of a non-enumerated power as a means for carrying into effect an enumerated one. The thing may be done, and has been done, and well done, without this assumption; therefore, it does not stand on that degree of *necessity* which can honestly justify it.

It may be said that a bank whose bills would have a currency all over the States, would be more convenient than one whose currency is limited to a single State. So it would be still more convenient that there should be a bank, whose bills should have a currency all over the world. But it does not follow from this superior conveniency, that there exists anywhere a power to establish such a bank; or that the world may not go on very well without it.

Can it be thought that the Constitution intended that for a shade or two of *convenience,* more or less, Congress should be authorized to break down the most ancient and fundamental laws of the several States; such as those against mortmain, the laws of alienage, the rules of descent, the acts of distribution, the laws of escheat and forfeiture, the laws of monopoly? Nothing but a necessity invincible by any other means, can justify such a prostitution of laws, which constitute the pillars of our whole system of jurisprudence. Will

Congress be too straight-laced to carry the Constitution into honest effect, unless they may pass over the foundation-laws of the State government for the slightest convenience of theirs?

The negative of the President is the shield provided by the Constitution to protect against the invasions of the legislature: 1. The right of the Executive. 2. Of the Judiciary. 3. Of the States and State legislatures. The present is the case of a right remaining exclusively with the States, and consequently one of those intended by the Constitution to be placed under its protection.

It must be added, however, that unless the President's mind on a view of everything which is urged for and against this bill, is tolerably clear that it is unauthorised by the Constitution; if the pro and the con hang so even as to balance his judgment, a just respect for the wisdom of the legislature would naturally decide the balance in favor of their opinion. It is chiefly for cases where they are clearly misled by error, ambition, or interest, that the Constitution has placed a check in the negative of the President.

We Have Differed As Friends

To John Adams, July 17, 1791

Paine's The Rights of Man *unavoidably affected Jefferson's political life. The Philadelphia printer of Paine's work affixed to it a comment sent by Jefferson: "I am extremely pleased to find it will be reprinted here, and that something is at length to be publickly said against the political heresies which have sprung up among us. I have no doubt that our citizens will rally round the standard of* Common Sense." "Political heresies" *must have referred to John Adams' strongly federalist* Discourses on Davila, *which appeared serially in a Philadelphia newspaper. Under the name Publicola, the Vice-President's son, John Quincy Adams, wrote a spirited criticism of Paine and his ideas. A host of pseudonymous writers then came to Paine's defense. Many thought that Publicola was John Adams and that Jefferson was one of his critics. Here Jefferson attempts to set the record straight.*

Dear Sir,—I have a dozen times taken up my pen to write to you, and as often laid it down again, suspended between opposing considerations. I determine, however, to write from a conviction that truth, between candid minds, can never do harm. The first of Paine's pamphlets on the rights of man, which came to hand here, belonged to Mr. Beckley. He lent it to Mr. Madison, who lent it to me; and while I was reading it, Mr. Beckley called on me for it, and, as I had not finished it, he desired me, as soon as I should have done so, to send it to Mr. Jonathan B. Smith, whose brother meant to reprint it. I finished reading it, and, as I had no acquaintance with Mr. Jonathan B. Smith, propriety required that I should explain to him why I, a stranger to him, sent him the pamphlet. I accordingly wrote a note of compliment, informing him that I did it at the desire of Mr. Beckley, and, to take off a little of the dryness of the note, I added that I was glad it was to be reprinted here, and that something was to be publicly said against the political heresies which had sprung up among us, etc. I thought so little of this note, that I did not even keep a copy of it; nor ever heard a tittle more of it, till, the week following, I was thunderstruck with seeing it come out at the head of the pamphlet. I hoped, however, it would not attract notice. But I found, on my return from a journey of a month, that a writer came forward, under the signature of Publicola, attacking not only the author and principles of the pamphlet, but myself as its sponsor, by name. Soon after came hosts of other writers, defending the pamphlet, and attacking you, by name, as the writer of Publicola. Thus were our names known on the public stage as public antagonists. That you and I differ in our ideas of the best form of government, is well known to us both; but we have differed as friends should do, respecting the purity of each other's motives, and confining our difference of opinion to private conversation. And I can declare with truth, in the presence of the Almighty, that nothing was further from my intention or expectation than to have either my own or your name brought before the public on this occasion. The friendship and confidence which has so long existed between us, required this explanation from me, and I know you too well to fear any misconstruction of the motives of it. Some people here, who would wish me to be, or to be thought, guilty of improprieties, have suggested that I was Agricola, that I was Brutus, etc., etc. I never did in my life, either by myself or by any other, have a sentence of mine inserted in a newspaper without putting my name to it; and I believe I never shall.

It Is Not Near Enough for My Wishes

To Martha Jefferson Randolph, January 15, 1792

From now on Jefferson's letters grow more plaintive, reflecting the intensity of his desire to return to private life. Anne was the first of twelve children born to his daughter and son-in-law.

My Dear Martha,—Having no particular subject for a letter, I find none more soothing to my mind than to indulge itself in expressions of the love I bear you, and the delight with which I recall the various scenes through which we have passed together in our wanderings over the world. These reveries alleviate the toils and inquietudes of my present situation, and leave me always impressed with the desire of being at home once more, and of exchanging labor, envy, and malice for ease, domestic occupation, and domestic love and society; where I may once more be happy with you, with Mr. Randolph and dear little Anne, with whom even Socrates might ride on a stick without being ridiculous. Indeed it is with difficulty that my resolution will bear me through what yet lies between the present day and that which, on mature consideration of all circumstances respecting myself and others, my mind has determined to be the proper one for relinquishing my office. Though not very distant, it is not near enough for my wishes. The ardor of these, however, would be abated if I thought that, on coming home, I should be left alone. On the contrary, I hope that Mr. Randolph will find a convenience in making only leisurely preparations for a settlement, and that I shall be able to make you both happier than you have been at Monticello, and relieve you of désagréments to which I have been sensible you were exposed, without the power in myself to prevent it, but by my own presence. Remember me affectionately to Mr. Randolph, and be assured of the tender love of yours.

They Had Chained It About Our Necks

Anas, February 28—March 1, 1792

Though his conflict with Hamilton had long been gathering force, Jefferson for the first time reveals it fully to Washington in this private conversation.

February the 28th, 1792. I was to have been with him [Washington] long enough before three o'clock (which was the hour and day he received visits), to have opened to him a proposition for doubling the velocity of the post riders, who now travel about fifty miles a day, and might, without difficulty, go one hundred, and for taking measures (by way bills) to know where the delay is, when there is any. I was delayed by business, so as to have scarcely time to give him the outlines. I run over them rapidly, and observed afterwards, that I had hitherto never spoken to him on the subject of the post office, not knowing whether it was considered as a revenue law, or a law for the general accommodation of the citizens: that the law just passed seemed to have removed the doubt, by declaring that the whole profits of the office should be applied to extending the posts, and that even the past profits should be refunded by the treasury for the same purpose: that I therefore conceive it was now in the department of the Secretary of State: that I thought it would be advantageous so to declare it for another reason, to wit: that the department of the Treasury possessed already such an influence as to swallow up the whole executive powers, and that even the future Presidents (not supported by the weight of character which himself possessed), would not be able to make head against this department. That in urging this measure I had certainly no personal interest, since, if I was supposed to have any appetite for power, yet as my career would certainly be exactly as short as his own, the intervening time was too short to be an object. My real wish was to avail the public of every occasion, during the residue of the President's period, to place things on a safe footing. . . .

I told him, that in my opinion, there was only a single source of these discontents. Though they had indeed appeared to spread themselves over the War department also, yet I considered that as an overflowing only from their real channel, which would never have taken place, if they had not first been generated in another department, to wit, that of the Treasury. That a system had there been contrived, for deluging the States with paper money instead of gold and silver, for withdrawing our citizens from the pursuits of commerce, manufactures, buildings, and other branches of useful industry, to occupy themselves and their capitals in a species of gambling, destructive of morality, and which had introduced its poison into the government itself. That it was a fact, as certianly known as that he and I were then conversing, that particular members of the legislature, while those laws were on the carpet, had feathered their nests with paper, had then voted for the laws, and constantly since lent all the energy of their talents, and instrumentality of their offices, to the establishment and enlargement of this system; that they had chained it about our necks for a great length of time, and in order to keep the game in their hands had, from time to time, aided in making such legislative constructions of the constitution, as made it a very different thing from what the people thought they had submitted to; that they had now brought forward a proposition far beyond any one ever yet advanced, and to which the eyes of many were turned, as the decision which was to let us know, whether we live under a limited or an unlimited government. He asked me to what proposition I alluded? I answered, to that in the report on manufactures, which, under color of giving *bounties* for the encouragement of particular manufactures, meant to establish the doctrine, that the power given by the constitution to collect taxes to provide for the *general welfare* of the United States, permitted Congress to take everything under their management which *they* should deem for the *public welfare,* and which is susceptible of the application of money; consequently, that the subsequent enumeration of their powers was not the description to which resort must be had, and did not at all constitute the limits of their authority; that this was a very different question from that of the bank, which was thought an incident to an enumerated power; that, therefore, this decision was expected with great anxiety; that, indeed, I hoped the proposition would be rejected, believing there was a majority in both Houses against it, and that if it should be, it would be considered as a proof that things were returning into their true channel; and that, at any rate, I looked forward to the broad representation which would shortly take place, for keeping the general constitution on its true ground; and that this would remove a great deal of the discontent which had shown itself. The conversation ended with this last topic. It is here stated nearly as much at length as it really was; the expressions preserved where I could recollect them, and their substance always faithfully stated.

March 1, 1792. . . .

1791. Towards the latter end of November, Hamilton had drawn Ternant into a conversation on the subject of the treaty of commerce recommended by the National Assembly of France to be negotiated with us, and, as he had no ready instructions on the subject, he led him into a proposal that Ternant should take the thing up as a volunteer with me, that we should arrange conditions, and let them go for confirmation or refusal. Hamilton communicated this to the President, who came into it, and proposed it to me. I disapproved of it, observing, that such a volunteer project would be binding on us, and not them; that it would enable them to find out how far we would go, and avail themselves of it. However, the President thought it worth trying, and I acquiesced. I prepared a plan of treaty for exchanging the privileges of native subjects, and fixing all duties forever as they now stood. Hamilton did not like this way of fixing the duties, because, he said, many articles here would bear to be raised, and therefore, he would prepare a tariff. He did so, raising duties for the French, from twenty-five to fifty per cent. So they were to give us the privileges of native subjects, and we, as a compensation, were to make them pay higher duties. Hamilton, having made his arrangements with Hammond to pretend that though he had no powers to conclude a treaty of commerce, yet his general commission authorized him to enter into the discussion of one, then proposed to the President at one of our meetings, that the business should be taken up with Hammond in the same informal way. I now discovered the trap which he had laid, by first getting the President into that step with Ternant. I opposed the thing warmly. Hamilton observed, if we did it with Ternant we should also with Hammond. The President thought this reasonable. I desired him to recollect, I had been against it with Ternant, and only acquiesced under his opinion. So the matter went off as to both. His scheme evidently was, to get us engaged first with Ternant, merely that he might have a pretext to engage us on the same ground with Hammond, taking care, at the same time, by an extravagant tariff, to render it impossible we should come to any conclusion with Ternant: probably meaning, at the same time, to propose terms so favorable to Great Britain, as would attach us to that country by treaty. On one of those occasions he asserted, that our commerce with Great Britain and her colonies was put on a much more favorable footing than with France and her colonies. I therefore prepared the tabular comparative view of the footing of our commerce with those nations, which see among my papers. See also my project of a treaty and Hamilton's tariff.

Committed to writing March the 11th, 1792. . . .

This Is the Event at Which I Tremble

To George Washington, May 23, 1792

Jefferson's motive in writing this important letter was to help dissuade Washington from retiring at the end of the year. Jefferson used the opportunity to disclose further, in a catalogue of grievances, his antipathy to Hamilton's "system." For his part, Washington, though he engaged in no dispute with Jefferson, stood by policies for which he, as President, was responsible. Nonetheless, on July 29 Washington sent Hamilton twenty-one "objections" without mentioning Jefferson as their source. Hamilton's answer, while vituperative toward the opposition (he mentioned no names), satisfied Washington that Jefferson's charges were incorrect or exaggerated.

Dear Sir,—I have determined to make the subject of a letter what for some time past has been a subject of inquietude to my mind, without having found a good occasion of disburthening itself to you in conversation, during the busy scenes which occupied you here. Perhaps, too, you may be able in your present situation, or on the road, to give it more time and reflection than you could do here at any moment.

When you first mentioned to me your purpose of retiring from the government, though I felt all the magnitude of the event, I was in a considerable degree silent. I knew that, to such a mind as yours, persuasion was idle and impertinent; that before forming your decision you had weighed all the reasons for and against the measure, had made up your mind on full view of them, and that there could be little hope of changing the result. Pursuing my reflections, too, I knew we were some day to try to walk alone, and if the essay should be made while you should be alive and looking on, we should derive confidence from that circumstance, and resource, if it failed. The public mind, too, was calm and confident, and therefore in a favorable state for making the experiment. Had no change of circumstances intervened, I should not, with any hopes of success, have now ventured to propose to you a

change of purpose. But the public mind is no longer confident and serene; and that from causes in which you are no
ways personally mixed. Though these causes have been hack-
neyed in the public papers in detail, it may not be amiss, in
order to calculate the effect they are capable of producing,
to take a view of them in the mass, giving to each the form,
real or imaginary, under which they have been presented.

It has been urged, then, that a public debt, greater than
we can possibly pay, before other causes of adding new debt
to it will occur, has been artificially created by adding together the whole amount of the debtor and creditor sides of
accounts, instead of only taking their balances, which could
have been paid off in a short time: that this accumulation
of debt has taken forever out of our power those easy sources
of revenue which, applied to the ordinary necessities and exigencies of government, would have answered them habitually,
and covered us from habitual murmurings against taxes and
tax-gatherers, reserving extraordinary calls for those extraordinary occasions which would animate the people to meet
them: that though the calls for money have been no greater
than we must expect generally, for the same or equivalent
exigencies, yet we are already obliged to strain the impost
till it produces clamor, and will produce evasion and war on
our own citizens to collect it, and even to resort to an *excise*
law of odious character with the people, partial in its operation, unproductive unless enforced by arbitrary and vexatious
means, and committing the authority of the government in
parts where resistance is most probable and coercion least
practicable. They cite propositions in Congress, and suspect
other projects on foot still to increase the mass of debt. They
say, that by borrowing at two-thirds of the interest, we might
have paid off the principal in two-thirds of the time; but that
from this we are precluded by its being made irredeemable
but in small portions and long terms; that this irredeemable
quality was given it for the avowed purpose of inviting its
transfer to foreign countries. They predict that this transfer of the principal, when completed, will occasion an
exportation of three millions of dollars annually for the
interest, a drain of coin, of which, as there has been no
examples, no calculation can be made of its consequences:
that the banishment of our coin will be complicated by the
creation of ten millions of paper money, in the form of bank
bills now issuing into circulation. They think the ten or twelve

per cent. annual profit paid to the lenders of this paper medium taken out of the pockets of the people, who would have had without interest the coin it is banishing: that all the capital employed in paper speculation is barren and useless, producing, like that on a gaming table, no accession to itself, and is withdrawn from commerce and agriculture, where it would have produced addition to the common mass: that it nourishes in our citizens habits of vice and idleness, instead of industry and morality: that it has furnished effectual means of corrupting such a portion of the legislature as turns the balance between the honest voters, whichever way it is directed: that this corrupt squadron, deciding the voice of the legislature, have manifested their dispositions to get rid of the limitations imposed by the Constitution on the general legislature, limitations, on the faith of which, the States acceded to that instrument: that the ultimate object of all this is to prepare the way for a change from the present republican form of government to that of monarchy, of which the English Constitution is to be the model: that this was contemplated by the convention is no secret, because its partisans have made more of it. To effect it then was impracticable, but they are still eager after their object, and are predisposing everything for its ultimate attainment. So many of them have got into the Legislature, that, aided by the corrupt squadron of paper dealers, who are at their devotion, they make a majority in both houses. The republican party, who wish to preserve the government in its present form, are fewer in number; they are fewer even when joined by the two, three, or half dozen anti-federalists, who, though they dare not avow it, are still opposed to any General Government; but, being less so to a republican than a monarchical one, they naturally join those whom they think pursuing the lesser evil.

Of all the mischiefs objected to the system of measures before mentioned, none is so afflicting and fatal to every honest hope, as the corruption of the Legislature. As it was the earliest of these measures, it became the instrument for producing the risk, and will be the instrument for producing in future a king, lords and commons, or whatever else those who direct it may choose. Withdrawn such a distance from the eye of their constituents, and these so dispersed as to be inaccessible to public information, and particularly to that of the conduct of their own representatives, they will form the most corrupt government on earth, if the means of their corruption be not prevented. The only hope of safety hangs now on the numerous representation which is to come forward the ensuing year. Some of the new members will be, probably, either in principle or interest, with the present majority; but it is expected that the great mass will form an accession to the republican party. They will not be able to undo all which the two preceding Legislatures, and especially the first, have done. Public faith and right will oppose this. But some parts of the system may be rightfully reformed, a liberation from the rest unremittingly pursued as fast as right will permit, and the door shut in future against similar commitments of the nation. Should the next Legislature take this course, it will draw upon them the whole monarchical and paper interest; but the latter, I think, will not go all lengths with the former, because creditors will never, of their own accord, fly off entirely from their debtors; therefore, this is the alternative least likely to produce convulsion. But should the majority of the new members be still in the same principles with the present, and show that we have nothing to expect but a continuance of the same practices, it is not easy to conjecture what would be the result, nor what means would be resorted to for correction of the evil. True wisdom would direct that they should be temperate and peaceable; but the division of sentiment and interest happens unfortunately to be so geographical, that no mortal can say that what is most wise and temperate would prevail against what is most easy and obvious? I can scarcely contemplate a more incalculable evil than the breaking of the Union into two or more parts. Yet when we consider the mass which opposed the original coalescence; when we consider that it lay chiefly in the Southern quarter; that the Legislature have availed themselves of no occasion of allaying it, but on the contrary, whenever Northern and Southern prejudices have come into conflict, the latter have been sacrificed and the former soothed; that the owners of the debt are in the Southern, and the holders of it in the Northern division; that the anti-federal champions are now strengthened in argument by the fulfillment of their predictions; that this has been brought about by the monarchical federalists themselves, who, having been for the new government merely as a stepping stone to monarchy, have themselves adopted the very constructions of the Constitution, of which, when advocating its acceptance before the tribunal of the people, they declared it unsusceptible; that the republican federalists who espoused the same government for its intrinsic merits, are disarmed of their weapons; that which they denied as prophecy, having now become true history, who can be sure that these things may not proselyte the small number which was wanting to place the majority on the other side? And this is the event at which I tremble, and to prevent which I consider your continuing at the head of affairs as of the last importance. The confidence of the whole Union is centred in you. Your being at the helm will be more than an answer to every argument which can be used to alarm and lead the people in any quarter, into violence and secession. North and South will hang together if they have you to hang on; and if the first correction of a numerous representation should fail in its effect, your presence will give time for trying others, not inconsistent with the union and peace of the States.

I am perfectly aware of the oppression under which your present office lays your mind, and of the ardor with which you pant for domestic life. But there is sometimes an eminence of character on which society have such peculiar claims as to control the predilections of the individual for a particular walk of happiness, and restrain him to that alone arising from the present and future benedictions of mankind. This seems to be your condition, and the law imposed on you by providence in forming your character, and fashioning the events on which it was to operate; and it is to motives like these, and not to personal anxieties of mine or others who have no right to call on you for sacrifices, that I appeal, and urge a revisal of it, on the ground of change in the aspect of things. Should an honest majority result from the new and enlarged representation; should those acquiesce whose principles or interest they may control, your wishes for retirement would be gratified with less danger, as soon as that shall be manifest, without awaiting the completion of the second period of four years. One or two sessions will determine the crises; and I cannot but hope that you can resolve to add more to the many years you have already sacrificed to the good of mankind.

The fear of suspicion that any selfish motive of continuance in office may enter into this solicitation on my part, obliges me to declare that no such motive exists. It is a thing of mere indifference to the public whether I retain or relinquish my purpose of closing my tour with the first periodical renovation of the government. I know my own measure too well to suppose that my services contribute anything to the public confidence, or the public utility. Multitudes can fill the office in which you have been pleased to place me, as much to their advantage and satisfaction. I have, therefore, no motive to consult but my own inclination, which is bent irresistibly on the tranquil enjoyment of my family, my farm and my books. I should repose among them, it is true, in far greater security, if I were to know that you remained at the watch; and I hope it will be so. To the inducements urged from a view of our domestic affairs, I will add a bare mention, of what indeed need only to be mentioned, that weighty motives for your continuance are to be found in our foreign affairs. I think it probable that both the Spanish and English negotiations, if not completed before your purpose is known, will be suspended from the moment it is known, and that the latter nation will then use double diligence in fomenting the Indian War. With my wishes for the future, I shall at the same time express my gratitude for the past, at least my portion in it; and beg permission to follow you, whether in public or private life, with those sentiments of sincere attachment and respect, with which I am unalterably, dear Sir, your affectionate friend and humble servant.

Go on Doing with Your Pen

To Thomas Paine, June 19, 1792

Jefferson here refers to the second part of Paine's Rights of Man. *His encomia of Paine reflect the increasingly ideological nature of his own contest with Hamilton.*

I received with great pleasure the present of your pamphlets, as well as for the thing itself as that it was a testimony of your recollection. Would you believe it possible that in this country there should be high & important characters who need your lessons in republicanism, & who do not heed them? It is but too true that we have a sect preaching up & pouting after an English constitution of king, lords, & commons, & whose heads are itching for crowns, coronets & mitres. But our people, my good friend, are firm and unanimous in their principles of republicanism & there is no better proof of it than that they love what you write and read it with delight. The printers season every newspaper with extracts from your last, as they did before from your first part of the *Rights of Man*. They have both served here to separate the wheat from the chaff, and to prove that tho' the latter appears on the surface, it is on the surface only. The bulk below is sound & pure. Go on then in doing with your pen what in other times was done with the sword: shew that reformation is more practicable by operating on the mind than on the body of man, and be assured that it has not a more sincere votary nor you a more ardent well-wisher than Yrs. &c.

His System Flowed from Principles
Adverse to Liberty

To George Washington, September 9, 1792

In letters to Jefferson and Hamilton, Washington sought to quiet their mutual antipathy. He asked Jefferson to show more tolerance and to accept less critically the policies of the government. But in his reply below Jefferson abates hardly a jot of his differences with Hamilton. To the charge he has levelled at Hamilton's general economic "system," he adds blatant interference in his own department.

. . . I now take the liberty of proceeding to that part of your letter wherein you notice the internal dissensions which have taken place within our government, and their disagreeable effect on its movements. That such dissensions have taken place is certain, and even among those who are nearest to you in the administration. To no one have they given deeper concern than myself; to no one equal mortification at being myself a part of them. Though I take to myself no more than my share of the general observations of your letter, yet I am so desirous ever that you should know the whole truth, and believe no more than the truth, that I am glad to seize every occasion of developing to you whatever I do or think relative to the government; and shall, therefore, ask permission to be more lengthy now than the occasion particularly calls for, or could otherwise perhaps justify.

When I embarked in the government, it was with a determination to intermeddle not at all with the Legislature, and as little as possible with my co-departments. The first and only instance of variance from the former part of my resolution, I was duped into by the Secretary of the Treasury, and made a tool for forwarding his schemes, not then sufficiently understood by me; and of all the errors of my political life, this has occasioned me the deepest regret. It has ever been my purpose to explain this to you, when, from being actors on the scene, we shall have become uninterested spectators only. The second part of my resolution has been religiously observed with the War Department; and as to that of the

Treasury, has never been further swerved from than by the mere enunciation of my sentiments in conversation, and chiefly among those who, expressing the same sentiments, drew mine from me. If it has been supposed that I have ever intrigued among the members of the Legislature to defeat the plans of the Secretary of the Treasury, it is contrary to all truth. As I never had the desire to influence the members, so neither had I any other means than my friendships, which I valued too highly to risk by usurpation on their freedom of judgment, and the conscientious pursuit of their own sense of duty. That I have utterly, in my private conversations, disapproved of the system of the Secretary of the Treasury, I acknowledge and avow; and this was not merely a speculative difference. His system flowed from principles adverse to liberty, and was calculated to undermine and demolish the Republic, by creating an influence of his department over the members of the Legislature. I saw this influence actually produced, and its first fruits to be the establishment of the great outlines of his project by the votes of the very persons who, having swallowed his bait, were laying themselves out to profit by his plans; and that had these persons withdrawn, as those interested in a question ever should, the vote of the disinterested majority was clearly the reverse of what they made it. These were no longer the votes then of the representatives of the people, but of deserters from the rights and interests of the people; and it was impossible to consider their decisions, which had nothing in view but to enrich themselves, as the measures of the fair majority, which ought always to be respected. If, what was actually doing, begat uneasiness in those who wished for virtuous government, what was further proposed was not less threatening to the friends of the Constitution. For, in a report on the subject of manufactures (still to be acted on), it was expressly assumed that the General Government has a right to exercise all powers which may be for the *general welfare,* that is to say, all the legitimate powers of government; since no government has a legitimate right to do what is not for the welfare of the governed. There was, indeed, a sham limitation of the universality of this power *to cases where money is to be employed.* But about what is it that money cannot be employed? Thus the object of these plans, taken together, is to draw all the powers of government into the hands of the general Legislature, to establish means for corrupting a sufficient corps in that Legislature to divide the honest votes, and preponderate, by their own, the scale which suited, and to have the corps under the command of the Secretary of the Treasury, for the purpose of subverting, step by step, the principles of the Constitution which he has so often declared to be a thing of nothing, which must be changed. Such views might have justified something more than mere expressions of dissent, beyond which, nevertheless, I never went. Has abstinence from the department, committed to me, been equally observed by him? To say nothing of other interferences equally known, in the case of the two nations, with which we have the most intimate connections, France and England, my system was to give some satisfactory distinctions to the former, of little cost to us, in return for the solid advantages yielded us by them; and to have met the English with some restrictions which might induce them to abate their severities against our commerce. I have always supposed this coincided with your sentiments. Yet the Secretary of the Treasury, by his cabals with members of the Legislature, and by high-toned declamations on other occasions, has forced down his own system, which was exactly the reverse. He undertook, of his own authority, the conferences with the ministers of those two nations, and was, on every consultation, provided with some report of a conversation with the one or the other of them, adapted to his views. These views, thus made to prevail, their execution fell, of course, to me; and I can safely appeal to you, who have seen all my letters and proceedings, whether I have not carried them into execution as sincerely as if they had been my own, though I ever considered them as inconsistent with the honor and interest of our country. That they have been inconsistent with our interest is but too fatally proved by the stab to our navigation given by the French. So that if the question be by whose fault is it that Colonel Hamilton and myself have not drawn together? the answer will depend on that to two other questions, whose principles of administration best justify, by their purity, conscientious adherence? and which of us has, notwithstanding, stepped farthest into the control of the department of the other?

To this justification of opinions, expressed in the way of conversation, against the views of Colonel Hamilton, I beg leave to add some notice of his late charges against me in Fenno's Gazette; for neither the style, matter, nor venom of the pieces alluded to, can leave a doubt of their author. Spelling my name and character at full length to the public, while he conceals his own under the signature of "An American," he charges me, 1st. With having written letters from Europe to my friends to oppose the present Constitution, while depending. 2d. With a desire of not paying the public debt. 3d. With setting up a paper to decry and slander the government. 1st. The first charge is most false. No man in the United States, I suppose, approved of every tittle in the Constitution; no one, I believe, approved more of it than I did, and more of it was certainly disapproved by my accuser than by me, and of its parts most vitally republican. Of this the few letters I wrote on the subject (not half a dozen I believe) will be a proof; and for my own satisfaction and justification, I must tax you with the reading of them when I return to where they are. You will there see that my objection to the Constitution was, that it wanted a bill of rights securing freedom of religion, freedom of the press, freedom from standing armies, trial by jury, and a constant habeas corpus act. Colonel Hamilton's was, that it wanted a king and house of lords. The sense of America has approved my objection and added the bill of rights, not the king and lords. I also thought a longer term of service, insusceptible of renewal, would have made a President more independent. My country has thought otherwise, I have acquiesced implicitly. He wishes the General Government should have power to make laws binding the States in all cases whatsoever. Our country has thought otherwise: has he acquiesced? Notwithstanding my wish for a bill of rights, my letters strongly urged the adoption of the Constitution, by nine States at least, to secure the good it contained. I at first thought that the best method of securing the bill of rights would be for four States to hold off till such a bill should be agreed to. But the moment I saw Mr. Hancock's proposition to pass the Constitution as it stood, and give perpetual instructions to the representatives of every State to insist on a bill of rights, I acknowledged the superiority of his plan, and advocated universal adoption. 2d. The second charge is equally untrue. My whole correspondence while in France, and every word, letter and act on the subject, since my return, prove that no man is more ardently intent to see the public debt soon and sacredly paid off than I am. This exactly marks the difference between Colonel Hamilton's views and mine, that I would wish the debt paid tomorrow; he wishes it never to be paid, but always to be a thing wherewith to corrupt and manage the Legislature. 3d. I have never enquired what number of sons, relatives and friends of Senators, Representatives, printers or other useful partisans Colonel Hamilton has provided for among the hundred clerks of his department, the thousand excisemen, at his nod, and spread over the Union; nor could ever have imagined that the man who has the shuffling of millions backwards and forwards from paper into money and money into paper, from Europe to America, and America to Europe, the dealing out of treasury secrets among his friends in what time and measure he pleases, and who never slips an occasion of making friends with his means, that such an one, I say, would have brought forward a charge against me for having appointed the poet, Freneau, translating clerk to my office, with a salary of 250 dollars a year. That fact stands thus. While the government was at New York I was applied to on behalf of Freneau to know if there was any place within my department to which he could be appointed. I answered there were but four clerkships, all of which I found full, and continued without any change. When we removed to Philadelphia, Mr. Pintard, the translating clerk, did not choose to remove with us. His office then became vacant. I was again applied to there for Freneau, and had no hesitation to promise the clerkship for him. I cannot recollect whether it was at the same time, or afterwards, that I was told he had a thought of setting up a newspaper there. But whether then, or afterwards, I consider it a circumstance of some value, as it might enable me to do, what I had long wished to have done, that is, to have the material parts of the Leyden Gazette brought under your eye, and that of the public, in order to possess yourself and them of a juster view of the affairs of Europe than could be obtained from any other public source. This I had ineffectually attempted through the press of Mr. Fenno, while in New York, selecting and translating passages myself at first, then having it done by Mr. Pintard, the translating clerk, but they found their way too slowly into Mr. Fenno's papers. Mr. Bache essayed it for me in Philadelphia, but his being a daily paper, did not circulate sufficiently in the other States. He even tried, at my request, the plan of a weekly paper of recapitulation from his daily paper, in hopes that that might go into the other States, but in this too we failed. Freneau, as translating clerk, and the printer of a periodical paper likely to circulate through the States (uniting in one person the parts of Pintard and Fenno), revived my hopes that the thing could at length be effected.

On the establishment of his paper, therefore, I furnished him with the Leyden Gazette, with an expression of my wish that he could always translate and publish the material intelligence they contained, and have continued to furnish them from time to time, as regularly as I received them. But as to any other direction or indication of my wish how his press should be conducted, what sort of intelligence he should give, what essays encourage, I can protest, in the presence of heaven, that I never did by myself, or any other, or indirectly, say a syllable, nor attempt any kind of influence. I can further protest, in the same awful presence, that I never did, by myself, or any other, directly or indirectly, write, dictate or procure any one sentence or sentiment to be inserted *in his, or any other gazette,* to which my name was not affixed or that of my office. I surely need not except here a thing so foreign to the present subject as a little paragraph about our Algerine captives, which I put once into Fenno's paper. Freneau's proposition to publish a paper, having been about the time that the writings of Publicola, and the discourses on Davila, had a good deal excited the public attention, I took for granted from Freneau's character, which had been marked as that of a good whig, that he would give free place to pieces written against the aristocratical and monarchical principles these papers had inculcated. This having been in my mind, it is likely enough I may have expressed it in conversation with others, though I do not recollect that I did. To Freneau I think I could not, because I had still seen him but once, and that was at a public table, at breakfast, at Mrs. Elsworth's, as I passed through New York the last year. And I can safely declare that my expectations looked only to the chastisement of the aristocratical and monarchical writers, and not to any criticisms on the proceedings of government.

Colonel Hamilton can see no motive for any appointment, but that of making a convenient partizan. But you, Sir, who have received from me recommendations of a Rittenhouse, Barlow, Paine, will believe that talents and science are sufficient motives with me in appointments to which they are fitted; and that Freneau, as a man of genius, might find a preference in my eye to be a translating clerk, and make good title to the little aids I could give him as the editor of a gazette, by procuring subscriptions to his paper, as I did some before it appeared, and as I have with pleasure done for the labors of other men of genius. I hold it to be one of the distinguishing excellences of elective over hereditary successions, that the talents which nature has provided in sufficient proportion, should be selected by the society for the government of their affairs, rather than that this should be transmitted through the loins of knaves and fools, passing from the debauches of the table to those of the bed. Colonel Hamilton, alias "Plain Facts," says, that Freneau's salary began before he resided in Philadelphia. I do not know what quibble he may have in reserve on the word "residence." He may mean to include under that idea the removal of his family; for I believe he removed himself, before his family did, to Philadelphia. But no act of mine gave commencement to his salary before he so far took up his abode in Philadelphia, as to be sufficiently in readiness for the duties of the office. As to the merits or demerits of his paper, they certainly concern me not. He and Fenno are rivals for the public favor. The one courts them by flattery, the other by censure, and I believe it will be admitted that the one has been as servile, as the other severe. But is not the dignity, and even decency of government committed, when one of its principal ministers enlists himself as an anonymous writer or paragraphist for either the one or the other of them? No government ought to be without censors; and where the press is free, no one ever will. If virtuous, it need not fear the fair operation of attack and defence. Nature has given to man no other means of sifting out the truth, either in religion, law, or politics. I think it as honorable to the government neither to know, nor notice, its sycophants or censors, as it would be undignified and criminal to pamper the former and persecute the latter. So much for the past, a word now of the future.

When I came into this office, it was with a resolution to retire from it as soon as I could with decency. It pretty early appeared to me that the proper moment would be the first of those epochs at which the Constitution seems to have contemplated a periodical change or renewal of the public servants. In this I was confirmed by your resolution respecting the same period; from which, however, I am happy in hoping you have departed. I look to that period with the longing of a wave-worn mariner, who has at length the land in view, and shall count the days and hours which still lie between me and it. In the meanwhile, my main object will be to wind up the business of my office, avoiding as much as possible all new enterprise. With the affairs of the Legislature, as I never did intermeddle, so I certainly shall not now begin. I am more desirous to predispose everything for the repose to which I am withdrawing, than expose it to be disturbed by newspaper contests. If these however cannot be avoided altogether, yet a regard for your quiet will be a sufficient motive for my deferring it till I become merely a private citizen, when the propriety or impropriety of what I may say or do, may fall on myself alone. I may then, too, avoid the charge of misapplying that time which now, belonging to those who employ me, should be wholly devoted to their service. If my own justification, or the interests of the republic shall require it, I reserve to myself the right of then appealing to my country, subscribing my name to whatever I write, and using with freedom and truth the facts and names necessary to place the cause in its just form before that tribunal. To a thorough disregard of the honors and emoluments of office, I join as great a value for the esteem of my countrymen, and conscious of having merited it by an integrity which cannot be reproached, and by an enthusiastic devotion to their rights and liberty, I will not suffer my retirement to be clouded by the slanders of a man whose history, from the moment at which history can stoop to notice him, is a tissue of machinations against the liberty of the country which has not only received and given him bread, but heaped its honors on his head. Still, however, I repeat the hope that it will not be necessary to make such an appeal. Though little known to the people of America, I believe, that as far as I am known, it is not as an enemy to the Republic, nor an intriguer against it, nor a waster of its revenue, nor prostitutor of it to the purposes of corruption, as the "American" represents me; and I confide that yourself are satisfied that as to dissension in the newspapers, not a syllable of them has ever proceeded from me, and that no cabals or intrigues of mine have produced those in the Legislature, and I hope I may promise both to you and myself, that none will receive aliment from me during the short space I have to remain in office, which will find ample employment in closing the present business of the department.

Observing that letters written at Mount Vernon on the Monday, and arriving at Richmond on the Wednesday, reach me on Saturday, I have now the honor to mention that the 22d instant will be the last of our post days that I shall be here, and consequently that no letter from you after the 17th, will find me here. Soon after that I shall have the honor of receiving at Mount Vernon your orders for Philadelphia, and of there also delivering you the little matter which occurs to me as proper for the opening of Congress, exclusive of what has been recommended in former speeches, and not yet acted on. In the meantime and ever I am, with great and sincere affection and respect, dear Sir, your most obedient, and most humble servant.

A Numerous Sect

Anas, October 1, 1792

The dialogue between Jefferson and Washington continues on the subject of their retirement and of Hamilton's alleged subversion of republicanism. Hamilton's connections in Virginia, his seeming attempt to influence the upcoming elections to the House, especially rankled Jefferson at this time.

Bladensburg, October the 1st, 1792. This morning, at Mount Vernon, I had the following conversation with the President. He opened it by expressing his regret at the resolution in which I appeared so fixed, in the letter I had written him, of retiring from public affairs. He said, that he should be extremely sorry that I should do it, as long as he was in office, and that he could not see where he should find another character to fill my office. That, as yet, he was quite undecided whether to retire in March or not. His inclination led him strongly to do it. Nobody disliked more the ceremonies of his office, and he had not the least taste or gratification in the execution of its functions. That he was happy at home alone, and that his presence there was now peculiarly called for by the situation of Major Washington, whom he thought irrecoverable, and should he get well, he would remove into another part of the country, which might better agree with him. That he did not believe his presence necessary; that there were other characters who would do the business as well or better. Still, however, if his aid was thought necessary to save the cause to which he had devoted his life principally, he would make the sacrifice of a longer continuance. That he therefore reserved himself for future decision, as his declaration would be in time if made a month before the day of election. He had desired Mr. Lear to find out from conversation, without appearing to make the inquiry, whether any other person would be desired by any body. He had informed him, he judged from conversation that it was the universal desire he should continue, and he believed that those who expressed a doubt of his continuance, did it in the language of apprehension, and not of desire. But this, says he, is only from the north; it may be very different in the south. I thought this meant as an opening to me to say what was the sentiment in the south, from which quarter I came. I told him, that as far as I knew, there was but one voice there, which was for his continuance. That as to myself, I had ever preferred the pursuits of private life to those of public, which had nothing in them agreeable to me. I explained to him the circumstances of the war which had first called me into public life, and those following the war, which had called me from a retirement on which I had determined. That I had constantly kept my eye on my own home, and could no longer refrain from returning to it. As to himself, his presence was important; that he was the only man in the United States who possessed the confidence of the whole; that government was founded in opinion and confidence and that the longer he remained, the stronger would become the habits of the people in submitting to the government, and in thinking it a thing to be maintained; that there was no other person who would be thought anything more than the head of a party.

He then expressed his concern at the difference which he found to subsist between the Secretary of the Treasury and myself, of which he said he had not been aware. He knew, indeed, that there was a marked difference in our political sentiments, but he had never suspected it had gone so far in producing a personal difference, and he wished he could be the mediator to put an end to it. That he thought it important to preserve the check of my opinions in the administration, in order to keep things in their proper channel, and prevent them from going too far. That as to the idea of transforming this government into a monarchy, he did not believe there were ten men in the United States whose opinions were worth attention, who entertained such a thought. I told him there were many more than he imagined. I recalled to his memory a dispute at his own table, a little before we left Philadelphia, between General Schuyler on one side and Pinckney and myself on the other, wherein the former maintained the position, that hereditary descent was as likely to produce good magistrates as election. I told him, that though the people were sound, there was a numerous sect who had monarchy in contemplation; that the Secretary of the Treasury was one of these. That I had heard him say that this constitution was a shilly shally thing, of mere milk and water, which could not last, and was only good as a step to something better. That when we reflected, that he had endeavored in the convention, to make an English constitution of it, and when failing in that, we saw all his measures tending to bring it to the same thing, it was natural for us to be jealous; and particularly, when we saw that these measures had established corruption in the legislature, where there was a squadron devoted to the nod of the Treasury, doing whatever he had directed, and ready to do what he should direct. That if the equilibrium of the three great bodies, legislative, executive and judiciary, could be preserved, if the legislature could be kept independent, I should never fear the result of such a government; but that I could not but be uneasy, when I saw that the executive had swallowed up the legislative branch.

He said, that as to that interested spirit in the legislature, it was what could not be avoided in any government, unless we were to exclude particular descriptions of men, such as the holders of the funds, from all office. I told him, there was great difference between the little accidental schemes of self-interest, which would take place in every body of men, and influence their votes, and a regular system for forming a corps of interested persons, who should be steadily at the orders of the Treasury. He touched on the merits of the funding system, observed there was a difference of opinion about it, some thinking it very bad, others very good; that experience was the only criterion of right which he knew, and this alone would decide which opinion was right. That for himself, he had seen our affairs desperate and our credit lost, and that this was in a sudden and extraordinary degree raised to the highest pitch. I told him, all that was ever necessary to establish our credit, was an efficient government and an honest one, declaring it would sacredly pay our debts, laying taxes for this purpose, and applying them to it. I avoided going further into the subject. He finished by another exhortation to me not to decide too positively on retirement, and here we were called to breakfast. . . .

The Arm of the People

To William Short, January 3, 1793

Jefferson's former secretary, William Short, now ambassador to Holland, had written a series of letters critical of Jacobinism. These had reached Washington whose views of the Revolution were unknown, perhaps unformed. Jefferson believed that if Washington were to oppose the Revolution, the cause of republicanism would suffer in America. Accordingly, Jefferson, here and in the future, emphasizes his solidarity with the Jacobins despite their crimes.

My last private letter to you was of October 16, since which I have received your Nos. 103, 107, 108, 109, 110, 112, 113 and 114 and yesterday your private one of September 15, came to hand. The tone of your letters had for some time given me pain, on account of the extreme warmth with which they censured the proceedings of the Jacobins of France. I considered that sect as the same with the Republican patriots, and the Feuillants as the Monarchical patriots, well known in the early part of the Revolution, and but little distant in their views, both having in object the establishment of a free constitution, differing only on the question whether their chief Executive should be hereditary or not. The Jacobins (as since called) yielded to the Feuillants, and tried the experiment of retaining their hereditary Executive. The experiment failed completely, and would have brought on the re-establishment of despotism had it been pursued. The Jacobins knew this, and that the expunging that office was of absolute necessity. And the nation was with them in opinion, for however they might have been formerly for the constitution framed by the first assembly, they were come over from their hope in it, and were now generally Jacobins. In the struggle which was necessary, many guilty persons fell without the forms of trial, and with them some innocent. These I deplore as much as any body, and shall deplore some of them to the day of my death. But I deplore them as I should have done had they fallen in battle. It was necessary to use the arm of the people, a machine not quite

329

so blind as balls and bombs, but blind to a certain degree. A few of their cordial friends met at their hands the fate of enemies.

But time and truth will rescue and embalm their memories, while their posterity will be enjoying that very liberty for which they would never have hesitated to offer up their lives. The liberty of the whole earth was depending on the issue of the contest, and was ever such a prize won with so little innocent blood? My own affections have been deeply wounded by some of the martyrs to this cause, but rather than it should have failed I would have seen half the earth desolated; were there but an Adam and an Eve left in every country, and left free, it would be better than as it now is. I have expressed to you my sentiments, because they are really those of ninety-nine in an hundred of our citizens. The universal feasts, and rejoicings which have lately been, had on account of the successes of the French, showed the genuine effusions of their hearts. You have been wounded by the sufferings of your friends, and have by this circumstance been hurried into a temper of mind which would be extremely disrelished if known to your countrymen. . . .

A Corrupt Squadron of Voters in Congress

Anas, February 7, 1793

In late January, Jefferson decided to stay on somewhat longer as Secretary of State. But, as he explains—or serves notice—here to Washington, his delay in retiring would result in no diminution of his conflict with Hamilton.

I waited on the President with letters and papers from Lisbon. After going through these, I told him that I had for some time suspended speaking with him on the subject of my going out of office, because I had understood that the bill for intercourse with foreign nations was likely to be rejected by the Senate, in which case, the remaining business of the department would be too inconsiderable to make it worth while to keep it up. But that the bill being now passed, I was freed from the considerations of propriety which had embarrassed me. That &c. [nearly in the words of a letter to Mr. T. M. Randolph, of a few days ago], and that I should be willing, if he had taken no arrangements to the contrary, to continue somewhat longer, how long I could not say, perhaps till summer, perhaps autumn. He said, so far from taking arrangements on the subject, he had never mentioned to any mortal the design of retiring which I had expressed to him, till yesterday, when having heard that I had given up my house, and that it was rented by another, he thereupon mentioned it to Mr. E. Randolph, and asked him, as he knew my retirement had been talked of, whether he had heard any persons suggested in conversation to succeed me. He expressed his satisfaction at my change of purpose, and his apprehensions that my retirement would be a new source of uneasiness to the public. He said Governor Lee had that day informed him of the general discontent prevailing in Virginia, of which he never had had any conception, much less sound information. That it appeared to him very alarming. He proceeded to express his earnest wish that Hamilton and myself could coalesce in the measures of the government, and urged here the general reasons for it which he had done to me in two former conversations. He said he had proposed the same thing to Hamilton, who expressed his readiness, and he thought our coalition would secure the general acquiescence of the public.

I told him my concurrence was of much less importance than he seemed to imagine, that I kept myself aloof from all cabal and correspondence on the subject of the government, and saw and spoke with as few as I could. That as to a coalition with Mr. Hamilton, if by that was meant that either was to sacrifice his general system to the other, it was impossible. We had both, no doubt, formed our conclusions after the most mature consideration; and principles conscientiously adopted, could not be given up on either side. My wish was, to see both Houses of Congress cleansed of all persons interested in the bank or public stocks; and that a pure legislature being given us, I should always be ready to acquiesce under their determinations, even if contrary to my own opinions; for that I subscribe to the principle, that the will of the majority, honestly expressed, should give law. I confirmed him in the fact of the great discontents to the south; that they were grounded on seeing that their judgments and interests were sacrificed to those of the eastern States on every occasion, and their belief that it was the effect of a corrupt squadron of voters in Congress, at the command of the Treasury; and they see that if the votes of those members who had any interest distinct from, and contrary to the general interest of their constituents, had been withdrawn, as in decency and honesty they should have been, the laws would have been the reverse of what they are on all the great questions. I instanced the new Assumption carried in the House of Representatives by the Speaker's vote. On this subject he made no reply. He explained his remaining in office to have been the effect of strong solicitations after he returned here; declaring that he had never mentioned his purpose of going out but to the Heads of departments and Mr. Madison; he expressed the extreme wretchedness of his existence while in office, and went lengthily into the late attacks on him for levees, &c., and explained to me how he had been led into them by the persons he consulted at New York; and that if he could but know what the sense of the public was, he would most cheerfully conform to it. . . .

The Source of All Authority

Opinion on French Treaties, April 28, 1793

On April 17, shortly after he learned that France had declared war on England, Washington, with Hamilton's assistance, placed thirteen questions before the Cabinet. These revolved around one central question of whether and how America should honor her treaty of military alliance with France. Hamilton argued that a revolutionary change in the government voided treaties made with its predecessor. Against Hamilton's opinion Jefferson wrote the one below. Washington accepted Jefferson's as the more valid.

I proceed in compliance with the requisition of the President to give an opinion in writing on the general question, whether the United States have a right to renounce their treaties with France, or to hold them suspended till the government of that country shall be established?

In the consultation at the President's on the 19th inst., the Secretary of the Treasury took the following positions and consequences. France was a monarchy when we entered into treaties with it; but it has declared itself a republic, and is preparing a republican form of government. As it may issue in a republic or a military despotism, or something else which may possibly render our alliance with it dangerous to ourselves, we have a right of election to renounce the treaty altogether, or to declare it suspended till their government shall be settled in the form it is ultimately to take; and then we may judge whether we will call the treaties into operation again, or declare them forever null. Having that right of election, now, if we receive their minister without any qualifications, it will amount to an act of election to continue the treaties; and if the change they are undergoing should issue in a form which should bring danger on us, we shall not be then free to renounce them. To elect to continue them is equivalent to the making a new treaty, at this time, in the same form, that is to say, with a clause of guarantee; but to make a treaty with a clause of guarantee, during a war, is a departure from neutrality, and would make us associates in the war. To renounce or suspend the treaties, therefore, is a necessary act of neutrality.

If I do not subscribe to the soundness of this reasoning, I do most fully to its ingenuity. I shall now lay down the principles which, according to my understanding, govern the case.

I consider the people who constitute a society or nation as the source of all authority in that nation; as free to transact their common concerns by any agents they think proper; to change these agents individually, or the organization of them in form or function whenever they please; that all the acts done by these agents under the authority of the nation, are the acts of the nation, are obligatory to them and enure to their use, and can in no wise be annulled or affected by any change in the form of the government, or of the persons administering it, consequently the treaties between the United States and France, were not treaties between the United States and Louis Capet, but between the two nations of America and France; and the nations remaining in existence, though both of them have since changed their forms of government, the treaties are not annulled by these changes. The law of nations, by which this question is to be determined, is composed of three branches. 1. The moral law of our nature. 2. The usages of nations. 3. Their special conventions. The first of these only concerns this question, that is to say the moral law to which man has been subjected by his creator, and of which his feelings or conscience, as it is sometimes called, are the evidence with which his creator has furnished him. The moral duties which exist between individual and individual in a state of nature, accompany them into a state of society, and the aggregate of the duties of all the individuals composing the society constitutes the duties of that society towards any other; so that between society and society the same moral duties exist as did between the individuals composing them, while in an unassociated state, and their maker not having released them from those duties on their forming themselves into a nation. Compacts then, between nation and nation, are obligatory on them by the same moral law which obliges individuals to observe their compacts. There are circumstances, however, which sometimes excuse the nonperformance of contracts between man and man; so are there also between nation and nation. When performance, for instance, becomes *impossible,* non-performance is not immoral; so if performance becomes *self-destructive* to the party, the law of self-preservation overrules the laws of obligation in others. For the reality of these principles I appeal to the true fountains of evidence, the head and heart of every rational and honest man. It is there nature has written her moral laws, and where every man may read them for himself. He will never read there the permission to annul his obligations for a time, or forever, whenever they become dangerous, useless, or disagreeable; certainly not when merely useless or disagreeable, as seems to be said in an authority which has been quoted, (Vattel, p. 2, 197) and though he may, under certain degrees of danger, yet the danger must be imminent, and the degree great. Of these, it is true, that nations are to be judges for themselves; since no one nation has a right to sit in judgment over another, but the tribunal of our consciences remains, and that also of the opinion of the world. These will revise the sentence we pass in our own case, and as we respect these, we must see that in judging ourselves we have honestly done the part of impartial and rigorous judges.

But reason which gives this right of self-liberation from a contract in certain cases, has subjected it to certain just limitations.

I. The danger which absolves us must be great, inevitable and imminent. Is such the character of that now apprehended from our treaties with France? What is that danger? 1st. Is it that if their government issues in a military despotism, an alliance with them may taint us with despotic principles? But their government when we allied ourselves to it, was perfect despotism, civil, and military, yet the treaties were made in that very state of things, and, therefore, that danger can furnish no just cause.

2d. It is that their government may issue in a republic, and too much strengthen our republican principles? But this is the hope of the great mass of our constituents, and not their dread. They do not look with longing to the happy mean of a limited monarchy.

3d. But, says the doctrine I am combatting, the change the French are undergoing, may possibly end in something we know not what, and may bring on us danger we know not whence. In short, it may end in a Raw-head and bloody bones in the dark. Very well—let Raw-head and bloody bones come. We shall be justified in making our peace with him by renouncing our ancient friends and his enemies; for observe, it is not the *possibility of danger* which absolves a party from his contract, for that possibility always exists, and in every case. It existed in the present one, at the moment of making the contract. If *possibilities* would void contracts, there never could be a valid contract, for possibilities hang over everything. Obligation is not suspended till the danger is become real, and the moment of it so imminent, that we can no longer avoid decision without forever losing the opportunity to do it. But can a danger which has not yet taken its shape, which does not yet exist, and never may exist which cannot therefore be defined—can such a danger, I ask, be so imminent that if we fail to pronounce on it in this moment, we can never have another opportunity of doing it? . . .

[To] whom is it that the treaties with France have become *disagreeable?* How will it be proved that they are *useless?*

The conclusion of the sentence suggests a reflection too strong to be suppressed, "for the party may say with truth that it would not have allied itself with this nation if it had been under the present form of its government." The republic of the United States allied itself with France when under a despotic government. She changes her government, and declares it shall be a republic; prepares a form of republic extremely free, and in the meantime is governing herself as such. And it is proposed that America shall declare the treaties void, because it may say with truth that it would not have allied itself with that nation if it had been under the present form of its government. Who is the American who can say with truth that he would not have allied himself to France if she had been a republic? Or that a republic of any form would be as *disagreeable* as her ancient despotism?

Upon the whole I conclude, that the treaties are still binding, notwithstanding the change of government in France; that no part of them but the clause of guarantee holds up *danger,* even at a distance, and consequently that a liberation from no other part would be prepared in any case; that if that clause may ever bring *danger,* it is neither extreme nor imminent, nor even probable that the authority for renouncing a treaty, when *useless or disagreeable,* is either misunderstood or in opposition to itself, to all other writers, and to every moral feeling; that were it not so, these treaties are in fact neither useless or disagreeable; that the receiving a minister from France at this time is an act of no significance with respect to the treaties, amounting neither to an admission nor denial of them, forasmuch as he comes not under any stipulation in them; that were it an explicit admission, or were it an express declaration of their obligation now to be made, it would not take from us that right which exists at all times, of liberating ourselves when an adherence to the treaties would be *ruinous* or *destructive* to the society; and that the not renouncing the treaties now is so far from being a breach of neutrality, that the doing it would be the breach, by giving just cause of war to France.

A Manly Neutrality

To James Madison, May 13, 1793

To his closest political cohort, Jefferson sharply adumbrates the economic and social bases for the conflict in foreign policy.

A manly neutrality, claiming the liberal rights ascribed to that condition by the very persons at war, was the part we should have taken, and would I believe have given satisfaction to our allies. If anything prevents its being a mere English neutrality, it will be that the penchant of the President is not that way, and above all, the ardent spirit of our constituents. The line is now drawn so clearly as to show on one side, 1. The fashionable circles of Philadelphia, New York, Boston and Charleston, (natural aristocrats.) 2. Merchants trading on British capital. 3. Paper men, (all the old tories are found in some one of the three descriptions.) On the other side are, 1. Merchants trading on their own capital. 2. Irish merchants. 3. Tradesmen, mechanics, farmers, and every other possible description of our citizens. Genett is not yet arrived though hourly expected. I have just heard that the workmen I had desired from Europe were engaged and about to embark. Another strong motive for making me uneasy here. Adieu.

His Paper Has Saved Our Constitution

Anas, May 23, 1793

Washington directed his most critical language to Jefferson on the occasion and for the reason given below. Philip Freneau, who worked as an employee in the State Department, edited and wrote political poetry for The National Gazette, *the Jeffersonian newspaper in Philadelphia.*

. . . He [President Washington] adverted to a piece in Freneau's paper of yesterday; he said he despised all their attacks on him personally, but that there never had been an act of the Government, not meaning in the executive line only, but in any line, which that paper had not abused. He had also marked the word republic thus, where it was applied to the French republic. . . . He was evidently sore and warm, and I took his intention to be, that I should interpose in some way with Freneau, perhaps withdraw his appointment of translating clerk to my office. But I will not do it. His paper has saved our Constitution, which was galloping fast into monarchy, and has been checked by no one means so powerfully as by that paper. It is well and universally known, that it has been that paper which has checked the career of the monocrats; and the President, not sensible of the designs of the party, has not with his usual good sense and *sang froid,* looked on the efforts and effects of this free press, and seen that, though some bad things have passed through it to the public, yet the good have preponderated immensely.

Et Tu Brute

Anas, August 2, 1793

"Citizen" Edmond Charles Genêt, the French Ambassador to the United States, provided grist for Hamilton's mill. Genêt had deceived the government in the Little Sarah *affair, and, moreover, in the course of the dispute, threatened to take his case to the people. This was an unprecedented insult to the government. The whole Cabinet agreed that Genêt had to go. But how should he be sent home? More important— since he had become a public celebrity—should the government present its case against him to the people?*

Met again. Hamilton spoke again three-quarters of an hour. I answered on these topics. *Object* of the appeal.— The democratic society; this the great circumstance of alarm; afraid it would extend its connections over the continent; chiefly meant for the local object of the ensuing election of Governor. If left alone, would die away after that is over. If opposed, if proscribed, would give it importance and vigor; would give it a new object, and multitudes would join it merely to assert the right of voluntary associations. That the measure was calculated to make the President assume the station of the head of a party; instead of the head of the nation. *Plan* of the appeal.—To consist of *facts* and the *decisions* of the President. As to facts we are agreed; but as to the decisions, there have been great differences of opinion among us. Sometimes as many opinions as persons. This proves there will be ground to attack the decisions. Genet will appeal also; it will become a contest between the President and Genet—anonymous writers—will be same difference of opinion in *public*, as in our cabinet—will be same difference in *Congress*, for it must be laid before them—would, therefore, work very unpleasantly *at home*. How would it work *abroad*? France— unkind—after such proofs of her friendship, should rely on that friendship, and her justice. Why appeal to the world? Friendly nations always negotiate little differences in private. Never appeal to the world, but when they appeal to the sword. Confederacy of Pillnitz was to overthrow the government of France. The interference of France to disturb other governments and excite insurrections, was a measure of reprisal. Yet these Princes have been able to make it believed to be the system of France. Colonel Hamilton supposes Mr. Genet's proceedings here are in pursuance of that system; and we are so to declare it to the world, and to add our testimony to this base calumny of the Princes.

What a triumph to them to be backed by our testimony. What a fatal stroke at the cause of liberty; *et tu Brute.* We indispose the French government, and they will retract their offer of the treaty of commerce. The President manifestly inclined to the appeal to the people. Knox, in a foolish incoherent sort of a speech, introduced the pasquinade lately printed, called the funeral of George W—n, and James W—n, King and Judge, &c., where the President was placed on a guillotine. The President was much inflamed; got into one of those passions when he cannot command himself; ran on much on the personal abuse which had been bestowed on him; defied any man on earth to produce one single act of his since he had been in the government, which was not done on the purest motives; that he had never repented but once the having slipped the moment of resigning his office, and that was every moment since; that *by God* he had rather be in his grave than in his present situation; that he had rather be on his farm than to be made *Emperor of the world;* and yet that they were charging him with wanting to be a King. That that *rascal Freneau* sent him three of his papers every day, as if he thought he would become the distributor of his papers; that he could see in this, nothing but an impudent design to insult him: he ended in this high tone. There was a pause. Some difficulty in resuming our question; it was, however, after a little while, presented again, and he said there seemed to be no necessity for deciding it now; the propositions before agreed on might be put into a train of execution, and perhaps events would show whether the appeal would be necessary or not. He desired we would meet at my office the next day, to consider what should be done with the vessels armed in our ports by Mr. Genet, and their prizes. . . .

I Would Have Chosen Them to Be Doubtful

Anas, November 18, 28, 1793

The matter before the Cabinet on November 18 was Washington's forthcoming message to Congress. Could the President proclaim neutrality without consulting Congress? Hamilton thought he could, or rather should in view of the possible effects of Genêt's revolutionary propaganda on Congress. Hamilton was charged with drafting this section of the message. Jefferson drafted the section on relations with France and England (presented to the Cabinet on November 28) wherein he condemned Genêt but upheld France. Jefferson stood alone on the issue of whether the documents relating to our dispute with England should be made public (Hamilton wanting them kept secret). Here Washington supported Jefferson.

[We] met at his [Washington's] house; read new volumes of Genet's letters, received since the President's departure; then took up the discussion of the subjects of communication to Congress. 1. The Proclamation. E. Randolph read the statement he had prepared; Hamilton did not like it; said much about his own views; that the President had a right to declare his opinion to our citizens and foreign nations; that it was not the interest of this country to join in the war, and that we were under no obligation to join in it; that though the declaration would not legally bind Congress, yet the President had a right to give his opinion of it, and he was against any explanation in the speech, which should yield that he did not intend that foreign nations should consider it as a declaration of neutrality, future as well as present; that he understood it as meant to give them that sort of assurance and satisfaction, and to say otherwise now, would be a deception on them. He was for the President's using such expressions, as should neither affirm his right to make such a declaration to foreign nations, nor yield it. Randolph and myself opposed the right of the President to declare anything future on the question, shall there or shall there not be war, and that no such thing was intended; that Hamilton's construction of the effect of the proclamation, would have been a determination of the question of the *guarantee*, which we both denied to have intended, and I had at the time declared the executive incompetent to. Randolph said he meant that foreign nations should understand it as an intimation of the President's opinion, that neutrality would be our interest. I declared my meaning to have been, that foreign nations should understand no such thing; that on the contrary, I would have chosen them to be doubtful, and to come and bid for our neutrality. I admitted the President, having received the nation at the close of Congress in a state of peace, was bound to preserve them in that state till Congress should meet again, and might proclaim anything which went no farther. The President declared he never had an idea that he could bind Congress against declaring war, or that anything contained in his proclamation could look beyond the first day of their meeting. His main view was to keep our people in peace; he apologized for the use of the term neutrality in his answers, and justified it, by having submitted the first of them (that to the merchants, wherein it was used) to our consideration, and we had not objected to the term. He concluded in the end, that Colonel Hamilton should prepare a paragraph on this subject for the speech, and it should then be considered. We were here called to dinner. . . .

[November 28] After dinner, I produced the draught of messages on the subject of France and England, proposing that that relative to Spain should be subsequent and secret.

Hamilton objected to the draught *in toto;* said that the contrast drawn between the conduct of France and England amounted to a declaration of war; he denied that France had ever done us favors; that it was mean for a nation to acknowledge favors; that the dispositions of the people of this country towards France, he considered as a serious calamity; that the executive ought not, by an echo of this language, to nourish that disposition in the people; that the offers in commerce made us by France, were the offspring of the moment, of circumstances which would not last, and it was wrong to receive as permanent, things merely temporary; that he could demonstrate that Great Britain showed us more favors than France. In complaisance to him I whittled down the expressions without opposition; struck out that of "favors ancient and recent" from France; softened some terms, and omitted some sentiments respecting Great Britain. He still was against the whole, but insisted that, at any rate, it should be a secret communication, because the matters it stated were still depending. These were, 1, the inexecution of the treaty; 2, the restraining our commerce to their own ports and those of their friends. Knox joined Hamilton in everything. Randolph was for the communications; that the documents respecting the first should be given in as public; but that those respecting the second should not be given to the legislature at all, but kept secret. I began to tremble now for the whole, lest all should be kept secret. I urged, especially, the duty now incumbent on the President, to lay before the legislature and the public what had passed on the inexecution of the treaty, since Mr. Hammond's answer of this month might be considered as the last we should ever have; that, therefore, it could no longer be considered as a negotiation pending. I urged that the documents respecting the stopping our corn ought also to go, but insisted that if it should be thought better to withhold them, the restrictions should not go to those respecting the treaty; that neither of those subjects was more in a state of *pendency* that the recall of Mr. Genet, on which, nevertheless, no scruples had been expressed. The President took up the subject with more vehemence than I have seen him show, and decided without reserve, that not only what had passed on the inexecution of the treaty should go in as public (in which Hamilton and Knox had divided in opinion from Randolph and myself), but also that those respecting the stopping our corn should go in as public (wherein, Hamilton, Knox, and Randolph had been against me). This was the first instance I had seen of his deciding on the opinion of one against that of three others, which proved his own to have been very strong. . . .

PART VII

DEMOCRATIC—REPUBLICAN: 1794—1801

Introduction

JEFFERSON RETURNED TO Monticello in January 1794 desiring nothing more than to be with his daughter and grandchildren and to tend his plantation of ten thousand acres and 154 slaves. His property badly needed attention. He began rotating his crops and otherwise experimenting with scientific agriculture, then in a rudimentary stage. He took particular pride in setting up a nail manufactory, for which slaves supplied the labor. But after a while the idyl of private life bored him. He could no more keep away from politics than he could avoid complaining of politics.

His Republican friends, chief among them Madison, kept him thoroughly informed of the drift of things in Philadelphia. Washington was taking an increasingly Hamiltonian position at home and abroad (though Hamilton himself resigned in January 1795). Washington personally recoiled from the tide of insolence and libertinism which the French Revolution called forth in the United States: the burgeoning number of Jacobin clubs, the sharp criticism which Republican papers, especially Philip Freneau's *National Gazette,* made of his administration, and—as the seditious fruit of radicalism—the Whiskey Rebellion of 1794. Washington gave full support to Jay's Treaty (signed on November 19, 1794), which excited furious opposition throughout the country, especially among planters and farmers producing staple crops, and did more to consolidate the Republican Party than any single event prior to Jefferson's assumption of the Presidency.

In a famous letter of 1795, Jefferson analyzed with remarkable accuracy the differences between the two parties. The Republicans, he said, consisted of: "1. The entire body of landholders throughout the United States. 2. The body of labourers, not being landholders, whether in husbanding or the arts." The Federalists, he said, with less objectivity, consisted of: "1. The old refugees and tories. 2. British merchants residing among us, and composing the main body of our merchants. 3. American merchants trading on British capital. Another great portion. 4. Speculators and holders in the banks and public funds. 5. Officers of the federal government with some exceptions. 6. Office-hunters, willing to give up principles for places. A numerous and noisy tribe. 7. Nervous persons, whose languid fibres have more analogy with a passive than active state of things." Thanks to Hamilton, leadership of the Republican Party had been organized well before it attracted a mass following. In May 1791 Jefferson and Madison visited the anti-Hamilton faction in New York led by George Clinton, Robert Livingston and Aaron Burr. An unusual alliance of Virginia squires and New York politicos thus sprung up, providing the elite for a party that was to dominate American political life for a quarter of a century.

Elected Vice-President in 1796, after having lost the Presidential contest to John Adams by only three electoral votes, Jefferson was confident that time favored the Republicans, and that, with Washington in retirement, the breach between Adams and Hamilton would widen. That is precisely what happened.

Federalism foundered on the issue of whether or not to go to war with France. Soon after the Directory learned of the contents of Jay's Treaty it ordered the interdiction of American trade with the Indies. In May 1797 President Adams appointed a commission of three—C. C. Pinckney, John Marshall and Elbridge Gerry, only the last was a Republican of sorts—to treat with France on the differences between the two countries. Negotiations collapsed when the French government, through Foreign Minister Talleyrand, surreptitiously asked for a bribe as the price for better relations with the United States. In April 1798 Adams presented the XYZ correspondence to Congress (X, Y and Z were Talleyrand's agents). A great hue and cry went up throughout the land. The blast of indignation carried the United States to the verge of war.

Preparations for war raised the spector of a Hamiltonian dictatorship. An army was about to be called up in which Hamilton was to be the aged Washington's second in command. But Adams averted war when, in February 1799, he took up France's proposal to receive an American minister. Adams thereupon appointed a commission to do what the previous commission had failed to do. This time negotiations proved successful. The signing, on September 30, 1800, of the Treaty of Morfontaine settled the outstanding differences between the two countries. Adams had done a courageous thing. But the split with Hamilton, whose hopes of conquest died forever, was irreparable.

Perhaps the severity of the struggle within the Federalist party was symptomatic of its growing alienation from the majority of the people. Had a war with France occurred, it might have been possible to put across the Alien and Sedition Acts of 1798 and the higher taxes to pay for war preparations. Jefferson himself failed to gauge the temper of the people when he wrote the Kentucky Resolutions, hoping that they would call forth a massive protest of the states against federal usurpation. But in only one other state did the Resolutions find favor—Virginia whose legislature passed a milder version of them. As the war scare passed so did Federalist chances for victory in the election of 1800.

Jefferson's election was an act of extraordinary irony. Could he have ever imagined that his election would depend on Hamilton's approval? The tie in the electoral college between Jefferson and Burr had thrown the election into the House of Representatives where a majority of the states— each with one vote—would make the decision. Most Federalists favored Burr. But Hamilton, who detested Burr's person more than he did Jefferson's principles, persuaded the Federalist caucus to allow Jefferson the victory. And so the man who had despised politics for most of the three decades that he had been in it and who had recently advised the states to join in nullifying Federal law became President of the United States.

They Will Triumph Completely

To Tench Coxe, May 1, 1794

Jefferson's warm support of revolutionary France in her war with "the foreign powers," reflected his bitterness towards Britain. For Britain was now effectively preventing American trade with the French West Indies. Tench Coxe was an economist of note who later broke with the Federalist Party to become a Jeffersonian.

. . . Your letters give a comfortable view of French affairs, and later events seem to confirm it. Over the foreign powers I am convinced they will triumph completely, and I cannot but hope that that triumph, and the consequent disgrace of the invading tyrants, is destined, in order of events, to kindle the wrath of the people of Europe against those who have dared to embroil them in such wickedness, and to bring at length, kings, nobles and priests to the scaffolds which they have been so long deluging with human blood. I am still warm whenever I think of these scoundrels, though I do it as seldom as I can, prefering infinitely to contemplate the tranquil growth of my lucerne and potatoes. I have so completely withdrawn myself from these spectacles of usurpation and misrule, that I do not take a single newspaper, nor read one a month; and I feel myself infinitely the happier for it. . . .

The Glittering of Crowns and Coronets

To James Madison, December 28, 1794

Washington had recently suppressed "The Whiskey Rebellion" in western Pennsylvania—the rebellion of farmers objecting to a tax on whiskey which served as their means of exchange. Hamilton attributed the rebellion to the factious influence of "democratic societies." In his annual message to Congress, Washington incorporated Hamilton's opinion of them. To Jefferson the coupling of the rebellion, of which he disapproved, with democratic societies was part of the monocratic plot.

. . . The denunciation of the democratic societies is one of the extraordinary acts of boldness of which we have seen so many from the faction of monocrats. It is wonderful indeed, that the President should have permitted himself to be the organ of such an attack on the freedom of discussion, the freedom of writing, printing and publishing. It must be a matter of rare curiosity to get at the modifications of these rights proposed by them, and to see what line their ingenuity would draw between democratical societies, whose avowed object is the nourishment of the republican principles of our Constitution, and the society of the Cincinnati, *a self-created* one, carving out for itself hereditary distinctions, lowering over our Constitution eternally, meeting together in all parts of the Union, periodically, with closed doors, accumulating a capital in their separate treasury, corresponding secretly and regularly, and of which society the very persons denouncing the democrats are themselves the fathers, founders and high officers. Their sight must be perfectly dazzled by the glittering of crowns and coronets, not to see the extravagance of the proposition to suppress the friends of general freedom, while those who wish to confine that freedom to the few, are permitted to go on in their principles and practices. I here put out of sight the persons whose misbehavior has been taken advantage of to slander the friends of popular rights; and I am happy to observe, that as far as the circle of my observation and information extends, everybody has lost sight of them, and views the abstract attempt on their natural and constitutional rights in all its nakedness. I have never heard, or heard of, a single expression or opinion which did not condemn it as an inexcusable aggression. . . .

Two Parties Then Do Exist

Notes on Christoph Daniel Ebeling's letter of July 30, 1795

Ebeling, a German scholar, was collecting data for his treatise (later published in five volumes), Geography and History of North America. *He consulted a number of prominent Americans, among them Ezra Stiles, Joel Barlow, Jebediah Morse and Noah Webster, and then asked Jefferson to evaluate their statements. Ebeling's request gave Jefferson an opportunity to set down his reflections on the conflict of political parties in America.*

. . . The people of America, before the revolution-war, being attached to England, had taken up, without examination, the English ideas of the superiority of their constitution over every thing of the kind which ever had been or ever would be tried. The revolution forced them to consider the subject for themselves, and the result was an universal conversion to republicanism. Those who did not come over to this opinion, either left us, and were called Refugees, or staid with us under the name of tories; and some, preferring profit to principle took side with us and floated with the general tide. Our first federal constitution, or Confederation as it was called, was framed in the first moments of our separation from England, in the highest point of our jealousies of independence as to her and as to each other. It formed therefore too weak a bond to produce an union of action as to foreign nations. This appeared at once on the establishment of peace, when the pressure of a common enemy which had hooped us together during the war, was taken away. Congress was found to be quite unable to point the action of the several states to a common object. A general desire therefore took place of amending the federal constitution. This was opposed by some of those who wished for monarchy, to wit, the Refugees now returned, the old tories, and the timid whigs who prefer tranquility to freedom, hoping monarchy might be the remedy if a state of complete anarchy could be brought on. A Convention however being decided on, some of the monocrats got elected, with a hope of introducing an English constitution as nearly as was attainable. In this they were not altogether without success; insomuch that the monarchical features of the new constitution produced a violent opposition to it from the most zealous republicans in the several states. For this reason, and because they also thought it carried the principle of a consolidation of the states farther than was requisite for the purpose of producing an union of action as to foreign powers, it is still doubted by some whether a majority of the people of the U.S. were not against adopting it. However it was carried through all the assemblies of the states, though by very small majorities in the largest states.

The inconveniences of an inefficient government, driving the people as is usual, into the opposite extreme, the elections to the first Congress ran very much in favor of those who were known to favor a very strong government. Hence the anti-republicans appeared a considerable majority in both houses of Congress. They pressed forward the plan therefore of strengthening all the features of the government which gave it resemblance to an English constitution, of adopting the English forms and principles of administration, and of forming like them a monied interest, by means of a funding system, not calculated to pay the public debt, but to render it perpetual, and to make it an engine in the hands of the executive branch of government which, added to the great patronage it possessed in the disposal of public offices, might enable it to assume by degrees a kingly authority. The biennial period of Congress being too short to betray to the people, spread over this great continent, this train of things during the first Congress, little change was made in the members to the second. But in the mean time two very distinct parties had formed in Congress; and before the third election, the people in general became apprised of the game which was playing for drawing over them a kind of government which they never had in contemplation. At the 3d election therefore a decided majority of Republicans were sent to the lower house of Congress; and as information spread still farther among the people after the 4th election the anti-republicans have become a weak minority. But the members of the Senate being changed but once in 6 years, the completion of that body will be much slower in its assimilation to that of the people. This will account for the differences which may appear in the proceedings and spirit of the two houses.

Still however it is inevitable that the Senate will at length be formed to the republican model of the people, and the two houses of the legislature, once brought to act on the true principles of the Constitution, backed by the people, will be able to defeat the plan of sliding us into monarchy, and to keep the Executive within republican bounds, notwithstanding the immense patronage it possesses in the disposal of public offices, notwithstanding it has been able to draw into this vortex the judiciary branch of the government and by their expectancy of sharing the other offices in the Executive gift to make them auxiliary to the Executive in all its views instead of forming a balance between that and the legislature as it was originally intended and notwithstanding the funding phalanx which a respect for public faith must protect, though it was engaged by false brethren. Two parties then do exist within the U.S. they embrace respectively the following descriptions of persons.

The Anti-republicans consist of

1. The old refugees and tories.

2. British merchants residing among us, and composing the main body of our merchants.

3. American merchants trading on British capital. Another great portion.

4. Speculators and holders in the banks and public funds.

5. Officers of the federal government with some exceptions.

6. Office-hunters, willing to give up principles for places. A numerous and noisy tribe.

7. Nervous persons, whose languid fibres have more analogy with a passive than active state of things.

The Republican part of our Union comprehends

1. The entire body of landholders throughout the United States.

2. The body of labourers, not being landholders, whether in husbanding or the arts.

The latter is to the aggregate of the former party probably as 500 to one; but their wealth is not as disproportionate, though it is also greatly superior, and is in truth the foundation of that of their antagonists. Trifling as are the numbers of the Anti-republican party, there are circumstances which give them an appearance of strength and numbers. They all live in cities, together, and can act in a body readily and at all times; they give chief employment to the newspapers, and therefore have most of them under their command. The

Agricultural interest is dispersed over a great extent of country, have little means of intercommunication with each other, and feeling their own strength and will, are conscious that a single exertion of these will at any time crush the machinations against their government. As in the commerce of human life, there are commodities adapted to every demand, so there are newspapers adapted to the Anti-republican palate, and others to the republican. Of the former class are the *Columbian Centinel*, the Hartford newspaper, Webster's *Minerva*, Fenno's *Gazette of the U.S.*, Davies's Richmond paper &c. Of the latter are Adams's Boston paper, Greenleaf's of New York, Freneau's of New Jersey, Bache's of Philadelphia, Pleasant's of Virginia &c. Pleasant's paper comes out twice a week, Greenleaf's and Freneau's once a week, Bache's daily. I do not know how often Adams's. I shall according to your desire endeavor to get Pleasant's for you for 1794, and 95 and will have it forwarded through 96 from time to time to your correspondent at Baltimore. . . .

A Burst of Dissatisfaction

To James Monroe, September 6, 1795

The Jay Treaty, discussed here cursorily, was signed on November 14, 1794, presumably to end Britain's interdiction of American trade and impressment of American seamen. But when its provisions became known in June, it provoked an uproar. Republicans construed it as a surrender to Britain dictated by Northern mercantile interests. As much as any single event, it crystallized party differences in America.

. . . Mr. Jay's treaty has at length been made public. So general a burst of dissatisfaction never before appeared against any transaction. Those who understand the particular articles of it, condemn these articles. Those who do not understand them minutely, condemn it generally as wearing a hostile face to France. This last is the most numerous class, comprehending the whole body of the people, who have taken a greater interest in this transaction than they were ever known to do in any other. It has in my opinion completely demolished the monarchial party here. The Chamber of Commerce in New York, against the body of the town, the merchants in Philadelphia, against the body of their town, also, and our town of Alexandria have come forward in it's support. Some individual champions also appear. Marshall, Carrington, Harvey, Bushrod Washington, Doctor Stewart. A more powerful one is Hamilton, under the signature of Camillas. Adams holds his tongue with an address above his character. We do not know whether the President has signed it or not. If he has it is much believed the H. of representatives will oppose it as constitutionally void, and thus bring on an embarrassing and critical state in our government. . . .

Their Heads Shorn by the Harlot England

To Phillip Mazzei, April 24, 1796

The so-called "Mazzei letter" became a cause célèbre *in 1797 which embarrassed Jefferson. Mazzei, Jefferson's old friend and neighbor, who had returned to Italy in 1785, printed an Italian translation of the letter below in a Florence newspaper. Soon after, the Paris* Moniteur *published it in French. On May 14, 1797, the anti-Republican* Minerva *presented an English retranslation of it, accompanied by the wry suggestion that its author should have "an opportunity to disavow it." Jefferson's position was especially delicate in view of his recent denial to Washington (see his letter of June 19, 1796) of ever having betrayed the government's confidence. But the Mazzei letter gave Washington reason to distrust Jefferson's protestations. Thereafter, the two Virginians did not exchange another word.*

. . . The aspect of our politics has wonderfully changed since you left us. In place of that noble love of liberty and republican government which carried us triumphantly through the war, an Anglican monarchical aristocratical party has sprung up, whose avowed object is to draw over us the substance, as they have already done the forms, of the British government. The main body of our citizens, however, remain true to their republican principles; the whole landed interest is republican, and so is a great mass of talents. Against us are the Executive, the Judiciary, two out of three branches of the Legislature, all the officers of the government, all who want to be officers, all timid men who prefer the calm of despotism to the boisterous sea of liberty, British merchants and Americans trading on British capital, speculators and holders in the banks and public funds, a contrivance invented for the purposes of corruption, and for assimilating us in all things to the rotten as well as the sound parts of the British model. It would give you a fever were I to name to you the apostates who have gone over to these heresies, men who were Samsons in the field and Solomons in the council, but who have had their heads shorn by the harlot England. In short, we are likely to preserve the liberty we have obtained only by unremitting labors and perils. But we shall preserve it; and our mass of weight and wealth on the good side is so great, as to leave no danger that force will ever be attempted against us. We have only to awake and snap the Lilliputian cords with which they have been entangling us during the first sleep which succeeded our labors. . . .

This Has Never Been from Under My Own Lock and Key

To George Washington, June 19, 1796

In the pro-Republican Aurora *of June 9, 1796, there appeared a complete report of the questions on French policy which Washington had asked his Cabinet on April 18, 1793. How did the* Aurora *get hold of it? Jefferson was quick to attest his innocence to Washington who believed him until the appearance of the Mazzei letter a year later.*

Dear Sir,—In Bache's Aurora, of the 9th inst which came here by the last post, a paper appears, which, having been confided, as I presume, to but few hands, makes it truly wonderful how it should have got there. I cannot be satisfied as to my own part, till I relieve my mind by declaring, and I attest everything sacred & honorable to the declaration, that it has got there neither thro' me nor the paper confided to me. This has never been from under my own lock & key, or out of my own hands. No mortal ever knew from me, that these questions had been proposed. Perhaps I ought to except one person, who possesses all my confidence, as he has possessed yours. I do not remember, indeed, that I communicated it even to him. But as I was in the habit of unlimited trust & council with him, it is possible I may have read it to him; no more: for the quire of which it makes a part was never in any hand but my own, nor was a word ever copied or taken down from it, by any body. I take on myself, without fear, any divulgation on his part. We both know him incapable of it. From myself, then, or my paper, this publication has never been derived. I have formerly mentioned to you, that from a very early period of my life, I had laid it down as a rule of conduct, never to write a word for the public papers. From this, I have never departed in a single instance; & on a late occasion, when all the world seemed to be writing, besides a rigid adherence to my own rule, I can say with truth, that not a line for the press was ever communicated to me, by any other, except a single petition referred for my correction which I did not correct, however, though the contrary, as have heard, was said in a public place, by one person through error, thro' malice by another. I learn that this last has thought it worth his while to try to sow tares between you & me, by representing me as still engaged in the bustle of politics, & in turbulence & intrigue against the government. I never believed for a moment that this could make any impression on you, or that your knowledge of me would not overweigh the slander of an intriguer, dirtily employed in sifting the conversations of my table, where alone he could hear of me; and seeking to atone for his sins against you by sins against another, who had never done him any other injury than that of declining his confidences. Political conversations I really dislike, & therefore avoid where I can without affectation. But when urged by others, I have never conceived that having been in public life requires me to belie my sentiments, or even to conceal them. When I am led by conversation to express them, I do it with the same independence here which I have practiced everywhere, and which is inseparable from my nature. But enough of this miserable tergiversator, who ought indeed either to have been of more truth, or less trusted by his country. . . .[1]

[1] Jefferson is referring to General Henry Lee, his old enemy.

The Only Sure Barrier

To James Madison, January 1, 1797

Though differences had arisen between Adams and Jefferson, each believed he could get along with the other; enough affection still remained to justify such a belief. Jefferson, for his own part, shrewdly calculated the political advantages of good relations with Adams, as the letter below indicates. It was inevitable that a schism should develop in Federalist ranks between Adams and Hamilton.

Yours of Dec. 19 has come safely. The event of the election has never been a matter of doubt in my mind. I knew that the Eastern States were disciplined in the schools of their town meetings to sacrifice differences of opinion to the great object of operating in phalanx, and that the more free and moral agency practiced in the other States would always make up the supplement of their weight. Indeed the vote comes much nearer an equality than I had expected. I know the difficulty of obtaining belief to one's declarations of a disinclination to honors, and that it is greatest with those who still remain in the world. But no arguments were wanting to reconcile me to a relinquishment of the first office or acquiescence under the second. As to the first it was impossible that a more solid unwillingness settled on full calculation, could have existed in any man's mind, short of the degree of absolute refusal. The only view on which I would have gone into it for awhile was to put our vessel on her republican tack before she should be thrown too much to leeward of her true principles. As to the second, it is the only office in the world about which I am unable to decide in my own mind whether I had rather have it or not have it. Pride does not enter into the estimate; for I think with the Romans that the general of to-day should be a soldier to-morrow if necessary. I can particularly have no feelings which would revolt at a secondary position to Mr. Adams. I am his junior in life, was his junior in Congress, his junior in the diplomatic line, his junior lately in the civil government. . . . If Mr. Adams can be induced to administer the government on its true principles, and to relinquish his bias to an English constitution, it is to be considered whether it would not be on the whole for the public good to come to a good understanding with him as to his future elections. He is perhaps the only sure barrier against Hamilton's getting in. . . .

It Could Not Brook Contradiction

To Archibold Stuart, January 4, 1797

Jefferson was, of course, increasingly disturbed about Washington's identification with Federalism. But what was to be done? For the Republicans to openly break with Washington might drive him further to the "right" and isolate them. Yet to avoid doing so might render their criticism ineffective and so deny them the possibility of leadership. Following is Jefferson's explanation of the tactic to be applied.

Dear Sir,—In answer to your favor of Dec. 31. & to the question whether adviseable to address the President on the subject of war against France, I shall speak explicitly, because I know I may do it safely to you. Such is the popularity of the President that the people will support him in whatever he will do or will not do, without appealing to their own reason or to anything but their feelings toward him. His mind has been so long used to unlimited applause that it could not brook contradiction, or even advice offered unasked. To advice, when asked, he is very open. I have long thought therefore it was best for the republican interest to soothe him by flattering where they could approve his measures, & to be silent where they disapprove, that they may not render him desperate as to their affections, & entirely indifferent to their wishes, in short to lie on their oars while he remains at the helm, and let the bark drift as his will and a superintending providence shall direct. By his answer to the House of Representatives on the subject of the French war, & also by private information, it seems he is earnest that the war should be avoided, & to have the credit of leaving us in full peace. I think then it is best to leave him to his own movements, & not to risk the ruffling them by what he might deem an improper interference with the constituted authorities. The rather too because we do not hear of any movement in any other quarter concurrent with what you suggest, & because it would scarcely reach him before his departure from office. As to the President elect, there is reason to believe that he (Mr. Adams I mean) is detached from Hamilton, & there is a possibility he may swerve from his politics in a great or less degree. Should the British faction attempt to urge him to the war by addresses of support with life & fortune, as may happen, it would then be adviseable to counteract their endeavors by dissuasive addresses. At this moment therefore, at our distance from the scene of information & influence, I should think it most adviseable to be silent till we see what turn the new administration will take. At the same time I mix so little with the world, that my opinion merits less attention than anybody's else, and ought not to be weighed against your own good judgment. If therefore I have given it freely, it is because you have desired it, & not because I think it worth your notice. . . .

My Zealous Attachment to the Constitution

Vice-Presidential Inaugural Address, March 4, 1797

*Jefferson wanted no official welcome, nor did he want even
the slightest formalities to take place during his inaugural
ceremony; he would have preferred, in fact, to receive official word of his election by mail.*

Gentlemen of the Senate,—Entering on the duties of the
office to which I am called, I feel it incumbent on me to
apologize to this honorable House for the insufficient manner in which I fear they may be discharged. At an earlier
period of my life, and through some considerable portion of
it, I have been a member of legislative bodies, and not altogether inattentive to the forms of their proceedings. But much
time has elapsed since that: other duties have occupied my
mind, and, in a great degree, it has lost its familiarity with
this subject. I fear that the House will have but too frequent
occasion to perceive the truth of this acknowledgment. If
a diligent attention, however, will enable me to fulfil the
functions now assigned me, I may promise that diligence
and attention shall be sedulously employed. For one portion
of my duty I shall engage with more confidence, because it
will depend on my will and not on my capacity. The rules
which are to govern the proceedings of this House, so far
as they shall depend on me for their application, shall be
applied with the most rigorous and inflexible impartiality, re-
garding neither persons, their views, or principles, and seeing
only the abstract proposition subject to my decision. If, in
forming that decision, I concur with some and differ from
others, as must of necessity happen, I shall rely on the liberality and candor of those from whom I differ, to believe
that I do it on pure motives.

I might here proceed, and with the greatest truth, to declare my zealous attachment to the Constitution of the United
States; that I consider the union of these States as the first
of blessings, and, as the first of duties, the preservation of
that Constitution which secures it; but I suppose these declarations not pertinent to the occasion of entering into an

office whose primary business is merely to preside over the forms of this House, and no one more sincerely prays that no accident may call me to the higher and more important functions which the Constitution eventually devolves on this office. These have been justly confided to the eminent character which has preceded me here, whose talents and integrity have been known and revered by me through a long course of years; have been the foundation of a cordial and uninterrupted friendship between us; and I devoutly pray he may be long preserved for the government, the happiness, and prosperity of our common country.

He Returned to His Former Party Views

Anas, March 2–6, 1797

Jefferson's account below reveals the difficulties which Adams labored under. To accommodate Jefferson would have meant alienating the dominant Hamiltonian wing of the Federalist party. It was a notorious fact that the members of Adam's Cabinet gave their entire loyalty to Hamilton.

. . . I arrived at Philadelphia to qualify as Vice-President, and called instantly on Mr. Adams, who lodged at Francis's, in Fourth street. The next morning he returned my visit at Mr. Madison's, where I lodged. He found me alone in my room, and shutting the door himself, he said he was glad to find me alone, for that he wished a free conversation with me. He entered immediately on an explanation of the situation of our affairs with France, and the danger of rupture with that nation, a rupture which would convulse the attachments of this country; that he was impressed with the necessity of an immediate mission to the Directory; that it would have been the first wish of his heart to have got me to go there, but that he supposed it was out of the question, as it did not seem justifiable for him to send away the person destined to take his place in case of accident to himself, nor decent to remove from competition one who was a rival in the public favor. That he had, therefore, concluded to send a mission, which, by its dignity, should satisfy France, and by its selection from the three great divisions of the continent, should satisfy all parts of the United States; in short, that he had determined to join Gerry and Madison to Pinckney, and he wished me to consult Mr. Madison for him. I told him that as to myself, I concurred in the opinion of the impropriety of my leaving the post assigned me, and that my inclinations, moreover, would never permit me to cross the Atlantic again; that I would, as he desired, consult Mr. Madison, but I feared it was desperate, as he had refused that mission on my leaving it, in General Washington's time, though it was kept open a twelvemonth for him. He said that if Mr. Madison should refuse, he would still appoint him, and leave the responsibility on him. I consulted Mr. Madison, who declined as I expected. I think it was on Monday the 6th of March, Mr. Adams and myself met at dinner at General Washington's, and we happened, in the evening, to rise from table and come away together. As soon as we got into the street, I told him the event of my negotiation with Mr. Madison. He immediately said, that, on consultation, some objections to that nomination had been raised which he had not contemplated; and was going on with excuses which evidently embarrassed him, when we came to Fifth street, where our road separated, his being down Market street, mine off along Fifth, and we took leave; and he never after that said one word to me on the subject, or ever consulted me as to any measures of the government. The opinion I formed at the time on this transaction, was, that Mr. Adams, in the first moments of the enthusiasm of the occasion (his inauguration), forgot party sentiments, and as he never acted on any system, but was always governed by the feeling of the moment, he thought, for a moment, to steer impartially between the parties; that Monday, the 6th of March, being the first time he had met his cabinet, on expressing ideas of this kind, he had been at once diverted from them, and returned to his former party views. . . .

That There Were an Ocean of Fire Between Us

To Elbridge Gerry, May 13, 1797

France replaced Britain as chief offender against American shipping. Hamilton and other extreme Federalists favored a tough policy toward France—including the imposition of an embargo and the raising of a navy and army—though they had, for a similar provocation, favored a lenient policy toward Britain. Jefferson and the Republicans plumped for neutrality now though they had been reluctant to concede it before to Britain. Adams sent three negotiators to France: John Marshall, C. C. Pinckney and Elbridge Gerry. Of the three, Gerry (who had refused to sign the Constitution in 1787) alone was more or less a Republican.

. . . I do sincerely wish with you, that we could take our stand on a ground perfectly neutral and independent towards all nations. It has been my constant object through my public life; and with respect to the English and French, particularly, I have too often expressed to the former my wishes, and made to them propositions verbally and in writing, officially and privately, to official and private characters, for them to doubt of my views, if they would be content with equality. Of this they are in possession of several written and formal proofs, in my own handwriting. But they have wished a monopoly of commerce and influence with us; and they have in fact obtained it. When we take notice that theirs is the workshop to which we go for all we want; that with them centre either immediately or ultimately all the labors of our hands and lands; that to them belongs either openly or secretly the great mass of our navigation; that even the factorage of their affairs here, is kept to themselves by factitious citizenships; that these foreign and false citizens now constitute the great body of what are called our merchants, fill our sea ports, are planted in every little town and district of the interior country, sway everything in the former places by their own votes, and those of their dependants, in the latter, by their insinuations and the influence of their ledgers; that they are advancing fast to a monopoly of our banks and public funds, and thereby placing our public finances under their control; that they have in their alliance the most influential characters in and out of office; when they have shown that by all these bearings on the different branches of the government, they can force it to proceed in whatever direction they dictate, and bend the interests of this country entirely to the will of another; when all this, I say, is attended to, it is impossible for us to say we stand on independent ground, impossible for a free mind not to see and to groan under the bondage in which it is bound. If anything after this could excite surprise, it would be that they have been able so far to throw dust in the eyes of our own citizens, as to fix on those who wish merely to recover self-government the charge of subserving one foreign influence, because they resist submission to another. But they possess our printing presses, a powerful engine in their government of us. At this very moment, they would have drawn us into a war on the side of England, had it not been for the failure of her bank. Such was their open and loud cry, and that of their gazettes till this event. After plunging us in all the broils of the European nations, there would remain but one act to close our tragedy, that is, to break up our Union; and even this they have ventured seriously and solemnly to propose and maintain by arguments in a Connecticut paper. I have been happy, however, in believing, from the stifling of this effort, that that dose was found too strong, and excited as much repugnance there as it did horror in other parts of our country, and that whatever follies we may be led into as to foreign nations, we shall never give up our Union, the last anchor of our hope, and that alone which is to prevent this heavenly country from becoming an arena of gladiators. Much as I abhor war, and view it as the greatest scourge of mankind, and anxiously as I wish to keep out of the broils of Europe, I would yet go with my brethren into these, rather than separate from them. But I hope we may still keep clear of them, notwithstanding our present thraldom, and that time may be given us to reflect on the awful crisis we have passed through, and to find some means of shielding ourselves in future from foreign influence, political, commercial, or in whatever other form it may be attempted. I can scarcely withhold myself from joining in the wish of Silas Deane, that there were an ocean of fire between us and the old world.

A perfect confidence that you are as much attached to

peace and union as myself, that you equally prize independence of all nations, and the blessings of self-government, has induced me freely to unbosom myself to you, and let you see the light in which I have viewed what has been passing among us from the beginning of the war. And I shall be happy, at all times, in an intercommunication of sentiments with you, believing that the dispositions of the different parts of our country have been considerably misrepresented and misunderstood in each part, as to the other, and that nothing but good can result from an exchange of information and opinions between those whose circumstances and morals admit no doubt of the integrity of their views.

I remain, with constant and sincere esteem, dear Sir, your affectionate friend and servant.

Against All Popular Storms and Passions

Anas, February 15, 1798

The following discussion between Adams and Jefferson was not abstract. The Senate, so warmly extolled by Adams, happened to be Federalist-dominated (it was a trial for Jefferson to preside over such a body), while the Republicans barely controlled the House.

February the 15th, 1798. I dined this day with Mr. Adams (the President). The company was large. After dinner I was sitting next to him, and our conversation was first on the enormous price of labor, house rent, and other things. We both concurred in ascribing it chiefly to the floods of bank paper now afloat, and in condemning those institutions. We then got on the constitution; and in the course of our conversation he said, that no republic could ever last which had not a Senate, and a Senate deeply and strongly rooted, strong enough to bear up against all popular storms and passions; that he thought our Senate as well constituted as it could have been, being chosen by the legislatures; for if these could not support them, he did not know what could do it; that perhaps it might have been as well for them to be chosen by the State at large, as that would insure a choice of distinguished men, since none but such could be known to a whole people; that the only fault in our Senate was, that it was not durable enough; that hitherto, it had behaved very well; however, he was afraid they would give way in the end. That as to trusting to a popular assembly for the preservation of our liberties, it was the merest chimera imaginable; they never had any rule of decision but their own will; that he would as lieve be again in the hands of our old committees of safety, who made the law and executed it at the same time; that it had been observed by some writer (I forget whom he named), that anarchy did more mischief in one night, than tyranny in an age; and that in modern times we might say with truth, that in France, anarchy had done more harm in one night, than all the despotism of their Kings had ever done in twenty or thirty years. The point in which he views our Senate, as the colossus of the constitution, serves as a key to the politics of the Senate, who are two-thirds of them in his sentiments, and accounts for the bold line of conduct they pursue. . . .

Will the Evil Stop There?

To John Taylor, June 1, 1798

John Taylor, the planter-philosopher, had suggested precisely the secessionist course Jefferson was to follow only a few months later. But in rejecting that course now Jefferson eloquently presages the unionist argument of Webster, Jackson and Lincoln.

. . . Mr. New showed me your letter on the subject of the patent, which gave me an opportunity of observing what you said, as to the effect, with you, of public proceedings, and that it was not unwise now to estimate the separate mass of Virginia and North Carolina, with a view to their separate existence. It is true that we are completely under the saddle of Massachusetts and Connecticut, and that they ride us very hard, cruelly insulting our feelings, as well as exhausting our strength and subsistence. Their natural friends, the three other eastern States, join them from a sort of family pride, and they have the art to divide certain other parts of the Union, so as to make use of them to govern the whole. This is not new, it is the old practice of despots; to use a part of the people to keep the rest in order. And those who have once got an ascendancy, and possessed themselves of all the resources of the nation, their revenues and offices, have immense means for retaining their advantage. But our present situation is not a natural one. The republicans, through every part of the Union, say, that it was the irresistible influence and popularity of General Washington played off by the cunning of Hamilton, which turned the government over to anti-republican hands, or turned the republicans chosen by the people into anti-republicans. He delivered it over to his successor in this state, and very untoward events since, improved with great artifice, have produced on the public mind the impressions we see. But still I repeat it, this is not the natural state. Time alone would bring round an order of things more correspondent to the sentiments of our constituents. But are there no events impending, which will do it within a few months? The crisis with England, the public and authentic avowal of sentiments hostile to the leading principles of our Constitution, the prospect of a war, in which we shall stand alone, land tax, stamp tax, increase of public debt, &c. Be this as it may, in every free and deliberating society, there must, from the nature of man, be opposite parties, and violent dissensions and discords; and one of these, for the most part, must prevail over the other for a longer or shorter time. Perhaps this party division is necessary to induce each to watch and delate to the people the proceedings of the other. But if on a temporary superiority of the one party, the other is to resort to a scission of the Union, no federal government can ever exist. If to rid ourselves of the present rule of Massachusetts and Connecticut, we break the Union, will the evil stop there? Suppose the New England States alone cut off, will our nature be changed? Are we not men still to the south of that, and with all the passions of men? Immediately, we shall see a Pennsylvania and a Virginia party arise in the residuary confederacy, and the public mind will be distracted with the same party spirit. What a game too will the one party have in their hands, by eternally threatening the other that unless they do so and so, they will join their northern neighbors. If we reduce our Union to Virginia and North Carolina, immediately the conflict will be established between the representatives of these two States, and they will end by breaking into their simple units. Seeing, therefore, that an association of men who will not quarrel with one another is a thing which never yet existed, from the greatest confederacy of nations down to a town meeting or a vestry; seeing that we must have somebody to quarrel with, I had rather keep our New England associates for that purpose, than to see our bickerings transferred to others. They are circumscribed within such narrow limits, and their population so full, that their numbers will ever be the minority, and they are marked, like the Jews, with such a perversity of character, as to constitute, from that circumstance, the natural division of our parties. A little patience, and we shall see the reign of witches pass over, their spells dissolved, and the people recovering their true sight, restoring their government to its true principles. It is true, that in the meantime, we are suffering deeply in spirit, and incurring the horrors of a war, and long oppressions of enormous public debt. But who can say what would be the evils of a scission, and when and where they would end? Better keep together as we are, haul off from Europe as soon as we can, and from all attachments to any portions of it; and if they show their power just sufficiently to hoop us together, it will be the happiest situation in which we can exist. If the game runs sometimes against us at home, we must have patience till luck turns, and then we shall have an opportunity of winning back the *principles* we have lost. For this is a game where principles are the stake. Better luck, therefore, to us all, and health, happiness and friendly salutations to yourself. Adieu.

P.S. It is hardly necessary to caution you to let nothing of mine get before the public; a single sentence got hold of by the Porcupines, will suffice to abuse and persecute me in their papers for months.

To Nullify of Their Own Authority

The Kentucky Resolutions, November 1798

In his letter to John Taylor of June 1, Jefferson had advised against secession. But events since then had moved swiftly. During the summer the Alien Act, the Sedition Act, the Naturalization Act had been passed by an aroused or intimidated Congress. To Jefferson the fearful moment—overthrow of Republicanism in America—seemed at hand. In late summer he met in high secrecy with Wilson Nicholas of Virginia and John Breckinridge of Kentucky to determine how Federalist policy could best be combated. If Republicanism was the end, states-rights would be the means. In drawing up the Kentucky Resolutions Jefferson hoped to generate a broad protest among the states reminiscent of the colonies' protest against Britain. The Kentucky legislature adopted them on November 13 only after having omitted mention of committees of correspondence, immediate nullification, or resistance. Apart from Virginia, which in late December passed Madison's more cautious version of the Kentucky Resolutions, state legislatures elsewhere either repudiated or disregarded them.

1. *Resolved,* That the several States composing the United States of America, are not united on the principle of unlimited submission to their general government; but that, by a compact under the style and title of a Constitution for the United States, and of amendments thereto, they constituted a general government for special purposes—delegated to that government certain definite powers, reserving, each State to itself, the residuary mass of right to their own self-government; and that whensoever the general government assumes undelegated powers, its acts are unauthoritative, void, and of no force: that to this compact each State acceded as a State, and is an integral party, its co-States forming, as to itself, the other party: that the government created by this compact was not made the exclusive or final judge of the extent of the powers delegated to itself; since that would have made its discretion, and not the Constitution, the measure of its

powers; but that, as in all other cases of compact among powers having no common judge, each party has an equal right to judge for itself, as well of infractions as of the mode and measure of redress.

2. *Resolved*, That the Constitution of the United States, having delegated to Congress a power to punish treason, counterfeiting the securities and current coin of the United States, piracies, and felonies committed on the high seas, and offences against the law of nations, and no other crimes whatsoever; and it being true as a general principle, and one of the amendments to the Constitution having also declared, that "the powers not delegated to the United States by the Constitution, nor prohibited by it to the States, are reserved to the States respectively, or to the people," therefore the act of Congress, passed on the 14th day of July, 1798, and intituled "An Act in addition to the act intituled An Act for the punishment of certain crimes against the United States," as also the act passed by them on the—day of June, 1798, intituled "An Act to punish frauds committed on the bank of the United States," (and all their other acts which assume to create, define, or punish crimes, other than those so enumerated in the Constitution,) are altogether void, and of no force; and that the power to create, define, and punish such other crimes is reserved, and, of right, appertains solely and exclusively to the respective States, each within its own territory.

3. *Resolved*, That it is true as a general principle, and is also expressly declared by one of the amendments to the Constitution, that "the powers not delegated to the United States by the Constitution, nor prohibited by it to the States, are reserved to the States respectively, or to the people"; and that no power over the freedom of religion, freedom of speech, or freedom of the press being delegated to the United States by the Constitution, nor prohibited by it to the States, all lawful powers respecting the same did of right remain, and were reserved to the States or the people: that thus was manifested their determination to retain to themselves the right of judging how far the licentiousness of speech and of the press may be abridged without lessening their useful freedom, and how far those abuses which cannot be separated from their use should be tolerated, rather than the use be destroyed. And thus also they guarded against all abridgment by the United States of the freedom of religious opinions and

exercises, and retained to themselves the right of protecting the same, as this State, by a law passed on the general demand of its citizens, had already protected them from all human restraint or interference. And that in addition to this general principle and express declaration, another and more special provision has been made by one of the amendments to the Constitution, which expressly declares, that "Congress shall make no law respecting an establishment of religion, or prohibiting the free exercise thereof, or abridging the freedom of speech or of the press": thereby guarding in the same sentence, and under the same words, the freedom of religion, of speech, and of the press: insomuch, that whatever violated either, throws down the sanctuary which covers the others, and that libels, falsehood, and defamation, equally with heresy and false religion, are withheld from the cognizance of federal tribunals. That, therefore, the act of Congress of the United States, passed on the 14th day of July, 1798, intituled "An Act in addition to the act intituled An Act for the punishment of certain crimes against the United States," which does abridge the freedom of the press, is not law, but is altogether void, and of no force.

4. *Resolved,* That alien friends are under the jurisdiction and protection of the laws of the State wherein they are: that no power over them has been delegated to the United States, nor prohibited to the individual States, distinct from their power over citizens. And it being true as a general principle, and one of the amendments to the Constitution having also declared, that "the powers not delegated to the United States by the Constitution, nor prohibited by it to the States, are reserved to the States respectively, or to the people," the act of the Congress of the United States, passed on the — day of July, 1798, intituled "An Act concerning aliens," which assumes powers over alien friends, not delegated by the Constitution, is not law, but is altogether void, and of no force.

5. *Resolved,* That in addition to the general principle, as well as the express declaration, that powers not delegated are reserved, another and more special provision, inserted in the Constitution from abundant caution, has declared that "the migration or importation of such persons as any of the States now existing shall think proper to admit, shall not be prohibited by the Congress prior to the year 1808": that this commonwealth does admit the migration of alien friends, described as the subject of the said act concerning aliens: that

a provision against prohibiting their migration, is a provision against all acts equivalent thereto, or it would be nugatory: that to remove them when migrated, is equivalent to a prohibition of their migration, and is, therefore, contrary to the said provision of the Constitution, and void.

6. *Resolved,* That the imprisonment of a person under the protection of the laws of this commonwealth, on his failure to obey the simple *order* of the President to depart out of the United States, as is undertaken by said act intituled "An Act concerning aliens," is contrary to the Constitution, one amendment to which has provided that "no person shall be deprived of liberty without due progress of law"; and that another having provided that "in all criminal prosecutions the accused shall enjoy the right to public trial by an impartial jury, to be informed of the nature and cause of the accusation, to be confronted with the witnesses against him, to have compulsory process for obtaining witnesses in his favor, and to have the assistance of counsel for his defence," the same act, undertaking to authorize the President to remove a person out of the United States, who is under the protection of the law, on his own suspicion, without accusation, without jury, without public trial, without confrontation of the witnesses against him, without hearing witnesses in his favor, without defence, without counsel, is contrary to the provision also of the Constitution, is therefore not law, but utterly void, and of no force: that transferring the power of judging any person, who is under the protection of the laws, from the courts to the President of the United States, as is undertaken by the same act concerning aliens, is against the article of the Constitution which provides that "the judicial power of the United States shall be vested in courts, the judges of which shall hold their offices during good behavior"; and that the said act is void for that reason also. And it is further to be noted, that this transfer of judiciary power is to that magistrate of the general government who already possesses all the Executive, and a negative on all Legislative powers.

7. *Resolved,* That the construction applied by the General Government (as is evidenced by sundry of their proceedings) to those parts of the Constitution of the United States which delegate to Congress a power "to lay and collect taxes, duties, imports, and excises, to pay the debts, and provide for the common defence and general welfare of the United States,"

and "to make all laws which shall be necessary and proper for carrying into execution the powers vested by the Constitution in the government of the United States, or in any department or officer thereof," goes to the destruction of all limits prescribed to their power by the Constitution: that words meant by the instrument to be subsidiary only to the execution of limited powers, ought not to be so construed as themselves to give unlimited powers, nor a part to be so taken as to destroy the whole residue of that instrument: that the proceedings of the General Government under color of these articles, will be a fit and necessary subject of revisal and correction, at a time of greater tranquillity, while those specified in the preceding resolutions call for immediate redress.

8. *Resolved*, That a committee of conference and correspondence be appointed, who shall have in charge to communicate the preceding resolutions to the Legislatures of the several States; to assure them that this commonwealth continues in the same esteem of their friendship and union which it has manifested from that moment at which a common danger first suggested a common union: that it considers union, for specified national purposes, and particularly to those specified in their late federal compact, to be friendly to the peace, happiness and prosperity of all the States: that faithful to that compact, according to the plain intent and meaning in which it was understood and acceded to by the several parties, it is sincerely anxious for its preservation: that it does also believe, that to take from the States all the powers of self-government and transfer them to a general and consolidated government, without regard to the special delegations and reservations solemnly agreed to in that compact, is not for the peace, happiness or prosperity of these States; and that therefore this commonwealth is determined, as it doubts not its co-States are, to submit to undelegated, and consequently unlimited powers in no man, or body of men on earth: that in cases of an abuse of the delegated powers, the members of the general government, being chosen by the people, a change by the people would be the constitutional remedy; but, where powers are assumed which have not been delegated, a nullification of the act is the rightful remedy: that every State has a natural right in cases not within the compact, (*casus non fœderis*,) to nullify of their own authority all assumptions of power by others within their limits:

that without this right, they would be under the dominion, absolute and unlimited, of whosoever might exercise this right of judgment for them: that nevertheless, this commonwealth, from motives of regard and respect for its co-States, has wished to communicate with them on the subject: that with them alone it is proper to communicate, they alone being parties to the compact, and solely authorized to judge in the last resort of the powers exercised under it, Congress being not a party, but merely the creature of the compact, and subject as to its assumptions of power to the final judgment of those by whom, and for whose use itself and its powers were all created and modified: that if the acts before specified should stand, these conclusions would flow from them; that the general government may place any act they think proper on the list of crimes, and punish it themselves whether enumerated or not enumerated by the constitution as cognizable by them: that they may transfer its cognizance to the President, or any other person, who may himself be the accuser, counsel, judge and jury, whose *suspicions* may be the evidence, his *order* the sentence, his *officer* the executioner, and his breast the sole record of the transaction: that a very numerous and valuable description of the inhabitants of these States being, by this precedent, reduced, as outlaws, to the absolute dominion of one man, and the barrier of the Constitution thus swept away from us all, no rampart now remains against the passions and the powers of a majority in Congress to protect from a like exportation, or other more grievous punishment, the minority of the same body, the legislatures, judges, governors and counsellors of the States, nor their other peaceable inhabitants, who may venture to reclaim the constitutional rights and liberties of the States and people, or who for other causes, good or bad, may be obnoxious to the views, or marked by the suspicions of the President, or be thought dangerous to his or their election, or other interests, public or personal: that the friendless alien has indeed been selected as the safest subject of a first experiment; but the citizen will soon follow, or rather, has already followed, for already has a sedition act marked him as its prey: that these and successive acts of the same character, unless arrested at the threshold, necessarily drive these States into revolution and blood, and will furnish new calumnies against republican government, and new pretexts for those who wish it to be believed that man cannot be governed but by a rod of iron: that it would be a dangerous delusion were a confidence in the men of our choice to silence our fears for the safety of our rights: that confidence is everywhere the parent of despotism—free government is founded in jealousy, and not in confidence; it is jealousy and not confidence which prescribes limited constitutions, to bind down those whom we are obliged to trust with power: that our Constitution has accordingly fixed the limits to which, and no further, our confidence may go; and let the honest advocate of confidence read the Alien and Sedition acts, and say if the Constitution has not been wise in fixing limits to the government it created, and whether we should be wise in destroying those limits. Let him say what the government is, if it be not a tyranny, which the men of our choice have conferred on our President, and the President of our choice has assented to, and accepted over the friendly strangers to whom the mild spirit of our country and its laws have pledged hospitality and protection: that the men of our choice have more respected the bare *suspicions* of the President, than the solid right of innocence, the claims of justification, the sacred force of truth, and the forms and substance of law and justice. In questions of power, then, let no more be heard of confidence in man, but bind him down from mischief by the chains of the Constitution. That this commonwealth does therefore call on its co-States for an expression of their sentiments on the acts concerning aliens, and for the punishment of certain crimes herein before specified, plainly declaring whether these acts are or are not authorized by the federal compact. And it doubts not that their sense will be so announced as to prove their attachment unaltered to limited government, whether general or particular. And that the rights and liberties of their co-States will be exposed to no dangers by remaining embarked in a common bottom with their own. That they will concur with this commonwealth in considering the said acts as so palpably against the Constitution as to amount to an undisguised declaration that that compact is not meant to be the measure of the powers of the General Government, but that it will proceed in the exercise over these States, of all powers whatsoever: that they will view this as seizing the rights of the States, and consolidating them in the hands of the General Government, with a power assumed to bind the States (not merely as the cases made federal, *casus fœderis* but), in all cases whatsoever, by laws made, not with their consent, but by others against their consent: that this would be to surrender the form of government we have chosen, and live under one deriving its powers from its own will, and not from our authority; and that the co-States, recurring to their natural right in cases not made federal, will concur in declaring these acts void, and of no force, and will each take measures of its own for providing that neither these acts, nor any others of the General Government not plainly and intentionally authorized by the Constitution, shall be exercised within their respective territories.

9. *Resolved,* That the said committee be authorized to communicate by writing or personal conferences, at any times or places whatever, with any person or persons who may be appointed by any one or more co-States to correspond or confer with them; and that they lay their proceedings before the next session of Assembly.

There, My Friend, Are My Principles

To Elbridge Gerry, January 26, 1799

In the course of this summary presentation of his political philosophy, Jefferson accurately gauges the mood of the American people: the growing hostility to Federalism and to the preparation for war against France, with the prospect of a large standing army, high taxes and submission to Hamilton's military leadership. Elbridge Gerry, who had remained behind to negotiate further with Talleyrand, was surprised, on his return home, to find how close the nation stood to war.

. . . I do then, with sincere zeal, wish an inviolable preservation of our present federal Constitution, according to the true sense in which it was adopted by the States, that in which it was advocated by its friends, and not that which its enemies apprehended, who therefore became its enemies; and I am opposed to the monarchising its features by the forms of its administration, with a view to conciliate a first transition to a President and Senate for life, and from that to an hereditary tenure of these offices, and thus to worm out the elective principle. I am for preserving to the States the powers not yielded by them to the Union, and to the legislature of the Union its constitutional share in the division of powers; and I am not for transferring all the powers of the States to the General Government, and all those of that government to the executive branch. I am for a government rigorously frugal and simple, applying all the possible savings of the public revenue to the discharge of the national debt; and not for a multiplication of officers and salaries merely to make partisans, and for increasing, by every device, the public debt, on the principle of its being a public blessing. I am for relying, for internal defence, on our militia solely, till actual invasion, and for such a naval force only as may protect our coasts and harbors from such depredations as we have experienced; and not for a standing army in time of peace, which may overawe the public sentiment; nor for a navy, which, by its own expenses and the eternal wars in which it will implicate us, will grind us with public burthens, and sink us under them. I am for free commerce with all nations; political connection with none; and little or no diplomatic establishment. And I am not for linking ourselves by new treaties with the quarrels of Europe; entering that field of slaughter to preserve their balance, or joining in the confederacy of kings to war against the principles of liberty. I am for freedom of religion, and against all manœuvres to bring about a legal ascendancy of one sect over another: for freedom of the press, and against all violations of the Constitution to silence by force and not by reason the complaints or criticisms, just or unjust, of our citizens against the conduct of their agents. And I am for encouraging the progress of science in all its branches; and not for raising a hue and cry against the sacred name of philosophy; for awing the human mind by stories of raw-head and bloody bones to a distrust of its own vision, and to repose implicitly on that of others; to go backwards instead of forwards to look for improvement; to believe that government, religion, morality, and every other science were in the highest perfection in ages of the darkest ignorance, and that nothing can ever be devised more perfect than what was established by our forefathers. To these I will add, that I was a sincere well-wisher to the success of the French revolution, and still wish it may end in the establishment of a free and well-ordered republic; but I have not been insensible under the atrocious depredations they have committed on our commerce. The first object of my heart is my own country. In that is embarked my family, my fortune, and my own existence. I have not one farthing of interest, nor one fibre of attachment out of it, nor a single motive of preference of any one nation to another, but in proportion as they are more or less friendly to us. But though deeply feeling the injuries of France, I did not think war the surest means of redressing them. I did believe, that a mission sincerely disposed to preserve peace, would obtain for us a peaceable and honorable settlement and retribution; and I appeal to you to say, whether this might not have been obtained, if either of your colleagues had been of the same sentiment with yourself.

These, my friend, are my principles; they are unquestionably the principles of the great body of our fellow-citizens, and I know there is not one of them which is not yours also. In truth, we never differed but on one ground, the funding system; and as, from the moment of its being adopted by the constituted authorities, I became religiously principled in the sacred discharge of it to the uttermost farthing, we are united now even on that single ground of difference. . . .

Doing Nothing Which May Hoop
Them Together

To Madison, November 26, 1799

*This memorandum reveals Jefferson as the shrewd politician
he was. The alarums of nullification are replaced by quite
moderate party strategy.*

. . . Our objects, according to my ideas, should be these.
1. peace even with Great Britain. 2. a sincere cultivation of
the Union. 3. the disbanding of the army on principles of
economy and safety. 4. protestations against violations of
the true principles of our constitution, merely to save them,
and prevent precedent and acquiescence from being pleaded
against them; but nothing to be said or done which shall look
or lead to force, and give any pretext for giving up the army.
If we find the monarchical party really split into pure Monocrats & Anglo-monocrats, we should leave them alone to
manage all those points of difference which they may
chuse to take between themselves, only arbitrating between
them by our votes, but doing nothing which may hoop
them together. . . .

Signs of It Will Be Their Respect for You

To Joseph Priestley, January 27, 1800

Priestley, the great scientist, had fled his native England for the sake of his republicanism and atheism and settled in Pennsylvania. He long corresponded with Jefferson on a host of subjects. In 1799 and 1800, in lengthy exchanges with Priestley, Jefferson returned to his cynosure: a truly republican system of education.

Dear Sir,—In my last letter of the 18th, I omitted to say any thing of the languages as part of our proposed University. It was not that I think, as some do, that they are useless. I am of a very different opinion. I do not think them very essential to the obtaining eminent degrees of science; but I think them very useful towards it. I suppose there is a portion of life during which our faculties are ripe enough for this, and for nothing more useful. I think the Greeks and Romans have left us the present models which exist of fine composition, whether we examine them as works of reason, or of style and fancy; and to them we probably owe these characteristics of modern composition. I know of no composition of any other ancient people, which merits the least regard as a model for its matter or style. To all this I add, that to read the Latin and Greek authors in their original, is a sublime luxury; and I deem luxury in science to be at least as justifiable as in architecture, painting, gardening, or the other arts. I enjoy Homer in his own language infinitely beyond Pope's translation of him, and both beyond the dull narrative of the same events by Dares Phrygius; and it is an innocent enjoyment. I thank on my knees, Him who directed my early education, for having put into my possession this rich source of delight; and I would not exchange it for anything which I could then have acquired, and have not since acquired. With this regard for those languages, you will acquit me of meaning to omit them. About twenty years ago, I drew a bill for our legislature, which proposed to lay off every county into hundreds or townships of five or six miles square, in the centre of each of them was to be a free English school;

the whole State was further laid off into ten districts, in each of which was to be a college for teaching the languages, geography, surveying, and other useful things of that grade; and then a single University for the sciences.

It was received with enthusiasm; but as I had proposed that William and Mary, under an improved form, should be the University, and that was at that time pretty highly Episcopal, the dissenters after awhile began to apprehend some secret design of a preference to that sect. About three years ago they enacted that part of my bill which related to English schools, except that instead of obliging, they left it optional in the court of every county to carry it into execution or not. I think it probable that part of the plan for the middle grade of education, may also be brought forward in due time. In the meanwhile, we are not without a sufficient number of good country schools, where the languages, geography, and the first elements of mathematics, are taught. Having omitted this information in my former letter, I thought it necessary now to supply it, that you might know on what base your superstructure was to be reared. I have a letter from Mr. Dupont, since his arrival at New York, dated the 20th, in which he says he will be in Philadelphia within about a fortnight from that time; but only on a visit. How much would it delight me if a visit from you at the same time, were to show us two such illustrious foreigners embracing each other in my country, as the asylum for whatever is great and good. Pardon, I pray you, the temporary delirium which has been excited here, but which is fast passing away. The Gothic idea that we are to look backwards instead of forwards for the improvement of the human mind, and to recur to the annals of our ancestors for what is most perfect in government, in religion and in learning, is worthy of those bigots in religion and government, by whom it has been recommended, and whose purposes it would answer. But it is not an idea which this country will endure; and the moment of their showing it is fast ripening; and the signs of it will be their respect for you, and growing detestation of those who have dishonored our country by endeavors to disturb our tranquillity in it. No one has felt this with more sensibility than, my dear Sir, your respectful and affectionate friend and servant.

This Simple and Economical Mode of Government

To Gideon Granger, August 13, 1800

Following is an excellent statement of Jefferson's philosophy of government. He could now rest easier that the country would not become monarchical, that it would remain at once intact and republican. But it remained to be seen how the strongly Federalist northeast would take to a change in regimes. Gideon Granger was a Connecticut Republican.

Dear Sir,—I received with great pleasure your favor of June 4, and am much comforted by the appearance of a change of opinion in your state; for tho' we may obtain, & I believe shall obtain, a majority in the legislature of the United States, attached to the preservation of the Federal constitution according to it's obvious principles, & those on which it was known to be received; attached equally to the preservation to the states of those rights unquestionably remaining with them; friends to the freedom of religion, freedom of the press, trial by jury & to economical government; opposed to standing armies, paper systems, war, & all connection, other than commerce, with any foreign nation; in short, a majority firm in all those principles which we have espoused and the federalists have opposed uniformly; still, should the whole body of New England continue in opposition to these principles of government, either knowingly or through delusion, our government will be a very uneasy one. It can never be harmonious & solid, while so respectable a portion of it's citizens support principles which go directly to a change of the federal constitution, to sink the state governments, consolidate them into one, and to monarchize that. Our country is too large to have all its affairs directed by a single government. Public servants at such a distance, & from under the eye of their constituents, must, from the circumstance of distance, be unable to administer & overlook all the details necessary for the good government of the citizens, and the same circumstance, by rendering detection impossible to their constituents, will invite the public agents to corruption, plunder & waste. And I do verily believe, that if the principle were to prevail, of a common law being in force in the U S, (which principle possesses the general government at once of all the powers of the state governments, and reduces us to a single consolidated government,) it would become the most corrupt government on the earth. You have seen the practises by which the public servants have been able to cover their conduct, or, where that could not be done, delusions by which they have varnished it for the eye of their constituents. What an augmentation of the field for jobbing, speculating, plundering, office-building & office-hunting would be produced by an assumption of all the state powers into the hands of the general government. The true theory of our constitution is surely the wisest & best, that the states are independent as to everything within themselves, & united as to everything respecting foreign nations. Let the general government be reduced to foreign concerns only, and let our affairs be disentangled from those of all other nations, except as to commerce, which the merchants will manage the better, the more they are left free to manage for themselves, and our general government may be reduced to a very simple organization, & a very unexpensive one; a few plain duties to be performed by a few servants. But I repeat, that this simple & economical mode of government can never be secured, if the New England States continue to support the contrary system. I rejoice, therefore, in every appearance of their returning to those principles which I had always imagined to be almost innate in them. In this State, a few persons were deluded by the X. Y. Z. duperies. You saw the effect of it in our last Congressional representatives, chosen under their influence. This experiment on their credulity is now seen into, and our next representation will be as republican as it has heretofore been. On the whole, we hope, that by a part of the Union having held on to the principles of the constitution, time has been given to the states to recover from the temporary frenzy into which they had been decoyed, to rally round the constitution, & to rescue it from the destruction with which it had been threatened even at their own hands. . . .

I Have Sworn upon the Altar of God . . .

To Dr. Benjamin Rush, September 23, 1800

During an electoral campaign of unrestrained calumny against his "atheism," Jefferson explained his ideas on religion only to Dr. Rush, the Philadelphia doctor and philosopher. The "letter on Christianity" to which Jefferson refers below, was not to be written for several years (See letter to Rush, April 21, 1803).

. . . I promised you a letter on Christianity, which I have not forgotten. On the contrary, it is because I have reflected on it, that I find much more time necessary for it than I can at present dispose of. I have a view of the subject which ought to displease neither the rational Christian nor Deists, and would reconcile many to a character they have too hastily rejected. I do not know that it would reconcile the *genus irritabile vatum*[1] who are all in arms against me. Their hostility is on too interesting ground to be softened. The delusion into which the X. Y. Z. plot showed it possible to push the people; the successful experiment made under the prevalence of that delusion on the clause of the Constitution, which, while it secured the freedom of the press, covered also the freedom of religion, had given to the clergy a very favorite hope of obtaining an establishment of a particular form of Christianity through the United States; and as every sect believes its own form the true one, every one perhaps hoped for his own, but especially the Episcopalians and Congregationalists. The returning good sense of our country threatens abortion to their hopes, and they believe that any portion of power confided to me, will be exerted in opposition to their schemes. And they believe rightly: for I have sworn upon the altar of God, eternal hostility against every form of tyranny over the mind of man. But this is all they have to fear from me: and enough too in their opinion. . . .

[1] The angry tribe of poets.

I Avoided Giving Any Answer

Anas, April 15, 1806

*Most Federalists supported Burr against Jefferson, thus caus-
ing the long deadlock in the House of Representatives. Some
Federalists, obedient to Hamilton's urgings, offered to go
over to Jefferson in exchange for a promise not to turn
Federalists out of office, nor to eliminate the navy and public
debt. The two go-betweens who treated with Jefferson on
February 16 got the impression that he would be amenable
to a quid pro quo. Later, however, Jefferson emphatically
denied that he made or implied any deal. In any case, on
February 17 Federalist forces in the House broke ranks.
Jefferson was elected President on the 36th ballot.*

. . . [The] following transactions took place . . . while the
Presidential election was in suspense in Congress, which,
though I did not enter at the time, they made such an impression on my mind, that they are now as fresh, as to their
principal circumstances, as if they had happened yesterday.
Coming out of the Senate chamber one day, I found Gouverneur Morris on the steps. He stopped me, and began a
conversation on the strange and portentous state of things
then existing, and went on to observe, that the reasons why
the minority of States was so opposed to my being elected,
were, that they apprehended that, 1, I would turn all federalists out of office; 2, put down the navy; 3, wipe off the
public debt. That I need only to declare, or authorize my
friends to declare, that I would not take these steps, and instantly the event of the election would be fixed. I told him,
that I should leave the world to judge of the course I meant
to pursue by that which I had pursued hitherto, believing it to
be my duty to be passive and silent during the present scene;
that I should certainly make no terms; should never go into
the office of President by capitulation, nor with my hands
tied by any conditions which should hinder me from pursuing
the measures which I should deem for the public good. It
was understood that Gouverneur Morris had entirely the
direction of the vote of Lewis Morris of Vermont, who, by

coming over to Matthew Lyon, would have added another vote, and decided the election. About the same time, I called on Mr. Adams. We conversed on the state of things. I observed to him, that a very dangerous experiment was then in contemplation, to defeat the Presidential election by an act of Congress declaring the right of the Senate to name a President of the Senate, to devolve on him the government during any interregnum; that such a measure would probably produce resistance by force, and incalculable consequences, which it would be in his power to prevent by negativing such an act. He seemed to think such an act justifiable, and observed, it was in my power to fix the election by a word in an instant, by declaring I would not turn out the federal officers, nor put down the navy, nor spunge the national debt. Finding his mind made up as to the usurpation of the government by the President of the Senate, I urged it no further, observed the world must judge as to myself of the future by the past, and turned the conversation to something else. About the same time, Dwight Foster of Massachusetts called on me in my room one night, and went into a very long conversation on the state of affairs, the drift of which was to let me understand, that the fears above mentioned were the only obstacle to my election, to all of which I avoided giving any answer the one way or the other. From this moment he became most bitterly and personally opposed to me, and so has ever continued. . . .

I Will Give to That Will a Faithful Execution

Reply to Notification of Election, February 20, 1801

Following are Jefferson's remarks to the Congressional Committee, led by Charles C. Pinckney of South Carolina—who had been a rival in the campaign—notifying him of his election on February 17.

I receive, gentlemen, with profound thankfulness this testimony of confidence from the great representative council of our nation. It fills up the measure of that grateful satisfaction which had already been derived from the suffrages of my fellow-citizens themselves, designating me as one of those to whom they were willing to commit this charge, the most important of all others to them. In deciding between the candidates whom their equal vote presented to your choice, I am sensible that age has been respected rather than more active and useful qualifications.

I know the difficulties of the station to which I am called, and feel and acknowledge my incompetence to them. But whatsoever of understanding, whatsoever of diligence, whatsoever of justice or of affectionate concern for the happiness of man, it has pleased Providence to place within the compass of my faculties shall be called forth for the discharge of the duties confided to me, and for procuring to my fellow-citizens all the benefits which our Constitution has placed under the guardianship of the General Government.

Guided by the wisdom and patriotism of those to whom it belongs to express the legislative will of the nation, I will give to that will a faithful execution.

I pray you, gentlemen, to convey to the honorable body from which you are deputed the homage of my humble acknowledgements and the sentiments of zeal and fidelity by which I shall endeavor to merit these proofs of confidence from the nation and its Representatives; and accept yourselves my particular thanks for the obliging terms in which you have been pleased to communicate their will.

Introduction

JEFFERSON AND HIS ENEMIES agreed on one thing, that his taking power was a revolutionary event. In the strongholds of Federalism he was reputed a dangerous man, an atheist and a demagogue who threatened to overthrow the carefully wrought political and social order. Jefferson believed that his election had dealt a crushing blow to monarchist pretensions in this country, had vindicated "science . . . philosophy and republicanism," and had renewed humanity's faith in itself. "A just and solid republican government maintained here," he affirmed soon after his inauguration, "will be a standing monument and example for the aim and imitation of the people of other countries. . . ."

To Jefferson, the true effects of the Republican revolution would be measured by the extent to which Federalism lost its following. For die-hards and leaders he had no hopes of apostasy. His political strategy was to win over the moderates. At the outset, in his First Inaugural Address, he extended a conciliatory hand to the opposition. A difference in party names, he emphasized, need not mean a difference in principles.

To match his words with deeds, he forebore removing Federalist officeholders en masse. But this raised difficulties with Republican faithful. The problem, an exceedingly delicate one, continually occupied Jefferson's attention. He dealt with it not by removing Federalists, except those "most marked for their bitterness and active zeal in slandering and in electioneering," but by appointing qualified Republicans to fill offices that fell vacant. The spoils system was repugnant to him.

To be sure, Jefferson wanted nothing more than to reconcile Federalists and Republicans—on Republican terms. He and his closest associates in the Cabinet—Madison, the Secretary of State, and Albert Gallatin, the Secretary of the Treasury—faithfully carried out the aims of the party as set forth in the Inaugural Address: economy and retrenchment in the Federal Government, restoration of powers usurped from states and individuals, and obedience to the will of the majority. Accordingly, in Jefferson's first term the Judiciary Act of 1801 was repealed, the national debt was reduced as government operations were cut back, internal taxes were abolished and the Alien and Sedition Acts were allowed to expire.

Jefferson's political strategy bore rich fruit in the peace and prosperity of his first term. The Federalist Party collapsed, ceasing even to be a viable opposition. Republican majorities in Congress and in nearly all state legislatures were overwhelming throughout Jefferson's years as President. In the election of 1804, which he won by 162 to 14 in the electoral college, he carried every New England state except Connecticut. In 1801 the Republicans had eighteen Senators to the Federalists' fourteen and sixty-nine Representatives to the Federalists' thirty-six. After the election of 1804 the Republicans had twenty-seven Senators to the Federalists' seven and 116 Representatives to the Federalists' twenty-five. Despite a show of slightly increased strength at the time of the Embargo Acts of 1807–9 and the War of 1812, the Federalists never overcame their parlous deficit and withered to a corporal's guard before disappearing altogether in 1820.

But if Jefferson succeeded in Republicanizing the Federalists, he succeeded even more in Federalizing the Republicans. Hamilton had anticipated this possibility in 1800 when, in supporting Jefferson over Burr, he wrote: "It is a fact which I have frequently mentioned, that, while we were in the administration together, he [Jefferson] was generally for a large construction of the Executive authority. . . ." In his eight years of office, Jefferson considerably enlarged the scope of Presidential authority, often under conditions which left him no choice. Congress was completely submissive to him. He dominated the tightly-knit Congressional party caucus, which made policy for the party as a whole and determined the legislation to be passed. Senate and House leaders accounted to Jefferson personally. Their names are for the most part unknown because he chose men least likely to stand up to him. John Randolph of Roanoke, for a long time floor leader of the House, was promptly jettisoned on opposing Jefferson for the same reasons that Jefferson had opposed the Federalists. In short, Presidential-Congressional relations during Jefferson's regime might be compared to the British Cabinet system during the regime of a strong Prime Minister.

Jefferson's overmastering support for westward expansion impelled him to make decisions which stretched the limits of Constitutional powers. His authorization of the Lewis and Clark expedition to the Pacific coast, secured clandestinely from Congress, was a trifle. But his approval of the Louisiana Purchase involved him in a Constitutional crisis. Jefferson resolved it after a fashion by first doing the deed and then asking for a Constitutional amendment. As between the prospect of adding nearly a million square miles of virgin territory by a broad construction of his powers and letting the opportunity slip by for the sake of Republican consistency, he had no choice. The Federalists, for their part, rightly fearing the long-term consequences of the purchase, opposed it on the grounds of states-rights—on grounds, that is, that had been orthodox Republican before 1801.

Politically, Jefferson and the Republicans failed to rule in only one area—the federal judiciary which the imperious John Marshall dominated like a colossus. In Marbury v. Madison, Marshall asserted the supremacy of the Court to decide Constitutional questions at the same time as he shrewdly avoided contesting Jefferson's power. He embarrassed Jefferson by requesting him to be a witness at the Aaron Burr trial of 1807. Moreover, by his strict interpretation of the treason clause of the Constitution, Marshall made it nearly impossible to convict Burr; Marshall knew that Jefferson badly wanted Burr's conviction. The Republicans, finally, failed in their effort to discipline a flagrantly Federalist judiciary in 1804. Though Congress impeached and removed Judge John Pickering for obvious incompetence, it failed, in a subsequent trial, to remove the nasty and partisan Federalist Judge Samuel Chase. Thus ended Jefferson's assault on the bench.

Foreign affairs forced Jefferson to exercise power vaster than any President until Lincoln. In 1803 war was resumed between Napoleon and Britain. By 1806 each was drastically interfering with American trade. Britain compounded the assault by impressing American seamen. Should the United States go to war with either of these giants or should some other method be attempted? Jefferson decided on a policy of peaceable coercion through a trade embargo against both. Altogether, Congress passed three Embargo Acts between December 1807 and March 1808. The numerous violations, particularly in the coastal trade and along the Canadian border, led to the passage of two Enforcement Acts which gave the administration extraordinary powers of inspection, apprehension, even confiscation of property. Force was applied in direct proportion to the frequency of the violations. Jefferson thus confronted the cruel logic of his embargo: to avoid war with a foreign power it became necessary to war upon a larger and larger segment of the American people. He repealed the Embargo Acts four days before quitting office.

We Are All Republicans, We Are All Federalists

First Inaugural Address, March 4, 1801

On March 4, at twelve noon, Jefferson, accompanied by Republican friends, walked from his boarding house to the Senate for his inauguration. He was dressed plainly to emphasize the Republican solemnity of the occasion. Conspicuously absent from the scene, indeed from Washington, was John Adams, his predecessor and erstwhile friend. Jefferson read his great address in a voice too low for most present to hear it. He had labored hard in writing the address in order to be certain that his proffer of conciliation and good will to like-intentioned Federalists should come through clearly.

Friends and Fellow Citizens,—Called upon to undertake the duties of the first executive office of our country, I avail myself of the presence of that portion of my fellow citizens which is here assembled, to express my grateful thanks for the favor with which they have been pleased to look toward me, to declare a sincere consciousness that the task is above my talents, and that I approach it with those anxious and awful presentiments which the greatness of the charge and the weakness of my powers so justly inspire. A rising nation, spread over a wide and fruitful land, traversing all the seas with the rich productions of their industry, engaged in commerce with nations who feel power and forget right, advancing rapidly to destinies beyond the reach of mortal eye— when I contemplate these transcendent objects, and see the honor, the happiness, and the hopes of this beloved country committed to the issue and the auspices of this day, I shrink from the contemplation, and humble myself before the magnitude of the undertaking. Utterly indeed, should I despair, did not the presence of many whom I here see remind me, that in the other high authorities provided by our constitution, I shall find resources of wisdom, of virtue, and of zeal, on which to rely under all difficulties. To you, then, gentlemen, who are charged with the sovereign functions of legislation, and to those associated with you, I look with encouragement for that guidance and support which may enable us to steer with safety the vessel in which we are all embarked amid the conflicting elements of a troubled world.

During the contest of opinion through which we have passed, the animation of discussion and of exertions has sometimes worn an aspect which might impose on strangers unused to think freely and to speak and to write what they think; but this being now decided by the voice of the nation, announced according to the rules of the constitution, all will, of course, arrange themselves under the will of the law, and unite in common efforts for the common good. All, too, will bear in mind this sacred principle, that though the will of the majority is in all cases to prevail, that will, to be rightful, must be reasonable; that the minority possess their equal rights, which equal laws must protect, and to violate which would be oppression. Let us, then, fellow-citizens, unite with one heart and one mind. Let us restore to social intercourse that harmony and affection without which liberty and even life itself are but dreary things. And let us reflect that having banished from our land that religious intolerance under which mankind so long bled and suffered, we have yet gained little if we countenance a political intolerance as despotic, as wicked, and capable of as bitter and bloody persecutions. During the throes and convulsions of the ancient world, during the agonizing spasms of infuriated man, seeking through blood and slaughter his long-lost liberty, it was not wonderful that the agitation of the billows should reach even this distant and peaceful shore; that this should be more felt and feared by some and less by others; that this should divide opinions as to measures of safety. But every difference of opinion is not a difference of principle. We have called by different names brethren of the same principle. We are all republicans—we are all federalists. If there be any among us who would wish to dissolve this Union or to change its republican form, let them stand undisturbed as monuments of the safety with which error of opinion may be tolerated where reason is left free to combat it. I know, indeed, that some honest men fear that a republican government cannot be strong; that this government is not strong enough. But would the honest patriot, in the full tide of successful experiment, abandon a government which has so far kept us free and firm, on the theoretic and visionary fear that this government, the world's best hope, may by possibility want energy to preserve itself? I trust not. I believe this, on the contrary, the strongest government on earth. I believe it is the only one where every man, at the call of the laws, would fly to the standard of the law, and would meet invasions of the public order as his own personal concern. Sometimes it is said that man cannot be trusted with the government of himself. Can he, then, be trusted with the government of others? Or have we found angels in the forms of kings to govern him? Let history answer this question.

Let us, then, with courage and confidence pursue our own federal and republican principles, our attachment to our union and representative government. Kindly separated by nature and a wide ocean from the exterminating havoc of one quarter of the globe; too high-minded to endure the degradations of the others; possessing a chosen country, with room enough for our descendants to the hundredth and thousandth generation; entertaining a due sense of our equal right to the use of our own faculties, to the acquisitions of our industry, to honor and confidence from our fellow citizens, resulting not from birth but from our actions and their sense of them; enlightened by a benign religion, professed, indeed, and practiced in various forms, yet all of them including honesty, truth, temperance, gratitude, and the love of man; acknowledging and adoring an overruling Providence, which by all its dispensations proves that it delights in the happiness of man here and his greater happiness hereafter; with all these blessings, what more is necessary to make us a happy and prosperous people? Still one thing more, fellow citizens—a wise and frugal government, which shall restrain men from injuring one another, which shall leave them otherwise free to regulate their own pursuits of industry and improvement, and shall not take from the mouth of labor the bread it has earned. This is the sum of good government, and this is necessary to close the circle of our felicities.

About to enter, fellow citizens, on the exercise of duties which comprehend everything dear and valuable to you, it is proper that you should understand what I deem the essential principles of our government, and consequently those which ought to shape its administration. I will compress them within the narrowest compass they will bear, stating the general principle, but not all its limitations. Equal and exact justice to all men, of whatever state or persuasion, religious or political; peace, commerce, and honest friendship with all nations—entangling alliances with none; the support of the State gov-

ernments in all their rights, as the most competent administrations for our domestic concerns and the surest bulwarks
against anti-republican tendencies; the preservation of the
general government in its whole constitutional vigor, as the
sheet anchor of our peace at home and safety abroad; a
jealous care of the right of election by the people—a mild
and safe corrective of abuses which are lopped by the sword
of the revolution where peaceable remedies are unprovided;
absolute acquiescence in the decisions of the majority—the
vital principle of republics, from which there is no appeal but to force, the vital principle and immediate parent
of despotism; a well-disciplined militia—our best reliance
in peace and for the first moments of war, till regulars
may relieve them; the supremacy of the civil over the
military authority; economy in the public expense, that
labor may be lightly burdened; the honest payment of
our debts and sacred preservation of the public faith; encouragement of agriculture, and of commerce as its hand-
maid; the diffusion of information and the arraignment
of all abuses at the bar of public reason; freedom of religion;
freedom of the press; freedom of person under the protection of the *habaes corpus;* and trial by juries impartially selected—these principles form the bright constellation
which has gone before us, and guided our steps through
an age of revolution and reformation. The wisdom of our
sages and the blood of our heroes have been devoted to their
attainment. They should be the creed of our political faith—
the text of civil instruction—the touchstone by which to try
the services of those we trust; and should we wander from
them in moments of error or alarm, let us hasten to retrace
our steps and to regain the road which alone leads to peace,
liberty, and safety.

I repair, then, fellow citizens, to the post you have assigned
me. With experience enough in subordinate offices to have
seen the difficulties of this, the greatest of all, I have learned
to expect that it will rarely fall to the lot of imperfect man
to retire from this station with the reputation and the favor
which bring him into it. Without pretensions to that high
confidence reposed in our first and great revolutionary
character, whose preëminent services had entitled him to the
first place in his country's love, and destined for him the
fairest page in the volume of faithful history, I ask so much
confidence only as may give firmness and effect to the legal

administration of your affairs. I shall often go wrong through defect of judgment. When right, I shall often be thought wrong by those whose positions will not command a view of the whole ground. I ask your indulgence for my own errors, which will never be intentional; and your support against the errors of others, who may condemn what they would not if seen in all its parts. The approbation implied by your suffrage is a consolation to me for the past; and my future solicitude will be to retain the good opinion of those who have bestowed it in advance, to conciliate that of others by doing them all the good in my power, and to be instrumental to the happiness and freedom of all.

Relying, then, on the patronage of your good will, I advance with obedience to the work, ready to retire from it whenever you become sensible how much better choice it is in your power to make. And may that Infinite Power which rules the destinies of the universe, lead our councils to what is best, and give them a favorable issue for your peace and prosperity.

The Band Is Removed

To John Dickinson, March 6, 1801

In this letter to one of the argonauts of the Revolution, Jefferson conveys a somewhat different tone and spirit than he conveyed in the Inaugural Address.

Dear Sir,—No pleasure can exceed that which I received from reading your letter of the 21st ultimo. It was like the joy we expect in the mansions of the blessed, when received with the embraces of our forefathers, we shall be welcomed with their blessing as having done our part not unworthily of them. The storm through which we have passed, has been tremendous indeed. The tough sides of our Argosy have been thoroughly tried. Her strength has stood the waves into which she was steered, with a view to sink her. We shall put her on her republican tack, and she will now show by the beauty of her motion the skill of her builders. Figure apart, our fellow-citizens have been led hoodwinked from their principles, by a most extraordinary combination of circumstances. But the band is removed, and they now see for themselves. I hope to see shortly a perfect consolidation to effect which, nothing shall be spared on my part, short of the abandonment of the principles of our revolution. A just and solid republican government maintained here, will be a standing monument and example for the aim and imitation of the people of other countries; and I join with you in the hope and belief that they will see, from our example, that a free government is of all others the most energetic; that the inquiry which has been excited among the mass of mankind by our revolution and its consequences, will ameliorate the condition of man over a great portion of the globe. What a satisfaction have we in the contemplation of the benevolent effects of our efforts, compared with those of the leaders on the other side, who have discountenanced all advances in science as dangerous innovations, have endeavored to render philosophy and republicanism terms of reproach, to persuade us that man cannot be governed but by the rod, etc. I shall have the happiness of living and dying in the contrary hope. Accept assurances of my constant and sincere respect and attachment, and my affectionate salutations.

Sentiments Worthy of Former Times

To Thomas Paine, March 18, 1801

Tom Paine had recently written a series of articles advising against United States entanglement in conflicts between European despotisms. It was truly an event that an incorrigible radical like Paine should live to see the head of a state honor his ideals.

. . . Determined as we are to avoid, if possible, wasting the energies of our people in war and destruction, we shall avoid implicating ourselves with the powers of Europe, even in support of principles which we mean to pursue. They have so many other interests different from ours we must avoid being entangled in them. . . . We believe that we can enforce those principles as to ourselves by peaceful means, now that we are likely to have our public councils detached from foreign views. The return of our citizens from the phrenzy into which they have been wrought, partly by ill-conduct in France, partly by artifices practiced upon them, is almost extinct, and will, I believe, become quite so. . . . I am in hopes you will find us returned generally to sentiments worthy of former times. In these it will be your glory to have steadily laboured and with as much effect as any man living. That you may long live to continue your useful labours and to reap the reward in the thankfulness of nations is my sincere prayer. Accept assurances of my high esteem and affectionate attachment.

The Barbarians Really Flattered Themselves

To Joseph Priestley, March 21, 1801

Attacks upon Jefferson's "atheism," particularly by New England Calvinist divines, did not end with his election. To Jefferson and Priestley, two typical sons of the Enlightenment, they only pointed up the need for scientific truth to prevail over religious superstition.

Dear Sir,—I learned some time ago that you were in Philadelphia, but that it was only for a fortnight; and I supposed you were gone. It was not till yesterday I received information that you were still there, had been very ill, but were on the recovery. I sincerely rejoice that you are so. Yours is one of the few lives precious to mankind, and for the continuance of which every thinking man is solicitous. Bigots may be an exception. What an effort, my dear Sir, of bigotry in politics and religion have we gone through! The barbarians really flattered themselves they should be able to bring back the times of Vandalism, when ignorance put everything into the hands of power and priestcraft. All advances in science were proscribed as innovations. They pretended to praise and encourage education, but it was to be the education of our ancestors. We were to look backwards, not forwards, for improvement; the President himself declaring, in one of his answers to addresses, that we were never to expect to go beyond them in real science. This was the real ground of all the attacks on you. Those who live by mystery and *charlatanerie,* fearing you would render them useless by simplifying the Christian philosophy,—the most sublime and benevolent, but most perverted system that ever shone on man,—endeavored to crush your well-earned and well-deserved fame. But it was the Lilliputians upon Gulliver. Our countrymen have recovered from the alarm into which art and industry had thrown them; science and honesty are replaced on their high ground; and you, my dear Sir, as their great apostle, are on its pinnacle. It is with heartfelt satisfaction that, in the first moments of my public action, I can hail you with welcome to our land, tender to you the homage of its respect and esteem, cover you under the protection of those laws which were made for the wise and good like you, and disdain the legitimacy of that libel on legislation, which, under the form of a law, was for some time placed among them.

As the storm is now subsiding, and the horizon becoming serene, it is pleasant to consider the phenomenon with attention. We can no longer say there is nothing new under the sun. For this whole chapter in the history of man is new. The great extent of our republic is new. Its sparse habitation is new. The mighty wave of public opinion which has rolled over it is new. But the most pleasing novelty is, its so quietly subsiding over such an extent of surface to its true level again. The order and good sense displayed in this recovery from delusion, and in the momentous crisis which lately arose, really bespeaks a strength of character in our nation which augurs well for the duration of our republic; and I am much better satisfied now of its stability than I was before it was tried. . . .

The Storm Is Over, and We Are in Port

To Samuel Adams, March 29, 1801

Samuel Adams was nearly eighty now. In recent struggles and as governor of Massachusetts from 1794 to 1797 he was a staunch Jeffersonian.

I addressed a letter to you, my very dear and ancient friend, on the 4th of March: not indeed to you by name, but through the medium of some of my fellow-citizens, whom occasion called on me to address. In meditating the matter of that address, I often asked myself, is this exactly in the spirit of the patriarch, Samuel Adams? Is it as he would express it? Will he approve of it? I have felt a great deal for our country in the times we have seen. But individually for no one so much as yourself. When I have been told that you were avoided, insulted, frowned on, I could but ejaculate, "Father, forgive them, for they know not what they do." I confess I felt an indignation for you, which for myself I have been able, under every trial, to keep entirely passive. However, the storm is over, and we are in port. The ship was not rigged for the service she was put on. We will show the smoothness of her motions on her republican tack. I hope we shall once more see harmony restored among our citizens, and an entire oblivion of past feuds. Some of the leaders who have most committed themselves cannot come into this. But I hope the great body of our fellow-citizens will do it. I will sacrifice everything but principle to procure it. A few examples of justice on officers who have perverted their functions to the oppression of their fellow-citizens, must, in justice to those citizens, be made. But opinion, and the just maintenance of it, shall never be a crime in my view; nor bring injury on the individual. Those whose misconduct in office ought to have produced their removal even by my predecessor, must not be protected by the delicacy due only to honest men. How much I lament that time has deprived me of your aid! It would have been a day of glory which should have called you to the first office of the administration. But give us your counsel, my friend, and give us your blessing; and be assured that there exists not in the heart of man a more faithful esteem than mine to you, and that I shall ever bear you the most affectionate veneration and respect.

Their Total Exclusion Calls for Prompter Corrections

To A Committee of the Merchants of New Haven, July 12, 1801

Jefferson's first dilemma was how to satisfy Republican Party faithful without alienating Federalists willing to take up his proffer of conciliation. But the heavily Federalist Connecticut legislature seemed bent on hounding out every Republican officeholder. "There then we will retaliate," said Jefferson. In the final days of his Administration, President Adams had appointed a Federalist, Elijah Goodrich, Collector of New Haven. Jefferson promptly replaced Goodrich with Samuel Bishop, an old Republican faithful. The merchants of New Haven thereupon drew up a remonstrance. Jefferson welcomed the chance to reassure the Republican Party as a whole.

Gentlemen,—I have received the remonstrance you were pleased to address to me, on the appointment of Samuel Bishop to the office of collector of New Haven, lately vacated by the death of David Austin. The right of our fellow citizens to represent to the public functionaries their opinion on proceedings interesting to them, is unquestionably a constitutional right, often useful, sometimes necessary, and will always be respectfully acknowledged by me.

Of the various executives duties, no one excites more anxious concern than that of placing the interests of our fellow citizens in the hands of honest men, with understandings sufficient for their stations. No duty, at the same time, is more difficult to fulfil. The knowledge of characters possessed by a single individual is, of necessity, limited. To seek out the best through the whole Union, we must resort to other information, which, from the best of men, acting disinterestedly and with the purest motives, is sometimes incorrect. In the case of Samuel Bishop, however, the subject of your remonstrance, time was taken, information was sought, and such obtained as could leave no room for doubt of his fitness. From private sources it was learned that his understanding was sound, his integrity pure, his character unstained. And the offices confided to him within his own State, are public evidences of the estimation in which he is held by the State in general, and the city and township particularly in which he lives. He is said to be the town clerk, a justice of the peace, mayor of the city of New Haven, an office held at the will of the legislature, chief judge of the court of common pleas for New Haven county, a court of high criminal and civil jurisdiction wherein most causes are decided without the right of appeal or review, and sole judge of the court of probates, wherein he singly decides all questions of wills, settlement of estates, testate and intestate, appoints guardians, settles their accounts, and in fact has under his jurisdiction and care all the property real and personal of persons dying. The two last offices, in the annual gift of the legislature, were given to him in May last. Is it possible that the man to whom the legislature of Connecticut has so recently committed trusts of such difficulty and magnitude, is "unfit to be the collector of the district of New Haven," though acknowledged in the same writing, to have obtained all this confidence "by a long life of usefulness"? It is objected, indeed, in the remonstrance, that he is seventy-seven years of age; but at a much more advanced age, our Franklin was the ornament of human nature. He may not be able to perform in person, all the details of his office; but if he gives us the benefit of his understanding, his integrity, his watchfulness, and takes care that all the details are well performed by himself or his necessary assistants, all public purposes will be answered. The remonstrance, indeed, does not allege that the office *has been* illy conducted, but only apprehends that it *will be* so. Should this happen in event, be assured I will do in it what shall be just and necessary for the public service. In the meantime, he should be tried without being prejudged.

The removal, as it is called, of Mr. Goodrich, forms another subject of complaint. Declarations by myself in favor of *political tolerance*, exhortations to *harmony* and affection in social intercourse, and to respect for the *equal rights* of the minority, have, on certain occasions, been quoted and misconstrued into assurances that the tenure of offices was to be undisturbed. But could candor apply such a construction? It is not indeed in the remonstrance that we find it; but it leads to the explanations which that calls for. When it is considered, that during the late administration, those who were not of a particular sect of politics were excluded from all office; when, by a steady pursuit of this measure, nearly the whole offices of the United States were monopolized by that sect; when the public sentiment at length declared itself, and burst open the doors of honor and confidence to those whose opinions they more approved, was it to be imagined that this monopoly of office was still to be continued in the hands of the minority? Does it violate their *equal rights*, to assert some rights in the majority also? Is it *political intolerance* to claim a proportionate share in the direction of the public affairs? Can they not *harmonize* in society unless they have everything in their own hands? If the will of the nation, manifested by their various elections, calls for an administration of government according with the opinions of those elected; if, for the fulfilment of that will, displacements are necessary, with whom can they so justly begin as with persons appointed in the last moments of an administration, not for its own aid, but to begin a career at the same time with their successors, by whom they had never been approved, and who could scarcely expect from them a cordial cooperation? Mr. Goodrich was one of these. Was it proper for him to place himself in office, without knowing whether those whose agent he was to be would have confidence in his agency? Can the preference of another, as the successor to Mr. Austin, be candidly called a removal of Mr. Goodrich? If a due participation of office is a matter of right, how are vacancies to be obtained? Those by death are few; by resignation, none. Can any other mode than that of removal be proposed? This is a painful office; but it is made my duty, and I meet it as such. I proceed in the operation with deliberation and inquiry, that it may injure the best men least, and effect the purposes of justice and public utility with the least private distress; that it may be thrown, as much as possible, on delinquency, on oppression, on intolerance, on anti-revolutionary adherence to our enemies.

The remonstrance laments "that a change in the administration must produce a change in the subordinate officers"; in other words, that it should be deemed necessary for all officers to think with their principal? But on whom does this imputation bear? On those who have excluded from office every shade of opinion which was not theirs? Or on those who have been so excluded? I lament sincerely that unessential differences of opinion should ever have been deemed sufficient to interdict half the society from the rights and the blessings of self-government, to proscribe them as unworthy of every trust. It would have been to me a circumstance of great relief, had I found a moderate participation of office in the hands of the majority. I would gladly have left to time and accident to raise them to their just share. But their total exclusion calls for prompter corrections. I shall correct the procedure; but that done, return with joy to that state of things, when the only questions concerning a candidate shall be, is he honest? Is he capable? Is he faithful to the Constitution?

I tender you the homage of my high respect.

I Have Begun the Reduction of What Was Deemed Necessary

First Annual Message to Congress, December 8, 1801

Things had gone well in the first nine months of Jefferson's Administration. In recent elections Republicans had scored heavily, even in New England. Napoleon and the other powers had signed a truce which augured peace at long last. Jefferson took pains in drafting his First Annual Message to Congress. He showed it to members of the Cabinet who advised removing some of the stronger passages—the passage in particular on the Sedition Act—so as to emphasize the theme of conciliation. Chastened by his poor performance at the Inaugural Address, he had the Message read to Congress by a clerk, thus setting a precedent which lasted until 1913.

Fellow Citizens of the Senate and House of Representatives, —It is a circumstance of sincere gratification to me that on meeting the great council of our nation, I am able to announce to them, on the grounds of reasonable certainty, that the wars and troubles which have for so many years afflicted our sister nations have at length come to an end, and that the communications of peace and commerce are once more opening among them. While we devoutly return thanks to the beneficent Being who has been pleased to breathe into them the spirit of conciliation and forgiveness, we are bound with peculiar gratitude to be thankful to him that our own peace has been preserved through so perilous a season, and ourselves permitted quietly to cultivate the earth and to practice and improve those arts which tend to increase our comforts. The assurances, indeed, of friendly disposition, received from all the powers with whom we have principal relations, had inspired a confidence that our peace with them would not have been disturbed. But a cessation of the irregularities which had affected the commerce of neutral nations, and of the irritations and injuries produced by them, cannot but add to this confidence; and strengthens, at the same time, the hope, that wrongs committed on unoffending friends, under a pressure of circumstances, will now be reviewed with candor, and will be considered as founding just claims of retribution for the past and new assurance for the future.

Among our Indian neighbors, also, a spirit of peace and friendship generally prevails; and I am happy to inform you that the continued efforts to introduce among them the implements and the practice of husbandry, and of the household arts, have not been without success; that they are becoming more and more sensible of the superiority of this dependence for clothing and subsistence over the precarious resources of hunting and fishing; and already we are able to announce, that instead of that constant diminution of their numbers, produced by their wars and their wants, some of them begin to experience an increase of population.

To this state of general peace with which we have been blessed, one only exception exists. Tripoli, the least considerable of the Barbary States, had come forward with demands unfounded either in right or in compact, and had permitted itself to denounce war, on our failure to comply before a given day. The style of the demand admitted but one answer. I sent a small squadron of frigates into the Mediterranean, with assurances to that power of our sincere desire to remain in peace, but with orders to protect our commerce against the threatened attack. The measure was seasonable and salutary. The bey had already declared war in form. His cruisers were out. Two had arrived at Gibraltar. Our commerce in the Mediterranean was blockaded, and that of the Atlantic in peril. The arrival of our squadron dispelled the danger. One of the Tripolitan cruisers having fallen in with, and engaged the small schooner *Enterprise*, commanded by Lieutenant Sterret, which had gone as a tender to our larger vessels, was captured, after a heavy slaughter of her men, without the loss of a single one on our part. The bravery exhibited by our citizens on that element, will, I trust, be a testimony to the world that it is not the want of that virtue which makes us seek their peace, but a conscientious desire to direct the energies of our nation to the multiplication of the human race, and not to its destruction. Unauthorized by the Constitution, without the sanction of Congress, to go beyond the line of defence, the vessel being disabled from committing further hostilities, was liberated with its crew. The legislature will doubtless consider whether, by authorizing measures of offence, also, they will place our force on an equal footing with that of its adversaries. I communicate all material information on this subject, that in the exercise of the important function confided by the Constitution to the legislature exclusively, their judgment may form itself on a knowledge and consideration of every circumstance of weight.

I wish I could say that our situation with all the other Barbary states was entirely satisfactory. Discovering that some delays had taken place in the performance of certain articles stipulated by us, I thought it my duty, by immediate measures for fulfilling them, to vindicate to ourselves the right of considering the effect of departure from stipulation on their side. From the papers which will be laid before you, you will be enabled to judge whether our treaties are regarded by them as fixing at all the measure of their demands, or as guarding from the exercise of force our vessels within their power; and to consider how far it will be safe and expedient to leave our affairs with them in their present posture. . . .

When we consider that this government is charged with the external and mutual relations only of these states; that the states themselves have principal care of our persons, our property, and our reputation, constituting the great field of human concerns, we may well doubt whether our organization is not too complicated, too expensive; whether offices and officers have not been multiplied unnecessarily, and sometimes injuriously to the service they were meant to promote. I will cause to be laid before you an essay toward a statement of those who, under public employment of various kinds, draw money from the treasury or from our citizens. Time has not permitted a perfect enumeration, the ramifications of office being too multiplied and remote to be completely traced in a first trial. Among those who are dependent on executive discretion, I have begun the reduction of what was deemed necessary. The expenses of diplomatic agency have been considerably diminished. The inspectors of internal revenue who were found to obstruct the accountability of the institution, have been discontinued. Several agencies created by executive authority, on salaries fixed by that also, have been suppressed, and should suggest the expediency of regulating that power by law, so as to subject its exercises to legislative inspection and sanction. Other reformations of the same kind will be pursued with that caution which is requisite in removing useless things, not to injure what is retained. But the great mass of public offices is established by law, and, therefore, by law alone can be abolished. Should the legislature think it expedient to pass this roll in review, and try all its parts by the test of public utility, they may be assured of every aid and light which executive information can yield. Considering the general tendency to multiply offices and dependencies, and to increase expense to the ultimate term of burden which the citizen can bear, it behooves us to avail ourselves of every occasion which presents itself for taking off the surcharge; that it never may be seen here that, after leaving to labor the smallest portion of its earnings on which it can subsist, government shall itself consume the residue of what it was instituted to guard.

In our care, too, of the public contributions intrusted to our direction, it would be prudent to multiply barriers against their dissipation, by appropriating specific sums to every specific purpose susceptible of definition; by disallowing all applications of money varying from the appropriation in object, or transcending it in amount; by reducing the undefined field of contingencies, and thereby circumscribing discretionary powers over money; and by bringing back to a single department all accountabilities for money where the examination may be prompt, efficacious, and uniform. . . .

Agriculture, manufactures, commerce, and navigation, the four pillars of our prosperity, are the most thriving when left most free to individual enterprise. Protection from casual embarrassments, however, may sometimes be seasonably interposed. If in the course of your observations or inquiries they should appear to need any aid within the limits of our constitutional powers, your sense of their importance is a sufficient assurance they will occupy your attention. We cannot, indeed, but all feel an anxious solicitude for the difficulties under which our carrying trade will soon be placed. How far it can be relieved, otherwise than by time, is a subject of important consideration.

The judiciary system of the United States, and especially that portion of it recently erected, will of course present itself to the contemplation of Congress; and that they may be able to judge of the proportion which the institution bears to the business it has to perform, I have caused to be procured from the several States, and now lay before Congress, an exact statement of all the causes decided since the first establishment of the courts, and of those which were depending when additional courts and judges were brought in to their aid.

And while on the judiciary organization, it will be worthy your consideration, whether the protection of the inestimable institution of juries has been extended to all the cases involving the security of our persons and property. Their impartial selection also being essential to their value, we ought further to consider whether that is sufficiently secured in those States where they are named by a marshal depending on executive will, or designated by the court or by officers dependent on them.

I cannot omit recommending a revisal of the laws on the subject of naturalization. Considering the ordinary chances of human life, a denial of citizenship under a residence of fourteen years is a denial to a great proportion of those who ask it, and controls a policy pursued from their first settlement by many of these States, and still believed of consequence to their prosperity. And shall we refuse the unhappy fugitives from distress that hospitality which the savages of the wilderness extended to our fathers arriving in this land? Shall oppressed humanity find no asylum on this globe? The constitution, indeed, has wisely provided that, for admission to certain offices of important trust, a residence shall be required sufficient to develop character and design. But might not the general character and capabilities of a citizen be safely communicated to everyone manifesting a *bonâ fide* purpose of embarking his life and fortunes permanently with us? with restrictions, perhaps, to guard against the fraudulent usurpation of our flag; an abuse which brings so much embarrassment and loss on the genuine citizen, and so much danger to the nation of being involved in war, that no endeavor should be spared to detect and suppress it.

These, fellow citizens, are the matters respecting the state of the nation, which I have thought of importance to be submitted to your consideration at this time. Some others of less moment, or not yet ready for communication, will be the subject of separate messages. I am happy in this opportunity of committing the arduous affairs of our government to the collected wisdom of the Union. Nothing shall be wanting on my part to inform, as far as in my power, the legislative judgment, nor to carry that judgment into faithful execution. The prudence and temperance of your discussions will promote, within your own walls, that conciliation which so much befriends national conclusion; and by its example will encourage among our constituents that progress of opinion which is tending to unite them in object and in will. That all should be satisfied with any one order of things is not to be expected, but I indulge the pleasing persuasion that the great body of our citizens will cordially concur in honest and disinterested efforts, which have for their object to preserve the general and State governments in their constitutional form and equilibrium; to maintain peace abroad, and order and obedience to the laws at home; to establish principles and practices of administration favorable to the security of liberty and prosperity, and to reduce expenses to what is necessary for the useful purposes of government.

A Haven for the Oppressed

To Mazzei, December 30, 1801

To his old Republican friend and erstwhile neighbor, Jefferson presents a good summary of what his administration accomplished in its first year.

. . . You cannot imagine what progress republican principles have made here. Business is conducted calmly, and with unanimous consent in both Chambers. The Tories are generally either converted or silenced by rational evidence or by prudence.

All the excess expenditures which were turning the ship of state toward monarchy are being rapidly abolished, and the fundamental principles of 1775 once more assert themselves vigorously. Briefly, there is every proof that people are enjoying life, although none have exclusive privileges, nor are there proscriptions for any except those guilty of infamous conduct.

Our country will be a haven for the oppressed, without fourteen years being necessary for qualification, and we have found a way of carrying on affairs without any need for an Act of Sedition. The appointments made by Mr. Adams to the District Courts, will, necessarily, have to be abandoned; the taxes on press and other things will be abolished; the '94 are suppressed; and, finally, all that is oppressive will be removed, and every encouragement will be given to naturalization, to commerce, to industry and to right conduct. You would really be surprised by the change which followed your departure. Those who wanted to burn the Jacobins now confess that the present government clearly shows a better knowledge of what is most salutary for this country than any which preceded it. . . .

To Restore to Man All His Natural Rights

Reply to a Committee of the Danbury, Connecticut Baptist Association, January 11, 1802

The Danbury Baptist Association had asked Jefferson to declare a day of Thanksgiving. Denying the request, Jefferson used the opportunity to publicly reaffirm his belief in the complete separation of church and state. "I know," he wrote Attorney-General Levi Lincoln, who had advised against the message, "it will give great offense to the New England clergy; but the advocate of religious freedom is to expect neither peace nor forgiveness from them."

Gentlemen: The affectionate sentiments of esteem and approbation which you are so good as to express towards me, on behalf of the Danbury Baptist Association, give me the highest satisfaction. My duties dictate a faithful and zealous pursuit of the interests of my constituents, and in proportion as they are persuaded of my fidelity to those duties, the discharge of them becomes more and more pleasing.

Believing with you that religion is a matter which lies solely between man and his God, that he owes account to none other for his faith or his worship, that the legislative powers of government reach actions only, and not opinions, I contemplate with sovereign reverence that act of the whole American people which declared that their legislature should "make no law respecting an establishment of religion, or prohibiting the free exercise thereof," thus building a wall of separation between church and State. Adhering to this expression of the supreme will of the nation in behalf of the rights of conscience, I shall see with sincere satisfaction the progress of those sentiments which tend to restore to man all his natural rights, convinced he has no natural right in opposition to his social duties.

I reciprocate your kind prayers for the protection and blessing of the common Father and Creator of man, and tender you for yourselves and your religious association, assurances of my high respect and esteem.

From That Moment We Must Marry Ourselves to the British Fleet and Nation

To Robert R. Livingston, April 18, 1802

France's repossession of the Louisiana Territory from Spain alarmed the United States. It was well known that Napoleon's ambitions vaulted over oceans and compassed the New World as well as the old ones. Jefferson makes it clear in this letter to Livingston, the minister to France, that the appearance of French troops in New Orleans must drive the United States into the arms of Britain. But Napoleon's plans ran aground in little "San Domingo" and he no longer had any use for Louisiana.

. . . The session of Louisiana and the Floridas by Spain to France works most sorely on the U. S. On this subject the Secretary of State has written to you fully. Yet I cannot forbear recurring to it personally, so deep is the impression it makes in my mind. It compleatly reverses all the political relations of the U. S. and will form a new epoch in our political course. Of all nations of any consideration France is the one which hitherto has offered the fewest points on which we could have any conflict of right, and the most points of a communion of interests. From these causes we have ever looked to her as our *natural friend,* as one with which we never could have an occasion of difference. Her growth therefore we viewed as our own, her misfortunes ours. There is on the globe one single spot, the possessor of which is our natural and habitual enemy. It is New Orleans, through which the produce of three-eighths of our territory must pass to market, and from its fertility it will ere long yield more than half of our whole produce and contain more than half our inhabitants. France placing herself in that door assumes to us the attitude of defiance. Spain might have retained it quietly for years. Her pacific dispositions, her feeble state, would induce her to increase our facilities there, so that her possession of the place would be hardly felt by us, and it would not perhaps be very long before some circumstance might arise which might make the cession of it to us the price of something of more worth to her. Not so can it ever be in the hands of France. The impetuosity of her temper, the energy and restlessness of her character, placed in a point of eternal friction with us, and our character, which though quiet, and loving peace and the pursuit of wealth, is high-minded, despising wealth in competition with insult or injury, enterprising and energetic as any nation on earth, these circumstances render it impossible that France and the U. S. can continue long friends when they meet in so irritable a position. They as well as we must be blind if they do not see this; and we must be very improvident if we do not begin to make arrangements on that hypothesis. The day that France takes possession of N. Orleans fixes the sentence which is to restrain her forever within her low water mark. It seals the union of two nations who in conjunction can maintain exclusive possession of the ocean. From that moment we must marry ourselves to the British fleet and nation. We must turn all our attentions to a maritime force, for which our resources place us on very high grounds: and having formed and cemented together a power which may render reinforcement of her settlements here impossible to France, make the first cannon, which shall be fired in Europe the signal for tearing up any settlement she may have made, and for holding the two continents of America in sequestration for the common purposes of the united British and American nations. This is not a state of things we seek or desire. It is one which this measure, if adopted by France, forces on us, as necessarily as any other cause, by the laws of nature, brings on its necessary effect. It is not from a fear of France that we deprecate this measure proposed by her. For however greater her force is than ours compared in the abstract, it is nothing in comparison of ours when to be exerted on our soil. But it is from a sincere love of peace, and a firm persuasion that bound to France by the interests and the strong sympathies still existing in the minds of our citizens, and holding relative positions which ensure their continuance we are secure of a long course of peace. Whereas the change of friends, which will be rendered necessary if France changes that position, embarks us necessarily as a belligerent power in the first war of Europe. In that case France will have held possession of New Orleans during the interval of a peace, long or short, at the end of which it will be wrested from her. Will this short-lived possession have been an equivalent to her for the transfer of such a weight into the scale of her enemy? Will not the amalgamation of a young, thriving, nation continue to that enemy the health and force which are at present so evidently on the decline? And will a few years possession of N. Orleans add equally to the strength of France? She may say she needs Louisiana for the supply of her West Indies. She does not need it in time of peace. And in war she could not depend on them because they would be so easily intercepted. I should suppose that all these considerations might in some proper form be brought into view of the government of France. Tho' stated by us, it ought not to give offence; because we do not bring them forward as a menace, but as consequences not controulable by us, but inevitable from the course of things. We mention them not as things which we desire by any means, but as things we deprecate; and we beseech a friend to look forward and to prevent them for our common interests.

If France considers Louisiana however as indispensable for her views she might perhaps be willing to look about for arrangements which might reconcile it to our interests. If anything could do this it would be the ceding to us the island of New Orleans and the Floridas. This would certainly in a great degree remove the causes of jarring and irritation between us, and perhaps for such a length of time as might produce other means of making the measure permanently conciliatory to our interests and friendships. It would at any rate relieve us from the necessity of taking immediate measures for countervailing such an operation by arrangements in another quarter. Still we should consider N. Orleans and the Floridas as equivalent for the risk of a quarrel with France produced by her vicinage. I have no doubt you have urged these considerations on every proper occasion with the government where you are. They are such as must have effect if you can find the means of producing thorough reflection on them by that government. The idea here is that the troops sent to St. Domingo, were to proceed to Louisiana after finishing their work in that island. If this were the arrangement, it will give you time to return again and again to the charge, for the conquest of St. Domingo will not be a short work. It will take considerable time to wear down a great number of souldiers. Every eye in the U. S. is now fixed on this affair of Louisiana. Perhaps nothing since the revolutionary war has produced more uneasy sensations through the body of the nation. Notwithstanding temporary bickerings have taken place with France, she has still a strong hold on the affections of our citizens generally. I have thought it not amiss, by way of supplement to the letters of the Secretary of State to write you this private one to impress you with the importance we affix to this transaction. . . .

Even to the Western Ocean

Confidential Message to Congress on a Western Exploring Expedition, January 18, 1803

In 1793 André Michaux, a Frenchman, had suggested to the Philosophical Society that he lead an exploratory mission into the interior of the Louisiana territory. The interest Jefferson had then shown in the idea continued through the years. Now, as President, he was in a position to act on it. Waiting for the right moment, he sent a confidential message to Congress which masked his real intention. Congress acceded to his request for appropriations to set up trading posts with the Indians. With the money at hand he brought together Merriwether Lewis, his private secretary, and William Clark of Virginia to lead the small expedition to the "western ocean."

The Indian tribes residing within the limits of the United States, have, for a considerable time, been growing more and more uneasy at the constant diminution of the territory they occupy, although effected by their own voluntary sales; and the policy has long been gaining strength with them, of refusing absolutely all further sale, on any conditions; insomuch that, at this time, it hazards their friendship, and excites dangerous jealousies and perturbations in their minds to make any overture for the purchase of the smallest portions of their land. A very few tribes only are not yet obstinately in these dispositions. In order peaceably to counteract this policy of theirs, and to provide an extension of territory which the rapid increase of our numbers will call for, two measures are deemed expedient. First: to encourage them to abandon hunting, to apply to the raising stock, to agriculture and domestic manufactures, and thereby prove to themselves that less land and labor will maintain them in this, better than in their former mode of living. The extensive forests necessary in the hunting life will then become useless, and they will see advantage in exchanging them for the means of improving their farms and of increasing their domestic comforts. Secondly: to multiply trading-houses among them, and

place within their reach those things which will contribute
more to their domestic comfort than the possession of extensive but uncultivated wilds. Experience and reflection will
develop to them the wisdom of exchanging what they can
spare and we want, for what we can spare and they want.
In leading them thus to agriculture, to manufactures, and
civilization; in bringing together their and our settlements,
and in preparing them ultimately to participate in the benefits of our government, I trust and believe we are acting for
their greatest good. . . .

While the extension of the public commerce among the
Indian tribes, may deprive of that source of profit such of our
citizens as are engaged in it, it might be worthy the attention of Congress, in their care of individual as well as of the
general interest, to point in another direction the enterprise
of these citizens, as profitably for themselves, and more use-
fully for the public. The river Missouri, and the Indians in-
habiting it, are not as well known as is rendered desirable by
their connection with the Mississippi, and consequently with
us. It is, however, understood, that the country on that river
is inhabited by numerous tribes, who furnish great supplies
of furs and peltry to the trade of another nation, carried on
in a high latitude, through an infinite number of portages and
lakes, shut up by ice through a long season. The commerce
on that line could bear no competition with that of the Missouri, traversing a moderate climate, offering, according to
the best accounts, a continued navigation from its source,
and possibly with a single portage, from the western ocean,
and finding to the Atlantic a choice of channels through the
Illinois or Wabash, the lakes and Hudson, through the Ohio
and Susquehanna, or Potomac or James rivers, and through
the Tennessee and Savannah rivers. An intelligent officer, with
ten or twelve chosen men, fit for the enterprise, and willing to
undertake it, taken from our posts, where they may be
spared without inconvenience, might explore the whole line,
even to the western ocean; have conferences with the natives
on the subject of commercial intercourse; get admission
among them for our traders, as others are admitted; agree on
convenient deposits for an interchange of articles; and return
with the information acquired, in the course of two summers.
Their arms and accoutrements, some instruments of observation, and light and cheap presents for the Indians, would be all
the apparatus they could carry, and with an expectation of a

soldier's portion of land on their return, would constitute the whole expense. Their pay would be going on, whether here or there. While other civilized nations have encountered great expense to enlarge the boundaries of knowledge, by undertaking voyages of discovery, and for other literary purposes, in various parts and directions, our nation seems to owe to the same object, as well as to its own interests, to explore this, the only line of easy communication across the continent, and so directly traversing our own part of it.

Love, Charity, Peace

To Dr. Benjamin Rush, April 21, 1803

Jefferson's reflections on religion, put in the form of a "syllabus," fulfilled a promise made to Rush four years earlier. For obvious reasons, he wanted it kept from the public. After Rush died, Jefferson asked that it be returned to him. Only after his own death was it published.

Dear Sir,—In some of the delightful conversations with you, in the evenings of 1798–99, and which served as an anodyne to the afflictions of the crisis through which our country was then laboring, the Christian religion was sometimes our topic; and I then promised you, that one day or other, I would give you my views of it. They are the result of a life of inquiry and reflection, and very different from that anti-Christian system imputed to me by those who know nothing of my opinions. To the corruptions of Christianity I am, indeed, opposed; but not to the genuine precepts of Jesus himself. I am a Christian, in the only sense in which he wished any one to be; sincerely attached to his doctrines, in preference to all others; ascribing to himself every *human* excellence; and believing he never claimed any other. At the short interval since these conversations, when I could justifiably abstract my mind from public affairs, the subject has been under my contemplation. But the more I considered it, the more it expanded beyond the measure of either my time or information. In the moment of my late departure from Monticello, I received from Dr. Priestley, his little treatise of "Socrates and Jesus Compared." This being a section of the general view I had taken of the field, it became a subject of reflection while on the road, and unoccupied otherwise. The result was, to arrange in my mind a syllabus, or outline of such an estimate of the comparative merits of Christianity, as I wished to see executed by some one of more leisure and information for the task, than myself. This I now send you, as the only discharge of my promise I can probably ever execute. And in confiding it to you, I know it will not be exposed to the malignant perversions of those who make every word from me a text for new misrepresentations and calumnies. I am moreover averse to the communication of my religious tenets to the public; because it would countenance the presumption of those who have endeavored to draw them before that tribunal, and to seduce public opinion to erect itself into that inquisition over the rights of conscience, which the laws have so justly proscribed. It behooves every man who values liberty of conscience for himself, to resist invasions of it in the case of others; or their case may, by change of circumstances, become his own. It behooves him, too, in his own case, to give no example of concession, betraying the common right of independent opinion, by answering questions of faith, which the laws have left between God and himself. Accept my affectionate salutations.

SYLLABUS OF AN ESTIMATE OF THE MERIT OF THE DOCTRINES OF JESUS, COMPARED WITH THOSE OF OTHERS

In a comparative view of the Ethics of the enlightened nations of antiquity, of the Jews and of Jesus, no notice should be taken of the corruptions of reason among the ancients, to wit, the idolatry and superstition of the vulgar, nor of the corruptions of Christianity by the learned among its professors.

Let a just view be taken of the moral principles inculcated by the most esteemed of the sects of ancient philosophy, or of their individuals; particularly Pythagoras, Socrates, Epicurus, Cicero, Epictetus, Seneca, Antoninus.

I. Philosophers. 1. Their precepts related chiefly to ourselves, and the government of those passions which, unrestrained, would disturb our tranquillity of mind.[1] In this branch of philosophy they were really great.

[1] To explain, I will exhibit the heads of Seneca's and Cicero's philosophical works, the most extensive of any we have received from the ancients. Of ten heads in Seneca, seven relate to ourselves, viz., de ira consolatio, de tranquillitate, de constantia sapientis, de otio sapientis, de vita beata, de brevitate vitae; two relate to others, de clementia, de beneficiis; and one relates to the government of the world, de providentia. Of eleven tracts of Cicero, five respect ourselves, viz., de finibus, Tusculana, academica, paradoxa, de senectute; one, de officiis, relates partly to ourselves, partly to others; one, de amicitia relates to others; and four are on different subjects, to wit, de natura deorum, de divinatione, de fato, and somnium Scipionis. [Jefferson].

2. In developing our duties to others, they were short and defective. They embraced, indeed, the circles of kindred and friends, and inculcated patriotism, or the love of our country in the aggregate, as a primary obligation; towards our neighbors and countrymen they taught justice, but scarcely viewed them as within the circle of benevolence. Still less have they inculcated peace, charity, and love to our fellowmen, or embraced with benevolence the whole family of mankind.

II. Jews. 1. Their system was Deism; that is, the belief in one only God. But their ideas of him and of his attributes were degrading and injurious.

2. Their Ethics were not only imperfect, but often irreconcilable with the sound dictates of reason and morality, as they respect intercourse with those around us; and repulsive and anti-social, as respecting other nations. They needed reformation, therefore, in an eminent degree.

III. Jesus. In this state of things among the Jews, Jesus appeared. His parentage was obscure; his condition poor; his education null; his natural endowments great; his life correct and innocent; he was meek, benevolent, patient, firm, disinterested, and of the sublimest eloqence.

The disadvantages under which his doctrines appear are remarkable.

1. Like Socrates and Epictetus, he wrote nothing himself.

2. But he had not, like them, a Xenophon or an Arrian to write for him. I name not Plato, who only used the name of Socrates to cover the whimsies of his own brain. On the contrary, all the learned of his country, entrenched in its power and riches, were opposed to him, lest his labors should undermine their advantages; and the committing to writing of his life and doctrines fell on unlettered and ignorant men; who wrote, too, from memory, and not till long after the transactions had passed.

3. According to the ordinary fate of those who attempt to enlighten and reform mankind, he fell an early victim to the jealousy and combination of the altar and the throne, at about thirty-three years of age, his reason having not yet attained the maximum of its energy, nor the course of his preaching, which was but of three years at most, presented occasions for developing a complete system of morals.

4. Hence the doctrines which he really delivered were defective as a whole, and fragments only of what he did deliver

have come to us mutilated, misstated, and often unintelligible.

5. They have been still more disfigured by the corruptions of schismatizing followers, who have found an interest in sophisticating and perverting the simple doctrines he taught, by engrafting on them the mysticisms of a Grecian sophist, frittering them into subleties, and obscuring them with jargon, until they have caused good men to reject the whole in disgust, and to view Jesus himself as an impostor.

Notwithstanding these disadvantages, a system of morals is presented to us, which, if filled up in the style and spirit of the rich fragments he left us, would be the most perfect and sublime that has ever been taught by man.

The question of his being a member of the Godhead, or in direct communication with it, claimed for him by some of his followers, and denied by others, is foreign to the present view, which is merely an estimate of the intrinsic merits of his doctrines.

1. He corrected the Deism of the Jews, confirming them in their belief of one only God, and giving them juster notions of his attributes and government.

2. His moral doctrines, relating to kindred and friends, were more pure and perfect than those of the most correct of the philosophers, and greatly more so than those of the Jews; and they went far beyond both in inculcating universal philanthropy not only to kindred and friends, to neighbors and countrymen, but to all mankind, gathering all into one family, under the bonds of love, charity, peace, common wants and common aids. A development of this head will evince the peculiar superiority of the system of Jesus over all others.

3. The precepts of philosophy, and of the Hebrew code, laid hold of actions only. He pushed his scrutinies into the heart of man; erected his tribunal in the region of his thoughts, and purified the waters at the fountain head.

4. He taught, emphatically, the doctrines of a future state, which was either doubted, or disbelieved by the Jews; and wielded it with efficacy, as an important incentive, supplementary to the other motives to moral conduct.

Let Us Receive Them

Article on Conciliation with the Federalists, June 1, 1803

Again Jefferson addresses himself to party affairs, this time in response to a critical feuilleton in the Federalist New York Evening Post. He wrote a pseudonymous article in reply designed "to reconcile the parties among the republicans." He sent it to Attorney-General Levi Lincoln of Massachusetts, hoping to print it in a state where Federalists were most numerous.

. . . Federalism returning to reason, tho' not to good manners. No matter. Decency will come in turn, when outrages on it are found to reflect only on those who commit them.

The symptom of returning reason to those pitiable maniacs is the following paragraph in the N. York evening post of May 24, where, speaking of the removal of Mr. Rogers, the naval officer, a revolutionary tory, an Englishman and not even a citizen, till the expectation of office suggested to him the expediency of becoming one, and of the appointment of Mr. Osgood, a member of the Old Congress and President of its board of treasury, and postmaster general under the administration of General Washington, Mr. Coleman says "The Democrats have not long since had the imprudence and *contempt of truth* to declare, that, notwithstanding the removals, the Federalists hold still a greater number of offices than they do themselves. In answer to which we have sometimes replied that, in point of value there was no comparison, and that every office of any value, *in this city* at least, if not in the U. S. except one, had been transferred to the Jeffersonian sect, and that one is now gone." And then he goes on with his usual scurrilities against the chief magistrate of his country, which shall not be here repeated; and with references to the President's reply to the New Haven remonstrance. I remember that in that reply it was asked whether it is political intolerance for the majority to claim a *proportionate share* in the direction of the public affairs? And, if a *due participation* of office is a matter of right, how is it to be obtained but by some removals, when nearly the whole offices of the U. S. are monopolized by a particular political sect? The reasonableness of this claim of *due proportion* of office was felt by every candid man at the first blush. But it did not accord with the feelings of Federalists. Nothing but a continuance in their monopoly of office could satisfy them: and, on the removal of the first individual, the whole band opened on the violation of their sanctuary of office, as if a general sweep had been made of every Federalist within its pale. After much uproar however repeated on every single removal, not finding in the President that want of nerve which with atheism, hypocrisy, malice, &c &c 'c, they have so liberally lent him, but that on the contrary, regardless of their barking he proceeded steadily towards his object of restoring to the excluded republicans some participation in office, they find it expedient to lower their tone a little. They can now bear to talk themselves on an *equal number,* instead of a monopoly of offices. This is well, as a first symptom; and we hope, in the progress of convalescence, they will become able to bear the idea of a *due proportion.* . . .

Hitherto I have spoken of the Federalists as if they were a homogeneous body, but this is not the truth. Under that name lurks the heretical sect of monarchists. Afraid to wear their own name they creep under the mantle of federalism, and the federalists, like sheep, permit the fox to take shelter among them, when pursued by the dogs. These men have no right to office. If a monarchist be in office anywhere, and it be known to the President, the oath he has taken to support the constitution imperiously requires the instantaneous dismission of such officer; and I should hold the President highly criminal if he permitted such to remain. To appoint a monarchist to conduct the affairs of a republic, is like appointing an atheist to the priesthood, but as to the real Federalists, I take them to my bosom as brothers: I view them as honest men, friends to the present constitution. Our difference has been about measures only, which now having passed away should no longer divide us. It was how we should treat France for the injuries offered us. They thought the occasion called for Armies and navies, that we should burthen ourselves with taxes, and our posterity with debts at exorbitant interest: that we should pass alien and sedition laws, punishing men with exile without trial by jury, and usurping the regulation of the press, exclusively belonging to the state governments. We

thought some of these measures inexpedient, others unconstitutional. They, however, were the majority, they carried
their opinions into effect, and we submitted. The measures
themselves are now done with, except the debts contracted,
which we are honestly proceeding to pay off. Why then
should we longer be opposed to each other? I confess myself
of opinion that this portion of our fellow-citizens should have
a just participation of office, and am far from concurring
with those who advocate a general sweep, without discriminat-
ing between Federalist and Monarchist. Should not these
recollect their own complaints against the late administration
for proscribing them from all public trust? And shall we now
be so inconsistent as to act ourselves on the very principle
we then so highly condemned! To countenance the anti-social
doctrine that a minority has no rights? Never let *us* do
wrong, because our opponents did so. Let us, rather, by doing
right, shew them what they ought to have done, and establish a rule the dictates of reason and conscience, rather than
of the angry passions.

If the Federalists will amalgamate with us on these terms,
let us receive them, and once more unite our country into one
mass. But, as they seem to hold off with a remarkable
repugnance, I agree that in the meantime both justice and
safety require a due proportion of office in republican hands.
Whether it is best to effect this by a single stroke, or to await
the operation of deaths, resignations, and removals for delinquency, for virulent opposition, and monarchism, I am
not satisfied: but am willing to leave it to the constitutional
authorities, who, though they proceeded slower than I have
expected, yet are probably better judges than I am of the
comparative merits of the two methods. The course they
seem to have preferred tends more perhaps to allay the passions which so unpleasantly divide and disquiet us; and
trusted as they are, with the care of the public happiness,
they are bound so to modify jarring principles as to affect
that happiness as far as the state of things will admit. This
seems too to be a fair ground of compromise between the
extremes of opinion, even among republicans, some of whom
think there should be a general removal, and others none at
all. The latter opinion, I am told, is much entertained in the
southern states. Still I think it will be useful to go into the
examination of the question which party holds an over-
proportion of office? And I therefore, again invite Mr. Cole-

man to take the field for the state of New York, not doubting that some champion there will enter the lists for the opposite interest. In my own state the fact is so obvious that I believe no Federalists here will undertake to question it. Should anyone however appear, he will certainly find persons able and ready to confront him with facts. "FAIR PLAY"

I Prefer That Which Is Safe and Precise

To Wilson C. Nicholas, September 7, 1803

Jefferson gives a full presentation of his constitutional position on the Louisiana Purchase. He wanted no liberties taken with the doctrine of narrow construction, though there could be no question over whether the purchase should be made; the question was how it could be best justified. Nicholas was an old friend and close political helpmate of Jefferson's.

. . . Whatever Congress shall think it necessary to do, should be done with as little debate as possible, and particularly so far as respects the constitutional difficulty. I am aware of the force of the observations you make on the power given by the Constitution to Congress, to admit new States into the Union, without restraining the subject to the territory then constituting the United States. But when I consider that the limits of the United States are fixed by the treaty of 1783, that the Constitution expressly declares itself to be made for the United States, I cannot help believing the intention was not to permit Congress to admit into the Union new States, which should be formed out of the territory for which, and under whose authority alone, they were then acting. I do not believe it was meant that they might receive England, Ireland, Holland, etc. into it, which would be the case on your construction. When an instrument admits two constructions, the one safe, the other dangerous, the one precise, the other indefinite, I prefer that which is safe and precise. I had rather ask an enlargement of power from the nation, where it is found necessary, than to assume it by a construction which would make our powers boundless. Our peculiar security is in the possession of a written Constitution. Let us not make it a blank paper by construction. I say the same as to the opinion of those who consider the grant of the treaty making power as boundless. If it is, then we have no Constitution. If it has bounds, they can be no others than the definitions of the powers which that instrument gives. It specifies and delineates the operations permitted to the federal government, and gives all the powers necessary to carry these into execution. Whatever of these enumerated objects is proper for a law, Congress may make the law; whatever is proper to be executed by way of a treaty, the President and Senate may enter into the treaty; whatever is to be done by a judicial sentence, the judges may pass the sentence. Nothing is more likely than that their enumeration of powers is defective. This is the ordinary case of all human works. Let us go on then perfecting it, by adding, by way of amendment to the Constitution, those powers which time and trial show are still wanting. But it has been taken too much for granted, that by this rigorous construction the treaty power would be reduced to nothing. . . . I confess, then, I think it important, in the present case, to set an example against broad construction, by appealing for new power to the people. If, however, our friends shall think differently, certainly I shall acquiesce with satisfaction; confiding, that the good sense of our country will correct the evil of construction when it shall produce ill effects. . . .

The Property and Sovereignty of All Louisiana

Third Annual Message, October 17, 1803

The prospective purchase of Louisiana naturally dominated the Third Annual Message. Jefferson had hoped to secure a constitutional sanction for an act clearly not expressed by the language of the Constitution. But time was essential. Napoleon might change his mind. Accordingly, Jefferson omitted mention in the Message of the purchase's constitutionality. The Senate now had the task of approving the treaty; the House that of appropriating the money to execute it.

Third Annual Message.—October 17, 1803

To the Senate and House of Representatives of the United States,—

In calling you together, fellow citizens, at an earlier day than was contemplated by the act of the last session of Congress, I have not been insensible to the personal inconveniences necessarily resulting from an unexpected change in your arrangements. But matters of great public concernment have rendered this call necessary, and the interest you feel in these will supersede in your minds all private considerations.

Congress witnessed, at their last session, the extraordinary agitation produced in the public mind by the suspension of our right of deposit at the port of New Orleans, no assignment of another place having been made according to treaty. They were sensible that the continuance of that privation would be more injurious to our nation than any consequences which could flow from any mode of redress, but reposing just confidence in the good faith of the government whose officer had committed the wrong, friendly and reasonable representations were resorted to, and the right of deposit was restored.

Previous, however, to this period, we had not been unaware of the danger to which our peace would be perpetually exposed while so important a key to the commerce of the western country remained under foreign power. Difficulties, too, were presenting themselves as to the navigation of other streams, which, arising within our territories, pass through those adjacent. Propositions had, therefore, been authorized for obtaining, on fair conditions, the sovereignty of New Orleans, and of other possessions in that quarter interesting to our quiet, to such extent as was deemed practicable; and the provisional appropriation of two millions of dollars, to be applied and accounted for by the president of the United States, intended as part of the price, was considered as conveying the sanction of Congress to the acquisition proposed. The enlightened Government of France saw, with just discernment, the importance to both nations of such liberal arrangements as might best and permanently promote the peace, friendship, and interests of both; and the property and sovereignty of all Louisiana, which had been restored to them, have on certain conditions been transferred to the United States by instruments bearing date the 30th of April last. When these shall have received the constitutional sanction of the senate, they will without delay be communicated to the representatives also, for the exercise of their functions, as to those conditions which are within the powers vested by the constitution in Congress. While the property and sovereignty of the Mississippi and its waters secure an independent outlet for the produce of the western States, and an uncontrolled navigation through their whole course, free from collision with other powers and the dangers to our peace from that source, the fertility of the country, its climate and extent, promise in due season important aids to our treasury, an ample provision for our posterity, and a widespread field for the blessings of freedom and equal laws.

With the wisdom of Congress it will rest to take those ulterior measures which may be necessary for the immediate occupation and temporary government of the country; for its incorporation into our Union; for rendering the change of government a blessing to our newly-adopted brethren; for securing to them the rights of conscience and of property; for confirming to the Indian inhabitants their occupancy and self-government, establishing friendly and commercial relations with them, and for ascertaining the geography of the country acquired. Such materials for your information, relative to its affairs in general, as the short space of time has permitted me to collect, will be laid before you when the subject shall be in a state for your consideration. . . .

All Are Perfectly Equal

Rules of Etiquette in Washington, November [7], 1803

Jefferson's rules of etiquette describe a true revolution wrought in Washington. Republican informality—or "pêle mêle"—replaced ordered ceremony in the relations between government officials, with the result that Jefferson alienated foreign diplomats, particularly the British Ambassador, Anthony Merry, to the point of outright antagonism.

i. In order to bring the members of society together in the first instance, the custom of the country has established that residents shall pay the first visit to strangers, and, among strangers, first comers to later comers, foreign and domestic; the character of stranger ceasing after the first visits. To this rule there is a single exception. Foreign ministers, from the necessity of making themselves known, pay the first visit to the ministers of the nation, which is returned.

ii. When brought together in society, all are perfectly equal, whether foreign or domestic, titled or untitled, in or out of office.

All other observances are but exemplifications of these two principles.

I. 1st. The families of foreign ministers, arriving at the seat of government, receive the first visit from those of the national ministers, as from all other residents.

2d. Members of the Legislature and of the Judiciary, independent of their offices, have a right as strangers to receive the first visit.

II. 1st. No title being admitted here, those of foreigners give no precedence.

2d. Differences of grade among diplomatic members, give no precedence.

3d. At public ceremonies, to which the government invites the presence of foreign ministers and their families, a convenient seat or station will be provided for them, with any other strangers invited and the families of the national ministers, each taking place as they arrive, and without any precedence.

4th. To maintain the principle of equality, or of pêle mêle, and prevent the growth of precedence out of courtesy, the members of the Executive will practice at their own houses, and recommend an adherence to the ancient usage of the country, of gentlemen in mass giving precedence to the ladies in mass, in passing from one apartment where they are assembled into another.

Morality Listens to This

To Jean Baptiste Say, February 1, 1804

Jefferson carefully read the avant-garde political economists whose liberal ideas were akin to his own. Say was the leading proponent of laissez-faire economics in France. Jefferson's recent reading of Malthus gave him a chance to expatiate on a favorite theme: the virtue, abundance and freedom of American agriculture.

Dear Sir,—I have to acknowledge the receipt of your obliging letter, and with it, of two very interesting volumes on Political Economy. These found me engaged in giving the leisure moments I rarely find, to the perusal of Malthus' work on population, a work of sound logic, in which some of the opinions of Adam Smith, as well as of the economists, are ably examined. I was pleased, on turning to some chapters where you treat the same questions, to find his opinions corroborated by yours. I shall proceed to the reading of your work with great pleasure. In the meantime, the present conveyance, by a gentleman of my family going to Paris, is too safe to hazard a delay in making my acknowledgements for this mark of attention, and for having afforded to me a satisfaction, which the ordinary course of literary communications could not have given me for a considerable time.

The differences of circumstance between this and the old countries of Europe, furnish differences of fact whereon to reason, in questions of political economy, and will consequently produce sometimes a difference of result. There, for instance, the quantity of food is fixed, or increasing in a slow and only arithmetical ratio, and the proportion is limited by the same ratio. Supernumerary births consequently add only to your mortality. Here the immense extent of uncultivated and fertile lands enables every one who will labor, to marry young, and to raise a family of any size. Our food, then, may increase geometrically with our laborers, and our births, however multiplied, become effective. Again, there the best distribution of labor is supposed to be that which places the manufacturing hands alongside the agricultural; so that the one part shall feed both, and the other part furnish both with clothes and other comforts. Would that be best here? Egoism and first appearances say yes. Or would it be better that all our laborers should be employed in agriculture? In this case a double or treble portion of fertile lands would be brought into culture; a double or treble creation of food be produced, and its surplus go to nourish the now perishing births of Europe, who in return would manufacture and send us in exchange our clothes and other comforts. Morality listens to this, and so invariably do the laws of nature create our duties and interests, that when they seem to be at variance, we ought to suspect some fallacy in our reasonings. In solving this question, too, we should allow its just weight to the moral and physical preference of the agricultural, over the manufacturing, man. My occupations permit me only to ask questions. They deny me the time, if I had the information, to answer them. Perhaps, as worthy the attention of the author of the *Traité d'Economie Politique,* I shall find them answered in that work. If they are not, the reason will have been that you wrote for Europe; while I shall have asked them because I think for America. Accept, Sir, my respectful salutations, and assurances of great consideration.

Proofs of My Great Respect for You

To Mrs. John Adams, September 11, 1804

Mrs. Adams revealed why she was angry with Jefferson: his administration had removed her son, John Quincy Adams, from an office to which one of the midnight judges—himself removed—had appointed him. Jefferson here exonerates himself from what he admits was a wrong done to her son and also justifies not having prosecuted the Sedition Act. This attempt to renew the old friendship between Jefferson and the Adamses failed. It would be eight years before another attempt would be made.

Your letter, Madam, of the 18th of August has been some days received, but a press of business has prevented the acknowledgment of it! perhaps, indeed, I may have already trespassed too far on your attention. With those who wish to think amiss of me, I have learned to be perfectly indifferent; but where I know a mind to be ingenuous, and to need only truths to set it to rights, I cannot be as passive.

The act of personal unkindness alluded to in your former letter, is said in your last to have been the removal of your eldest son from some office to which the judges had appointed him. I conclude then he must have been a commissioner of bankruptcy. But I declare to you, on my honor, that this is the first knowledge I have ever had that he was so. It may be thought, perhaps, that I ought to have inquired who were such, before I appointed others. But it is to be observed, that the former law permitted the judges to name commissioners occasionally, only for every case as it arose, and not to make them permanent officers. Nobody, therefore, being in office, there could be no removal. The judges, you well know, have been considered as highly federal; and it was noted that they confined their nominations exclusively to federalists. The Legislature, dissatisfied with this, transferred the nomination to the President, and made the offices permanent. The very object in passing the law was, that he should correct, not confirm, what was deemed the partiality of the judges. I thought it therefore proper to inquire, not whom they had employed, but whom I ought to appoint to fulfil the intentions of the law. In making these appointments, I put in a proportion of federalists, equal, I believe, to the proportion they bear in numbers through the Union generally. Had I known that your son had acted, it would have been a real pleasure to me to have preferred him to some who were named in Boston, in what was deemed the same line of politics. To this I should have been led by my knowledge of his integrity, as well as my sincere dispositions towards yourself and Mr. Adams.

You seem to think it devolved on the judges to decide on the validity of the sedition law. But nothing in the Constitution has given them a right to decide for the Executive, more than to the Executive to decide for them. Both magistrates are equally independent in the sphere of action assigned to them. The judges, believing the law constitutional, had a right to pass a sentence of fine and imprisonment; because the power was placed in their hands by the Constitution. But the Executive, believing the law to be unconstitutional, were bound to remit the execution of it; because that power has been confined to them by the Constitution. That instrument meant that its co-ordinate branches should be checks on each other. But the opinion which gives to the judges the right to decide what laws are constitutional, and what are not, not only for themselves in their own sphere of action, but for the legislature and executive also, in their spheres, would make the judiciary a despotic branch. Nor does the opinion of the unconstitutionality, and consequent nullity, of that law, remove all restraint from the overwhelming torrent of slander, which is confounding all vice and virtue, all truth and falsehood, in the United States. The power to do that is fully possessed by the several State Legislatures. It was reserved to them, and was denied to the General Government, by the Constitution, according to our construction of it. While we deny that Congress have a right to control the freedom of the press, we have ever asserted the right of the States, and their exclusive right, to do so. They have accordingly, all of them, made provisions for punishing slander, which those who have time and inclination, resort to for the vindication of their characters. In general, the State laws appear to have made the presses responsible for slander as far as is consistent with its useful freedom. In those States where they do not admit even the truth of the allegations to protect the printer, they have gone too far.

The candor manifested in your letter, and which I ever believed you to possess, has alone inspired the desire of calling your attention, once more, to those circumstances of fact and motive by which I claim to be judged. I hope you will see these intrusions on your time to be, what they really are, proofs of my great respect for you. I tolerate with the utmost latitude the right of others to differ from me in opinion without imputing to them criminality. I know too well the weakness and uncertainty of human reason to wonder at its different results. Both of our political parties, at least the honest part of them, agree conscientiously in the same object—the public good. One side believes it best done by one side of the governing powers; the other, by a different one. One fears most the ignorance of the people; the other, the selfishness of rulers independent of them. Which is right, time and experience will prove. We think that one side of this experiment has been long enough tried, and proved not to promote the good of the many; and that the other has not been fairly and sufficiently tried. Our opponents think the reverse. With whichever opinion the body of the nation concurs, that must prevail. My anxieties on the subject will never carry me beyond the use of fair and honorable means, of truth and reason; nor have they ever lessened my esteem for moral worth, nor alienated my affections from a single friend, who did not first withdraw himself. Whenever this has happened, I confess that I have not been insensible to it; yet have ever kept myself open to a return of their justice. I conclude with a sincere prayer for your health and happiness, that yourself and Mr. Adams may long enjoy the tranquility you desire and merit, and see in the prosperity of your family what is the consummation of the last and warmest of human wishes.

The Disposition to Be Just

To William Burwell, January 28, 1805

Jefferson could not have been more wrong in thinking that the slave-owning interest was going over to the side of morality. The tobacco interest was in the doldrums, but the cotton interest had not yet sprung up. Burwell was Jefferson's secretary.

. . . I have long since given up the expectation of any early provision for the extinguishment of slavery among us. There are many virtuous men who would make any sacrifices to affect it, many equally virtuous who persuade themselves either that the thing is not wrong, or that it cannot be remedied, and very many with whom interest is morality. The older we grow, the larger we are disposed to believe the last party to be. But interest is really going over to the side of morality. The value of the slave is every day lessening; his burden on his master dayly increasing. Interest is therefore preparing the disposition to be just; and this will be goaded from time to time by the insurrectionary spirit of the slaves. This is easily quelled in it's first efforts; but from being local it will become general, and whenever it does it will rise more formidable after every defeat, until we shall be forced, after dreadful scenes & sufferings to release them in their own way, which, without such sufferings we might now model after our own convenience. Accept my affectionate salutations.

Facts Are Piercing Through

Second Inaugural Address, March 4, 1805

In Jefferson's view, the "promise" of the First Inaugural was being fulfilled, and he intended the Second Inaugural to announce this fact. In one respect certainly his policy had proved masterful: the Federalist Party lay nearly in ruins; only in Connecticut among New England states did its strength exceed Jefferson's. Yet Jefferson's own policies had taken on a Federalist coloration. This is reflected in his proposal that surplus revenue "be applied in times of peace, to rivers, canals, roads, arts, manufacture, education and other great objects within each state." Jefferson, accompanied by a large crowd, walked to the Capitol to be inaugurated. Once again he read his speech in a voice that was hardly audible.

Proceeding, fellow citizens, to that qualification which the constitution requires, before my entrance on the charge again conferred upon me, it is my duty to express the deep sense I entertain of this new proof of confidence from my fellow citizens at large, and the zeal with which it inspires me, so to conduct myself as may best satisfy their just expectations.

On taking this station on a former occasion, I declared the principles on which I believed it my duty to administer the affairs of our commonwealth. My conscience tells me that I have, on every occasion, acted up to that declaration, according to its obvious import, and to the understanding of every candid mind.

In the transaction of your foreign affairs, we have endeavored to cultivate the friendship of all nations, and especially of those with which we have the most important relations. We have done them justice on all occasions, favored where favor was lawful, and cherished mutual interests and intercourse on fair and equal terms. We are firmly convinced, and we act on that conviction, that with nations, as with individuals, our interests soundly calculated, will ever be found inseparable from our moral duties; and history bears witness to the fact, that a just nation is taken on its word, when recourse is had to armaments and wars to bridle others.

451

At home, fellow citizens, you best know whether we have done well or ill. The suppression of unnecessary offices, of useless establishments and expenses, enabled us to discontinue our internal taxes. These covering our land with officers, and opening our doors to their intrusions, had already begun that process of domiciliary vexation which, once entered, is scarcely to be restrained from reaching successively every article of produce and property. If among these taxes some minor ones fell which had not been inconvenient, it was because their amount would not have paid the officers who collected them, and because, if they had any merit, the state authorities might adopt them, instead of others less approved.

The remaining revenue on the consumption of foreign articles, is paid cheerfully by those who can afford to add foreign luxuries to domestic comforts, being collected on our seaboards and frontiers only, and incorporated with the transactions of our mercantile citizens, it may be the pleasure and pride of an American to ask, what farmer, what mechanic, what laborer, ever sees a tax-gatherer of the United States? These contributions enable us to support the current expenses of the government, to fulfil contracts with foreign nations, to extinguish the native right of soil within our limits, to extend those limits, and to apply such a surplus to our public debts, as places at a short day their final redemption, and that redemption once effected, the revenue thereby liberated may, by a just repartition among the states, and a corresponding amendment of the constitution, be applied, *in time of peace,* to rivers, canals, roads, arts, manufactures, education, and other great objects within each state. *In time of war,* if injustice, by ourselves or others, must sometimes produce war, increased as the same revenue will be increased by population and consumption, and aided by other resources reserved for that crisis, it may meet within the year all the expenses of the year, without encroaching on the rights of future generations, by burdening them with the debts of the past. War will then be but a suspension of useful works, and a return to a state of peace, a return to the progress of improvement.

I have said, fellow citizens, that the income reserved had enabled us to extend our limits; but that extension may possibly pay for itself before we are called on, and in the mean-time, may keep down the accruing interest; in all events, it will repay the advances we have made. I know that the acquisition of Louisiana has been disapproved by some, from a candid apprehension that the enlargement of our territory would endanger its union. But who can limit the extent to which the federative principle may operate effectively? The larger our association, the less will it be shaken by local passions; and in any view, is it not better that the opposite bank of the Mississippi should be settled by our own brethren and children, than by strangers of another family? With which shall we be most likely to live in harmony and friendly intercourse?

In matters of religion, I have considered that its free exercise is placed by the constitution independent of the powers of the general government. I have therefore undertaken, on no occasion, to prescribe the religious exercises suited to it; but have left them, as the constitution found them, under the direction and discipline of state or church authorities acknowledged by the several religious societies.

The aboriginal inhabitants of these countries I have regarded with the commiseration their history inspires. Endowed with the faculties and the rights of men, breathing an ardent love of liberty and independence, and occupying a country which left them no desire but to be undisturbed, the stream of overflowing population from other regions directed itself on these shores; without power to divert, or habits to contend against, they have been overwhelmed by the current, or driven before it; now reduced within limits too narrow for the hunter's state, humanity enjoins us to teach them agriculture and the domestic arts; to encourage them to that industry which alone can enable them to maintain their place in existence, and to prepare them in time for that state of society, which to bodily comforts adds the improvement of the mind and morals. We have therefore liberally furnished them with the implements of husbandry and household use; we have placed among them instructors in the arts of first necessity; and they are covered with the ægis of the law against aggressors from among ourselves.

But the endeavors to enlighten them on the fate which awaits their present course of life, to induce them to exercise their reason, follow its dictates, and change their pursuits with the change of circumstances, have powerful obstacles to encounter; they are combated by the habits of their bodies, prejudice of their minds, ignorance, pride, and the influence of interested and crafty individuals among them, who feel themselves something in the present order of things, and fear to become nothing in any other. These persons inculcate a sanctimonious reverence for the customs of their ancestors; that whatsoever they did, must be done through all time; that reason is a false guide, and to advance under its counsel, in their physical, moral, or political condition, is perilous innovation; that their duty is to remain as their Creator made them, ignorance being safety, and knowledge full of danger; in short, my friends, among them is seen the action and counteraction of good sense and bigotry; they, too, have their anti-philosophers, who find an interest in keeping things in their present state, who dread reformation, and exert all their faculties to maintain the ascendency of habit over the duty of improving our reason, and obeying its mandates.

In giving these outlines, I do not mean, fellow citizens, to arrogate to myself the merit of the measures; that is due, in the first place, to the reflecting character of our citizens at large, who, by the weight of public opinion, influence and strengthen the public measures; it is due to the sound discretion with which they select from among themselves those to whom they confide the legislative duties; it is due to the zeal and wisdom of the characters thus selected, who lay the foundations of public happiness in wholesome laws, the execution of which alone remains for others; and it is due to the able and faithful auxiliaries, whose patriotism has associated with me in the executive functions.

During this course of administration, and in order to disturb it, the artillery of the press has been levelled against us, charged with whatsoever its licentiousness could devise or dare. These abuses of an institution so important to freedom and science, are deeply to be regretted, inasmuch as they tend to lessen its usefulness, and to sap its safety; they might, indeed, have been corrected by the wholesome punishments reserved and provided by the laws of the several States against falsehood and defamation; but public duties more urgent press on the time of public servants, and the offenders have therefore been left to find their punishment in the public indignation.

Nor was it uninteresting to the world, that an experiment should be fairly and fully made, whether freedom of discussion, unaided by power, is not sufficient for the propagation and protection of truth—whether a government, conducting itself in the true spirit of its constitution, with zeal and purity, and doing no act which it would be unwilling the whole world should witness, can be written down by falsehood and defamation. The experiment has been tried; you have witnessed the scene; our fellow citizens have looked on, cool and collected; they saw the latent source from which these outrages proceeded; they gathered around their public functionaries, and when the constitution called them to the decision by suffrage, they pronounced their verdict, honorable to those who had served them, and consolatory to the friend of man, who believes he may be intrusted with his own affairs.

No inference is here intended, that the laws, provided by the State against false and defamatory publications, should not be enforced; he who has time, renders a service to public morals and public tranquillity, in reforming these abuses by the salutary coercions of the law; but the experiment is noted, to prove that, since truth and reason have maintained their ground against false opinions in league with false facts, the press, confined to truth, needs no other legal restraint; the public judgment will correct false reasonings and opinions, on a full hearing of all parties; and no other definite line can be drawn between the inestimable liberty of the press and its demoralizing licentiousness. If there be still improprieties which this rule would not restrain, its supplement must be sought in the censorship of public opinion.

Contemplating the union of sentiment now manifested so generally, as auguring harmony and happiness to our future course, I offer to our country sincere congratulations. With those, too, not yet rallied to the same point, the disposition to do so is gaining strength; facts are piercing through the veil drawn over them; and our doubting brethren will at length see, that the mass of their fellow citizens, with whom they cannot yet resolve to act, as to principles and measures, think as they think, and desire what they desire; that our wish, as well as theirs, is, that the public efforts may be directed honestly to the public good, that peace be cultivated, civil and religious liberty unassailed, law and order preserved, equality of rights maintained, and that state of property, equal or unequal, which results to every man from his own industry, or that of his fathers. When satisfied of these views, it is not in human nature that they should not approve and support them; in the meantime, let us cherish them with patient affection; let us do them justice, and more than justice, in all competitions of interest; and we need not doubt that truth, reason, and their own interests, will at length prevail, will gather them into the fold of their country, and will complete their entire union of opinion, which gives to a nation the blessing of harmony, and the benefit of all its strength.

I shall now enter on the duties to which my fellow citizens have again called me, and shall proceed in the spirit of those principles which they have approved. I fear not that any motives of interest may lead me astray; I am sensible of no passion which could seduce me knowingly from the path of justice; but the weakness of human nature, and the limits of my own understanding, will produce errors of judgment sometimes injurious to your interests. I shall need, therefore, all the indulgence I have heretofore experienced—the want of it will certainly not lessen with increasing years. I shall need, too, the favor of that Being in whose hands we are, who led our forefathers, as Israel of old, from their native land, and planted them in a country flowing with all the necessaries and comforts of life; who has covered our infancy with his providence, and our riper years with his wisdom and power; and to whose goodness I ask you to join with me in supplications, that he will so enlighten the minds of your servants, guide their councils, and prosper their measures, that whatsoever they do, shall result in your good, and shall secure to you the peace, friendship, and approbation of all nations.

New Principles Have Been Interloped into the Law of Nations

Fifth Annual Message, December 3, 1805

Almost at once Jefferson's second administration was swept into a maelstrom of troubles. After the Napoleonic Wars resumed in 1803, Britain laid down a series of Orders in Council, each more severe than the preceding one, restricting American trade with the French and Spanish West Indies. France, for her part, imposed, where possible, similar restrictions on American trade with the British West Indies. Controversy with Spain arose out of her mistreatment of Americans in the recently acquired Louisiana territory and her refusal to include West Florida in the Louisiana purchase. The American government thus found itself compelled to take steps at variance with Jefferson's hopes for peace, frugality and liberty. On the other hand, a treaty of peace was signed with Tripoli on June 4, which ended the depredations on American shipping along the North African coast.

. . . Since our last meeting the aspect of our foreign relations has considerably changed. Our coasts have been infested and our harbors watched by private armed vessels, some of them without commissions, some with illegal commissions, others with those of legal form but committing piratical acts beyond the authority of their commissions. They have captured in the very entrance of our harbors, as well as on the high seas, not only the vessels of our friends coming to trade with us, but our own also. They have carried them off under pretence of legal adjudication, but not daring to approach a court of justice, they have plundered and sunk them by the way, or in obscure places where no evidence could arise against them; maltreated the crews, and abandoned them in boats in the open sea or on desert shores without food or covering. These enormities appearing to be unreached by any control of their sovereigns, I found it necessary to equip a force to cruise within our own seas, to arrest all vessels of these descriptions found hovering on our coast within the limits of the Gulf Stream, and to bring the offenders in for trial as pirates.

The same system of hovering on our coasts and harbors under color of seeking enemies, has been also carried on by public armed ships, to the great annoyance and oppression of our commerce. New principles, too, have been interloped into the law of nations, founded neither in justice nor the usage or acknowledgment of nations. According to these, a belligerent takes to himself a commerce with its own enemy which it denies to a neutral, on the ground of its aiding that enemy in the war. But reason revolts at such an inconsistency, and the neutral having equal right with the belligerent to decide the question, the interest of our constituents and the duty of maintaining the authority of reason, the only umpire between just nations, impose on us the obligation of providing an effectual and determined opposition to a doctrine so injurious to the rights of peaceable nations. Indeed, the confidence we ought to have in the justice of others, still countenances the hope that a sounder view of those rights will of itself induce from every belligerent a more correct observance of them.

With Spain our negotiations for a settlement of differences have not had a satisfactory issue. Spoliations during the former war, for which she had formally acknowledged herself responsible, have been refused to be compensated, but on conditions affecting other claims in nowise connected with them. Yet the same practices are renewed in the present war, and are already of great amount. On the Mobile, our commerce passing through that river continues to be obstructed by arbitrary duties and vexatious searches. Propositions for adjusting amicably the boundaries of Louisiana have not been acceded to. While, however, the right is unsettled, we have avoided changing the state of things by taking new posts or strengthening ourselves in the disputed territories, in the hope that the other power would not, by contrary conduct, oblige us to meet their example, and endanger conflicts of authority the issue of which may not be easily controlled. But in this hope we have now reason to lessen our confidence. Inroads have been recently made into the territories of Orleans and the Mississippi, our citizens have been seized and their property plundered in the very parts of the former which had been actually delivered up by Spain, and this by the regular officers and soldiers of that government. I have therefore found it necessary at length to give orders to our troops on that frontier to be in readiness to protect our citizens, and to repel by arms any similar aggression in future. Other details, necessary for your full information of the state of things between this country and that shall be the subject of another communication.

In reviewing these injuries from some of the belligerent powers, the moderation, the firmness, and the wisdom of the legislature will be all called into action. We ought still to hope that time and a more correct estimate of interest, as well as of character, will produce the justice we are bound to expect. But should any nation deceive itself by false calculations, and disappoint that expectation, we must join in the unprofitable contest of trying which party can do the other the most harm. Some of these injuries may perhaps admit a peaceable remedy. Where that is competent it is always the most desirable. But some of them are of a nature to be met by force only, and all of them may lead to it. I cannot, therefore, but recommend such preparations as circumstances call for. The first object is to place our seaport towns out of the danger of insult. Measures have been already taken for furnishing them with heavy cannon for the service of such land batteries as may make a part of their defence against armed vessels approaching them. In aid of these it is desirable that we should have a competent number of gunboats; and the number, to be competent, must be considerable. If immediately begun, they may be in readiness for service at the opening of the next season. Whether it will be necessary to augment our land forces will be decided by occurrences probably in the course of your session. In the meantime, you will consider whether it would not be expedient, for a state of peace as well as of war, so to organize or class the militia as would enable us, on a sudden emergency, to call for the services of the younger portions, unencumbered with the old and those having families. Upward of three hundred thousand able-bodied men, between the ages of eighteen and twenty-six years, which the last census shows we may now count within our limits, will furnish a competent number for offence or defence in any point where they may be wanted, and will give time for raising regular forces after the necessity of them shall become certain; and the reducing to the early period of life all its active service cannot but be desirable to our younger citizens, of the present as well as future times, inasmuch as it engages to them in more advanced age a quiet and undisturbed repose in the bosom of their families. I cannot, then, but earnestly recommend to your early consideration the expediency of so modifying our militia system as, by a separation of the more active part from that which is less so, we may draw from it, when necessary, an efficient corps fit for real and active service, and to be called to it in regular rotation.

Considerable provision has been made, under former authorities from Congress, of materials for the construction of ships of war of seventy-four guns. These materials are on hand, subject to the further will of the legislature.

An immediate prohibition of the exportation of arms and ammunition is also submitted to your determination.

Turning from these unpleasant views of violence and wrong, I congratulate you on the liberation of our fellow citizens who were stranded on the coast of Tripoli and made prisoners of war. In a government bottomed on the will of all, the life and liberty of every individual citizen become interesting to all. In the treaty, therefore, which has concluded our warfare with that State, an article for the ransom of our citizens has been agreed to. An operation by land, by a small band of our countrymen, and others—engaged for the occasion, in conjunction with the troops of the ex-bashaw of that country, gallantly conducted by our late consul Eaton, and their successful enterprise on the city of Derne, contributed, doubtless, to the impression which produced peace; and the conclusion of this prevented opportunities of which the officers and men of our squadron destined for Tripoli would have availed themselves, to emulate the acts of valor exhibited by their brethren in the attack of the last year. Reflecting with high satisfaction on the distinguished bravery displayed whenever occasion permitted in the Mediterranean service, I think it would be a useful encouragement, as well as a just reward, to make an opening for some present promotion by enlarging our peace establishment of captains and lieutenants.

With Tunis some misunderstandings have arisen, not yet sufficiently explained, but friendly discussions with their ambassador recently arrived, and a mutual disposition to do whatever is just and reasonable, cannot fail of dissipating these; so that we may consider our peace on that coast, generally, to be on as sound a footing as it has been at any preceding time. Still it will not be expedient to withdraw, immediately, the whole of our force from that sea.

The law for providing a naval peace establishment fixes the number of frigates which shall be kept in constant service in time of peace, and prescribes that they shall not be manned by more than two-thirds of their complement of seamen and ordinary seamen. Whether a frigate may be trusted to two-thirds only of her proper complement of men must depend on the nature of the service on which she is ordered; that may sometimes, for her safety, as well as to insure her object, require her fullest complement. In adverting to this subject, Congress will perhaps consider whether the best limitation on the executive discretion in this case would not be by the number of seamen which may be employed in the whole service, rather than by the number of vessels. Occasions oftener arise for the employment of small than of large vessels, and it would lessen risk as well as expense to be authorized to employ them of preference. The limitation suggested by the number of seamen would admit a selection of vessels best adapted to the service.

You Must Not Commit Yourself to Him

To James Monroe, May 4, 1806

Ambitious, restive James Monroe, now minister to Britain, was known to resent the favoritism Jefferson showed Madison as his successor. Rumor had it that Monroe was giving his ear to John Randolph, Jefferson's apostate enemy in the House of Representatives. Here Jefferson warns Monroe not to jeopardize his career by falling in with Randolph.

. . . Our old friend, Mercer, broke off from us some time ago; at first professing to disdain joining the federalists, yet, from the habit of voting together, becoming soon identified with them. Without carrying over with him one single person, he is now in a state of as perfect obscurity as if his name had never been known. Mr. J. Randolph is in the same track, and will end in the same way. His course has excited considerable alarm. Timid men consider it as a proof of the weakness of our government, & that it is to be rent into pieces by demagogues, & to end in anarchy. I survey the scene with a different eye, and draw a different augury from it. In a house of Representatives of a great mass of good sense, Mr. R's popular eloquence gave him such advantages as to place him unrivalled as the leader of the house; and, altho' not conciliatory to those whom he led, principles of duty & patriotism induced many of them to swallow the humiliations he subjected them to, and to vote as was right, as long as he kept the path of right himself. The sudden defection of such a man could not but produce a momentary astonishment, & even dismay; but for a moment only. The good sense of the house rallied around it's principles, & without any leader pursued steadily the business of the session, did it well, & by a strength of vote which has never before been seen. Upon all trying questions, exclusive of the federalists, the minority of republicans voting with him has been from 4. to 6. or 8., against from 90, to 100.; and altho' he yet treats the federalists with ineffable contempt, yet, having declared eternal opposition to this administration, & consequently associated with them, in his votes, he will, like

Mercer, end with them. The augury I draw from this is, that there is a steady, good sense in the Legislature, and in the body of the nation, joined with good intentions, which will lead them to discern & to pursue the public good under all circumstances which can arise, and that no *ignis fatuus* will be able to lead them long astray. In the present case, the public sentiment, as far as declarations of it have yet come in, is, without a single exception, in firm adherence to the administration. One popular paper is endeavoring to maintain equivocal ground; approving the administration in all it's proceedings, & Mr. R in all those which have heretofore merited approbation, carefully avoiding to mention his late aberrations. The ultimate view of this paper is friendly to you; & the editor, with more judgement than him who assumes to be at the head of your friends, sees that the ground of opposition to the administration is not that on which it would be advantageous to you to be planted. The great body of your friends are among the firmest adherents to the administration; and in their support of you, will suffer Mr. R to have no communications with them. My former letter told you the line which both duty & inclination would lead me sacredly to pursue. But it is unfortunate for you to be embarrassed with such a *soi-disant* friend. You must not commit yourself to him. . . .

The Articles of Public Care

Sixth Annual Message, December 2, 1806

This Message, in contrast to the previous one, was optimistic and equable. Jefferson wrote it at a time when Britain was relaxing her interdictions against American shipping and before he could possibly have received word of the denouement toward which Monroe's and Pinckney's negotiations with Britain were headed. Once again, Jefferson suggests a national program of internal improvements and of aid to education and the arts.

... The question, therefore, now comes forward,—to what other objects shall these surpluses be appropriated, and the whole surplus of impost, after the entire discharge of the public debt, and during those intervals when the purposes of war shall not call for them? Shall we suppress the impost and give that advantage to foreign over domestic manufactures? On a few articles of more general and necessary use, the suppression in due season will doubtless be right, but the great mass of the articles on which impost is paid is foreign luxuries, purchased by those only who are rich enough to afford themselves the use of them. Their patriotism would certainly prefer its continuance and application to the great purposes of the public education, roads, rivers, canals, and such other objects of public improvement as it may be thought proper to add to the constitutional enumeration of federal powers. By these operations new channels of communication will be opened between the States; the lines of separation will disappear, their interests will be identified, and their union cemented by new and indissoluble ties. Education is here placed among the articles of public care, not that it would be proposed to take its ordinary branches out of the hands of private enterprise, which manages so much better all the concerns to which it is equal; but a public institution can alone supply those sciences which, though rarely called for, are yet necessary to complete the circle, all the parts of which contribute to the improvement of the country, and some of them to its preservation. The subject is now proposed for the consideration of Congress, because, if approved by the time the State legislatures shall have deliberated on this extension of the federal trusts, and the laws shall be passed, and other arrangements made for their execution, the necessary funds will be on hand and without employment. I suppose an amendment to the constitution, by consent of the States, necessary, because the objects now recommended are not among those enumerated in the constitution, and to which it permits the public moneys to be applied.

The present consideration of a national establishment for education, particularly, is rendered proper by this circumstance also, that if Congress, approving the proposition, shall yet think it more eligible to found it on a donation of lands, they have it now in their power to endow it with those which will be among the earliest to produce the necessary income. This foundation would have the advantage of being independent on war, which may suspend other improvements by requiring for its own purposes the resources destined for them.

To Depart from the Same

Chesapeake Proclamation, July 2, 1807

On June 1, The British navy charged that the American frigate Chesapeake, *anchored in Norfolk, had hired four British deserters. On June 22, the British frigate* Leopard *confronted the* Chesapeake *outside the three mile limit. When the British Commander was refused the power of search, he ordered the* Leopard *to attack. As a result of the ensuing engagement, in which three American crewmen were killed, the* Chesapeake *surrendered, was searched, and the four alleged deserters pulled off. The country was shocked and humiliated. Jefferson called his Cabinet and read the following Proclamation.*

During the wars which for some time have unhappily prevailed among the powers of Europe, the U.S. of America, firm in their principles of peace, have endeavored by justice, by a regular discharge of all their national and social duties, and by every friendly office their situation admitted, to maintain, with all the belligerents, their accustomed relations of friendship, hospitality and commercial intercourse. Taking no part in the questions which animated these powers against each other, nor permitting themselves to entertain a wish, but for the restoration of general peace, they have observed with good faith the neutrality they assumed, and they believe that no instance of departure from its duties can be justly imputed to them by any nation. A free use of their harbours and waters, the means of refitting and of refreshment, of succour to their sick and suffering, have, at all times, and on equal principles been extended to all: and this too while the officers of one of the belligerents received among us have been in a continued course of insubordination to the laws, of violence to the persons, and of trespasses on the property of our citizens. These abuses of the laws of hospitality have become habitual to the Commanders of the British armed vessels hovering on our coasts and frequenting our harbours; they have been the subject of repeated representations to their government; assurances have been given that proper orders should restrain them within the limit of the rights, and of the respect belonging to a friendly nation: but those orders and assurances have been without effect; nor has a single instance of punishment for past wrongs taken place. And at length a deed, transcending all we have suffered, brings the public sensibility to a serious crisis, and forbearance to a necessary pause. A frigate of the U.S. trusting to a state of peace and leaving her harbor on a distant service, has been surprised and attacked by a British vessel of superior force, one of a squadron then lying in our waters to cover the transaction, and has been disabled from service with the loss of a number of men killed and wounded. This enormity was not only without provocation or justifiable cause; but was committed with the avowed purpose of taking by force from a ship of war of the U.S. a part of her crew: and that no circumstance might be wanting to make its character, the commander was apprised that the seamen thus forcibly [blank] were native citizens of the U.S. His purpose effected he returned to anchor with his squadron within our jurisdiction. Hospitality under such circumstances ceases to be a duty: and a continuance of it with such uncontrolled abuses would tend only, by multiplying injuries, and irritations, to bring on a rupture equally opposed to the interests of both nations, as to assurances of the most friendly dispositions on the part of the British government in the midst of which this outrage has been committed. The subject cannot but present itself to that government, and strengthen the motives to an honorable reparation of the wrong which has been done, and that effectual control, of its naval commanders which alone can justify the government of the U.S. in the exercise of those hospitalities it is now constrained to discontinue.

IN CONSIDERATION of these circumstances, and of the right of every nation to regulate its own police, to provide for its peace and for the safety of its citizens, and consequently to refuse the admission of armed vessels into its harbors or waters, either in such numbers, or of such descriptions, as are inconsistent with these, or with the maintenance of the authority of the laws, I have thought proper in pursuance of the authority specially given by law to issue this my PROCLAMATION, hereby requiring all armed vessels bearing commissions under the government of Great Britain now within the harbors or waters of the U.S. immediately and without any delay to depart from the same: and interdicting the entrance of all the said harbors and waters to the said armed vessels, and to all others bearing commissions under the authority of the British government.

And if the said vessels or any of them, shall fail to depart as aforesaid, or if they or any others, so interdicted, shall hereafter enter the harbors or waters aforesaid, I do in that case forbid all intercourse with either or any of them, their officers or crews, and do prohibit all supplies and aid from being furnished to them or any of them.

And I do declare and make known that if any person from, or within, the jurisdictional limits of the U.S. shall afford any aid to any such vessel contrary to the prohibition contained in this proclamation, either in repairing any such vessel, or in furnishing her, her officers or crew, with supplies of any kind, or in any manner whatever, or if any pilot shall assist in navigating any of the said armed vessels, unless it be for the purpose of carrying them in the first instance, beyond the limits and jurisdiction of the U.S. or unless it be in the case of a vessel forced by distress, or charged with public dispatches as hereinafter provided for, such person or persons shall, on conviction, suffer all the pains and penalties by the laws provided for such offences.

And I do hereby enjoin and require all persons bearing office civil or military within or under the authority of the U.S., and all others, citizens or inhabitants thereof, or being within the same, with vigilance and promptitude to exert their respective authorities and to be aiding and assisting to the carrying this Proclamation and every part thereof into full effect.

Provided nevertheless that if any such vessel shall be forced into the harbors or waters of the U.S. by distress, by the dangers of the sea, or by the pursuit of an enemy, or shall enter them charged with dispatches or business from their government, or shall be a public packet for the conveyance of letters and dispatches, the commanding officer, immediately reporting his vessel to the collector of the district, stating the object or causes of entering the said harbors or waters, and conforming himself to the regulations in that case prescribed under the authority of the laws, shall be allowed the benefit of such regulations respecting repairs, supplies, stay, intercourse, and departure as shall be permitted under the same authority.

In testimony whereof I have caused the seal of the U.S. to be affixed to these presents and sign the same.

Given at the city of Washington the 2d day of July in the year of our Lord 1807 and of the sovereignty and independence of the U.S. the 31st.

These Aggravations

Seventh Annual Message, October 27, 1807

This message is a toned-down version of a more bellicose previous draft. Treasury Secretary Gallatin had objected that it would be better to use mild words while preparing for the possibility of war. Jefferson acceded and substituted the cautious language of the Message below. A compliant Congress promptly adopted legislation to fortify harbors and increase the number of gunboats.

To the Senate and House of Representatives of the United States: Circumstances, fellow citizens, which seriously threatened the peace of our country, have made it a duty to convene you at an earlier period than usual. The love of peace, so much cherished in the bosoms of our citizens, which has so long guided the proceedings of the public councils, and induced forbearance under so many wrongs, may not insure our continuance in the quiet pursuits of industry. The many injuries and depredations committed on our commerce and navigation upon the high seas for years past, the successive innovations on those principles of public law which have been established by the reason and usage of nations as the rule of their intercourse, and the umpire and security of their rights and peace, and all the circumstances which induced the extraordinary mission to London, are already known to you. The instructions given to our ministers were framed in the sincerest spirit of amity and moderation. They accordingly proceeded, in conformity therewith, to propose arrangements which might embrace and settle all the points in difference between us, which might bring us to a mutual understanding on our neutral and national rights, and provide for a commercial intercourse on conditions of some equality. After long and fruitless endeavors to effect the purposes of their mission, and to obtain arrangements within the limits of their instructions, they concluded to sign such as could be obtained, and to send them for consideration, candidly declaring to the other negotiators, at the same time, that they were acting against their instructions, and that their government, therefore, could not be pledged for ratification. Some of the articles proposed might have been admitted on a principle of compromise, but others were too highly disadvantageous, and no sufficient provision was made against the principal source of the irritations and collisions which were constantly endangering the peace of the two nations. The question, therefore, whether a treaty should be accepted in that form could have admitted but of one decision, even had no declarations of the other party impaired our confidence in it. Still anxious not to close the door against friendly adjustment, new modifications were framed, and further concessions authorized than could before have been supposed necessary; and our ministers were instructed to resume their negotiations on these grounds. On this new reference to amicable discussion, we were reposing in confidence, when on the 22d day of June last, by a formal order from the British admiral, the frigate Chesapeake, leaving her port for distant service, was attacked by one of those vessels which had been lying in our harbors under the indulgences of hospitality, was disabled from proceeding, had several of her crew killed, and four taken away. On this outrage no commentaries are necessary. Its character has been pronounced by the indignant voice of our citizens with an emphasis and unanimity never exceeded. I immediately, by proclamation, interdicted our harbors and waters to all British armed vessels, forbade intercourse with them, and uncertain how far hostilities were intended, and the town of Norfolk, indeed, being threatened with immediate attack, a sufficient force was ordered for the protection of that place, and such other preparations commenced and pursued as the prospect rendered proper. An armed vessel of the United States was despatched with instructions to our ministers at London to call on that government for the satisfaction and security required by the outrage. A very short interval ought now to bring the answer, which shall be communicated to you as soon as received; then also, or as soon after as the public interests shall be found to admit, the unratified treaty, and the proceedings relative to it, shall be made known to you.

The aggression thus begun has been continued on the part of the British commanders, by remaining within our waters, in defiance of the authority of the country, by habitual violations of its jurisdiction, and at length by putting to death one of the persons whom they had forcibly taken from on board the Chesapeake. These aggravations necessarily lead to the policy, either of never admitting an armed vessel into our harbors, or of maintaining in every harbor such an armed force as may constrain obedience to the laws, and protect the lives and property of our citizens, against their armed guests. But the expense of such a standing force, and its inconsistence with our principles, dispense with those courtesies which would necessarily call for it, and leave us equally free to exclude the navy, as we are the army, of a foreign power, from entering our limits.

To former violations of maritime rights, another is now added of very extensive effect. The government of that nation has issued an order interdicting all trade by neutrals between ports not in amity with them; and being now at war with nearly every nation on the Atlantic and Mediterranean seas, our vessels are required to sacrifice their cargoes at the first port they touch, or to return home without the benefit of going to any other market. Under this new law of the ocean, our trade on the Mediterranean has been swept away by seizures and condemnations, and that in other seas is threatened with the same fate. . . .

Whether a regular army is to be raised, and to what extent, must depend on the information so shortly expected. In the meantime, I have called on the States for quotas of militia, to be in readiness for present defence; and have, moreover, encouraged the acceptance of volunteers; and I am happy to inform you that these have offered themselves with great alacrity in every part of the Union. They are ordered to be organized, and ready at a moment's warning to proceed on any service to which they may be called, and every preparation within the executive powers has been made to insure us the benefit of early exertions.

I informed Congress at their last session of the enterprises against the public peace, which were believed to be in preparation by Aaron Burr and his associates, of the measures taken to defeat them, and to bring the offenders to justice. Their enterprises were happily defeated by the patriotic exertions of the militia wherever called into action, by the fidelity of the army, and energy of the commander-in-chief in promptly arranging the difficulties presenting themselves on the Sabine, repairing to meet those arising on the Mississippi, and dissipating, before their explosion, plots engendering there. I shall think it my duty to lay before you the proceedings and the evidence publicly exhibited on the arraignment of the principal offenders before the circuit court of Virginia. You will be enabled to judge whether the defeat was in the testimony, in the law, or in the administration of the law; and wherever it shall be found, the legislature alone can apply or originate the remedy. The framers of our constitution certainly supposed they had guarded, as well their government against destruction by treason, as their citizens against oppression, under pretence of it; and if these ends are not attained, it is of importance to inquire by what means, more effectual, they may be secured. . . .

The Principles of Humanity

To Messrs. Thomas, Ellicot, et al., November 13, 1807

Jefferson expresses his liberal sentiments and his hopes for peace—soon to be struck hard blows—to a delegation of Quakers.

FRIENDS AND FELLOW CITIZENS,—I thank you for the address you have kindly presented me, on behalf of that portion of the Society of Friends of which you are the representatives, and I learn with satisfaction their approbation of the principles which have influenced the councils of the general government in their decisions on several important subjects confided to them.

The desire to preserve our country from the calamities and ravages of war, by cultivating a disposition, and pursuing a conduct, conciliatory and friendly to all nations, has been sincerely entertained and faithfully followed. It was dictated by the principles of humanity, the precepts of the gospel, and the general wish of our country, and it was not to be doubted that the Society of Friends, with whom it is a *religious* principle, would sanction it by their support.

The same philanthropic motives have directed the public endeavors to ameliorate the condition of the Indian natives, by introducing among them a knowledge of agriculture and some of the mechanic arts, by encouraging them to resort to these as more certain, and less laborious resources for subsistence than the chase; and by withholding from them the pernicious supplies of ardent spirits. They are our brethren, our neighbors; they may be valuable friends, and troublesome enemies. Both duty and interest then enjoin, that we should extend to them the blessings of civilized life, and prepare their minds for becoming useful members of the American family. In this important work I owe to your society an acknowledgement that we have felt the benefits of their zealous co-operation, and approved its judicious direction towards producing among those people habits of industry, comfortable subsistence, and civilized usages, as preparatory to religious instruction and the cultivation of letters.

Whatever may have been the circumstances which influenced our forefathers to permit the introduction of personal bondage into any part of these States, and to participate in the wrongs committed on an unoffending quarter of the globe, we may rejoice that such circumstances, and such a sense of them, exist no longer. It is honorable to the nation at large that their legislature availed themselves of the first practicable moment for arresting the progress of this great moral and political error; and I sincerely pray with you, my friends, that all the members of the human family may, in the time prescribed by the Father of us all, find themselves securely established in the enjoyment of life, liberty, and happiness.

To Do No Act Which Shall Impair That Principle

To The Representatives of The New Jersey Legislature, December 10, 1807

As time for Presidential nominations approached, Jefferson made it clear to a multitude of remonstrants that he would not run again. He had already served longer than he thought safe for republican government.

The sentiments, fellow citizens, which you are pleased to express in your address of the 4th inst., of attachment and esteem for the general government, and of confidence and approbation of those who direct its councils, cannot but be pleasing to the friends of union generally, and give a new claim on all those who direct the public affairs, for everything which zeal can effect for the good of their country.

It is indeed to be deplored that distant as we are from the storms and convulsions which agitate the European world, the pursuit of an honest neutrality, beyond the reach of reproach, has been insufficient to secure to us the certain enjoyment of peace with those whose interests as well as ours would be promoted by it. What will be the issue of present misunderstandings cannot as yet be foreseen; but the measures adopted for their settlement have been sincerely directed to maintain the rights, the honor, and the peace of our country. Should they fail, the ardor of our citizens to obey the summons of their country, and the offer which you attest, of their lives and fortunes in its support, are worthy of their patriotism, and are pledges of our safety.

The suppression of the late conspiracy by the hand of the people, uplifted to destroy it whenever it reared its head, manifests their fitness for self-government, and the power of a nation, of which every individual feels that his own will is a part of the public authority.

The effect of the public contributions in reducing the national debt, and liberating our resources from the canker of interest, has been so far salutary, and encourages us to continue in the same course; or, if necessarily interrupted, to resume it as soon as practicable.

I perceive with sincere pleasure that my conduct in the chief magistracy has so far met your approbation, that my continuance in that office, after its present term, would be acceptable to you. But that I should lay down my charge at a proper period is as much a duty as to have borne it faithfully. If some termination to the services of the chief magistrate be not fixed by the constitution, or supplied by practice, his office, nominally for years, will, in fact, become for life, and history shows how easily that degenerates into an inheritance. Believing that a representative government, responsible at short periods of election, is that which produces the greatest sum of happiness to mankind, I feel it a duty to do no act which shall essentially impair that principle; and I should unwillingly be the person who, disregarding the sound precedent set by an illustrious predecessor, should furnish the first example of prolongation beyond the second term of office.

Truth also obliges me to add, that I am sensible of that decline which advancing years bring on, and feeling their physical, I ought not to doubt their mental effect. Happy if I am the first to perceive and to obey this admonition of nature, and to solicit a retreat from cares too great for the wearied faculties of age.

Declining a re-election on grounds which cannot but be approved, I am sincerely thankful for the approbation which the Legislature of New Jersey are pleased to manifest of the principles and measures pursued in the management of their affairs; and should I be so fortunate as to carry into retirement the equal approbation and good will of my fellow citizens generally, it will be the comfort of my future days, and will close a service of forty years with the only reward it ever wished.

The Manufacturer and the Husbandman
Side by Side

To The Society of Tammany, or Columbian Order
No. 1, of the City of New York, February 29, 1808

*The consequences of the Embargo Acts, actual or potential,
forced Jefferson to make an about face in his attitude toward
cities and manufacturing.*

I have received your address, fellow citizens, and, thankful
for the expressions so personally gratifying to myself, I contemplate with high satisfaction the ardent spirit it breathes of
love to our country, and of devotion to its liberty and independence. The crisis in which it is placed, cannot but be
unwelcome to those who love peace, yet spurn at a tame
submission to wrong. So fortunately remote from the theatre
of European contests, and carefully avoiding to implicate
ourselves in them, we had a right to hope for an exemption
from the calamities which have afflicted the contending nations, and to be permitted unoffendingly to pursue paths of
industry and peace.

But the ocean, which, like the air, is the common birthright of mankind, is arbitrarily wrested from us, and maxims
consecrated by time, by usage, and by an universal sense of
right, are trampled on by superior force. To give time for
this demoralizing tempest to pass over, one measure only
remained which might cover our beloved country from its
overwhelming fury: an appeal to the deliberate understanding
of our fellow citizens in a cessation of all intercourse with the
belligerent nations, until it can be resumed under the protection of a returning sense of the moral obligations which constitute a law for nations as well as individuals. There can be
no question, in a mind truly American, whether it is best to
send our citizens and property into certain captivity, and then
wage war for their recovery, or to keep them at home, and
to turn seriously to that policy which plants the manufacturer
and the husbandman side by side, and establishes at the door
of everyone that exchange of mutual labors and comforts,
which we have hitherto sought in distant regions, and under

477

perpetual risk of broils with them. Between these alternatives your address has soundly decided, and I doubt not your aid, and that of every real and faithful citizen, towards carrying into effect the measures of your country, and enforcing the sacred principle, that in opposing foreign wrong there must be but one mind.

I receive with sensibility your kind prayers for my future happiness, and I supplicate a protecting providence to watch over your own and our country's freedom and welfare.

A Crop of Sudden and Rank Growth

To Gallatin, August 16, 1808

Secretary of the Treasury Gallatin had advised against the embargo on precisely the grounds of Jefferson's complaint. Better to go to war, said Gallatin, than to try to enforce such a law. Despite three Embargo Acts and one Enforcement Act the crop of frauds grew thicker than ever.

. . . This embargo law is certainly the most embarrassing one we have ever had to execute. I did not expect a crop of so sudden and rank growth of fraud and open opposition by force could have grown up in the U.S. I am satisfied with you that if orders and decrees are not repealed, and a continuance of the embargo is preferred to war (which sentiment is universal here), Congress must legalize all *means* which may be necessary to obtain its *end.* . . .

The Moderation and Firmness Which Govern Our Councils

Eighth Annual Message, November 8, 1808

Significantly, Jefferson's swan-song to Congress fails to mention the unhappy moral and economic consequences of the Embargo Acts. Jefferson reaffirms the need to stimulate "internal manufactures and improvements." Necessity and contingency, in short, had federalized Jefferson to a degree unthinkable before his second administration.

To the Senate and House of Representatives of the United States—It would have been a source, fellow citizens, of much gratification, if our last communications from Europe had enabled me to inform you that the belligerent nations, whose disregard of neutral rights has been so destructive to our commerce, had become awakened to the duty and true policy of revoking their unrighteous edicts. That no means might be omitted to produce this salutary effect, I lost no time in availing myself of the act authorizing a suspension, in whole or in part, of the several embargo laws. Our ministers at London and Paris were instructed to explain to the respective governments there, our disposition to exercise the authority in such manner as would withdraw the pretext on which the aggressions were originally founded, and open the way for a renewal of that commercial intercourse which it was alleged on all sides had been reluctantly obstructed. As each of those governments had pledged its readiness to concur in renouncing a measure which reached its adversary through the incontestable rights of neutrals only, and as the measure had been assumed by each as a retaliation for an asserted acquiescence in the aggressions of the other, it was reasonably expected that the occasion would have been seized by both for evincing the sincerity of their profession, and for restoring to the commerce of the United States its legitimate freedom. The instructions to our ministers with respect to the different belligerents were necessarily modified with reference to their different circumstances, and to the condition annexed by law to the executive power of suspension, requiring a degree of security to our commerce which would not result from a repeal of the decrees of France. Instead of a pledge, therefore, of a suspension of the embargo as to her in case of such a repeal, it was presumed that a sufficient inducement might be found in other considerations, and particularly in the change produced by a compliance with our just demands by one belligerent, and a refusal by the other, in the relations between the other and the United States. To Great Britain, whose power on the ocean is so ascendant, it was deemed not inconsistent with that condition to state explicitly, that on her rescinding her orders in relation to the United States their trade would be opened with her, and remain shut to her enemy, in case of his failure to rescind his decrees also. From France no answer has been received, nor any indication that the requisite change in her decrees is contemplated. The favorable reception of the proposition to Great Britain was the less to be doubted, as her orders of council had not only been referred for their vindication to an acquiescence on the part of the United States no longer to be pretended, but as the arrangement proposed, while it resisted the illegal decrees of France, involved, moreover, substantially, the precise advantages professedly aimed at by the British orders. The arrangement has nevertheless been rejected.

This candid and liberal experiment having thus failed, and no other event having occurred on which a suspension of the embargo by the executive was authorized, it necessarily remains in the extent originally given to it. We have the satisfaction, however, to reflect, that in return for the privations by the measure, and which our fellow citizens in general have borne with patriotism, it has had the important effects of saving our mariners and our vast mercantile property, as well as of affording time for prosecuting the defensive and provisional measures called for by the occasion. It has demonstrated to foreign nations the moderation and firmness which govern our councils, and to our citizens the necessity of uniting in support of the laws and the rights of their country, and has thus long frustrated those usurpations and spoliations which, if resisted, involve war; if submitted to, sacrificed a vital principle of our national independence.

Under a continuance of the belligerent measures which, in defiance of laws which consecrate the rights of neutrals, overspread the ocean with danger, it will rest with the wisdom of Congress to decide on the course best adapted to such a state of things; and bringing with them, as they do, from every part of the Union, the sentiments of our constituents, my confidence is strengthened, that in forming this decision they will, with an unerring regard to the essential rights and interests of the nation, weigh and compare the painful alternatives out of which a choice is to be made. Nor should I do justice to the virtues which on other occasions have marked the character of our fellow citizens, if I did not cherish an equal confidence that the alternative chosen, whatever it may be, will be maintained with all the fortitude and patriotism which the crisis ought to inspire.

The documents containing the correspondences on the subject of the foreign edicts against our commerce, with the instructions given to our ministers at London and Paris, are now laid before you.

The communications made to Congress at their last session explained the posture in which the close of the discussion relating to the attack by a British ship of war on the frigate Chesapeake left a subject on which the nation had manifested so honorable a sensibility. Every view of what had passed authorized a belief that immediate steps would be taken by the British government for redressing a wrong, which, the more it was investigated, appeared the more clearly to require what had not been provided for in the special mission. It is found that no steps have been taken for the purpose. On the contrary, it will be seen, in the documents laid before you, that the inadmissible preliminary which obstructed the adjustment is still adhered to; and, moreover, that it is now brought into connection with the distinct and irrelative case of the orders in council. The instructions which had been given to our ministers at London with a view to facilitate, if necessary, the reparation claimed by the United States, are included in the documents communicated. . . .

I have not thought it necessary in the course of the last season to call for any general detachments of militia or volunteers under the law passed for that purpose. For the ensuing season, however, they will require to be in readiness should their services be wanted. Some small and special detachments have been necessary to maintain the laws of embargo on that portion of our northern frontier which offered peculiar facilities for evasion, but these were replaced as soon as it could be done by bodies of new recruits. By the aid of these, and of the armed vessels called into actual service in other quarters, the spirit of disobedience and abuse which manifested itself early, and with sensible effect while we were unprepared to meet it, has been considerably repressed.

Considering the extraordinary character of the times in which we live, our attention should unremittingly be fixed on the safety of our country. For a people who are free, and who mean to remain so, a well-organized and armed militia is their best security. It is, therefore, incumbent on us, at every meeting, to revise the condition of the militia, and to ask ourselves if it is prepared to repel a powerful enemy at every point of our territories exposed to invasion. Some of the States have paid a laudable attention to this object; but every degree of neglect is to be found among others. Congress alone have power to produce a uniform state of preparation in this great organ of defence; the interests which they so deeply feel in their own and their country's security will present this as among the most important objects of their deliberation.

Under the acts of March 11th and April 23d, respecting arms, the difficulty of procuring them from abroad, during the present situation and dispositions of Europe, induced us to direct our whole efforts to the means of internal supply. The public factories have, therefore, been enlarged, additional machineries erected, and in proportion as artificers can be found or formed, their effect, already more than doubled, may be increased so as to keep pace with the yearly increase of the militia. The annual sums appropriated by the latter act, have been directed to the encouragement of private factories of arms, and contracts have been entered into with individual undertakers to nearly the amount of the first year's appropriation.

The suspension of our foreign commerce, produced by the injustice of the belligerent powers, and the consequent losses and sacrifices of our citizens, are subjects of just concern. The situation into which we have thus been forced, has impelled us to apply a portion of our industry and capital to internal manufactures and improvements. The extent of this conversion is daily increasing, and little doubt remains that the establishments formed and forming will—under the auspices of cheaper materials and subsistence, the freedom of labor from taxation with us, and of protecting duties and prohibitions—become permanent. The commerce with the Indians, too, within our own boundaries, is likely to receive abundant aliment from the same internal source, and will secure to them peace and the progress of civilization, undisturbed by practices hostile to both. . . .

Availing myself of this the last occasion which will occur of addressing the two houses of the legislature at their meeting, I cannot omit the expression of my sincere gratitude for the repeated proofs of confidence manifested to me by themselves and their predecessors since my call to the administration, and the many indulgences experienced at their hands. The same grateful acknowledgments are due to my fellow citizens generally, whose support has been my great encouragement under all embarrassments. In the transaction of their business I cannot have escaped error. It is incident to our imperfect nature. But I may say with truth, my errors have been of the understanding, not of intention; and that the advancement of their rights and interests has been the constant motive for every measure. On these considerations I solicit their indulgence. Looking forward with anxiety to their future destinies, I trust that, in their steady character unshaken by difficulties, in their love of liberty, obedience to law, and support of the public authorities, I see a sure guaranty of the permanence of our republic; and retiring from the charge of their affairs, I carry with me the consolation of a firm persuasion that Heaven has in store for our beloved country long ages to come of prosperity and happiness.

We Have Suffered Some Loss

Reply to Taber Fitch, November 21, 1808

Jefferson publicly defends the embargo. But he was to jettison it shortly as a failure.

Sir,—I have received with great pleasure the address of the republicans of the State of Connecticut, and am particularly sensible of the kindness with which they have viewed my conduct in the direction of their affairs. Having myself highly approved the example of an illustrious predecessor, in voluntarily retiring from a trust, which, if too long continued in the same hands, might become a subject of reasonable uneasiness and apprehension, I could not mistake my own duty when placed in a similar situation.

Our experience so far, has satisfactorily manifested the competence of a republican government to maintain and promote the best interests of its citizens; and every future year, I doubt not, will contribute to settle a question on which reason, and a knowledge of the character and circumstances of our fellow citizens, could never admit a doubt, and much less condemn them as fit subjects to be consigned to the dominion of wealth and force. Although under the pressure of serious evils at this moment, the governments of the other hemisphere cannot boast a more favorable situation. We certainly do not wish to exchange our difficultites for the sanguinary distresses of our fellow men beyond the water. In a state of the world unparalleled in times past, and never again to be expected, according to human probabilities, no form of government has, so far, better shielded its citizens from the prevailing afflictions. By withdrawing awhile from the ocean we have suffered some loss; but we have gathered home our immense capital. Exposed to foreign depredation, we have saved our seamen from the jails of Europe, and gained time to prepare for the defence of our country. The questions of submission, of war, or embargo, are now before our country as unembarrassed as at first. Submission and tribute, if that be our choice, will be no baser now than at the date of the embargo. But if, as I trust, that idea be spurned, we may now decide on the other alternatives of war and embargo, with the advantage of possessing all the means which have been rescued from the grasp of capture. These advantages certainly justify the approbation of the embargo declared in your address, and I have no doubt will ensure that of every candid citizen, who will correctly trace the consequences of any other course.

I thank you for the kind concern you are pleased to express for my future happiness, and offer my sincere prayers for your welfare and prosperity.

Get by Them As You Would by an
Angry Bull

To Thomas Jefferson Randolph, November 24, 1808

Once again Jefferson assumes the part of intellectual and moral cicerone to youth. Thomas Jefferson Randolph was his oldest grandchild.

. . . As much has been secured for you, by your particular position and the acquaintance to which you have been recommended, as could be done towards shielding you from the dangers which surround you. But thrown on a wide world, among entire strangers, without a friend or guardian to advise, so young too, and with so little experience of mankind, your dangers are great, and still your safety must rest on yourself. A determination never to do what is wrong, prudence and good humor, will go far towards securing to you the estimation of the world. When I recollect that at fourteen years of age, the whole care and direction of myself was thrown on myself entirely, without a relation or friend qualified to advise or guide me, and recollect the various sorts of bad company with which I associated from time to time, I am astonished I did not turn off with some of them, and become as worthless to society as they were. I had the good fortune to become acquainted very early with some characters of very high standing, and to feel the incessant wish that I could ever become what they were. Under temptations and difficulties, I would ask myself what would Dr. Small, Mr. Wythe, Peyton Randolph do in this situation? What course in it will insure me their approbation? I am certain that this mode of deciding on my conduct, tended more to correctness than any reasoning powers I possessed. Knowing the even and dignified line they pursued, I could never doubt for a moment which of two courses would be in character for them. Whereas, seeking the same object through a process of moral reasoning, and with the jaundiced eye of youth, I should often have erred. From the circumstances of my position, I was often thrown into the society of horse racers, card players, fox hunters, scientific and professional men, and of dignified men; and many a time have I asked myself, in the enthusiastic moment of the death of a fox, the victory of a favorite horse, the issue of a question eloquently argued at the bar, or in the great council of the nation, well, which of these kinds of reputation should I prefer? That of a horse jockey? a fox hunter? an orator? or the honest advocate of my country's rights? Be assured, my dear Jefferson, that these little returns into ourselves, this self-catechising habit, is not trifling nor useless, but leads to the prudent selection and steady pursuit of what is right.

I have mentioned good humor as one of the preservatives of our peace and tranquillity. It is among the most effectual, and its effect is so well imitated and aided, artificially, by politeness, that this also becomes an acquisition of first rate value. In truth, politeness is artificial good humor, it covers the natural want of it, and ends by rendering habitual a substitute nearly equivalent to the real virtue. It is the practice of sacrificing to those whom we meet in society, all the little conveniences and preferences which will gratify them, and deprive us of nothing worth a moment's consideration; it is the giving a pleasing and flattering turn to our expressions which will conciliate others, and make them pleased with us as well as themselves. How cheap a price for the good will of another! When this is in return for a rude thing said by another, it brings him to his senses, it mortifies and corrects him in the most salutary way, and places him at the feet of your good nature, in the eyes of the company. But in stating prudential rules for our government in society, I must not omit the important one of never entering into dispute or argument with another. I never saw an instance of one of two disputants convincing the other by argument. I have seen many, on their getting warm, becoming rude, and shooting one another. Conviction is the effect of our own dispassionate reasoning, either in solitude, or weighing within ourselves dispassionately, what we hear from others, standing uncommitted in argument ourselves. It was one of the rules which above all others, made Doctor Franklin the most amiable of men in society, "never to contradict anybody." If he was urged to announce an opinion, he did it rather by asking questions, as if for information, or by suggesting doubts. When I hear another express an opinion which is not mine, I say to myself, he has a right to his opinion, as I to mine, why should I question it? His error does me no injury, and shall I become a Don Quixote, to bring all men by force of argument to one opinion? If a fact be misstated, it is probable he is gratified by a belief of it, and I have no right to deprive him of the gratification. If he wants information, he will ask it, and then I will give it in measured terms; but if he still believes his own story, and shows a desire to dispute the fact with me, I hear him and say nothing. It is his affair, not mine, if he prefers error.

There are two classes of disputants most frequently to be met with among us. The first is of young students, just entered the threshold of science, with a first view of its outlines, not yet filled up with the details and modifications which a further progress would bring to their knowledge. The other consists of the ill-tempered and rude men in society, who have taken up a passion for politics. (Good humor and politeness never introduce into mixed society, a question on which they foresee there will be a difference of opinion.) From both of these classes of disputants, my dear Jefferson, keep aloof, as you would from the infected subjects of yellow fever or pestilence. Consider yourself, when with them, as among the patients of Bedlam, needing medical more than moral counsel. Be a listener only, keep within yourself, and endeavor to establish with yourself the habit of silence, especially on politics. In the fevered state of our country, no good can ever result from any attempt to set one of these fiery zealots to rights, either in fact or principle. They are determined as to the facts they will believe, and the opinions on which they will act. Get by them, therefore, as you would by an angry bull; it is not for a man of sense to dispute the road with such an animal. You will be more exposed than others to have these animals shaking their horns at you, because of the relation in which you stand with me. Full of political venom, and willing to see me and to hate me as a chief in the antagonist party, your presence will be to them what the vomit grass is to the sick dog, a nostrum for producing ejaculation. Look upon them exactly with that eye, and pity them as objects to whom you can administer only occasional ease. My character is not within their power. It is in the hands of my fellow citizens at large, and will be consigned to honor or infamy by the verdict of the republican mass of our country, according to what themselves will have seen, not what their enemies and mine shall have said. Never, therefore, consider these puppies in politics as requiring any notice from you, and always show that you are not afraid to leave my character to the umpirage of public opinion. Look steadily to the pursuits which have carried you to Philadelphia, be very select in the society you attach yourself to, avoid taverns, drinkers, smokers, idlers, and dissipated persons generally; for it is with such that broils and contentions arise; and you will find your path more easy and tranquil. The limits of my paper warn me that it is time for me to close with my affectionate adieu.

You Will Unite Yourselves with Us

To Captain Hendrick, the Delawares, Mohicans, and Munries, [n. d.]

Immensely concerned for the well-being of Indians, Jefferson never ceased exhorting them to solve their problems of poverty, infecundity, and loss of land by taking on the habits of white Americans.

My Son and My Children,—I am glad to see you here to receive your salutations, and to return them by taking you by the hand, and renewing to you the assurances of my friendship. I learn with pleasure that the Miamis and Powtawatamies have given you some of their lands on the White River to live on and that you propose to gather there your scattered tribes, and to dwell on it all your days.

The picture which you have drawn, my son, of the increase of our numbers and the decrease of yours is just, the causes are very plain, and the remedy depends on yourselves alone. You have lived by hunting the deer and buffalo—all these have been driven westward; you have sold out on the seaboard and moved westwardly in pursuit of them. As they became scarce there, your food has failed you; you have been a part of every year without food, except the roots and other unwholesome things you could find in the forest. Scanty and unwholesome food produce diseases and death among your children, and hence you have raised few and your numbers have decreased. Frequent wars, too, and the abuse of spirituous liquors, have assisted in lessening your numbers. The whites, on the other hand, are in the habit of cultivating the earth, of raising stocks of cattle, hogs, and other domestic animals, in much greater numbers than they could kill of deer and buffalo. Having always a plenty of food and clothing they raise abundance of children, they double their numbers every twenty years, the new swarms are continually advancing upon the country like flocks of pigeons, and so they will continue to do. Now, my children, if we wanted to diminish our numbers, we would give up the culture of the earth, pursue the deer and buffalo, and be always at war; this would soon reduce us to be as few as you are, and if you wish to increase your numbers you must give up the deer and buffalo, live in peace, and cultivate the earth. You see then, my children, that it depends on yourselves alone to become a numerous and great people. Let me entreat you, therefore, on the lands now given you to begin to give every man a farm; let him enclose it, cultivate it, build a warm house on it, and when he dies, let it belong to his wife and children after him. Nothing is so easy as to learn to cultivate the earth; all your women understand it, and to make it easier, we are always ready to teach you how to make ploughs, hoes, and necessary utensils. If the men will take the labor of the earth from the women they will learn to spin and weave and to clothe their families. In this way you will also raise many children, you will double your numbers every twenty years, and soon fill the land your friends have given you, and your children will never be tempted to sell the spot on which they have been born, raised, have labored and called their own. When once you have property, you will want laws and magistrates to protect your property and persons, and to punish those among you who commit crimes. You will find that our laws are good for this purpose; you will wish to live under them, you will unite yourselves with us, join in our great councils and form one people with us, and we shall all be Americans; you will mix with us by marriage, your blood will run in our veins, and will spread with us over this great island. Instead, then, my children, of the gloomy prospect you have drawn of your total disappearance from the face of the earth, which is true, if you continue to hunt the deer and buffalo and go to war, you see what a brilliant aspect is offered to your future history, if you give up war and hunting. Adopt the culture of the earth and raise domestic animals; you see how from a small family you may become a great nation by adopting the course which from the small beginning you describe has made us a great nation.

On an Equal Footing

To M. Henri Grégoire, Eveque et Senateur à Paris,
February 25, 1809

In this letter Jefferson goes further than ever before in recognizing the equality of Negroes.

Sir,—I have received the favor of your letter of August 17th, and with it the volume you were so kind as to send me on the "Literature of Negroes." Be assured that no person living wishes more sincerely than I do, to see a complete refutation of the doubts I have myself entertained and expressed on the grade of understanding allotted to them by nature, and to find that in this respect they are on a par with ourselves. My doubts were the result of personal observation on the limited sphere of my own State, where the opportunities for the development of their genius were not favorable, and those of exercising it still less so. I expressed them therefore with great hesitation; but whatever be their degree of talent it is no measure of their rights. Because Sir Isaac Newton was superior to others in understanding, he was not therefore lord of the person or property of others. On this subject they are gaining daily in the opinions of nations, and hopeful advances are making towards their re-establishment on an equal footing with the other colors of the human family. I pray you therefore to accept my thanks for the many instances you have enabled me to observe of respectable intelligence in that race of men, which cannot fail to have effect in hastening the day of their relief; and to be assured of the sentiments of high and just esteem and consideration which I tender to yourself with all sincerity.

The Hermit of Monticello

To M. Du Pont de Nemours, March 2, 1809

Several times before Jefferson had sighed relief when leaving public office—only to return to it again. Now he was retiring for good to his family, his farm, his books. Over the years he and Du Pont de Nemours, like himself a philosopher and scientist, carried on a famous correspondence.

. . . Never did a prisoner, released from his chains, feel such relief as I shall on shaking off the shackles of power. Nature intended me for the tranquil pursuits of science, by rendering them my supreme delight. But the enormities of the times in which I have lived, have forced me to take a part in resisting them, and to commit myself on the boisterous ocean of political passions. I thank God for the opportunity of retiring from them without censure, and carrying with me the most consoling proofs of public approbation. I leave everything in the hands of men so able to take care of them, that if we are destined to meet misfortunes, it will be because no human wisdom could avert them. Should you return to the United States, perhaps your curiosity may lead you to visit the hermit of Monticello. He will receive you with affection and delight; hailing you in the meantime with his affectionate salutations and assurances of constant esteem and respect. . . .

P. S. If you return to us, bring a couple of pair of true-bred shepherd's dogs. You will add a valuable possession to a country now beginning to pay great attention to the raising sheep.

PART IX
MONTICELLO: 1809–1826

Introduction

THE SEVENTEEN YEARS Jefferson spent at Monticello after he left the Presidency were full, active, creative years. Until his vigor diminished several months before his death, he wrote thousands of letters into which he poured the distilled essence of his political, social and moral philosophy. He kept abreast of political events, freely giving counsel when solicited, but avoiding criticism of his two close Virginia friends who, for sixteen years, succeeded him as President. He lived long enough to see his family multiply into twelve grandchildren and innumerable great-grandchildren. But he also saw his once great estate sink into insoluble debt.

Posterity is apt to find in his correspondence with John Adams the most impressive event of Jefferson's retirement. They had fallen out in 1800-1801 after twenty-five years of friendship. Adams was not even in Washington for Jefferson's inaugural. They were reconciled in 1812 thanks mostly to the good offices of their mutual friend, Dr. Benjamin Rush. For the next fourteen years these old friends or adversaries wrote each other on their careers, on the great men whom they had known, on theology, on political and moral philosophy, on life in general—their subjects were inexhaustible. Though their differences carried over from the past—Jefferson remaining the spirited radical, Adams the somber conservative—their entire lives had been and were still committed to similar republican principles: civil liberties, religious toleration, a system of strict checks and balances upon the government.

Jefferson's final achievement consisted in single-handedly creating the University of Virginia. From his Bill for the General Diffusion of Knowledge in 1779 to his famous letter to Peter Carr of September 7, 1814, Jefferson had always favored establishing a university as part of a comprehensive system of public education which would allow students to go as far as their talents could take them. Jefferson spent an incredible amount of energy in securing legislative approval for a university. The approval was not given until 1819 when Jefferson was seventy-six; but even this was only the first step. At every subsequent session of the legislature he entreated and cajoled for more money, his plans having in the meantime far outdistanced the available resources. He drew up a plan and a curriculum for the university and then got it under way by carefully bringing together a staff of the best men he could find, by designing the buildings (he was their architect) and by financing it. Jefferson was present at the ceremonies which opened the university in March 1825. Thereafter and until his health gave way he regularly invited the professors and often the students to dine with him at Monticello.

Jefferson's opinions, covering, as always, a multitude of subjects, lost nothing of their freshness, incisiveness and eloquence. To the last he maintained his solidarity with the ideals of the Enlightenment. Never having regarded Christ as divine, having always been a sort of Unitarian with a deistic bent, he readily applauded the Unitarianism of William Ellery Channing when it appeared in 1819. Jefferson's severe animadversions against the "usurpations" of the Supreme Court, of John Marshall in particular, continued a controversy that had begun with Hamilton three decades before. Jefferson remained the implacable defender of democracy, civil liberty, freedom of inquiry and thought and of the Southern, landed interest against the Northern, moneyed and mercantile interests. But he no longer maintained that farmers and planters alone had virtue on their side. The War of 1812, coming soon after his own Embargo Acts, convinced him of the need for manufacturing in the United States.

One event—apart from his personal misfortunes—filled him with anxiety: the conflict over the extension of slavery which eventuated in the Missouri Compromise of 1820. He heard, as he prophesied in his letter to John Holmes, "the fire bell in the night" sounding a tragic knell. Most tragic perhaps was the defeat of Jeffersonian liberalism in the South. His own reasoning in support of the Southern position was a good augur of it. He hoped that the "diffusion" of slaves "over a greater surface would make them individually happier, and proportionately facilitate the accomplishment of emancipation by dividing the burden on a greater number of coadjutors." But instead of emancipation the diffusion of slavery only resulted in its legitimation.

Jefferson's sturdy health began to give way in February 1826. Ten days before he died he received a letter from the mayor of Washington asking his attendance at the fiftieth anniversary celebration of the Declaration of Independence. His reply—his last public utterance—breathes the same heroic and optimistic spirit which nourished him throughout his life. "All eyes are opened, or opening, to the rights of man. The general spread of the light of science has already laid open the palpable truth, that the mass of mankind has not been born with saddles on their backs, nor a favored few booted and spurred, ready to ride them legitimately, by the grace of God. These are grounds of hope for others. For ourselves, let the annual return of this day forever refresh our recollections of these rights, and our undiminished devotion to them."

On Your Verdict I Rest

To the Inhabitants of Albemarle County, April 3, 1809

Jefferson replies to his neighbors' welcome on his return home.

Returning to the scenes of my birth and early life, to the society of those with whom I was raised, and who have been ever dear to me, I receive, fellow-citizens and neighbors, with inexpressible pleasure, the cordial welcome you were so good as to give me. Long absent on duties which the history of a wonderful era made incumbent on those called to them, the pomp, the turmoil, the bustle and splendor of office; have drawn but deeper sighs for the tranquil and irresponsible occupations of private life, for the enjoyment of an affectionate intercourse with you, my neighbors and friends, and the endearments of family love, which nature has given us all, as the sweetner of every hour. For these I gladly lay down the distressing burthen of power, and seek, with my fellow-citizens, repose and safety under the watchful cares, the labors and perplexities of younger and abler minds. The anxieties you express to administer to my happiness, do, of themselves, confer that happiness; and the measure will be complete, if any endeavors to fulfil my duties in the several public stations to which I have been called, have obtained for me the approbation of my country. The part which I have acted on the theatre of public life, has been before them; and to their sentence I submit it; but the testimony of my native county, of the individuals who have known me in private life, to my conduct in its various duties and relations, is the more grateful, as proceeding from eye-witnesses and observers, from triers of the vicinage. Of you, then, my neighbors, I may ask, in the face of the world, "Whose ox have I taken, or whom have I defrauded? Whom have I oppressed, or of whose hand have I received a bribe to blind mine eyes therewith?" On your verdict I rest with conscious security. Your wishes for my happiness are received with just sensibility, and I offer sincere prayers for your own welfare and prosperity.

Everything Which Has Passed Between Us

To Dr. Benjamin Rush, January 16, 1811

Rush, a friend of both Jefferson and Adams, sought to restore their friendship after an estrangement of eleven years. Rush played the shrewd diplomat: he convinced each that he had the confidence of the other; accordingly he gave each the impression that the other sought a reconciliation. Jefferson found it especially difficult—as he explains below—in view of his unhappy exchange with Abigail Adams some years before. In December 1811, Jefferson learned that Adams had said to two visitors: "I always loved Jefferson, and still love him." Jefferson then informed Rush that he needed only "an apposite occasion to express to Mr. Adams my unchanged affections for him." Rush conveyed Jefferson's feelings to Adams who, though skeptical, took up his pen on January 1, 1812. Thus commenced their great correspondence. Adams was seventy-six. Jefferson was sixty-nine.

I receive with sensibility your observations on the discontinuance of friendly correspondence between Mr. Adams and myself, and the concern you take in its restoration. This discontinuance has not proceeded from me, nor from the want of sincere desire and of effort on my part, to renew our intercourse. You know the perfect coincidence of principle and of action, in the early part of the Revolution, which produced a high degree of mutual respect and esteem between Mr. Adams and myself. Certainly no man was ever truer than he was, in that day, to those principles of rational republicanism which, after the necessity of throwing off our monarchy, dictated all our efforts in the establishment of a new government. And although he swerved, afterwards, towards the principles of the English constitution, our friendship did not abate on that account. While he was Vice-President, and I Secretary of State, I received a letter from President Washington, then at Mount Vernon, desiring me to call together the Heads of departments, and to invite Mr. Adams to join us (which, by-the-bye, was the only instance of that being done) in order to determine on some measure which required despatch; and he desired me to act on it, as decided, without again recurring to him. I invited them to dine with me, and after dinner, sitting at our wine, having settled our question, other conversation came on, in which a collision of opinion arose between Mr. Adams and Colonel Hamilton, on the merits of the British constitution, Mr. Adams giving it as his opinion, that, if some of its defects and abuses were corrected, it would be the most perfect constitution of government ever devised by man. Hamilton, on the contrary, asserted, that with its existing vices, it was the most perfect model of government that could be formed; and that the correction of its vices would render it an impracticable government. And this you may be assured was the real line of difference between the political principles of these two gentlemen. Another incident took place on the same occasion, which will further delineate Mr. Hamilton's political principles. The room being hung around with a collection of the portraits of remarkable men, among them were those of Bacon, Newton and Locke, Hamilton asked me who they were. I told him they were my trinity of the three greatest men the world had ever produced, naming them. He paused for some time: "the greatest man," said he, "that ever lived, was Julius Cæsar." Mr. Adams was honest as a politician, as well as a man; Hamilton honest as a man, but, as a politician, believing in the necessity of either force or corruption to govern men.

You remember the machinery which the federalists played off, about that time, to beat down the friends to the real principles of our Constitution, to silence by terror every expression in their favor, to bring us into war with France and alliance with England, and finally to homologize our Constitution with that of England. Mr. Adams, you know, was overwhelmed with feverish addresses, dictated by the fear, and often by the pen, of the *bloody buoy,* and was seduced by them into some open indications of his new principles of government, and in fact, was so elated as to mix with his kindness a little superciliousness towards me. Even Mrs. Adams, with all her good sense and prudence, was sensibly flushed. And you recollect the short suspension of our intercourse, and the circumstance which gave rise to it, which you were so good as to bring to an early explanation, and have set to rights, to the cordial satisfaction of us all. The nation at length passed condemnation on the political principles of the federalists, by refusing to continue Mr. Adams in the Presidency. On the day on which we learned in Philadelphia the vote of the city of New York, which it was well known would decide the vote of the State, and that, again, the vote of the Union, I called on Mr. Adams on some official business. He was very sensibly affected, and accosted me with these words: "Well, I understand that you are to beat me in this contest, and I will only say that I will be as faithful a subject as any you will have." "Mr. Adams," said I, "this is no personal contest between you and me. Two systems of principles on the subject of government divide our fellow citizens into two parties. With one of these you concur, and I with the other. As we have been longer on the public stage than most of those now living, our names happen to be more generally known. One of these parties, therefore, has put your name at its head, the other mine. Were we both to die to-day, to-morrow two other names would be in the place of ours, without any change in the motion of the machinery. Its motion is from its principle, not from you or myself." "I believe you are right," said he, "that we are but passive instruments, and should not suffer this matter to affect our personal dispositions." But he did not long retain this just view of the subject. I have always believed that the thousand calumnies which the federalists, in bitterness of heart, and mortification at their ejection, daily invented against me, were carried to him by their busy intriguers, and made some impression. When the election between Burr and myself was kept in suspense by the federalists, and they were meditating to place the President of the Senate at the head of the government, I called on Mr. Adams with a view to have this desperate measure prevented by his negative. He grew warm in an instant, and said with a vehemence he had not used towards me before, "Sir, the event of the election is within your own power. You have only to say you will do justice to the public creditors, maintain the navy, and not disturb those holding offices, and the government will instantly be put into your hands. We know it is the wish of the people it should be so." "Mr. Adams," said I, "I know not what part of my conduct, in either public or private life, can have authorized a doubt of my fidelity to the public engagements. I say, however, I will not come into the government by capitulation. I will not enter on it, but in perfect freedom to follow the dictates of my own judgment." I had before given the same answer to the same intimation from Gouverneur Morris. "Then," said he, "things must take their course." I turned the conversation to something else, and soon took my leave. It was the first time in our lives we had ever parted with anything like dissatisfaction. And then followed those scenes of midnight appointment, which have been condemned by all men. The last day of his political power, the last hours, and even beyond the midnight, were employed in filling all offices, and especially permanent ones, with the bitterest federalists, and providing for me the alternative, either to execute the government by my enemies, whose study it would be to thwart and defeat all my measures, or to incur the odium of such numerous removals from office, as might bear me down. A little time and reflection effaced in my mind this temporary dissatisfaction with Mr. Adams, and restored me to that just estimate of his virtues and passions, which a long acquaintance had enabled me to fix. And my first wish became that of making his retirement easy by any means in my power; for it was understood he was not rich. I suggested to some republican members of the delegation from his State, the giving him, either directly or indirectly, an office, the most lucrative in that State, and then offered to be resigned, if they thought he would not deem it affrontive. They were of opinion he would take great offence at the offer; and moreover, that the body of republicans would consider such a step in the outset as auguring very ill of the course I meant to pursue. I dropped the idea, therefore, but did not cease to wish for some opportunity of renewing our friendly understanding.

Two or three years after, having had the misfortune to lose a daughter, between whom and Mrs. Adams there had been a considerable attachment, she made it the occasion of writing me a letter, in which, with the tenderest expressions of concern at this event, she carefully avoided a single one of friendship towards myself, and even concluded it with the wishes "of her who *once* took pleasure in subscribing herself your friend, Abigail Adams." Unpromising as was the complexion of this letter, I determined to make an effort towards removing the cloud from between us. This brought on a correspondence which I now enclose for your perusal, after which be so good as to return it to me, as I have never communicated it to any mortal breathing, before. I send it to you, to convince you I have not been wanting either in the desire, or the endeavor to remove this misunderstanding. Indeed, I thought it highly disgraceful to us both, as indicating minds not sufficiently elevated to prevent a public competition from affecting our personal friendship. I soon found from the correspondence that conciliation was desperate, and yielding to an intimation in her last letter, I ceased from further explanation. I have the same good opinion of Mr. Adams which I ever had. I know him to be an honest man, an able one with his pen, and he was a powerful advocate on the floor of Congress. He has been alienated from me, by belief in the lying suggestions contrived for electioneering purposes, that I perhaps mixed in the activity and intrigues of the occasion. My most intimate friends can testify that I was perfectly passive. They would sometimes, indeed, tell me what was going on; but no man ever heard me take part in such conversations; and none ever misrepresented Mr. Adams in my presence, without my asserting his just character. With very confidential persons I have doubtless disapproved of the principles and practices of his administration. This was unavoidable. But never with those with whom it could do him any injury. Decency would have required this conduct from me, if disposition had not; and I am satisfied Mr. Adams' conduct was equally honorable towards me. But I think it part of his character to suspect foul play in those of whom he is jealous, and not easily to relinquish his suspicions.

I have gone, my dear friend, into these details, that you might know everything which had passed between us, might be fully possessed of the state of facts and dispositions, and judge for yourself whether they admit a revival of that friendly intercourse for which you are so kindly solicitous. I shall certainly not be wanting in anything on my part which may second your efforts, which will be the easier with me, inasmuch as I do not entertain a sentiment of Mr. Adams, the expression of which could give him reasonable offence. And I submit the whole to yourself, with the assurance, that whatever be the issue, my friendship and respect for yourself will remain unaltered and unalterable.

Their Minds Keep Pace with Their Bodies

To Dr. Benjamin Rush, August 17, 1811

Jefferson descants on the pleasures—and problems—of returning to his books and thoughts.

Dear Sir,—I write to you from a place ninety miles from Monticello, near the New London of this State, which I visit three or four times a year, and stay from a fortnight to a month at a time. I have fixed myself comfortably, keep some books here, bring others occasionally, am in the solitude of a hermit, and quite at leisure to attend to my absent friends. I note this to show that I am not in a situation to examine the dates of our letters, whether I have overgone the annual period of asking how you do? I know that within that time I have received one or more letters from you, accompanied by a volume of your introductory lectures, for which accept my thanks. I have read them with pleasure and edification, for I acknowledge facts in medicine as far as they go, distrusting only their extension by theory. Having to conduct my grandson through his course of mathematics, I have resumed that study with great avidity. It was ever my favorite one. We have no theories there, no uncertainties remain on the mind; all is demonstration and satisfaction. I have forgotten much, and recover it with more difficulty than when in the vigor of my mind I originally acquired it. It is wonderful to me that old men should not be sensible that their minds keep pace with their bodies in the progress of decay. Our old revolutionary friend Clinton, for example, who was a hero, but never a man of mind, is wonderfully jealous on this head. He tells eternally the stories of his younger days to prove his memory, as if memory and reason were the same faculty. Nothing betrays imbecility so much as the being insensible of it. Had not a conviction of the danger to which an unlimited occupation of the executive chair would expose the republican constitution of our government, made it conscientiously a duty to retire when I did, the fear of becoming a dotard and of being insensible of it, would of itself have resisted all solicitations to remain. I

have had a long attack of rheumatism, without fever and
without pain while I keep myself still. A total prostration of
the muscles of the back, hips and thighs, deprived me of the
power of walking, and leaves it still in a very impaired state.
A pain when I walk, seems to have fixed itself in the hip,
and to threaten permanence. I take moderate rides, without
much fatigue; but my journey to this place, in a hard-going
gig, gave me great sufferings which I expect will be renewed
on my return as soon as I am able. The loss of the power
of taking exercise would be a sore affliction to me. It has been
the delight of my retirement to be in constant bodily activity,
looking after my affairs. It was never damped as the pleasures
of reading are, by the question of *cui bono?* for what object?
I hope your health of body continues firm. Your works show
that of your mind. The habits of exercise which your calling
has given to both, will tend long to preserve them. The seden-
tary character of my public occupations sapped a constitution
naturally sound and vigorous, and draws it to an earlier close.
But it will still last quite as long as I wish it. There is a fulness
of time when men should go, and not occupy too long the
ground to which others have a right to advance. We must
continue while here to exchange occasionally our mutual good
wishes. I find friendship to be like wine, raw when new,
ripened with age, the true old man's milk and restorative
cordial. God bless you and preserve you through a long and
healthy old age.

You and I Have Been Wonderfully Spared

To John Adams, January 21, 1812

Following is Jefferson's reply to Adams' first letter. As Jefferson later explained to Rush, to whom he sent a copy, his letter was designed to offer Adams "ground of reciprocation." Adams was immensely pleased. He wrote Rush that Jefferson's letter contained "all the elegance, purity and sweetness of style of his youth and middle age, and with (what I envy more)—a firmness of finger, and steadiness of chirography, that to me are lost for ever." The "specimen of homespun" to which Jefferson refers below turned out to be not cloth but two volumes called Lectures on Rhetoric and Oratory *"spun from the brain" of Adams' son, John Quincy.*

Dear Sir,—I thank you beforehand (for they are not yet arrived) for the specimens of homespun you have been so kind as to forward me by post. I doubt not their excellence, knowing how far you are advanced in these things in your quarter. Here we do little in the fine way, but in coarse and middling goods a great deal. Every family in the country is a manufactory within itself, and is very generally able to make within itself all the stouter and middling stuffs for its own clothing and household use. We consider a sheep for every person in the family as sufficient to clothe it, in addition to the cotton, hemp and flax which we raise ourselves. For fine stuff we shall depend on your northern manufactories. Of these, that is to say, of company establishments, we have none. We use little machinery. The spinning jenny, and loom with the flying shuttle, can be managed in a family; but nothing more complicated. The economy and thriftiness resulting from our household manufactures are such that they will never again be laid aside; and nothing more salutary for us has ever happened than the British obstructions to our demands for their manufacures. Restore free intercourse when they will, their commerce with us will have totally changed its form, and the articles we shall in future want from them will not exceed their own consumption of our produce.

A letter from you calls up recollections very dear to my

mind. It carries me back to the times when, beset with difficulties and dangers, we were fellow laborers in the same cause, struggling for what is most valuable to man, his right of self-government. Laboring always at the same oar, with some wave ever ahead, threatening to overwhelm us, and yet passing harmless under our bark, we knew not how we rode through the storm with heart and hand, and made a happy port. Still we did not expect to be without rubs and difficulties; and we have had them. First, the detention of the western posts, then the coalition of Pilnitz, outlawing our commerce with France, and the British enforcement of the outlawry. In your day, French depredations; in mine, English, and the Berlin and Milan decrees; now, the English orders of council, and the piracies they authorize. When these shall be over, it will be the impressment of our seamen or something else; and so we have gone on, and so we shall go on, puzzled and prospering beyond example in the history of man. And I do believe we shall continue to grow, to multiply and prosper until we exhibit an association, powerful, wise and happy, beyond what has yet been seen by men. As for France and England, with all their preëminence in science, the one is a den of robbers, and the other of pirates. And if science produces no better fruits than tyranny, murder, rapine and destitution of national morality, I would rather wish our country to be ignorant, honest and estimable, as our neighboring savages are. But whither is senile garrulity leading me? Into politics, of which I have taken final leave. I think little of them and say less. I have given up newspapers in exchange for Tacitus and Thucydides, for Newton and Euclid, and I find myself much the happier. Sometimes, indeed, I look back to former occurrences, in remembrance of our old friends and fellow laborers, who have fallen before us. Of the signers of the Declaration of Independence, I see now living not more than half a dozen on your side of the Potomac, and on this side, myself alone. You and I have been wonderfully spared, and myself with remarkable health, and a considerable activity of body and mind. I am on horseback three or four hours of every day; visit three or four times a year a possession I have ninety miles distant, performing the winter journey on horseback. I walk little, however, a single mile being too much for me, and I live in the midst of my grandchildren, one of whom has lately promoted me to be a great-grandfather. I have heard with pleasure that you also retain good health, and a greater power of exercise in walking than I do. But I would rather have heard this from yourself, and that, writing a letter like mine, full of egotisms, and of details of your health, your habits, occupations and enjoyments, I should have the pleasure of knowing that in the race of life, you do not keep, in its physical decline, the same distance ahead of me which you have done in political honors and achievements. No circumstances have lessened the interest I feel in these particulars respecting yourself; none have suspended for one moment my sincere esteem for you, and I now salute you with unchanged affection and respect.

A Man of Debate Only

On Patrick Henry, 1812, 1824

During their long political careers, Jefferson and Patrick Henry were generally at odds. The first excerpt below is from a letter to William Wirt, who was collecting information on Henry for a biography. Jefferson's remarks of 1824 were taken down by Daniel Webster on his visit to Monticello.

1. April 12, 1812

. . . Another of the great occasions on which he exhibited examples of eloquence such as probably had never been exceeded, was on the question of adopting the new constitution in 1788. To this he was most violently opposed, as is well known; and after its adoption he continued hostile to it, expressing more than any other man in the U.S. his thorough contempt and hatred of General Washington. From being the most violent of all anti-federalists however he was brought over to the new constitution by his Yazoo speculation, before mentioned. The Georgia legislature having declared that transaction fraudulent and void, the depreciated paper which he had bought up to pay for the Yazoo purchase was likely to remain on his hands worth nothing. But Hamilton's founding system came most opportunely to his relief, and suddenly raised his paper from $\frac{2}{6}$ to $2\frac{7}{6}$ the pound. Hamilton became now his idol, and abandoning the republican advocates of the constitution, the federal government on federal principles became his political creed. General Washington flattered him by an appointment to a mission to Spain, which he declined; and by proposing to him the office of Secretary of State, on the most earnest solicitations of General Henry Lee, who pledged himself that Henry should not accept it; for General Washington knew that he was entirely unqualified for it, and moreover that his self-esteem had never suffered him to act as second to any man on earth. I had this fact from information, but that of the mission to Spain is of my own knowledge because after my retiring from the office of Secretary of State

General Washington passed the papers to Mr. Henry through my hands. Mr. Henry's apostasy sunk him to nothing in the estimation of his country. He lost at once all that influence which federalism had hoped, by cajoling him, to transfer with him to itself and a man who through a long and active life had been the idol of his country beyond anyone that ever lived, descended to the grave with less than its indifference, and verified the saying of the philosopher, that no man must be called happy till he is dead. . . .

2. December. 1824

Patrick Henry was originally a barkeeper. He was married very young, and going into some business, on his own account, was a bankrupt before the year was out. When I was about the age of fifteen, I left the school here, to go to college of Williamsburg. I stopped a few days at a friend's in the county of Louisa. There I first saw and became acquainted with Patrick Henry. Having spent the Christmas holidays there, I proceeded to Williamsburg. Some question arose about my admission, as my preparatory studies had not been pursued at the school connected with that institution. This delayed my admission a fortnight, at which time Henry appeared in Williamsburg, and applied for a license to practice law, having commenced the study of it subsequently to the time of my meeting him in Louisa. There were four examiners, Wythe, Pendleton, Peyton Randolph and John Randolph. Wythe and Pendleton at once rejected his application. The two Randolphs, by his importunity, were prevailed upon to sign the license; and having obtained their signatures, he applied again to Pendleton, and after much entreaty and many promises of future study, succeeded in obtaining his. He then turned out for a practising lawyer.

The first case which brought him into notice was a contested election, in which he appeared as counsel before a committee of the House of Burgesses. His second was the Parsons cause, already well known. These and similar efforts soon obtained for him so much reputation that he was elected a member of the legislature. He was as well suited to the times as any man ever was, and it is not now easy to say what we should have done without Patrick Henry. He was far before all in maintaining the spirit of the Revolution. His influence was most extensive with the members from the upper counties, and his boldness and their votes overawed and controlled the more cool or the more timid aristocratic gentlemen of the lower part of the State. His eloquence was peculiar, if indeed it should be called eloquence; for it was impressive and sublime, beyond what can be imagined. Although it was difficult when he had spoken to tell what he had said, yet, while he was speaking, it always seemed directly to the point. When he had spoken in opposition to my opinion, had produced a great effect, and I myself been highly delighted and moved, I have asked myself when he ceased: "what the d—l has he said?" I could never answer the inquiry. His person was of full size, and his manner and voice free and manly. His utterance neither very fast nor very slow. His speeches generally short, from a quarter to a half an hour. His pronunciation was vulgar and vicious, but it was forgotten while he was speaking.

He was a man of very little knowledge of any sort; he read nothing, and had no books. Returning one November from Albemarle court, he borrowed of me Hume's Essays, in two volumes, saying he should have leisure in the winter for reading. In the spring he returned them, and declared he had not been able to go further than twenty or thirty pages in the first volume. He wrote almost nothing—he could not write. The resolutions of '75, which have been ascribed to him, have by many been supposed to have been written by Mr. Johnson, who acted as his second in that occasion; but if they were written by Henry himself, they are not such as to prove any power of composition.

Neither in politics nor in his profession was he a man of business; he was a man of debate only. His biographer[1] says that he read Plutarch every year. I doubt whether he ever read a volume of it in his life. His temper was excellent, and he generally observed decorum in debate. On one or two occasions I have seen him angry, and his anger was terrible; those who witnessed it, were not disposed to rouse it again. In his opinions he was yielding and practicable and not disposed to differ from his friends. In private conversation, he was agreeable and facetious, and, while in genteel society, appeared to understand all the decencies and proprieties

[1] William Wirt (*Sketches of the Life and Character of Patrick Henry* [1817]). Jefferson commented on Wirt's *Sketches:* "It is a poor book written in bad taste, and gives so imperfect an idea of Patrick Henry, that it seems intended to show off the writer more than the subject."

of it; but, in his heart, he preferred low society, and sought it as often as possible. He would hunt in the pine woods of Fluvannah with overseers, and people of that description, living in a camp for a fortnight at a time without a change of raiment. I have been astonished at his command of proper language; how he attained the knowledge of it. I never could find out, as he read so little and conversed little with educated men. After all, it must be allowed that he was our leader in the measures of the Revolution, in Virginia. In that respect more was due to him than any other person. If we had not had him we should probably have got on pretty well, as you did, by a number of men of nearly equal talents, but he left us all far behind.

An American Dialect Will Be Formed

To John Waldo, August 16, 1813

Standing apart from most men of culture in his time, Jefferson had faith in the creative possibilities of the American language. John Waldo was the author of Rudiments of English Grammar.

. . . Grammar . . . [has] never been a favorite with me. The scanty foundation, laid in at school, has carried me through a life of much hasty writing, more indebted for style to reading and memory, than to rules of grammar. I have been pleased to see that in all cases you appeal to usage, as the arbiter of language; and justly consider that as giving law to grammar, and not grammar to usage. I concur entirely with you in opposition to Purists, who would destroy all strength and beauty of style, by subjecting it to a rigorous compliance with their rules. Fill up all the ellipses and syllepses of Tacitus, Sallust, Livy, &c., and the elegance and force of their sententious brevity are extinguished. *"Auferre, trucidare, rapere, falsis nominibus, imperium appellant." "Doerum injurias, diis curae." "Allieni appetens, sui profusus; ardens in cupiditatibus; satis loquentiae, sapientiae parum." "Annibal peto pacem." "Per diem Sol non* uret *te, neque Luna per noctem."*[1] Wire-draw these expressions by filling up the whole syntax and sense, and they become dull paraphrases on rich sentiments. We may say then truly with Quinctilian, *"Aliud est Grammaticé, aliud Latiné loqui."*[2] I am no friend, therefore, to what is called *Purism,* but a zealous one to the *Neology* which has introduced these two words without the authority of any dictionary. I consider

---

[1] "Robbery, slaughter, and plunder they label with the false name of 'empire.'" "The injuries of the gods are the concerns of the gods." "Ever niggardly with others, ever generous with himself; fiery in his desires; adequate in eloquence, inadequate in wisdom." "I, Hannibal, seek peace." "Let not the sun burn you during the day, nor the moon during the night."

[2] "It is one thing to be a professor of language, but another to speak Latin."

the one as destroying the nerve and beauty of language, while the other improves both, and adds to its copiousness. I have been not a little disappointed, and made suspicious of my own judgment, on seeing the Edinburgh Reviews, the ablest critics of the age, set their faces against the introduction of new words into the English language; they are particularly apprehensive that the writers of the United States will adulterate it. Certainly so great growing a population, spread over such an extent of country, with such a variety of climates, of productions, of arts, must enlarge their language, to make it answer its purpose of expressing all ideas, the new as well as the old. The new circumstances under which we are placed, call for new words, new phrases, and for the transfer of old words to new objects. An American dialect will therefore be formed; so will a West-Indian and Asiatic, as a Scotch and an Irish are already formed. But whether will these adulterate, or enrich the English language? Has the beautiful poetry of Burns, or his Scottish dialect, disfigured it? Did the Athenians consider the Doric, the Ionian, the Aeolic, and other dialects, as disfiguring or as beautifying their language? Did they fastidiously disavow Herodotus, Pindar, Theocritus, Sappho, Alcæus, or Grecian writers? On the contrary, they were sensible that the variety of dialects, still infinitely varied by poetical license, constituted the riches of their language, and made the Grecian Homer the first of poets, as he must ever remain, until a language equally ductile and copious shall again be spoken.

Every language has a set of terminations, which make a part of its peculiar idiom. Every root among the Greeks was permitted to vary its termination, so as to express its radical idea of the form of any one of the parts of speech; to wit, as a noun, an adjective, a verb, participle, or adverb; and each of these parts of speech again, by still varying the termination, could vary the shade of idea existing in the mind. . . .

The Grounds of This Are Virtue and Talents

To John Adams, October 28, 1813

*On July 9, 1813 Adams wrote Jefferson: ". . . I read in Greek
. . . a couplet, the sense of which was: 'Nobility in men is
worth as much as it is in horses, asses, or rams; but the
meanest blooded puppy in the world, if he gets a little money,
is as good a man as the best of them.' Yet birth and wealth
together have prevailed over virtue and talents in all ages.
The many will acknowledge no other* aristoi." *Adams returned to the same theme on September 15: "I asked you in
a former letter how far we were in the science of aristocracy
since Theognis' Stallions, Jacks and Rams? . . . How shall we
get rid of this aristocracy? It is entailed upon us forever."
Following is a part of Jefferson's famous reply.*

. . . The selecting the best male for a Harem of well chosen
females also, which Theognis seems to recommend from the
example of our sheep and asses, would doubtless improve the
human, as it does the brute animal, and produce a race of
veritable [aristoi]. For experience proves, that the moral and
physical qualities of man, whether good or evil, are trans-
missible in a certain degree from father to son. But I suspect
that the equal rights of men will rise up against this privileged
Solomon and his Harem, and oblige us . . . to content ourselves with the accidental aristoi produced by the fortuitous
concourse of breeders. For I agree with you that there is a
natural aristocracy among men. The grounds of this are virtue
and talents. Formerly, bodily powers gave place among the
aristoi. But since the invention of gunpowder has armed the
weak as well as the strong with missile death, bodily strength,
like beauty, good humor, politeness and other accomplishments, has become but an auxiliary ground of distinction.
There is also an artificial aristocracy, founded on wealth and
birth, without either virtue or talents; for with these it would
belong to the first class. The natural aristocracy I consider as
the most precious gift of nature, for the instruction, the trusts,
and government of society. And indeed, it would have been
inconsistent in creation to have formed man for the social

state, and not to have provided virtue and wisdom enough to manage the concerns of the society. May we not even say, that that form of government is the best, which provides the most effectually for a pure selection of these natural aristoi into the offices of government? The artificial aristocracy is a mischievous ingredient in government, and provision should be made to prevent its ascendency. On the question, what is the best provision, you and I differ; but we differ as rational friends, using the free exercise of our own reason, and mutually indulging its errors. You think it best to put the pseudo-aristoi into a separate chamber of legislation, where they may be hindered from doing mischief by their co-ordinate branches, and where, also, they may be a protection to wealth against the Agrarian and plundering enterprises of the majority of the people. I think that to give them power in order to prevent them from doing mischief, is arming them for it, and increasing instead of remedying the evil. For if the co-ordinate branches can arrest their action, so may they that of the co-ordinates. Mischief may be done negatively as well as positively. Of this, a cabal in the Senate of the United States has furnished many proofs. Nor do I believe them necessary to protect the wealthy; because enough of these will find their way into every branch of the legislation, to protect themselves. From fifteen to twenty legislatures of our own, in action for thirty years past, have proved that no fears of an equalization of property are to be apprehended from them. I think the best remedy is exactly that provided by all our constitutions, to leave to the citizens the free election and separation of the aristoi from the pseudo-aristoi, of the wheat from the chaff. In general they will elect the really good and wise. In some instances, wealth may corrupt, and birth blind them; but not in sufficient degree to endanger the society.

It is probable that our difference of opinion may, in some measure, be produced by a difference of character in those among whom we live. From what I have seen of Massachusetts and Connecticut myself, and still more from what I have heard, and the character given of the former by yourself (vol. 1, page 111), who know them so much better, there seems to be in those two States a traditionary reverence for certain families, which has rendered the offices of the government nearly hereditary in those families. I presume that from an early period of your history, members of those families happening to possess virtue and talents, have honestly exercised them for the good of the people, and by their services have endeared their names to them. In coupling Connecticut with you, I mean it politically only, not morally. For having made the Bible the common law of their land, they seem to have modeled their morality on the story of Jacob and Laban. But although this hereditary succession to office with you, may, in some degree, be founded in real family merit, yet in a much higher degree, it has proceeded from your strict alliance of Church and State. These families are canonised in the eyes of the people on common principles, "you tickle me, and I will tickle you." In Virginia we have nothing of this. Our clergy, before the revolution, having been secured against rivalship by fixed salaries, did not give themselves the trouble of acquiring influence over the people. Of wealth, there were great accumulations in particular families, handed down from generation to generation, under the English law of entails. But the only object of ambition for the wealthy was a seat in the King's Council. All their court then was paid to the crown and its creatures; and they Philipised in all collisions between the King and the people. Hence they were unpopular; and that unpopularity continues attached to their names. A Randolph, a Carter, or a Burwell must have great personal superiority over a common competitor to be elected by the people even at this day. At the first session of our legislature after the Declaration of Independence, we passed a law abolishing entails. And this was followed by one abolishing the privilege of primogeniture, and dividing the lands of intestates equally among all their children, or other representatives. These laws, drawn by myself, laid the axe to the foot of pseudo-aristocracy. And had another which I prepared been adopted by the legislature, our work would have been complete. It was a bill for the more general diffusion of learning. This proposed to divide every county into wards of five or six miles square, like your townships; to establish in each ward a free school for reading, writing and common arithmetic; to provide for the annual selection of the best subjects from these schools, who might receive, at the public expense, a higher degree of education at a district school; and from these district schools to select a certain number of the most promising subjects, to be completed at an University, where all the useful sciences should be taught. Worth and genius would thus have been sought out from every condition of life, and completely prepared by education for defeating the competition of wealth and birth for public trusts. My proposition had, for a further object, to impart to these wards those portions of self-government for which they are best qualified, by confiding to them the care of their poor, their roads, police, elections, the nomination of jurors, administration of justice in small cases, elementary exercises of militia; in short, to have made them little republics, with a warden at the head of each, for all those concerns which, being under their eye, they would better manage than the larger republics of the county or State. A general call of ward meetings by their wardens on the same day through the State, would at any time produce the genuine sense of the people on any required point, and would enable the State to act in mass, as your people have so often done, and with so much effect by their town meetings. The law for religious freedom, which made a part of this system, having put down the aristocracy of the clergy, and restored to the citizen the freedom of the mind, and those of entails and descents nurturing an equality of condition among them, this on education would have raised the mass of the people to the high ground of moral respectability necessary to their own safety, and to orderly government; and would have completed the great object of qualifying them to select the veritable aristoi, for the trusts of government, to the exclusion of the pseudalists; . . . Although this law has not yet been acted on but in a small and inefficient degree, it is still considered as before the legislature, with other bills of the revised code, not yet taken up, and I have great hope that some patriotic spirit will, at a favorable moment, call it up, and make it the key-stone of the arch of our government.

With respect to aristocracy, we should further consider, that before the establishment of the American States, nothing was known to history but the man of the old world, crowded within limits either small or overcharged, and steeped in the vices which that situation generates. A government adapted to such men would be one thing; but a very different one, that for the man of these States. Here every one may have land to labor for himself, if he chooses; or, preferring the exercise of any other industry, may exact for it such compensation as not only to afford a comfortable subsistence, but wherewith to provide for a cessation from labor in old age. Every one, by his property, or by his satisfactory situation, is interested in the support of law and order. And such men may safely and advantageously reserve to themselves a whole-some control over their public affairs, and a degree of free-dom, which, in the hands of the *canaille* of the cities of Europe, would be instantly perverted to the demolition and destruction of everything public and private. The history of the last twenty-five years of France and of the last forty years in America, nay of its last two hundred years, proves the truth of both parts of this observation.

But even in Europe a change has sensibly taken place in the mind of man. Science had liberated the ideas of those who read and reflect, and the American example had kindled feelings of right in the people. An insurrection has conse-quently begun, of science, talents, and courage, against rank and birth, which have fallen into contempt. It has failed in its first effort, because the mobs of the cities, the instrument used for its accomplishment, debased by ignorance, poverty, and vice, could not be restrained to rational action. But the world will recover from the panic of this first catastrophe. Science is progressive, and talents and enterprise on the alert. Resort may be had to the people of the country, a more governable power from their principles and subordination; and rank, and birth, and tinsel-aristocracy will finally shrink into insignificance, even there. This, however, we have no right to meddle with. It suffices for us, if the moral and physical condition of our own citizens qualifies them to select the able and good for the direction of their government, with a recurrence of elections at such short periods as will enable them to displace an unfaithful servant, before the mischief he meditates may be irremediable. . . .

A Wise, a Good, and a Great Man

On George Washington, January 2, 1814

The few words Jefferson requires to delineate Washington's character speak volumes. History has since then pretty much born out his judgments. The excerpts below are from a letter to Dr. Walter Jones.

. . . I think I knew General Washington intimately and thoroughly; and were I called on to delineate his character, it should be in terms like these.

His mind was great and powerful, without being of the very first order; his penetration strong, though not so acute as that of a Newton, Bacon, or Locke; and as far as he saw, no judgment was ever sounder. It was slow in operation, being little aided by invention or imagination, but sure in conclusion. Hence the common remark of his officers, of the advantage he derived from councils of war, where hearing all suggestions, he selected whatever was best; and certainly no General ever planned his battles more judiciously. But if deranged during the course of the action, if any member of his plan was dislocated by sudden circumstances, he was slow in readjustment. The consequence was, that he often failed in the field, and rarely against an enemy in station, as at Boston and York. He was incapable of fear, meeting personal dangers with the calmest unconcern. Perhaps the strongest feature in his character was prudence, never acting until every circumstance, every consideration, was maturely weighed; refraining if he saw a doubt, but, when once decided, going through with his purpose, whatever obstacles opposed. His integrity was most pure, his justice the most inflexible I have ever known, no motives of interest or consanguinity, of friendship or hatred, being able to bias his decision. He was, indeed, in every sense of the words, a wise, a good, and a great man. His temper was naturally high toned; but reflection and resolution had obtained a firm and habitual ascendency over it. If ever, however, it broke its bonds, he was most tremendous in his wrath. In his expenses he was honorable, but exact; liberal in contributions to whatever promised utility; but frowning and unyielding on all visionary projects, and all unworthy calls on his charity. His heart was not warm in its affections; but he exactly calculated every man's value, and gave him a solid esteem proportioned to it. His person, you know, was fine, his stature exactly what one would wish, his deportment easy, erect and noble; the best horseman of his age, and the most graceful figure that could be seen on horseback. Although in the circle of his friends, where he might be unreserved with safety, he took a free share in conversation, his colloquial talents were not above mediocrity, possessing neither copiousness of ideas, nor fluency of words. In public, when called on for a sudden opinion, he was unready, short and embarrassed. Yet he wrote readily, rather diffusely, in an easy and correct style. This he had acquired by conversation with the world, for his education was merely reading, writing and common arithmetic, to which he added surveying at a later day. His time was employed in action chiefly, reading little, and that only in agriculture and English history. His correspondence became necessarily extensive, and, with journalizing his agricultural proceedings, occupied most of his leisure hours within doors. On the whole, his character was, in its mass, perfect, in nothing bad, in few points indifferent; and it may truly be said, that never did nature and fortune combine more perfectly to make a man great, and to place him in the same constellation with whatever worthies have merited from man an everlasting remembrance. For his was the singular destiny and merit, of leading the armies of his country successfully through an arduous war, for the establishment of its independence; of conducting its councils through the birth of a government, new in its forms and principles, until it had settled down into a quiet and orderly train; and of scrupulously obeying the laws through the whole of his career, civil and military, of which the history of the world furnishes no other example.

How, then, can it be perilous for you to take such a man on your shoulders? I am satisfied the great body of republicans think of him as I do. We were, indeed, dissatisfied with him on his ratification of the British treaty. But this was short lived. We knew his honesty, the wiles with which he was encompassed, and that age had already began to relax the firmness of his purposes; and I am convinced he is more deeply seated in the love and gratitude of the republicans, than in the Pharisaical homage of the federal monarchists. For he was no monarchist from preference of his judgment. The soundness of that gave him correct views of the rights of man, and his severe justice devoted him to them. He has often declared to me that he considered our new constitution as an experiment on the practicability of republican government, and with what dose of liberty man could be trusted for his own good; that he was determined the experiment should have a fair trial, and would lose the last drop of his blood in support of it. And these declarations he repeated to me the oftener and more pointedly, because he knew my suspicions of Colonel Hamilton's views, and probably had heard from him the same declarations which I had, to wit, "that the British constitution, with its unequal representation, corruption and other existing abuses, was the most perfect government which had ever been established on earth, and that a reformation of those abuses would make it an impracticable government." I do believe that General Washington had not a firm confidence in the durability of our government. He was naturally distrustful of men, and inclined to gloomy apprehensions; and I was ever persuaded that a belief that we must at length end in something like a British constitution, had some weight in his adoption of the ceremonies of levees, birth-days, pompous meetings with Congress, and other forms of the same character, calculated to prepare us gradually for a change which he believed possible, and to let it come on with as little shock as might be to the public mind.

These are my opinions of General Washington, which I would vouch at the judgment seat of God, having been formed on an acquaintance of thirty years. I served with him in the Virginia legislature from 1769 to the Revolutionary war, and again, a short time in Congress, until he left us to take command of the army. During the war and after it we corresponded occasionally, and in the four years of my continuance in the office of Secretary of State, our intercourse was daily, confidential and cordial. After I retired from that office, great and malignant pains were taken by our federal monarchists, and not entirely without effect, to make him view me as a theorist, holding French principles of government, which would lead infallibly to licentiousness and anarchy. And to this he listened the more easily, from my known disapprobation of the British treaty. I never saw him afterwards, or these malignant insinuations should have been dissipated before his just judgment, as mists before the sun. I felt on his death, with my countrymen, that "verily a great man hath fallen this day in Israel. . . ."

Your Solitary but Welcome Voice

To Edward Coles, August 25, 1814

Coles, a friend and neighbor of Jefferson, now secretary to President Madison, had long favored abolishing slavery. Later, as governor of Illinois, he heroically won the fight to outlaw slavery in that state.

Dear Sir,—Your favour of July 31, was duly received, and was read with peculiar pleasure. The sentiments breathed through the whole do honor to both the head and heart of the writer. Mine on the subject of slavery of negroes have long since been in possession of the public, and time has only served to give them stronger root. The love of justice and the love of country plead equally the cause of these people, and it is a moral reproach to us that they should have pleaded it so long in vain, and should have produced not a single effort, nay I fear not much serious willingness to relieve them & ourselves from our present condition of moral & political reprobation. From those of the former generation who were in the fulness of age when I came into public life, which was while our controversy with England was on paper only, I soon saw that nothing was to be hoped. Nursed and educated in the daily habit of seeing the degraded condition, both bodily and mental, of those unfortunate beings, not reflecting that that degradation was very much the work of themselves & their fathers, few minds have yet doubted but that they were as legitimate subjects of property as their horses and cattle. The quiet and monotonous course of colonial life has been disturbed by no alarm, and little reflection on the value of liberty. And when alarm was taken at an enterprize on their own, it was not easy to carry them to the whole length of the principles which they invoked for themselves. In the first or second session of the Legislature after I became a member, I drew to this subject the attention of Col. Bland, one of the oldest, ablest, & most respected members, and he undertook to move for certain moderate extensions of the protection of the laws to these people. I seconded his motion, and, as a younger member, was more spared in the debate; but he was denounced as an enemy of his country, & was treated with the grossest indecorum. From an early stage of our revolution other & more distant duties were assigned to me, so that from that time till my return from Europe in 1789, and I may say till I returned to reside at home in 1809, I had little opportunity of knowing the progress of public sentiment here on this subject. I had always hoped that the younger generation receiving their early impressions after the flame of liberty had been kindled in every breast, & had become as it were the vital spirit of every American, that the generous temperament of youth, analogous to the motion of their blood, and above the suggestions of avarice, would have sympathized with oppression wherever found, and proved their love of liberty beyond their own share of it. But my intercourse with them, since my return has not been sufficient to ascertain that they had made towards this point the progress I had hoped. Your solitary but welcome voice is the first which has brought this sound to my ear; and I have considered the general silence which prevails on this subject as indicating an apathy unfavorable to every hope. Yet the hour of emancipation is advancing, in the march of time. . . .

Every Branch of Science

To Peter Carr, September 7, 1814

Jefferson was given the chance to return to a favorite project, a school system which would accept men of talent and virtue, with the establishment in 1813 of Central College in Charlottesville, the President of whose Board of Trustees was Peter Carr, his nephew. Gathering advice from many friends, Jefferson drew up the plan given below. The plan was soon after printed in the Richmond Enquirer. *In consequence, the state legislature incorporated Central College, appropriated $600,000 for it, and ordered a formal plan drafted on the lines of Jefferson's recommendations. It thus became the basis for the establishment of the University of Virginia in 1819.*

Dear Sir,—On the subject of the academy or college proposed to be established in our neighborhood, I promised the trustees that I would prepare for them a plan, adapted, in the first instance, to our slender funds, but susceptible of being enlarged, either by their own growth or by accession from other quarters.

I have long entertained the hope that this, our native State, would take up the subject of education, and make an establishment, either with or without incorporation into that of William and Mary, where every branch of science, deemed useful at this day, should be taught in its highest degree. With this view, I have lost no occasion of making myself acquainted with the organization of the best seminaries in other countries, and with the opinions of the most enlightened individuals, on the subject of the sciences worthy of a place in such an institution. In order to prepare what I have promised our trustees, I have lately revised these several plans with attention; and I am struck with the diversity of arrangement observable in them—no two alike. Yet, I have no doubt that these several arrangements have been the subject of mature reflection, by wise and learned men, who, contemplating local circumstances, have adapted them to the conditions of the section of society for which they have been framed. I am strengthened in this conclusion by an examination of each separately, and a conviction that no one of them, if adopted without change, would be suited to the circumstances and pursuit of our country. The example they set, then, is authority for us to select from their different institutions the materials which are good for us, and, with them, to erect a structure, whose arrangement shall correspond with our own social condition, and shall admit of enlargement in proportion to the encouragement it may merit and receive. As I may not be able to attend the meetings of the trustees, I will make you the depository of my ideas on the subject, which may be corrected, as you proceed, by the better view of others, and adapted, from time to time, to the prospects which open upon us, and which cannot be specifically seen and provided for.

In the first place, we must ascertain with precision the object of our institution, by taking a survey of the general field of science, and marking out the portion we mean to occupy at first, and the ultimate extension of our views beyond that, should we be enabled to render it, in the end, as comprehensive as we would wish.

1. Elementary schools.

It is highly interesting to our country, and it is the duty of its functionaries, to provide that every citizen in it should receive an education proportioned to the condition and pursuits of his life. The mass of our citizens may be divided into two classes—the laboring and the learned. The laboring will need the first grade of education to qualify them for their pursuits and duties; the learned will need it as a foundation for further acquirements. A plan was formerly proposed to the legislature of this State for laying off every county into hundreds or wards of five or six miles square, within each of which should be a school for the education of the children of the ward, wherein they should receive three years' instruction gratis, in reading, writing, arithmetic as far as fractions, the roots and ratios, and geography. The Legislature at one time tried an ineffectual expedient for introducing this plan, which having failed, it is hoped they will some day resume it in a more promising form.

2. General schools.

At the discharging of the pupils from the elementary schools, the two classes separate—those destined for labor will engage in the business of agriculture, or enter into apprenticeships to such handicraft art as may be their choice; their companions, destined to the pursuits of science, will proceed to the college, which will consist, 1st of general schools; and, 2d, of professional schools. The general schools will constitute the second grade of education.

The learned class may still be subdivided into two sections:

1, Those who are destined for learned professions, as means of livelihood; and, 2, The wealthy, who, possessing independent fortunes, may aspire to share in conducting the affairs of the nation, or to live with usefulness and respect in the private ranks of life. Both of these sections will require instruction in all the higher branches of science; the wealthy to qualify them for either public or private life; the professional section will need those branches, especially, which are the basis of their future profession, and a general knowledge of the others, as auxiliary to that, and necessary to their standing and association with the scientific class. All the branches, then, of useful science, ought to be taught in the general schools, to a competent degree, in the first instance. These sciences may be arranged into three departments, not rigorously scientific, indeed, but sufficiently so for our purposes. These are, I. Language; II. Mathematics; III. Philosophy.

I. Language. In the first department, I would arrange a distinct science. 1, Languages and History, ancient and modern; 2, Grammar; 3, Belles Lettres; 4, Rhetoric and Oratory; 5, A school for the deaf, dumb and blind. History is here associated with languages, not as a kindred subject, but on the principle of economy, because both may be attained by the same course of reading, if books are selected with that view.

II. Mathematics. In the department of Mathematics, I should give place distinctly: 1, Mathematics pure; 2, Physico-Mathematics; 3, Physics; 4, Chemistry; 5, Natural History, to wit: Mineralogy; 6, Botany; and 7, Zoology; 8, Anatomy; 9, the Theory of Medicine.

III. Philosophy. In the Philosophical department, I should distinguish: 1, Ideology; 2, Ethics; 3, the Law of Nature and Nations; 4, Government; 5, Political Economy.

But, some of these terms being used by different writers, in different degrees of extension, I shall define exactly what I mean to comprehend in each of them.

I. 3. Within the term of Belles Lettres I include poetry and composition generally, and criticism.

II. 1. I consider pure mathematics as the science of, 1, Numbers, and 2, Measure in the abstract; that of numbers comprehending Arithmetic, Algebra and Fluxions; that of Measure (under the general appellation of Geometry), comprehending Trigonometry, plane and spherical, conic sections, and transcendental curves.

II. 2. Physico-Mathematics treat of physical subjects by the aid of mathematical calculation. These are Mechanics, Statics, Hydrostatics, Hydrodynamics, Navigation, Astronomy, Geography, Optics, Pneumatics, Acoustics.

II. 3. Physics, or Natural Philosophy (not entering the limits of Chemistry) treat of natural substances, their properties, mutual relations and action. They particularly examine the subjects of motion, action, magnetism, electricity, galvanism, light, meteorology, with an etc. not easily enumerated. These definitions and specifications render immaterial the question whether I use the generic terms in the exact degree of comprehension in which others use them; to be understood is all that is necessary to the present object.

3. Professional Schools.

At the close of this course the students separate; the wealthy retiring, with a sufficient stock of knowledge, to improve themselves to any degree to which their views may lead them, and the professional section to the professional schools, constituting the third grade of education, and teaching the particular sciences which the individuals of this section mean to pursue, with more minuteness and detail than was within the scope of the general schools for the second grade of instruction. In these professional schools each science is to be taught in the highest degree it has yet attained. They are to be the

1st Department, the fine arts, to wit: Civil Architecture, Gardening, Painting, Sculpture, and the Theory of Music; the

2d Department, Architecture, Military and Naval; Projectiles, Rural Economy (comprehending Agriculture, Horticulture and Veterinary), Technical Philosophy, the Practice of Medicine, Materia Medica, Pharmacy and Surgery. In the

3d Department, Theology and Ecclesiastical History; Law, Municipal and Foreign.

To these professional schools will come those who separated at the close of their first elementary course, to wit:

The lawyer to the law school.

The ecclesiastic to that of theology and ecclesiastical history.

The physician to those of medicine, materia medica, pharmacy and surgery.

The military man to that of military and naval architecture and projectiles.

The agricultor to that of rural economy.

The gentleman, the architect, the pleasure gardener, painter and musician to the school of fine arts.

And to that of technical philosophy will come the mariner, carpenter, shipwright, pumpmaker, clockmaker, machinist, optician, metallurgist, founder, cutler, druggist, brewer, vintner, distiller, dyer, painter, bleacher, soapmaker, tanner, powdermaker, saltmaker, glassmaker, to learn as much as shall be necessary to pursue their art understandingly, of the sciences of geometry, mechanics, statics, hydrostatics, hydraulics, hydrodynamics, navigation, astronomy, geography, optics, pneumatics, physics, chemistry, natural history, botany, mineralogy and pharmacy.

The school of technical philosophy will differ essentially in its functions from the other professional schools. The others are instituted to ramify and dilate the particular sciences taught in the schools of the second grade on a general scale only. The technical school is to abridge those which were taught there too much *in extenso* for the limited wants of the artificer or practical man. These artificers must be grouped together, according to the particular branch of science in which they need elementary and practical instruction; and a special lecture or lectures should be prepared for each group. And these lectures should be given in the evening, so as not to interrupt the labors of the day. The school, particularly, should be maintained wholly at the public expense, on the same principles with that of the ward schools. Through the whole of the collegiate course, at the hours of recreation on certain days, all the students should be taught the manual exercise; military evolutions and manœuvers should be under a standing organization as a military corps, and with proper officers to train and command them.

A tabular statement of this distribution of the sciences will place the system of instruction more particularly in view:

1st or Elementary Grade in the Ward Schools.
Reading, Writing, Arithmetic, Geography.

2d, or General Grade.
1. Language and History, ancient and modern.
2. Mathematics, viz: Mathematics pure, Physico-Mathematics, Physics, Chemistry, Anatomy, Theory of Medicine, Zoology, Botany and Mineralogy.
3. Philosophy, viz: Ideology, and Ethics, Law of Nature and Nations, Government, Political Economy.

3d, or Professional Grades

Theology and Ecclesiastical History; Law, Municipal and Foreign; Practice of Medicine; Materia Medica and Pharmacy; Surgery; Architecture, Military and Naval, and Projectiles; Technical Philosophy; Rural Economy; Fine Arts.

On this survey of the field of science, I recur to the question, what portion of it we mark out for the occupation of our institution? With the first grade of education we shall have nothing to do. The sciences of the second grade are our first object; and, to adapt them to our slender beginnings, we must separate them into groups, comprehending many sciences each, and greatly more, in the first instance, than ought to be imposed on, or can be competently conducted by a single professor permanently. They must be subdivided from time to time, as our means increase, until each professor shall have no more under his care than he can attend to with advantage to his pupils and ease to himself. For the present, we may group the sciences into professorships, as follows, subject, however, to be changed, according to the qualifications of the persons we may be able to engage.

I. Professorship.

Languages and History, ancient and modern.
Belles-Lettres, Rhetoric and Oratory.

II. Professorship.

Mathematics pure, Physico-Mathematics.
Physics, Anatomy, Medicine, Theory.

III. Professorship.

Chemistry, Zoology, Botany, Mineralogy.

IV. Professorship.

Philosophy.

The organization of the branch of the institution which respects its government, police and economy, depending on principles which have no affinity with those of its institution, may be the subject of separate and subsequent consideration.

With this tribute of duty to the board of trustees, accept assurances of my great esteem and consideration.

Experience Has Taught Me

To Benjamin Austin, January 9, 1816

Jefferson explains his position now on manufacturing—a position toward which he had been tending since the turn of the century. Austin was a leader of the Massachusetts Republican party.

. . . You tell me I am quoted by those who wish to continue our dependence on England for manufactures. There was a time when I might have been so quoted with more candor, but within the thirty years which have since elapsed, how are circumstances changed! We were then in peace. Our independent place among nations was acknowledged. A commerce which offered the raw material in exchange for the same material after receiving the last touch of industry, was worthy of welcome to all nations. It was expected that those especially to whom manufacturing industry was important, would cherish the friendship of such customers by every favor, by every inducement, and particularly cultivate their peace by every act of justice and friendship. Under this prospect the question seemed legitimate, whether with such an immensity of unimproved land, courting the hand of husbandry, the industry of agriculture, or that of manufactures, would add most to the national wealth? And the doubt was entertained on this consideration chiefly, that to the labor of the husbandman a vast addition is made by the spontaneous energies of the earth on which it is employed: for one grain of wheat committed to the earth, she renders twenty, thirty, and even fifty fold, whereas to the labor of the manufacturer nothing is added. Pounds of flax, in his hands, yield, on the contrary, but pennyweights of lace. This exchange, too, laborious as it might seem, what a field did it promise for the occupations of the ocean; what a nursery for that class of citizens who were to exercise and maintain our equal rights on that element? This was the state of things in 1785, when the "Notes on Virginia" were first printed; when, the ocean being open to all nations, and their common right in it acknowledged and exercised under regulations sanctioned by

533

the assent and usage of all, it was thought that the doubt might claim some consideration. But who in 1785 could foresee the rapid depravity which was to render the close of that century the disgrace of the history of man? Who could have imagined that the two most distinguished in the rank of nations, for science and civilization, would have suddenly descended from that honorable eminence, and setting at defiance all those moral laws established by the Author of nature between nation and nation, as between man and man, would cover earth and sea with robberies and piracies, merely because strong enough to do it with temporal impunity; and that under this disbandment of nations from social order, we should have been despoiled of a thousand ships, and have thousands of our citizens reduced to Algerine slavery. Yet all this has taken place. One of these nations interdicted to our vessels all harbors of the globe without having first proceeded to some one of hers, there paid a tribute proportioned to the cargo, and obtained her license to proceed to the port of destination. The other declared them to be lawful prize if they had touched at the port, or been visited by a ship of the enemy nation. Thus were we completely excluded from the ocean.

Compare this state of things with that of '85, and say whether an opinion founded in the circumstances of that day can be fairly applied to those of the present. We have experienced what we did not then believe, that there exists both profligacy and power enough to exclude us from the field of interchange with other nations: that to be independent for the comforts of life we must fabricate them ourselves. We must now place the manufacturer by the side of the agriculturist. The former question is suppressed, or rather assumes a new form. Shall we make our own comforts, or go without them, at the will of a foreign nation? He, therefore, who is now against domestic manufacture, must be for reducing us either to dependence on that foreign nation, or to be clothed in skins, and to live like wild beasts in dens and caverns. I am not one of these; experience has taught me that manufactures are now as necessary to our independence as to our comfort; and if those who quote me as of a different opinion, will keep pace with me in purchasing nothing foreign where an equivalent of domestic fabric can be obtained, without regard to difference of price, it will not be our fault if we do not soon have a supply at home equal to our demand, and wrest that weapon of distress from the hand which has wielded it. If it shall be proposed to go beyond our own supply, the question of '85 will then recur, will our *surplus* labor be then most beneficially employed in the culture of the earth, or in the fabrications of art? We have time yet for consideration, before that question will press upon us; and the maxim to be applied will depend on the circumstances which shall then exist; for in so complicated a science as political economy, no one axiom can be laid down as wise and expedient for all times and circumstances, and for their contraries. . . .

More or Less of This Ingredient

To John Taylor, May 28, 1816

John Taylor of Caroline, Virginia, Jefferson's old friend and political coadjutor, sent Jefferson his radical, anti-Federalist book, An Inquiry into The Principles and Policy of the United States. *In the course of commenting on it, Jefferson defines the meaning of republicanism.*

... Indeed, it must be acknowledged, that the term *republic* is of very vague application in every language. Witness the self-styled republics of Holland, Switzerland, Genoa, Venice, Poland. Were I to assign to this term a precise and definite idea, I would say, purely and simply, it means a government by its citizens in mass, acting directly and personally, according to rules established by the majority; and that every other government is more or less republican, in proportion as it has in its composition more or less of this ingredient of the direct action of the citizens. Such a government is evidently restrained to very narrow limits of space and population. I doubt if it would be practicable beyond the extent of a New England township. The first shade from this pure element, which, like that of pure vital air, cannot sustain life of itself, would be where the powers of the government, being divided, should be exercised each by representatives chosen either *pro hac vice*, or for such short terms as should render secure the duty of expressing the will of their constituents. This I should consider as the nearest approach to a pure republic, which is practicable on a large scale of country or population. And we have examples of it in some of our State Constitutions, which, if not poisoned by priestcraft, would prove its excellence over all mixtures with other elements; and, with only equal doses of poison, would still be the best. Other shades of republicanism may be found in other forms of government, where the executive, judiciary and legislative functions, and the different branches of the latter, are chosen by the people more or less directly, for longer terms of years, or for life, or made hereditary; or where there are mixtures of authorities, some dependent on, and others independent of the people. The further the departure from direct and constant control by the citizens, the less has the government of the ingredient of republicanism; ...

If, then, the control of the people over the organs of their government be the measure of its republicanism, and I confess I know no other measure, it must be agreed that our governments have much less of republicanism than ought to have been expected; in other words, that the people have less regular control over their agents, than their rights and their interests require. And this I ascribe, not to any want of republican dispositions in those who formed these Constitutions, but to a submission of true principle to European authorities, to speculators on government, whose fears of the people have been inspired by the populace of their own great cities, and were unjustly entertained against the independent, the happy, and therefore orderly citizens of the United States. Much I apprehend that the golden moment is past for reforming these heresies. The functionaries of public power rarely strengthen in their dispositions to abridge it, and an unorganized call for timely amendment is not likely to prevail against an organized opposition to it. We are always told that things are going on well; why change them? *"Chista bene, non si muove,"* said the Italian, "let him who stands well, stand still." This is true; and I verily believe they would go on well with us under an absolute monarch, while our present character remains, of order, industry and love of peace, and restrained, as he would be, by the proper spirit of the people. But it is while it remains such, we should provide against the consequences of its deterioration. And let us rest in the hope that it will yet be done, and spare ourselves the pain of evils which may never happen.

On this view of the import of the term *republic, instead* of saying, as has been said, "that it may mean anything or nothing," we may say with truth and meaning, that governments are more or less republican, as they have more or less of the element of popular election and control in their composition; and believing, as I do, that the mass of the citizens is the safest depository of their own rights and especially, that the evils flowing from the duperies of the people, are less injurious than those from the egosim of their agents, I am a friend to that composition of government which has in it the most of this ingredient. And I sincerely believe, with you, that banking establishments are more dangerous than standing armies; and that the principle of spending money to be paid by posterity, under the name of funding, is but swindling futurity on a large scale.

I salute you with constant friendship and respect.

I Am Not Among Those Who Fear the People

To Samuel Kercheval, July 12, 1816

A constitutional convention was about to be called in Virginia. Jefferson's friend Kercheval solicited his opinion on it. Kercheval sent copies of Jefferson's letter to friends. On learning that a printer had it, Jefferson begged Kercheval to recall all copies and expunge his name from the lists of controversy. "I again throw the quiet of my life on your honor," he wrote.

Sir,—I duly received your favor of June the 13th, with the copy of the letters on the calling a convention, on which you are pleased to ask my opinion. I have not been in the habit of mysterious reserve on any subject, nor of buttoning up my opinions within my own doublet. On the contrary, while in public service especially, I thought the public entitled to frankness, and intimately to know whom they employed. But I am now retired: I resign myself, as a passenger, with confidence to those at present at the helm, and ask but for rest, peace and good will. The question you propose, on equal representation, has become a party one, in which I wish to take no public share. Yet, if it be asked for your own satisfaction only, and not to be quoted before the public, I have no motive to withhold it, and the less from you, as it coincides with your own. At the birth of our republic, I committed that opinion to the world, in the draught of a constitution annexed to the "Notes on Virginia," in which a provision was inserted for a representation permanently equal. The infancy of the subject at that moment, and our inexperience of self-government, occasioned gross departures in that draught from genuine republican canons. In truth, the abuses of monarchy had so much filled all the space of political contemplation, that we imagined everything republican which was not monarchy. We had not yet penetrated to the mother principle, that "governments are republican only in proportion as they embody the will of their people, and execute it." Hence, our first constitutions had really no leading principles in them. But experience and reflection have but more and more confirmed me in the particular importance of the equal representation then proposed. On that point, then, I am entirely in sentiment with your letters; and only lament that a copy-right of your pamphlet prevents their appearance in the newspapers, where alone they would be generally read, and produce general effect. The present vacancy too, of other matter, would give them place in every paper, and bring the question home to every man's conscience.

But inequality of representation in both Houses of our legislature, is not the only republican heresy in this first essay of our revolutionary patriots at forming a constitution. For let it be agreed that a government is republican in proportion as every member composing it has his equal voice in the direction of its concerns (not indeed in person, which would be impracticable beyond the limits of a city, or small township, but), by representatives chosen by himself, and responsible to him at short periods, and let us bring to the test of this canon every branch of our constitution.

In the legislature, the House of Representatives is chosen by less than half the people, and not at all in proportion to those who do choose. The Senate are still more disproportionate, and for long terms of irresponsibility. In the Executive, the Governor is entirely independent of the choice of the people, and for their control; his Council equally so, and at best but a fifth wheel to a wagon. In the Judiciary, the judges of the highest courts are dependent on none but themselves. In England, where judges were named and removable at the will of an hereditary executive, from which branch most misrule was feared, and has flowed, it was a great point gained, by fixing them for life, to make them independent of that executive. But in a government founded on the public will, this principle operates in an opposite direction, and against that will. There, too, they were still removable on a concurrence of the executive and legislative branches. But we have made them independent of the nation itself. They are irremovable, but by their own body, for any depravities of conduct, and even by their own body for the imbecilities of dotage. The justices of the inferior courts are self-chosen, are for life, and perpetuate their own body in succession forever, so that a faction once possessing themselves of the bench of a county, can never be broken up, but hold their county in chains, forever indissoluble. Yet these justices are the real executive as well as judiciary, in all our minor and most ordinary concerns. They tax us at will; fill the office of sheriff, the most important of all the executive officers of the county; name nearly all our military leaders, which leaders, once named, are removable but by themselves. The juries, our judges of all fact, and of law when they choose it, are not selected by the people, nor amenable to them. They are chosen by an officer named by the court and executive. Chosen, did I say? Picked up by the sheriff from the loungings of the court yard, after everything respectable has retired from it. Where then is our republicanism to be found? Not in our constitution certainly, but merely in the spirit of our people. That would oblige even a despot to govern us republicanly. Owing to this spirit, and to nothing in the form of our constitution, all things have gone well. But this fact, so triumphantly misquoted by the enemies of reformation, is not the fruit of our constitution, but has prevailed in spite of it. Our functionaries have done well, because generally honest men. If any were not so, they feared to show it.

But it will be said, it is easier to find faults than to amend them. I do not think their amendment so difficult as is pretended. Only lay down true principles, and adhere to them inflexibly. Do not be frightened into their surrender by the alarms of the timid, or the croakings of wealth against the ascendency of the people. If experience be called for, appeal to that of our fifteen or twenty governments for forty years, and show me where the people have done half the mischief in these forty years, that a single despot would have done in a single year; or show half the riots and rebellions, the crimes and the punishments, which have taken place in any single nation, under kingly government, during the same period. The true foundation of republican government is the equal right of every citizen, in his person and property, and in their management. Try by this, as a tally, every provision of our constitution, and see if it hangs directly on the will of the people. Reduce your legislature to a convenient number for full, but orderly discussion. Let every man who fights or pays, exercise his just and equal right in their election. Submit them to approbation or rejection at short intervals. Let the executive be chosen in the same way, and for the same term, by those whose agent he is to be; and leave no screen of a council behind which to skulk from responsibility. It has been thought that the people are not competent electors of judges *learned in the law.* But I do not know that this is true, and, if doubtful, we should follow principle. In this, as in many other elections, they would be guided by reputation, which would not err oftener, perhaps, than the present mode of appointment. In one State of the Union, at least, it has long been tried, and with the most satisfactory success. The judges of Connecticut have been chosen by the people every six months, for neary two centuries, and I believe there has hardly ever been an instance of change; so powerful is the curb of incessant responsibility. If prejudice, however, derived from a monarchical institution, is still to prevail against the vital elective principle of our own, and if the existing example among ourselves of periodical election of judges by the people be still mistrusted, let us at least not adopt the evil, and reject the good, of the English precedent; let us retain amovability on the concurrence of the executive and legislative branches, and nomination by the executive alone. Nomination to office is an executive function. To give it to the legislature, as we do, is a violation of the principle of the separation of powers. It swerves the members from correctness, by temptations to intrigue for office themselves, and to a corrupt barter of votes; and destroys responsibility by dividing it among a multitude. By leaving nomination in its proper place, among executive functions, the principle of the distribution of power is preserved, and responsibility weighs with its heaviest force on a single head.

The organization of our county administrations may be thought more difficult. But follow principle, and the knot unties itself. Divide the counties into wards of such size as that every citizen can attend, when called on, and act in person. Ascribe to them the government of their wards in all things relating to themselves exclusively. A justice, chosen by themselves, in each, a constable, a military company, a patrol, a school, the care of their own poor, their own portion of the public roads, the choice of one or more jurors to serve in some court, and the delivery, within their own wards, of their own votes for all elective officers of higher sphere, will relieve the county administration of nearly all its business, will have it better done, and by making every citizen an acting member of the government, and in the offices nearest and most interesting to him, will attach him by his strongest feelings to the independence of his country, and its republican constitution. The justices thus chosen by every ward, would constitute the county court, would do its judiciary business, direct roads and bridges, levy county and poor rates, and administer all the matters of common interest to the whole country. These wards, called townships in New England, are the vital principle of their governments, and have proved themselves the wisest invention ever devised by the wit of man for the perfect exercise of self-government, and for its preservation. We should thus marshal our government into, 1, the general federal republic, for all concerns foreign and federal; 2, that of the State, for what relates to our own citizens exclusively; 3, the county republics, for the duties and concerns of the county; and 4, the ward republics, for the small, and yet numerous and interesting concerns of the neighborhood; and in government, as well as in every other business of life, it is by division and subdivision of duties alone, that all matters, great and small, can be managed to perfection. And the whole is cemented by giving to every citizen, personally, a part in the administration of the public affairs.

The sum of these amendments is, 1. General suffrage. 2. Equal representation in the legislature. 3. An executive chosen by the people. 4. Judges elective or amovable. 5. Justices, jurors, and sheriffs elective. 6. Ward divisions. And 7. Periodical amendments of the constitution.

I have thrown out these as loose heads of amendment, for consideration and correction; and their object is to secure self-government by the republicanism of our constitution, as well as by the spirit of the people; and to nourish and perpetuate that spirit. I am not among those who fear the people. They, and not the rich, are our dependence for continued freedom. And to preserve their independence, we must not let our rulers load us with perpetual debt. We must make our election between *economy and liberty,* or *profusion and servitude.* If we run into such debts, as that we must be taxed in our meat and in our drink, in our necessaries and our comforts, in our labors and our amusements, for our callings and our creeds, as the people of England are, our people, like them, must come to labor sixteen hours in the twenty-four, give the earnings of fifteen of these to the government for their debts and daily expenses; and the sixteenth being insufficient to afford us bread, we must live, as they now do, on oatmeal and potatoes; have no time to think, no means of calling the mismanagers to account; but be glad to obtain subsistence by hiring ourselves to rivet their chains on the necks of our fellow suffers. Our land-holders, too, like theirs, retaining indeed the title and stewardship of estates called theirs, but held really in trust for the treasury, must wander, like theirs, in foreign countries, and be contented with penury, obscurity, exile, and the glory of the nation. This example reads to us the salutary lesson, that private fortunes are destroyed by public as well as by private extravagance. And this is the tendency of all human governments. A departure from principle in one instance becomes a precedent for a second; that second for a third; and so on, till the bulk of the society is reduced to be mere automatons of misery, to have no sensibilities left but for sinning and suffering. Then begins, indeed, the *bellum omnium in omnia*,[1] which some philosophers observing to be so general in this world, have mistaken it for the natural, instead of the abusive state of man. And the fore horse of this frightful team is public debt. Taxation follows that, and in its train wretchedness and oppression.

Some men look at constitutions with sanctimonious reverence, and deem them like the ark of the covenant, too sacred to be touched. They ascribe to the men of the preceding age a wisdom more than human, and suppose what they did to be beyond amendment. I knew that age well; I belonged to it, and labored with it. It deserved well of its country. It was very like the present, but without the experience of the present; and forty years of experience in government is worth a century of book-reading; and this they would say themselves, were they to rise from the dead. I am certainly not an advocate for frequent and untried changes in laws and constitutions. I think moderate imperfections had better be borne with; because, when once known, we accommodate ourselves to them, and find practical means of correcting their ill effects. But I know also, that laws and institutions must go hand in hand with the progress of the human mind. As that becomes more developed, more enlightened, as new discoveries are made, new truths disclosed, and manners and opinions change with the change of circumstances, institutions must advance also, and keep pace with the times. We might as well require a man to wear still the coat which fitted him when a boy, as civilized society to remain ever under

[1] Wars for everything.

the regimen of their barbarous ancestors. It is this preposterous idea which has lately deluged Europe in blood. Their monarchs, instead of wisely yielding to the gradual change of circumstances, of favoring progressive accommodation to progressive improvement, have clung to old abuses, entrenched themselves behind steady habits, and obliged their subjects to seek through blood and violence rash and ruinous innovations, which, had they been referred to the peaceful deliberations and collected wisdom of the nation, would have been put into acceptable and salutary forms.

Let us follow no such examples, nor weakly believe that one generation is not as capable as another of taking care of itself, and of ordering its own affairs. Let us, as our sister States have done, avail ourselves of our reason and experience, to correct the crude essays of our first and unexperienced, although wise, virtuous, and well-meaning councils. And lastly, let us provide in our Constitution for its revision at stated periods. What these periods should be, nature herself indicates. By the European tables of mortality, of the adults living at any one moment of time, a majority will be dead in about nineteen years. At the end of that period then, a new majority is come into place; or, in other words, a new generation. Each generation is as independent of the one preceding, as that was of all which had gone before. It has then, like them, a right to choose for itself the form of government it believes most promotive of its own happiness; consequently, to accommodate to the circumstances in which it finds itself, that received from its predecessors; and it is for the peace and good of mankind, that a solemn opportunity of doing this every nineteen or twenty years, should be provided by the Constitution; so that it may be handed on, with periodical repairs, from generation to generation, to the end of time, if anything human can so long endure.

It is now forty years since the constitution of Virginia was formed. The same tables inform us, that, within that period, two-thirds of the adults then living are now dead. Have then the remaining third, even if they had the wish, the right to hold in obedience to their will, and to laws heretofore made by them, the other two-thirds, who, with themselves, compose the present mass of adults? If they have not, who has? The dead? But the dead have no rights. They are nothing; and nothing cannot own something. Where there is no substance, there can be no accident. This corporeal globe, and everything upon it, belong to its present corporeal inhabitants, during their generation. They alone have a right to direct what is the concern of themselves alone, and to declare the law of that direction; and this declaration can only be made by their majority. That majority, then, has a right to depute representatives to a convention, and to make the Constitution what they think will be the best for themselves. But how collect their voice? This is the real difficulty. If invited by private authority, or county or district meetings, these divisions are so large that few will attend; and their voice will be imperfectly, or falsely, pronounced. Here, then, would be one of the advantages of the ward divisions I have proposed. The mayor of every ward, on a question like the present, would call his ward together, take the simple yea or nay of its members, convey these to the county court, who would hand on those of all its wards to be the proper general authority; and the voice of the whole people would be thus fairly, fully, and peaceably expressed, discussed, and decided by the common reason of the society. If this avenue be shut to the call of sufferance, it will make itself heard through that of force, and we shall go on, as other nations are doing, in the endless circle of oppression, rebellion, reformation; and oppression, rebellion, reformation, again; and so on forever. . . .

There Would Never Have Been an Infidel

To Mrs. Samuel Harrison Smith, August 6, 1816

Jefferson returns to an old theme. His hostility to priestcraft had not abated a jot over the years. Mrs. Smith was the wife of the editor of the Republican National Intelligencer.

. . . The Priests, indeed, have heretofore thought proper to ascribe to me religious, or rather anti-religious sentiments of their own fabric, but such as soothed their resentments against the Act of Virginia for establishing religious freedom. They wish him to be thought atheist, deeist, or devil, who could advocate freedom from their religious dictations, but I have ever thought religion a concern purely between our God and our consciences for which we were accountable to him, and not to the priests. I never told my own religion nor scrutinized that of another. I never attempted to make a convert, nor wish to change another's creed. I have ever judged of the religion of others by their lives; and by this test, my dear Madam, I have been satisfied yours must be an excellent one, to have produced a life of such exemplary virtue and correctness, for it is in our lives and not from our words, that our religion must be read. By the same test the world must judge me.

But this does not satisfy the priesthood, they must have a positive, a declared assent to all their interested absurdities. My opinion is that there would never have been an infidel, if there had never been a priest. The artificial structure they have built on the purest of all moral systems for the purpose of deriving from it pence and power revolts those who think for themselves and who read in that system only what is really there. These, therefore, they brand with such nicknames as their enmity chooses gratuitously to impute. I have left the world in silence, to judge of causes from their effects: and I am consoled in this course, my dear friend, when I perceive the candor with which I am judged by your justice and discernment; and that, notwithstanding the slander of the Saints, my fellow citizens have thought me worthy of trust. The imputations of irreligion having spent their force, they think an imputation of change might now be turned to account as a bolster for their duperies. I shall leave them as heretofore to grope on in the dark. . . .

Not Now Very Distant

To Abigail Adams, January 11, 1817

The antagonisms between Jefferson and Abigail Adams—they had once been close friends—melted in the glow of old age. This was to be their last exchange. Abigail Adams died the following year.

I owe you, dear Madam, a thousand thanks for the letters communicated in your favor of December 15th, and now returned. . . .

I communicated the letters, according to your permission, to my grand-daughter, Ellen Randolph, who read them with pleasure and edification. She is justly sensible of, and flattered by your kind notice of her; and additionally so, by the favorable recollections of our northern visiting friends. If Monticello has anything which has merited their remembrance, it gives it a value the more in our estimation; and could I, in the spirit of your wish, count backwards a score of years, it would not be long before Ellen and myself would pay our homage personally to Quincy. But those twenty years! Alas! where are they? With those beyond the flood. Our next meeting must then be in the country to which they have flown,—a country for us not now very distant. For this journey we shall need neither gold nor silver in our purse, nor scrip, nor coats, nor staves. Nor is the provision for it more easy than the preparation has been kind. Nothing proves more than this that the Being who presides over the world is essentially benevolent. Stealing from us, one by one, the faculties of enjoyment, searing our sensibilities, leading us, like the horse in his mill, round and round the same beaten circle,

> ——To see what we have seen,
> To taste the tasted, and at each return
> Less tasteful; o'er our palates to decant
> Another vintage—

Until satiated and fatigued with this leaden iteration, we ask our own *congé*. I heard once a very old friend, who had troubled himself with neither poets nor philosophers, say the same thing in plain prose, that he was tired of pulling off his shoes and stockings at night, and putting them on again in the morning. The wish to stay here is thus gradually extinguished; but not so easily that of returning once, in awhile, to see how things have gone on. Perhaps, however, one of the elements of future felicity is to be a constant and unimpassioned view of what is passing here. If so, this may well supply the wish of occasional visits. Mercier has given us a vision of the year 2440; but prophecy is one thing, and history another. On the whole, however, perhaps it is wise and well to be contented with the good things which the master of the feast places before us, and to be thankful for what we have, rather than thoughtful about what we have not. You and I, dear Madam, have already had more than an ordinary portion of life, and more, too, of health than the general measure. On this score I owe boundless thankfulness. Your health was, some time ago, not so good as it has been; and I perceive in the letters communicated some complaints still. I hope it is restored; and that life and health may be continued to you as many years as yourself shall wish, is the sincere prayer of your affectionate and respectful friend.

Your Heavy Affliction

To John Adams, November 13, 1818

In a moving and eloquent letter, Jefferson condoles Adams on the death of Abigail.

The public papers, my dear friend, announce the fatal event of which your letter of October the 20th had given me ominous foreboding. Tried myself in the school of affliction, by the loss of every form of connection which can rive the human heart, I know well, and feel what you have lost, what you have suffered, are suffering, and have yet to endure. The same trials have taught me that for ills so immeasurable, time and silence are the only medicine. I will not, therefore, by useless condolences, open afresh the sluices of your grief, nor, although mingling sincerely my tears with yours, will I say a word more where words are vain, but that it is of some comfort to us both, that the term is not very distant, at which we are to deposit in the same cerement, our sorrows and suffering bodies, and to ascend in essence to an ecstatic meeting with the friends we have loved and lost, and whom we shall still love and never lose again. God bless you and support you under your heavy affliction.

I Have Lived Temperately

To Dr. Vine Utley, March 21, 1819

Dr. Utley's inquiry into Jefferson's "physical habits" was not surprising in view of his reputation, borne out by the letter below, for possessing remarkably good health.

Sir,—Your letter of February the 18th came to hand on the 1st instant; and the request of the history of my physical habits would have puzzled me not a little, had it not been for the model with which you accompanied it, of Doctor Rush's answer to a similar inquiry. I live so much like other people, that I might refer to ordinary life as the history of my own. Like my friend the Doctor, I have lived temperately, eating little animal food, and that not as an aliment, so much as a condiment for the vegetables, which constitute my principal diet. I double however, the Doctor's glass and a half of wine, and even treble it with a friend; but halve its effects by drinking the weak wines only. The ardent wines I cannot drink, nor do I use ardent spirits in any form. Malt liquors and cider are my table drinks, and my breakfast, like that also of my friend, is of tea and coffee. I have been blest with organs of digestion which accept and concoct, without ever murmuring, whatever the palate chooses to consign to them, and I have not yet lost a tooth by age. I was a hard student until I entered on the business of life, the duties of which leave no idle time to those disposed to fulfil them; and now, retired, and at the age of seventy-six, I am again a hard student. Indeed, my fondness for reading and study revolts me from the drudgery of letter-writing. And a stiff wrist, the consequence of an early dislocation, makes writing both slow and painful. I am not so regular in my sleep as the Doctor says he was, devoting to it from five to eight hours, according as my company or the book I am reading interests me; and I never go to bed without an hour, or half hour's previous reading of something moral, whereon to ruminate in the intervals of sleep. But whether I retire to bed early or late, I rise with the sun. I use spectacles at night, but not necessarily in the day, unless in reading small print. My hearing is distinct

in particular conversation, but confused when several voices
cross each other, which unfits me for the society of the table.
I have been more fortunate than my friend in the article of
health. So free from catarrhs that I have not had one, (in
the breast, I mean) on an average of eight or ten years
through life. I ascribe this exemption partly to the habit of
bathing my feet in cold water every morning, for sixty years
past. A fever of more than twenty-four hours I have not had
above two or three times in my life. A periodical headache
has afflicted me occasionally, once, perhaps, in six or eight
years, for two or three weeks at a time, which seems now to
have left me; and except on a late occasion of indisposition,
I enjoy good health; too feeble, indeed, to walk much, but
riding without fatigue six or eight miles a day, and sometimes
thirty or forty. I may end these egotisms, therefore, as I
began, by saying that my life has been so much like that of
other people, that I might say with Horace, to every one
"*nomine mutato, narratur fabula de te.*"[1] I must not end,
however, without due thanks for the kind sentiments of regard you are so good as to express towards myself; and with
my acknowledgments for these, be pleased to accept the
assurances of my respect and esteem.

[1] Change the name and the same story may be told of you.

I Too Am an Epicurean

To William Short, October 31, 1819

Short, once Jefferson's secretary, complained that he was surrendering to epicurean ataraxia. Jefferson, however, bends the stoic-epicurean philosophy, of which he considered himself a true votary, to his own purposes by joining it to Unitarian Christianity.

Dear Sir,—Your favor of the 21st is received. My late illness, in which you are so kind as to feel an interest, was produced by a spasmodic stricture of the ileum, which came upon me on the 7th inst. The crisis was short, passed over favorably on the fourth day, and I should soon have been well but that a dose of calomel and jalap, in which were only eight or nine grains of the former, brought on a salivation. Of this, however, nothing now remains but a little soreness of the mouth. I have been able to get on horseback for three or four days past.

As you say of yourself, I too am an Epicurian. I consider the genuine (not the imputed) doctrines of Epicurus as containing everything rational in moral philosophy which Greece and Rome have left us. Epictetus indeed, has given us what was good of the Stoics; all beyond, of their dogmas, being hypocrisy and grimace. Their great crime was in their calumnies of Epicurus and misrepresentations of his doctrines; in which we lament to see the candid character of Cicero engaging as an accomplice. Diffuse, vapid, rhetorical, but enchanting. His prototype Plato, eloquent as himself, dealing out mysticisms incomprehensible to the human mind, has been deified by certain sects usurping the name of Christians; because, in his foggy conceptions, they found a basis of impenetrable darkness whereon to rear fabrications as delirious, of their own invention. These they fathered blasphemously on Him whom they claimed as their Founder, but who would disclaim them with the indignation which their caricatures of His religion so justly excite. Of Socrates we have nothing genuine but in the Memorabilia of Xenophon; for Plato makes him one of his Collocutors merely to cover his own whimsies under the mantle of his name; a liberty of which we are told Socrates himself complained. Seneca is indeed a fine moralist, disfiguring his work at times with some Stoicisms, and affecting too much of antithesis and point, yet giving us on the whole a great deal of sound and practical morality. But the greatest of all the reformers of the depraved religion of His own country, was Jesus of Nazareth. Abstracting what is really His from the rubbish in which it is buried, easily distinguished by its lustre from the dross of His biographers, and as separable from that as the diamond from the dunghill, we have the outlines of a system of the most sublime morality which has ever fallen from the lips of man; outlines which it is lamentable He did not live to fill up. Epictetus and Epicurus give laws for governing ourselves, Jesus a supplement of the duties and charities we owe to others. The establishment of the innocent and genuine character of this benevolent Moralist, and the rescuing it from the imputation of imposture, which has resulted from artificial systems,[1] invented by ultra-Christian sects, unauthorized by a single word ever uttered by Him, is a most desirable object, and one to which Priestley has successfully devoted his labors and learning. It would in time, it is to be hoped, effect a quiet euthanasia of the heresies of bigotry and fanaticism which have so long triumphed over human reason, and so generally and deeply afflicted mankind; but this work is to be begun by winnowing the grain from the chaff of the historians of His life. I have sometimes thought of translating Epictetus (for he has never been tolerably translated into English) by adding the genuine doctrines of Epicurus from the Syntagma of Gassendi, and an abstract from the Evangelists of whatever has the stamp of the eloquence and fine imagination of Jesus. The last I attempted too hastily some twelve or fifteen years ago. It was the work of two or three night only, at Washington, after getting through the evening task of reading the letters and papers of the day. But with one foot in the grave, these are now idle projects for me. My business is to beguile the wearisomeness of declining

[1] *E.g.* The immaculate conception of Jesus, His deification, the creation of the world by Him, His miraculous powers, His resurrection and visible ascension, His corporeal presence in the Eucharist, the Trinity, original sin, atonement, regeneration, election, orders of Hierarchy, etc. [Jefferson's note].

life, as I endeavor to do, by the delights of classical reading and of mathematical truths, and by the consolations of a sound philosophy, equally indifferent to hope and fear.

I take the liberty of observing that you are not a true disciple of our master Epicurus, in indulging the indolence to which you say you are yielding. One of his canons, you know, was that "that indulgence which presents a greater pleasure, or produces a greater pain, is to be avoided." Your love of repose will lead, in its progress, to a suspension of healthy exercise, a relaxation of mind, an indifference to everything around you, and finally to a debility of body, and hebetude of mind, the farthest of all things from the happiness which the well-regulated indulgences of Epicurus ensure; fortitude, you know, is one of his four cardinal virtues. That teaches us to meet and surmount difficulties; not to fly from them, like cowards; and to fly, too, in vain, for they will meet and arrest us at every turn of our road. Weigh this matter well; brace yourself up; take a seat with Correa, and come and see the finest portion of your country, which, if you have not forgotten, you still do not know, because it is no longer the same as when you knew it. It will add much to the happiness of my recovery to be able to receive Correa and yourself, and prove the estimation in which I hold you both. Come, too, and see our incipient University, which has advanced with great activity this year. By the end of the next, we shall have elegant accommodations for seven professors, and the year following the professors themselves. No secondary character will be received among them. Either the ablest which America or Europe can furnish, or none at all. They will give us the selected society of a great city separated from the dissipations and levities of its ephemeral insects.

I am glad the bust of Condorcet has been saved and so well placed. His genius should be before us; while the lamentable, but singular act of ingratitude which tarnished his latter days, may be thrown behind us.

I will place under this a syllabus of the doctrines of Epicurus, somewhat in the lapidary style, which I wrote some twenty years ago; a like one of the philosophy of Jesus, of nearly the same age, is too long to be copied. *Vale, et tibi persuade carissimum te esse mihi.*[2]

---

[2] Farewell, and believe among yourselves that you are most dear to me.

Syllabus of the doctrines of Epicurus

Physical.—The Universe eternal.

Its parts, great and small, interchangeable.

Matter and Void alone.

Motion inherent in matter which is weighty and declining.

Eternal circulation of the elements of bodies.

Gods, an order of beings next superior to man, enjoying in their sphere, their own felicities; but not meddling with the concerns of the scale of beings below them.

Moral.—Happiness the aim of life.

Virtue the foundation of happiness.

Utility the test of virtue.

Pleasure active and In-do-lent.

In-do-lence is the absence of pain, the true felicity.

Active, consists in agreeable motion; it is not happiness, but the means to produce it.

Thus the absence of hunger is an article of felicity; eating the means to obtain it.

The *summum bonum* is to be not pained in body, nor troubled in mind.

i.e. In-do-lence of body, tranquillity of mind.

To procure tranquillity of mind we must avoid desire and fear, the two principal diseases of the mind.

Man is a free agent.

Virtue consists in 1. Prudence. 2. Temperance. 3. Fortitude. 4. Justice.

To which are opposed, 1. Folly. 2. Desire. 3. Fear. 4. Deceit.

A Fire-bell in the Night

To John Holmes, April 22, 1820

Below are Jefferson's brief reflections on the expansion of slavery. The issue was moot at this time. The territories filled up and divided into free and slave states. But what was to be done about the Louisiana Territory now that Missouri, a part of it, was applying for admission? The Missouri Compromise temporarily cauterized the conflict. John Holmes was a congressman from the Maine district of Massachusetts and a friend of the Compromise.

I thank you, dear Sir, for the copy you have been so kind as to send me of the letter to your constituents on the Missouri question. It is a perfect justification to them. I had for a long time ceased to read newspapers, or pay any attention to public affairs, confident they were in good hands, and content to be a passenger in our bark to the shore from which I am not distant. But this momentous question, like a fire-bell in the night, awakened and filled me with terror. I considered it at once as the knell of the Union. It is hushed, indeed, for the moment. But this is a reprieve only, not a final sentence. A geographical line, coinciding with a marked principle, moral and political, once conceived and held up to the angry passions of men, will never be obliterated; and every new irritation will mark it deeper and deeper. I can say, with conscious truth, that there is not a man on earth who would sacrifice more than I would to relieve us from this heavy reproach, in any *practicable* way. The cession of that kind of property, for so it is misnamed, is a bagatelle which would not cost me a second thought, if, in that way, a general emancipation and *expatriation* could be effected; and, gradually, and with due sacrifices, I think it might be. But as it is, we have the wolf by the ears, and we can neither hold him, nor safely let him go. Justice is in one scale, and self-preservation in the other. Of one thing I am certain, that as the passage of slaves from one State to another, would not make a slave of a single human being who would not be so without it, so their diffusion over a greater surface would make them individually happier, and proportionally facilitate the accomplishment of their emancipation, by dividing the burden on a greater number of coadjutors. An abstinence too, from this act of power, would remove the jealousy excited by the undertaking of Congress to regulate the condition of the different descriptions of men composing a State. This certainly is the exclusive right of every State, which nothing in the Constitution has taken from them and given to the General Government. Could Congress, for example, say, that the non-freemen of Connecticut shall be freemen, or that they shall not emigrate into any other State?

I regret that I am now to die in the belief, that the useless sacrifice of themselves by the generation of 1776, to acquire self-government and happiness to their country, is to be thrown away by the unwise and unworthy passions of their sons, and that my only consolation is to be, that I live not to weep over it. If they would but dispassionately weigh the blessings they will throw away, against an abstract principle more likely to be effected by union than by scission, they would pause before they would perpetrate this act of suicide on themselves, and of treason against the hopes of the world. To yourself, as the faithful advocate of the Union, I tender the offering of my high esteem and respect.

The General Religion

To James Smith, December 8, 1822

To Jefferson, Christ had always been a moralist and Christianity a philosophy of right action. Unitarianism seemed to him entirely compatible with this belief. Smith was an Ohioan who frequently wrote on religion.

Sir,—I have to thank you for your pamphlets on the subject of Unitarianism, and to express my gratification with your efforts for the revival of primitive Christianity in your quarter. No historical fact is better established, than that the doctrine of one God, pure and uncompounded, was that of the early ages of Christianity; and was among the efficacious doctrines which gave it triumph over the polytheism of the ancients, sickened with the absurdities of their own theology. Nor was the unity of the Supreme Being ousted from the Christian creed by the force of reason, but by the sword of civil government, wielded at the will of the fanatic Athanasius. The hocus-pocus phantasm of a God like another Cerberus, with one body and three heads, had its birth and growth in the blood of thousands and thousands of martyrs. And a strong proof of the solidity of the primitive faith, is its restoration, as soon as a nation arises which vindicates to itself the freedom of religious opinion; and its external divorce from the civil authority. The pure and simple unity of the Creator of the universe, is now all but ascendant in the Eastern States; it is dawning in the West, and advancing towards the South; and I confidently expect that the present generation will see Unitarianism become the general religion of the United States. The Eastern presses are giving us many excellent pieces on the subject, and Priestley's learned writings on it are, or should be, in every hand. In fact, the Athanasian paradox that one is three, and three but one, is so incomprehensible to the human mind, that no candid man can say he has any idea of it, and how can he believe what presents no idea? He who thinks he does, only deceives himself. He proves, also, that man, once surrendering his reason, has no remaining guard against absurdities the most monstrous, and like a ship without rudder, is the sport of every wind. With such persons, gullibility which they call faith, takes the helm from the hand of reason, and the mind becomes a wreck.

I write with freedom, because while I claim a right to believe in one God, if so my reason tells me, I yield as freely to others that of believing in three. Both religions, I find, make honest men, and that is the only point society has any right to look to. Although this mutual freedom should produce mutual indulgence, yet I wish not to be brought in question before the public on this or any other subject, and I pray you to consider me as writing under that trust. I take no part in controversies, religious or political. At the age of eighty, tranquillity is the greatest good of life, and the strongest of our desires that of dying in the good will of all mankind. And with the assurance of all my good will to Unitarian and Trinitarian, to Whig and Tory, accept for yourself that of my entire respect.

That Wholesome Distribution of Powers

To William Johnson, June 12, 1823

Jefferson had long considered the Supreme Court a Federalist preserve whose reason for existence was to thwart the democratic will. His quarrel with Chief Justice John Marshall was of long standing. Each of Marshall's recent decisions—Dartmouth College v. Woodward (1819), Sturges v. Crowninshield (1819), McCullock v. Maryland (1819), Cohen v. Virginia (1821)—strengthened Jefferson's opinion that Marshall was using the Court to uphold property rights over human rights, the corporation over the community. William Johnson of South Carolina was himself a member of the Court, appointed to it by Jefferson in 1804.

. . . You request me confidentially, to examine the question, whether the Supreme Court has advanced beyond its constitutional limits, and trespassed on those of the State authorities? I do not undertake, my dear Sir, because I am unable. Age and the wane of mind consequent on it, had disqualified me from investigations so severe, and researches so laborious. And it is the less necessary in this case, as having been already done by others with a logic and learning to which I could add nothing. On the decision of the case of Cohen *vs.* The State of Virginia, in the Supreme Court of the United States, in March, 1821, Judge Roane, under the signature of Algernon Sidney, wrote for the Enquirer a series of papers on the law of that case. I considered these papers maturely as they came out, and confess that they appeared to me to pulverize every word which had been delivered by Judge Marshall, of the extra-judicial part of his opinion; and all was extra-judicial, except the decision that the act of Congress had not purported to give to the corporation of Washington the authority claimed by their lottery law, of controlling the laws of the States within the States themselves. But unable to claim that case, he could not let it go entirely, but went on gratuitously to prove that notwithstanding the eleventh amendment of the constitution, a State *could* be brought as a defendant, to the bar of his court; and again, that

Congress might authorize a corporation of its territory to exercise legislation within a State, and paramount to the laws of that State. . . .

This practice of Judge Marshall, of travelling out of his case to prescribe what the law would be in a moot case not before the court, is very irregular and very censurable. I recollect another instance, and the more particularly, perhaps, because it in some measure bore on myself. Among the midnight appointments of Mr. Adams, were commissions to some federal justices of the peace for Alexandria. These were signed and sealed by him, but not delivered. I found them on the table of the department of State, on my entrance into office, and forbade their delivery. Marbury, named in one of them, applied to the Supreme Court for a mandamus to the Secretary of State (Mr. Madison) to deliver the commission intended for him. The court determined at once, that being an original process, they had no cognizance of it; and therefore the question before them was ended. But the Chief Justice went on to lay down what the law would be, had they jurisdiction of the case, to wit: that they should command the delivery. The object was clearly to instruct any other court having the jurisdiction, what they should do if Marbury should apply to them. Besides the impropriety of this gratuitous interference, could anything exceed the perversion of law? For if there is any principle of law never yet contradicted it is that delivery is one of the essentials to the validity of the deed. Although signed and sealed, yet as long as it remains in the hands of the party himself, it is in *fieri* only, it is not a deed, and can be made so only by its delivery. In the hands of a third person it may be made an escrow. But whatever is in the executive offices is certainly deemed to be in the hands of the President; and in this case, was actually in my hands, because, when I countermanded them, there was as yet no Secretary of State. Yet this case of Marbury and Madison is continually cited by bench and bar, as if it were settled law, without any animadversion on its being merely an *obiter* dissertation of the Chief Justice.

It may be impracticable to lay down any general formula of words which shall decide at once, and with precision, in every case, this limit of jurisdiction. But there are two canons which will guide us safely in most of the cases. 1st. The capital and leading object of the constitution was to leave with the States all authorities which respected their own citizens only, and to transfer to the United States those which respected citizens of foreign or other States: to make us several as to ourselves, but one as to all others. In the latter case, then, constructions should lean to the general jurisdiction, if the words will bear it; and in favor of the States in the former, if possible to be so construed. And indeed, between citizens and citizens of the same State, and under their own laws, I know but a single case in which a jurisdiction is given to the General Government. That is, where anything but gold or silver is made a lawful tender, or the obligation of contracts is any otherwise impaired. The separate legislatures had so often abused that power, that the citizens themselves chose to trust it to the general, rather than to their own special authorities. 2d. On every question of construction, carry ourselves back to the time when the constitution was adopted, recollect the spirit manifested in the debates, and instead of trying what meaning may be squeezed out of the text, or invented against it, conform to the probable one in which it was passed. Let us try Cohen's case by these canons only, referring always, however, for full argument, to the essays before cited.

1. It was between a citizen and his own State, and under a law of his State. It was a domestic case, therefore, and not a foreign one.

2. Can it be believed, that under the jealousies prevailing against the General Government, at the adoption of the constitution, the States meant to surrender the authority of preserving order, of enforcing moral duties and restraining vice, within their own territory? And this is the present case, that of Cohen being under the ancient and general law of gaming. Can any good be effected by taking from the States the moral rule of their citizens, and subordinating it to the general authority, or to one of their corporations, which may justify forcing the meaning of words, hunting after possible constructions, and hanging inference on inference, from heaven to earth, like Jacob's ladder? Such an intention was impossible, and such a licentiousness of construction and inference, if exercised by both governments, as may be done with equal right, would equally authorize both to claim all power, general and particular, and break up the foundations of the Union. Laws are made for men of ordinary understanding, and should, therefore, be construed by the ordinary rules of common sense. Their meaning is not to be sought for in

metaphysical subtleties, which may make anything mean everything or nothing, at pleasure. It should be left to the sophisms of advocates, whose trade it is, to prove that a defendant is a plaintiff, though dragged into court, *torto collo*, like Bonaparte's volunteers, into the field in chains, or that a power has been given, because it ought to have been given, *et alia talia*. The States supposed that by their tenth amendment, they had secured themselves against constructive powers. They were not lessoned yet by Cohen's case, nor aware of the slipperiness of the eels of the law. I ask for no straining of words against the General Government, nor yet against the States. I believe the States can best govern our home concerns, and the General Government our foreign ones. I wish, therefore, to see maintained that wholesome distribution of powers established by the constitution for the limitation of both; and never to see all offices transferred to Washington, where, further withdrawn from the eyes of the people, they may more secretly be bought and sold as at market.

But the Chief Justice says, "there must be an ultimate arbiter somewhere." True, there must; but does that prove it is either party? The ultimate arbiter is the people of the Union, assembled by their deputies in convention, at the call of Congress, or of two-thirds of the States. Let them decide to which they mean to give an authority claimed by two of their organs. And it has been the peculiar wisdom and felicity of our constitution, to have provided this peaceable appeal, where that of other nations is at once to force. . . .

Through the Ocean of Time

To President James Monroe, October 24, 1823

President Monroe asked Jefferson's (and Madison's) advice on Britain's recent request to join with the United States in preventing the Holy Alliance from crushing the new republics of South America. Jefferson's answer is contained in the letter below. But Secretary of State, John Quincy Adams, skeptical of Britain's motives, thought that the United States should, if possible, act unilaterally. The Monroe Doctrine of December 2, 1823, was, in essence, the product of Adams' advice.

Dear Sir,—The question presented by the letters you have sent me, is the most momentous which has ever been offered to my contemplation since that of Independence. That made us a nation, this sets our compass and points the course which we are to steer through the ocean of time opening on us. And never could we embark on it under circumstances more auspicious. Our first and fundamental maxim should be, never to entangle ourselves in the broils of Europe. Our second, never to suffer Europe to intermeddle with cis-Atlantic affairs. America, North and South, has a set of interests distinct from those of Europe, and peculiarly her own. She should therefore have a system of her own, separate and apart from that of Europe. While the last is laboring to become the domicile of despotism, our endeavors should surely be, to make our hemisphere that of freedom. One nation, most of all, could disturb us in this pursuit; she now offers to lead, aid, and accompany us in it. By acceding to her proposition, we detach her from the bands, bring her mighty weight into the scale of free government, and emancipate a continent at one stroke, which might otherwise linger long in doubt and difficulty. Great Britain is the nation which can do us the most harm of any one, or all on earth; and with her on our side we need not fear the whole world. With her then, we should most sedulously cherish a cordial friendship; and nothing would tend more to knit our affections than to be fighting once more, side by side, in the same cause. Not that I would purchase even her amity at the price of taking part in her wars. But the war in which the present proposition might engage us, should that be its consequence, is not her war, but ours. Its object is to introduce and establish the American system, of keeping out of our land all foreign powers, of never permitting those of Europe to intermeddle with the affairs of our nations. It is to maintain our own principle, not to depart from it. And if, to facilitate this, we can effect a division in the body of the European powers, and draw over to our side its most powerful member, surely we should do it. But I am clearly of Mr. Canning's opinion, that it will prevent instead of provoking war. With Great Britain withdrawn from their scale and shifted into that of our two continents, all Europe combined would not undertake such a war. For how would they propose to get at either enemy without superior fleets? Nor is the occasion to be slighted which this proposition offers, of declaring our protest against the atrocious violations of the rights of nations, by the interference of any one in the internal affairs of another, so flagitiously begun by Bonaparte, and now continued by the equally lawless Alliance, calling itself Holy.

But we have first to ask ourselves a question. Do we wish to acquire to our own confederacy any one or more of the Spanish provinces? I candidly confess, that I have ever looked on Cuba as the most interesting addition which could ever be made to our system of States. The control which, with Florida Point, this island would give us over the Gulf of Mexico, and the countries and isthmus bordering on it, as well as all those whose waters flow into it, would fill up the measure of our political well-being. Yet, as I am sensible that this can never be obtained, even with her own consent, but by war; and its independence, which is our second interest, (and especially its independence of England,) can be secured without it, I have no hesitation in abandoning my first wish to future chances, and accepting its independence, with peace and the friendship of England, rather than its association, at the expense of war and her enmity.

I could honestly, therefore, join in the declaration proposed, that we aim not at the acquisition of any of those possessions, that we will not stand in the way of any amicable arrangement between them and the Mother country; but that we will oppose, with all our means, the forcible interposition of any other power, as auxiliary, stipendiary, or under any other form or pretext, and most especially, their transfer to any power by conquest, cession, or acquisition in any other way. I should think it, therefore, advisable, that the Executive should encourage the British government to a continuance in the dispositions expressed in these letters, by an assurance of his concurrence with them as far as his authority goes; and that as it may lead to war, the declaration of which requires an act of Congress, the case shall be laid before them for consideration at their first meeting, and under the reasonable aspect in which it is seen by himself.

I have been so long weaned from political subjects, and have so long ceased to take any interest in them, that I am sensible I am not qualified to offer opinions on them worthy of any attention. But the question now proposed involves consequences so lasting, and effects so decisive of our future destinies, as to rekindle all the interest I have heretofore felt on such occasions, and to induce me to the hazard of opinions, which will prove only my wish to contribute still my mite towards anything which may be useful to our country. And praying you to accept it at only what it is worth, I add the assurance of my constant and affectionate friendship and respect.

Nothing Then Is Unchangeable but the Inherent and Unalienable Rights of Man

To Major John Cartwright, June 5, 1824

In stirring words, Jefferson at eight-one, again affirms his radical ideal of the autonomy of each generation. He does so in the course of commenting on Cartwright's The English Constitution Produced and Illustrated.

. . . With respect to our State and federal governments, I do not think their relations correctly understood by foreigners. They generally suppose the former subordinate to the latter. But this is not the case. They are co-ordinate departments of one simple and integral whole. To the State governments are reserved all legislation and administration, in affairs which concern their own citizens only, and to the federal government is given whatever concerns foreigners, or the citizens of other States; these functions alone being made federal. The one is the domestic, the other the foreign branch of the same government; neither having control over the other, but within its own department. There are one or two exceptions only to this partition of power. But, you may ask, if the two departments should claim each the same subject of power, where is the common umpire to decide ultimately between them? In cases of little importance or urgency, the prudence of both parties will keep them aloof from the questionable ground; but if it can neither be avoided nor compromised, a convention of the States must be called, to ascribe the doubtful power to that department which they may think best. You will perceive by these details, that we have not yet so far perfected our constitutions as to venture to make them unchangeable. But still, in their present state, we consider them not otherwise changeable than by the authority of the people, on a special election of representatives for that purpose expressly: they are until then the *lex legum*.

But can they be made unchangeable? Can one generation bind another, and all others, in succession forever? I think not. The Creator has made the earth for the living, not the dead. Rights and powers can only belong to persons, not to things, not to mere matter, unendowed with will. The dead are not even things. The particles of matter which composed their bodies, make part now of the bodies of other animals, vegetables, or minerals, of a thousand forms. To what then are attached the rights and powers they held while in the form of men? A generation may bind itself as long as its majority continues in life; when that has disappeared, another majority is in place, holds all the rights and powers their predecessors once held, and may change their laws and institutions to suit themselves. Nothing then is unchangeable but the inherent and unalienable rights of man. . . .

Your Benefactor in Peace As Well As in War

Speech on Lafayette, November 4, 1824

In the fall of 1824, Lafayette came to America and visited Jefferson, his friend of almost fifty years. Lafayette arrived at Monticello accompanied by a crowd. Jefferson slowly walked down the steps of the portico to greet him. Jefferson's grandson describes the scene: "As they approached each other, their uncertain gait quickened itself into a shuffling run, and exclaiming, 'Ah, Jefferson!' 'Ah, Lafayette!' they burst into tears as they fell into each other's arms." Following are Jefferson's remarks, read by another, at a banquet in Lafayette's honor. Present also were Madison and President Monroe.

I will avail myself of this occasion, my beloved neighbors and friends, to thank you for the kindness which now, and at all times, I have received at your hands. Born and bred among your fathers, led by their partiality into the line of public life, I labored in fellowship with them through that arduous struggle which, freeing us from foreign bondage, established us in the rights of self-government; rights which have blessed ourselves, and will bless, in their sequence, all the nations of the earth. In this contest, all did our utmost, and, as none could do more, none had pretensions to superior merit.

I joy, my friends, in your joy, inspired by the visit of this our ancient and distinguished leader and benefactor. His deeds in the war of independence you have heard and read. They are known to you and embalmed in your memories, and in the pages of faithful history. His deeds, in the peace which followed that war, are perhaps not known to you; but I can attest them. When I was stationed in his country, for the purpose of cementing its friendship with ours, and of advancing our mutual interests, this friend of both, was my most powerful auxiliary and advocate. He made our cause his own, as in truth it was that of his native country also. His influence and connections there were great. All doors of all departments were open to him at all times; to me, only formally and at appointed times. In truth, I only held the nail, he drove it. Honor him then, as your benefactor in peace, as well as in war.

My friends, I am old, long in the disuse of making speeches, and without voice to utter them. In this feeble state, the exhausted powers of life leave little within my competence for your service. If, with the aid of my younger and abler coadjutors, I can still contribute anything to advance the Institution, within whose walls we are now mingling manifestations to this our guest, it will be, as it ever has been, cheerfully and zealously bestowed. And could I live to see it once enjoy the patronage and cherishment of our public authorities with undivided voice, I should die without a doubt of the future fortunes of my native State, and in the consoling contemplation of the happy influence of this institution on its character, its virtue, its prosperity, and safety.

To these effusions for the cradle and land of my birth, I add, for our nation at large, the aspirations of a heart warm with the love of country; whose invocations to heaven for its indissoluble union, will be fervent and unremitting while the pulse of life continues to beat, and, when that ceases, it will expire in prayers for the eternal duration of its freedom and prosperity.

Take Care of Me When Dead

To James Madison, February 17, 1826

Jefferson had good reason to despair over his personal affairs. Heavily in debt while supporting a large family, he requested permission of the state legislature to hold a lottery for sale of his property. The letter below describes his condition with the pathos of a Lear. The lottery, as it turned out, failed. When news of Jefferson's state became known a public subscription was held in New York, Philadelphia and Baltimore, which helped slightly. The bulk of his enormous debt, about a hundred thousand dollars, remained his legacy.

. . . You will have seen in the newspapers some proceedings in the legislature, which have cost me much mortification. My own debts had become considerable, but not beyond the effect of some lopping of property, which would have been little felt, when our friend Nicholas[1] gave me the *coup de grace*. Ever since that I have been paying twelve hundred dollars a year interest on his debt, which, with my own, was absorbing so much of my annual income, as that the maintenance of my family was making deep and rapid inroads on my capital, and had already done it. Still, sales at a fair price would leave me completely provided. Had crops and prices for several years been such as to maintain a steady competition of substantial bidders at market, all would have been safe. But the long succession of years of stunted crops, of reduced prices, the general prostration of the farming business, under levies for the support of manufacturers, etc., with the calamitous fluctuations of value in our paper medium, have kept agriculture in a state of abject depression, which has peopled the Western States by silently breaking up those on the Atlantic, and glutted the land market, while it drew off its bidders. In such a state of things, property has lost its character of being a resource for debts. High land in

---

[1] Jefferson had backed a $20,000 loan taken by his friend Wilson Cary Nicholas. Jefferson had to make it good when Nicholas defaulted.

Bedford, which, in the days of our plethory, sold readily for from fifty to one hundred dollars the acre, (and such sales were many then,) would not now sell for more than from ten to twenty dollars, or one-quarter or one-fifth of its former price. Reflecting on these things, the practice occurred to me, of selling, on fair valuation, and by way of lottery, often resorted to before the Revolution to effect large sales, and still in constant usage in every State for individual as well as corporation purposes. If it is permitted in my case, my lands here alone, with the mills, etc., will pay everything, and leave me Monticello and a farm free. If refused, I must sell everything here, perhaps considerably in Bedford, move thither with my family, where I have not even a log hut to put my head into, and whether ground for burial, will depend on the depredations which, under the form of sales, shall have been committed on my property. The question then with me was *ultrum horum?* But why afflict you with these details? Indeed, I cannot tell, unless pains are lessened by communication with a friend. The friendship which has subsisted between us, now half a century, and the harmony of our political principles and pursuits, have been sources of constant happiness to me through that long period. And if I remove beyond the reach of attentions to the University, or beyond the bourne of life itself, as I soon must, it is a comfort to leave that institution under your care, and an assurance that it will not be wanting. It has also been a great solace to me, to believe that you are engaged in vindicating to posterity the course we have pursued for preserving to them, in all their purity, the blessings of self-government, which we had assisted too in acquiring for them. If ever the earth has beheld a system of administration conducted with a single and steadfast eye to the general interest and happiness of those committed to it, one which, protected by truth, can never know reproach, it is that to which our lives have been devoted. To myself you have been a pillar of support through life. Take care of me when dead, and be assured that I shall leave with you my last affections.

The Choice We Made

To Roger C. Weightman, June 24, 1826

Three signers of the Declaration of Independence were still alive: Jefferson, John Adams and Charles Carroll. Weightman asked the three Fathers to appear at an Independence Day celebration in Washington of which he was chairman. Jefferson wrote this letter, his last, two weeks before he died.

Respected Sir,—The kind invitation I receive from you, on the part of the citizens of the city of Washington, to be present with them at their celebration on the fiftieth anniversary of American Independence, as one of the surviving signers of an instrument pregnant with our own, and the fate of the world, is most flattering to myself, and heightened by the honorable accompaniment proposed for the comfort of such a journey. It adds sensibly to the sufferings of sickness, to be deprived by it of a personal participation in the rejoicings of that day. But acquiescence is a duty, under circumstances not placed among those we are permitted to control. I should, indeed, with peculiar delight, have met and exchanged there congratulations personally with the small band, the remnant of that host of worthies, who joined with us on that day, in the bold and doubtful election we were to make for our country, between submission or the sword; and to have enjoyed with them the consolatory fact, that our fellow citizens, after half a century of experience and prosperity, continue to approve the choice we made. May it be to the world, what I believe it will be (to some parts sooner, to others later, but finally to all), the signal of arousing men to burst the chains under which monkish ignorance and superstition had persuaded them to bind themselves, and to assume the blessings and security of self-government. That form which we have substituted, restores the free right to the unbounded exercise of reason and freedom of opinion. All eyes are opened, or opening, to the rights of man. The general spread of the light of science has already laid open to every view the palpable truth, that the mass of mankind has not been born with saddles on their backs, nor a favored few booted and spurred, ready to ride them legitimately, by the grace of God. These are grounds of hope for others. For ourselves, let the annual return of this day forever refresh our recollections of these rights, and an undiminished devotion to them.

I will ask permission here to express the pleasure with which I should have met my ancient neighbors of the city of Washington and its vicinities, with whom I passed so many years of a pleasing social intercourse; an intercourse which so much relieved the anxieties of the public cares, and left impressions so deeply engraved in my affections, as never to be forgotten. With my regret that ill health forbids me the gratification of an acceptance, be pleased to receive for yourself and those for whom you write, the assurance of my highest respect and friendly attachments.

Bibliography

THE NUMBER of books and articles on Jefferson are voluminous beyond measure. (One bibliographer, in 1935, succeeded in counting 1,248 titles.) Below is only a faint sampling of those which may be consulted by the general reader. A good bibliography, chronologically organized, is contained in Merrill Peterson's *The Jefferson Image in The American Mind* (New York: Oxford University Press, 1960).

The definitive collection of Jefferson's writings, relied on wherever possible, is *The Papers of Thomas Jefferson*, Julian P. Boyd, editor (Princeton: Princeton University Press, 1950–1961), of which sixteen volumes, to the year 1790, are available.

The next best collection is *The Writings of Thomas Jefferson*, Paul L. Ford, editor (10 vols., New York: G. P. Putnam's Sons, 1892–1899). A more complete, though less reliable collection is *The Writings of Thomas Jefferson*, A. A. Lipscomb and A. E. Bergh, editors (20 vols., Washington, 1903).

A sound, well-balanced, general biography is Gilbert Chinard's *Thomas Jefferson* (Boston: Little, Brown and Co., 1929). Albert Jay Nock's *Jefferson* (New York: Harcourt, Brace and Co., 1926) is excellent on Jefferson's diverse interests and broad humanism. Dumas Malone's three volumes of a projected series—*Jefferson the Virginian* (Boston: Little, Brown and Co., 1948), *Jefferson and the Rights of Man* (Boston: Little, Brown and Co., 1951) and *Jefferson and the Ordeal of Liberty* (Boston: Little, Brown and Co., 1962)—are exhaustive in research and impeccable in style and judgment. Two valuable nineteenth century biographies are worth mentioning: James Parton's *Life of Thomas Jefferson* (Boston: Houghton, Mifflin and Co., 1884) and Henry Randall's *The Life of Thomas Jefferson* (3 vols., New York: Derby and Jackson, 1858).

Indispensable is Henry Adams' ironic, critical, masterfully written and composed *History of the United States of America During the Administration of Thomas Jefferson* (2 vols., New York: Albert and Charles Boni, 1930). For a lively and strongly partisan account of Jefferson as party leader and

President, see Claude Bower's *Jefferson and Hamilton* (Boston: Houghton, Mifflin and Co., 1925), and *Jefferson in Power* (Boston: Houghton, Mifflin and Co., 1936). Leonard White's *The Federalist* (New York: Macmillan and Co., 1948) and *The Jeffersonians* (New York: Macmillan and Co., 1951) are exceedingly important for an understanding of the whole period from the establishment of the Federal Government through Monroe's administration. Important for an understanding of the economic and social bases of Jefferson's radicalism are Charles A. Beard's classic studies: *An Economic Interpretation of the United States* (New York: Macmillan and Co., 1914) and *The Economic Origins of Jeffersonian Democracy* (New York: Macmillan and Co., 1952). Adrienne Koch's *Jefferson and Madison* (New York: Alfred A. Knopf and Co., 1950) makes clear the extent of their political and intellectual collaboration.

For good accounts of Jefferson's thought and the thought of the Enlightenment which it reflected, see Daniel Boorstin, *The Lost World of Thomas Jefferson* (New York: Henry Holt and Co., 1948); Adrienne Koch, *The Philosophy of Thomas Jefferson* (New York: Columbia University Press, 1943); and Carl Becker, *The Declaration of Independence* (New York: Harcourt, Brace and Co., 1922).

Finally, two essays may be recommended: Richard Hofstadter, "Thomas Jefferson: Aristocrat as Democrat," in *The American Political Tradition and The Men Who Made It* (New York: Alfred A. Knopf, 1948); and Vernon Louis Parrington, "Thomas Jefferson: Agrarian Democrat," in *Main Currents in American Thought* (New York: Harcourt, Brace and Co., 1927).